That Was The Life Th

FROST

The Authorised Biography

Neil Hegarty

WH
ALLEN

1 3 5 7 9 10 8 6 4 2

WH Allen, an imprint of Ebury Publishing,
20 Vauxhall Bridge Road,
London SW1V 2SA

WH Allen is part of the Penguin Random House group of companies whose
addresses can be found at global.penguinrandomhouse.com

Penguin
Random House
UK

First published in the United Kingdom by WH Allen in 2015
This edition first published by WH Allen in 2016

www.eburypublishing.co.uk

A CIP catalogue record for this book is available from the British Library

ISBN 9780753556726

Printed and bound in Great Britain by Clays Ltd, St Ives PLC

In Memory of Miles Frost (1984–2015)

By his brothers Wilfred and George

Dad died on Saturday August 31st, 2013. His death was a massive blow to us all. Since then, we have worked hard to celebrate Dad's life, and continue ours as he would have wanted. This book was one of the ways in which we chose to honour and remember the life of David Frost.

On Sunday 19th July, 2015, our older brother Miles died, having collapsed whilst out jogging. He was thirty-one years old, and his death was sudden, tragic and unfair. This has been another terrible blow to our family; it has been even more difficult to comprehend than losing Dad. Miles was in his prime: fit and healthy and with his life ahead of him. Since Dad left us, he had become the leader of our pack. He headed the family, and kept us together, balanced and solid. Above all he led us to being happy again.

Miles was exceptional – as a son, as a brother, as a friend. His strength was combined with qualities of generosity, kindness and wisdom that marked him unmistakably as Dad and Mum's son. We are left bereft by his death, but we are determined to be strong – both for our mother's sake, and in order to honour the memory of Miles himself, and the memory of our father.

As a family we all agreed we must continue to celebrate Dad's wonderful life as planned – despite this enormous setback. The final text of this book had already been signed off before Miles died, and we decided not to change a word. This is the book on Dad to which Mum and the three Frost boys have all contributed, thus Miles' voice is still very much present and unchanged from before his tragic passing.

It turns out Miles had a condition called Hypertrophic Cardiomyopathy, or HCM. Even more tragically we found out that Dad had HCM too, but since it was not the direct cause of Dad's death, the condition was not flagged to us. Regardless, we have set up the Miles Frost Fund in partnership with the British Heart Foundation in order to work to prevent similar tragedies of cardiac death in the young being experienced by other families. For more information please visit www.MilesFrostFund.com.

We dedicate this book to the wonderful memory of our beloved father, and our perfect-in-every-way brother. We live our lives to make you both proud.

Lady Carina Frost:

"Our beloved beautiful blue-eyed boy – we are with you and you are with Dad – forever and a day. All our love always."

Contents

Preface

It was with trepidation that David and I sneaked into the Donmar for *Frost/Nixon*. At first I felt like I was locked into a huge deep freeze – the air conditioning was on full – with no way out. And then the enormity, both of the play and the man I was married to, hit like a tornado. I was quite literally sitting next to a legend. I took his hand and watched his face, watching himself being played sublimely by Michael Sheen. It was an uncanny moment, and I began to relax and allow these incredible performances to pull me in. And there began the extraordinary journey of *Frost/Nixon* that David and I shared with our three boys. We were so proud, and we had such fun.

Carina Frost

On the evening of August 21st, 2006, a new play opened at the Donmar Warehouse theatre at Covent Garden in central London. *Frost/Nixon* was based on the meetings in 1977 between Richard Nixon, who, in the aftermath of the Watergate scandal, had resigned the office of President of the United States, and David Frost, the British interviewer and talk-show host who had sensationally beaten the big American networks to the prize of interviewing the disgraced former president.

Sir David Frost was now sixty-seven years old, and a very different man to the one who, three decades previously, had met and jousted with Richard Nixon on the coast of California. His career had morphed and moved in many directions: he had been there at the beginning of breakfast television in 1980s Britain; and he had gone on to carve out a crucial space at the heart – uniquely – both of current-affairs and light-entertainment broadcasting. He had sustained a profile on the other side of the Atlantic too, interviewing yet more presidents, celebrities and significant public figures – and in the process becoming a key and highly networked player in American television. This was all a far cry from Frost's earliest television experience as the fresh-faced anchor of *That Was the Week That Was*, the Establishment-cracking BBC satirical programme which had created a sensation in the Britain of the 1960s – and it demonstrated Frost's extraordinary energy, range and ambition, sustained year by year, decade by decade.

And crucially, David Frost's private life had changed utterly too: the playboy figure of the mid-1970s, tracked by tabloid journalists and photographers and habitually sporting a clutch of girlfriends – this era was over, and Frost was now a married man. He had married, indeed, into the heart of the British Establishment: his wife of twenty-two years was Lady Carina Fitzalan Howard, sister of the Duke of Norfolk; and the couple had three sons now on the cusp of adulthood. Nor was David Frost at the point of easing down his activities, assessing a life well-lived or contemplating retirement. On the contrary, he had just completed a move to a new Arabic-based satellite network, Al Jazeera, the stated intention of which was to provide an alternative source of news to the Western networks that had traditionally dominated the media market; it was a move both bold and lucrative, and it had startled media observers. And now, in the summer of 2006, David Frost had a West End play written about his life.

On the last night of the Donmar run, Carina and David Frost attended the performance once more, this time in the company of Alastair Campbell, press secretary at that time to Prime Minister Tony Blair. Campbell recalls the evening with amusement:

I hadn't for a variety of reasons had a chance to go to see *Frost/ Nixon* in the West End – and now the clock was ticking on the production, and so with just a few nights to go before it closed, I phoned David and said, "Look, you just have to get me a couple of tickets to see the play. Can you do that?" And he phoned back, and said, "Oh yes, I certainly can! – I have four tickets for the closing night!" And so, on closing night, Fiona [Millar,

Campbell's partner] and I were there sitting in row ten with Carina and David – and talk about life imitating art imitating life! Everyone in the audience was staring at David and clearly thinking how hilarious the situation was. And by this stage David had seen the play many times: so many times, in fact, that he practically knew the script by heart and was able to mouth Michael Sheen's lines, and sometimes even say his lines aloud. I had to nudge him and say, "Stop that!"[1]

The run at the Donmar had come to an end, but this chapter was far from at an end. The play would soon move to Broadway, before being turned into an Oscar-winning film directed by Ron Howard. Nor was the wider story of Frost's life, already packed as it was with the sort of public incident and drama and private stability of which few others can boast, coming to an end. *Frost/Nixon* was a most useful metaphor – for Frost's life had been lived on a stage and open to the view of all. And yet there were limits: for he guarded his privacy, kept many of his feelings and thoughts to himself, and many elements of the world at bay.

*

The reader's first question of the biographer is always going to be, What was she, or he, like?

Hermione Lee

Hermione Lee's question about the inquiry that drives biography has a special pertinence in the case of a figure who is that quintessentially modern phenomenon: a personality. About people in this category we all tend to know *something* – but, as a consequence, the real person becomes more obscure, and more difficult to distinguish from the public image. The story of David Frost fascinates because he was a man known for his ease and success in the media age: indeed, it was part of his character to be able to negotiate that virtual world. Such a talent has its roots in all the influences that shape an individual, and yet coexist with depths and complexities which are not revealed on camera or in public. And Frost's talent and success are also part of a larger story, of social change and cultural transformation, which partly explain and were in turn shaped by his innovations.

This, then, is the biography of a personality, though it is doubtful whether David Frost would have described himself in this way. He might have thought of himself as a showman, or an entertainer; as a listener and an asker of questions, though probably not as an interviewer, nor a journalist; a television man, and a ladies' man, and a family man; an international globetrotter – though also an Englishman through and through. An original, for an original medium: Frost had the good fortune to be present as television was taking off as a commanding cultural mode, a mass channel of communication. He was one of the first to see its possibilities, and to place himself at the centre of what it had to offer – and he was able to stay the course, as others fell away.

David Frost had, at first glance, no great advantages of birth, but was rather the product of moderate circumstances: carefully middle-middle class, according to the English form of reckoning, neither more nor less – and born of parents who understood their place in society and who commanded respect within it. They were devout Methodists, with all that this implied: broadminded, evangelical, passionate and socially aware, with a keen sense of justice and a dedication to a sacred idea of the universality of God's grace. And although his later lifestyle hardly gave the appearance of it, David Frost had an understanding with God too, and prayed to Him each night. He made his early reputation laughing at and satirising the British Establishment: but he died occupying a place at its centre – even if he would have denied such an observation, claiming instead that he had never changed his spots, that this self-same Establishment had moved instead in *his* direction. And when we look a little more carefully at his circumstances, we see that he did enjoy one tremendous advantage – the greatest. He enjoyed stability, security and unconditional family love of the sort that can bring with it confidence – and that in his case catapulted him forward into life.

He was elusive: that much is clear to his biographer, although he devoted a great deal of energy to veiling this same quality. *What you saw with David was what you got*: this is the mantra associated with him – and he would like to have heard such a declaration. For it was true – what you saw was indeed what you got: a man of great kindness, of sweetness of temper, of generosity and compassion; he seldom if ever lost his temper, and never pulled rank. He was loyal to his friends, regardless of their circumstances, and he attracted loyalty and discretion in return and in abundance. He asked questions, incessantly; was curious, ravenously so, about other people, their stories and their lives. He was interested in fame – in famous people and in what makes them tick – and he was interested in power, and enjoyed being close to its springs. He projected a *joie de vivre*, a life force that was almost tangible, and profoundly attractive. He enjoyed a love life that was varied and was made much of at various times in the press: he was no thrillingly handsome physical specimen, but he understood women, and – because he was empathetic in a way unusual in a man of his generation – many women were attracted to him.

And yet he was, to a degree, an enigma: as one girlfriend put it, "one very quickly learned that there was a private David: a place in his heart that was his, and that must remain his. One learned to keep a distance."[2] And it was for this reason too that he asked questions endlessly, that he was endlessly interested in and curious about those around him – in order to keep any questions about himself at bay, to remain behind a veil so transparent that more often than not it was invisible to those about him. He was in this sense chameleon-like, and certainly, he was difficult to pin down – politically and ideologically. Instead, he was an Everyman figure: he took on the colours of his context, the better to smooth his way through life, and to ease and comfort others in the process. He could not and would not deal with confrontation: and this in the end became his trademark, and a quality that attracted praise from many.

But David Frost attracted disdain too: from many of his peers in the Cambridge University of the late 1950s, who saw a grammar-school boy with ideas above his station, an ambition he made no effort to disguise, and a public manner not yet fully formed – and who reacted with dislike and a curdling envy that might have crushed him. Though it did not – and instead, it was the making of him: bolstered by a natural confidence and buoyed by the love of his family, he allowed no such negativity to find a chink; he carried on regardless. And yet: it is impossible not to gaze for long at David Frost without glimpsing a bruise or two, without divining a sense of hurt; and impossible also not to conclude that here was a man whose path was fuelled – in part – by reaction to the disdain he detected; driven all the more energetically as a consequence of this disdain to make as much of himself, and his life, as he possibly could.

David Frost was able to provide all the gags an audience could desire, and to set a room laughing; and he was able to work that same room, and discover where the power and influence lay within it. He lived a life which wanted for nothing, and he liked it that way: he liked his luxury, and his holidays, his fine wines and large cars and properties. But he worked hard for these luxuries – and he worked hard too, and frequently below the radar, to do what was needful for those less fortunate than himself. He was able to schmooze with the best of them; but equally, he was able to wave an index finger, in anger and disgust, in the face of a shady businessman live on television; or – like a dog with a bone – query a momentous Prime Ministerial decision again and again. He worked hard out of a sense of compulsion – and in the process, he shed much of the hinterland that keeps lives on the straight and narrow; and maintains equilibrium. And in the end, he lived too much, and died too young.

Every life ends in fragments – of public records and private ones, of voices, of stories, of anecdotes. I never met David Frost. Instead, I absorbed his public image osmotically through the television screen, and came to understand the significance of his earliest television work, created in the years before I was even born. As a result, I have had the advantage of approaching this project in an expansive frame of mind and open to all knowledge; and the inestimable advantage too of having the full cooperation of the Frost family, and of David Frost's friends and colleagues. Indeed, I came to understand rapidly that a biography written *without* this cooperation would quickly have foundered: the most striking element in this project has been the level of loyalty felt for the man and for his family, constituting a protection around David Frost that otherwise would simply have been impossible to penetrate. This element is significant in itself, suggesting as it does a life lived in a way that earned the gratitude and respect of those around him.

In piecing together this life story, I have been able to study the public David Frost through virtually the entire course of his adult life, watching him change from a quiffed and boundlessly energetic young man in the sixties, to the prematurely aged figure he became in his final years. I have listened to the testimonies – detailed and frequently, though not always, loving – of those who knew him, in order to understand the private boy and man; and I have tried to detect his own silences too, and to catch their meaning. The result is a canvas the surface of which has been pieced together, in the manner of all biographies, to create something that is, once more, solid and able to support the weight of a life.

Prologue

By Wilfred, on behalf of Miles, Wilfred and George Frost

Saturday, August 24th, 2013 was the last time we were all with Dad – and he was on sparkling form. It was the final night of our holiday in Spain, staying with Lady Annabel Goldsmith – a family tradition we have been lucky enough to experience every year of our lives.

Torre de Tramores is a magical place. It is a 2000-acre estate in southern Spain about thirty minutes north of Marbella. It is not grand, but rather luxurious and homely. It is a sporadic set of beautiful rooms set around an old tower (the "Torre"), which lends itself perfectly to the Mediterranean climate. We have regularly described our annual week spent with the Goldsmiths as the happiest week of our year – and 2013 was no exception. There is always the perfect mix of age groups – which leads to a holiday that balances family time with fun in the most perfect way.

There is never really a daily agenda at Tramores, which is what makes it so relaxing. But the one vaguely formal part of the day is dinner at 9pm (after Lady A has watched *EastEnders*). We say *vaguely* because dinner is always over in no time at all. The three of us eat quickly. But Jemima, Zac and Ben (Sir Jimmy and Lady Annabel's three children, who are five-to-ten years our senior) put us to shame, inhaling their food. Dinner is always fresh, Spanish cuisine, which typically would not have been Dad's dream meal. But everyone always catered to Dad's (very boring) preferences when it came to food, and if there was something he didn't like, there would usually be a special plate prepared for him. Then, after dinner, we would convene in Annabel's white drawing room. Cue the standard joke from George that he had spilt red wine on the sofa, and Lady A responding with a tirade of expletives before realising he was, for the fourth night in a row, yet again joking.

As fate would have it, on August 24th, 2013, the post-dinner discussion centred on Dad. Ben, who is Dad's godson, got him talking about certain moments of his career, and the anecdotes kept rolling. We even watched a clip on YouTube of him interviewing Muhammad Ali, and Ali had come up with the immortal phrase, "David, if you think the world was surprised when Nixon resigned, wait till I whip Foreman's behind." Hidden in that quote is so much – so epic. Dad of course had no idea what YouTube was. He had been a pioneer for the first thirty years of his fifty-year television career. But the digital age passed him by. He once said to Wilf, "What is the difference between digital and iPad?" – the language was totally alien to him. But that night, he was just delighted we had reviewed some of his clips and that everyone had enjoyed them.

In fact, even a regular television set oft defeated Dad. The number of times we would receive a phone call at 3.30 on a Sunday afternoon is countless. "How has your weekend been, my boy?" – he would try to pretend he was just calling for a catch up. Though we knew what was coming. "Since I've got you … I am trying to watch Sky Sports 1; has anyone changed the remote set-up? It doesn't seem to be working." What would follow can only be described as desperately simplistic instructions of how to turn a TV on and change the channel to 401. Anyone in earshot of our end of the phone call would look on in disbelief, as if we were talking to an alien. In fact, on the other end of the phone was the greatest broadcaster who ever lived. He was just useless with all forms of technology.

That night's flirtation with YouTube led Ben to encourage him to join Twitter. This is something we had long since given up on. Ben tried regardless. He informed Dad that someone like Stephen Fry had over five million followers on Twitter, and that Dad was probably more famous than him. Dad paused. Nodded slightly. And with a wry smile said, "Yes, I think I probably am." A few days later, we would realise how well known he truly was – more so than we had ever realised before.

Dad had definitely slowed down in the final years of his life, but his last three or four months he was on spectacular form. It was a joy for Mum and us to see. That final night in Spain was a perfect example of it. He was regaling us with stories with the same verve and charm as in his prime. Most of these stories were ones we had heard before. But we were always impressed and delighted to hear them again, and always laughed at the jokes we had heard before. We knew the incoming punchline, but it was always delivered with such genuine warmth that it was impossible not to laugh alongside his smile. Everyone was on his side: Mum and the three of us more than anyone else.

*

The last few years had seen a couple of changes in family life that had seen us move from both our childhood homes. The move from Carlyle Square in London had come about because the three of us had moved out into our own places, so the house where Mum and Dad had hosted their famous summer garden parties was feeling rather empty. And the move from our Hampshire home, Michelmersh Court, to somewhere closer to London had taken place just a few months before Dad died. Dad had not minded unduly about the London move. He *had* been apprehensive, however, about the move from Michelmersh. And so it delighted us all that this move had proceeded smoothly and that he had instantly fallen in love with the new place. And this in turn meant we had a summer of happy memories of him at our new home.

He had in fact scheduled his first Sunday lunch party for just a week after his death. As his old friend Michael Caine said in the BBC documentary that followed his passing: "I was meant to be going to lunch at his new house. But I went to his funeral instead." Dad lived for Sunday lunches. Having done a Sunday morning show for so long, Sunday lunch was really the only part of the week when he was totally free. He would rush home from doing the show, his car filled with two cigars' worth of smoke, and a fun gathering would be lined up for lunch each week. We would really only care about post-lunch activities, which would centre around football – both watching it and playing it. Dad's friends, from whatever walk of life, would be roped into a post-lunch game of football. David Seaman, Rory Bremner, Angus Deayton, Bush Sr, Michael Parkinson, Michael Howard, David Gower, Imran Khan and Tony Blair are some of the people we have battled in our back garden. It's a pretty extraordinary line-up, and indicative of some of the amazing people we have been lucky enough to meet thanks to Dad. (We once had a Frost vs Blair match at Chequers – we cannot remember who won, but are going to stake a claim that it was Team Frost, and await any appeal.)

There is no way we can ever thank our parents enough for what they have given us. Lovely homes. A wonderful education. Amazing holidays. All of those things on their own would give us more to thank them for than would ever be possible. But those aspects are not the most important. From the day we were born we have been surrounded by so much love and support that it would have been impossible not to have had the happiest of childhoods. That above all is what we are grateful for. Dad was an unbelievable father.

Wilf remembers: "After 9/11, the Queen wrote that, 'Grief is the price we pay for love.' That really resonated with us after Dad died – God, it hurt, but we were lucky that it did hurt, because it highlighted what amazing years we had had with him.

"Miles said shortly after Dad died that he had no regrets – his sentiment was spot on for all three of us. We all knew that Dad loved us, and he knew that we loved him. Many people have said that was patently obvious whenever we were with him. Despite that, I wish I had told him every day. I don't have regrets. But I do wish I had told him every chance I had how grateful I was for all he had done for me. He knew. But still ..."

*

The holiday in Spain came to an end. Wilf went back to work in London. Work at that time for him was as in the world of finance for a firm called Newton. Wilf: "I had in fact secretly been working to follow in Dad's footsteps for some time, something that had excited Dad hugely, but I had not got to the point of quitting my job in finance yet. On the Thursday of that week I had an important TV job interview, which had gone very well. It did not in fact lead to anything in the end, but I remember calling Dad to tell him it had gone well, and he was delighted for me. That was the last time I spoke to him."

Miles, George and Mum had dinner with him on Friday August 30th in the country – and this was particularly memorable for George: "I was desperately trying to convince my ex-girlfriend into going back out with me, and managed to persuade her to come home for the weekend. The five of us went for dinner at a local pub, and it was one of the happiest meals of my life. Dad was on as fabulous, energetic, loving form as I can remember. We were there for hours, and it was a riotous evening, with all of us in hysterics for most of it. Needless to say, the thought then that a man so wonderfully full of beans and energetic would be leaving us in the way that he did the next day couldn't have been further from my mind. And that, I suppose, is the solace that we can all draw on. Dad went out still full of life – it had nothing to do with who he interviewed, or what he had done professionally – my memory of my wonderful father will never be tainted by old age, he will always be the one at the centre of attention, his mere presence making everyone else feel better and have a better time."

The following morning, Dad set off to Southampton for his engagements on the *Queen Elizabeth*. Mum would normally accompany Dad on these trips, and in fact on any trip, but the prospect of a three-day sail from Southampton to Lisbon was this time rejected in favour of a summer weekend at home with two of her sons.

Dad had worked with Cunard for the last few years. He would board the ship, do his one-man show for a few nights in a row and then come home. It was well paid, but he didn't really do it for that; he did it because he ADORED it. His long-time producer, Trevor Poots, who still works with us at Paradine Productions today, often said that he thought Dad would have preferred to be a comedian than an interviewer. He certainly loved to make people laugh, and many of our own generation forget that he started his career as a comic satirist, not a serious interviewer. His one-man show was not stand-up in the mould of Eddie Izzard or Michael McIntyre. It was more like a one-man cabaret performance. He had such amazing stories to recount, and would use them to work in various funny anecdotes, which were more amusing than outright witty, but the way he told them would always elicit the response he was after from the crowd, even if you had heard them before! He would often start a speech by thanking the person who had introduced him by saying he did not always get such a warm welcome… "I was speaking at the Grosvenor House Hotel the other day, and rather than saying, 'Now, pray silence for Sir David Frost,' I am not sure if he was nervous or what, but the toast master said, 'PRAAAAAY for the silence of Sir David Frost.' He probably had it right, come to think of it."

A great example of his lack of understanding of modern technology, whilst talking of Thatcher, or the '80s, he would go off on a tangent in order to tell an extra joke: "Of course, back then, if you had a three and half inch floppy, that was something you kept VERY [in classic Frost drawl] quiet about." We tried to explain to him that the joke no longer worked, but he would gleefully come off stage and correctly inform us, "See: they still love it." – Wilf: "I maintain that it didn't work any more – HE got the laugh, not the joke. There are so many more of those jokes – and they bring a beaming smile to my face to think of them again."

Dad boarded the *Queen Elizabeth* at Southampton in the afternoon of Saturday, August 31st, 2013. Cunard tells us that he was in Cabin 5194 – a Queen's Suite. The ship's log records painstakingly that he boarded the *Queen Elizabeth* at 15:26, an hour before the ship sailed; that he ordered a panini, a pot of coffee and a glass of house wine at 16:40; a second coffee at 17:20; that he was last seen alive at 18:00; that he was found two and a half hours later; and pronounced dead five minutes after that. The ship did not reach Lisbon for another three days, arriving on September 3rd at 07:49. Dad's body was removed from the ship at approximately 10:00, and he was taken to the Legal Medicine Building in Lisbon, where a post mortem took place on the morning of Wednesday, September 4th. He had suffered a major heart attack.

Although he died on a Saturday evening, we did not find out until the following morning. Since we had moved house, the police did not have any contact details for us. And there was nobody at Dad's office, given the time of the week. In the end, the police reached Mum's cousin – who lived near us in Oxfordshire – in the early hours of Sunday morning. He then told Mum's brother Ed, who decided he would drive up first thing in the morning to break the devastating news.

As Ed pulled up at the house with a police car behind him, Mum knew something terrible must have happened, but did not think for a second it would be relating to Dad. Ed had the terrible task of telling Mum that Dad had died. He then went to tell Miles and George, since Mum was in no state to do so. Miles then drove up to London to tell Wilf. Wilf: "I remember the moment incredibly clearly. I was still in bed when I heard the buzzer going at my flat. It was about 8 o'clock on a Sunday morning. I heard that it was Miles, and knew he had been in the country, so immediately asked why he was there. 'Just let me in.' I honestly could not have prepared for the pain that was about to hit. 'Dad died last night.' I immediately broke down. Miles and I sobbed in each other's arms for a minute or two. We then rang Mum and George and sobbed again. And then we drove back down to see them both."

It is hard to express how empty we felt that day. It was an unbelievable shock. Whilst Dad had aged in his final years, he had still been on great form, and had never shown any sign of serious bad health. We knew he was no longer the athlete he once was, but nothing had suggested *this* was on the cards.

Now that Mum and us all knew, we set about telling a few other people. Cunard had managed to keep it under wraps for some twelve hours, so we knew we needed to make a press release immediately. Given that fact, too many people found out from the press, because we did not have time to tell everyone in advance, which was not ideal, but was impossible to avoid. We rang Dad's close friend Peter Chadlington and he notified the press for us. And what followed was totally and utterly overwhelming – in a good way. The outpouring of love and respect for Dad that day, and in the weeks and months afterwards, was astonishing. To this day it makes us so proud. He lived fifty years of his life in the public eye, and yet there was so little negativity, and instead so much warmth, respect and admiration for him. Of course it was small consolation, but nonetheless it helped.

Dad topped the news from midday to midnight that day. Not just a headline either, but a good meaty report and reaction in the 'A block'. His death dominated every UK newspaper the following day – and of course, it was not just in the UK. Unsurprisingly, his passing made big news in the US, too – page one of the *New York Times*, *Washington Post* and *LA Times*. Wilf: "I had friends in China and Hong Kong who told me his life made the front pages there too. My brothers and I didn't quite realise how famous he was until he died – I had never seen a public reaction quite like it before."

Given the shock of his death, nothing had been planned. One expects that post-death management is sorted by other people, but of course, it is not. With reflection, there are moments of lightness in the immediate days that followed. Dad had left no notes as to who he would want at his funeral and what should be in the service. Although Dad was the son of a Methodist minister, we are not a hugely religious family. We planned what we thought would be a good service, but it only lasted about 25 minutes. It was a small, intimate service at the church near our home, which means Dad's grave is walking distance for us whenever we need to speak to him. It certainly could have been very different: the Dean of Westminster offered to have the service at Westminster Abbey. This was an incredible offer, but we're glad we decided on the small funeral, and to follow it some months later with a memorial service at the Abbey.

Most of the administrative aspects of the days following his death were a complete nightmare. It took what felt like an inordinate amount of time for the authorities to process his body. Following the post mortem, Dad was released to the undertaker appointed by Cunard – and the company and the Foreign Office were fantastic at expediting his journey home. Nonetheless, it felt like an eternity until his body was finally returned from Lisbon. He was flown back (in the cargo bay, not his usual seat 1B!) on Thursday September 5th – on British Airways flight 503, which departed Lisbon at 19:04 and arrived at London Heathrow at 21:10. That allowed us to hold the funeral on September 12th.

The night before the funeral, we had the opportunity to go and see his body to say goodbye for the final time. Wilf: "I don't regret the decision to do so, but I was not prepared for it. Usually, if one wants to see the body of a loved one after they die, I guess you get to do so within 24 hours. This was nearly two weeks later, and more problematically, in order to prepare a body to travel on a plane, they do quite a lot to it. The exact forensic process escapes me, but the body we looked at was not "Dad". It was incredibly hard to see the face looking up at us that lay in the coffin. It was like a distorted waxwork, and did not resemble Dad. And it was frighteningly cold. Nonetheless, it was important to do, and to have a moment with him alone to say some important words."

I think the image of him in the coffin would have haunted Mum and us had we not had hours upon hours of glorious footage to be able to see, countless photographs and invaluable memories. We are incredibly lucky in that regard: he is always there, at the push of a button. Indeed, we have uncovered some absolute gems in his archives, which will be unveiled soon. We cannot describe how proud it makes us to be able to look back at his career. He was utterly unique: at the top of the most competitive industry out there for FIFTY years, and all the time everyone adored him; and most important of all, he was the best, most normal dad ever.

We smile now, as we remind each other that, today, we can have flavoursome food at home – Dad had the most boring taste when it came to food. Tomato, garlic, onion, pepper, pretty much any sauce – anything that added flavour, you name it, he wouldn't eat it. We no longer get the dreaded weekend phone call requesting explanation on how to turn up the volume. Nor do we have to negotiate an airport at an unthinkably slow pace. But we miss even these dull aspects terribly.

We need to thank all of the people who allowed Dad's life to be what it was. There are quite simply too many people to thank, and we hope they will forgive us for thanking them in private over many future encounters rather than listing their names on paper. We hope they know – in fact, we are sure they already do – that he was so grateful to them. We are talking about his producers, his make-up artists, directors, writers, cameramen … the list goes on. Above all, he would be so grateful to all of his friends, who have been so supportive to us.

For this book in particular, though, we must single out Michael Rosenberg, Trevor Poots and John Florescu for their hours of help and unrivalled knowledge of Dad's career and personality.

Most importantly, we want to thank Mum. Quite simply Dad would not have made it so far without her. Not many people in the life of such a public man were privy to their private intimacy: she was his everything. He began and ended every day by talking to her, whether in person or, for example, on a sat. phone from Benazir Bhutto's house in Pakistan. He respected Mum, relied on her, and totally adored her. She was the most amazing wife, and is the most amazing mother. We love you, Mum, and we live our lives to try to make you and Dad proud.

Finally, we would all like to thank Neil Hegarty. It was a long time ago that Wilfred set out on the path to find our biographer of Dad, and we could not be happier with the choice he made. Neil has brought together an extraordinary amount of material, given it historical context and relevance, and made it as exciting as the content warrants.

Dad always loved to find out what made people tick. The account that follows is our attempt to do that about Dad. We hope you enjoy it.

CHAPTER 1

Friday's Child

"David was born on Good Friday, and because of that and his name, he would get terribly teased: 'Cold Cross Bun', they used to call him."

Margaret Frost

Early April, 1939 was a busy time in the household of the Reverend Wilfred John Paradine Frost and his wife Mona. The Reverend Frost was the Methodist minister in the small town of Tenterden, Kent: and as was the case in churches and parishes up and down the land, so the approach of Easter in Tenterden meant increased activity, increased services, increased public devotion to the Lord – and increased workloads. Busy, ceaseless activity was of course nothing new to the Frosts: it went with the territory; and Wilfred and Mona were accustomed to – and indeed throve on – hard work. In addition, they had useful back-up in the form of two dutiful teenage daughters: Jean, aged sixteen, and fourteen-year-old Margaret could be relied upon to lend a hand, to do what was needful in the parish and in the family manse at Oaks Road. They were good girls, and this was a close, supportive family.

This Easter, however, was bringing with it a notable alteration in the life of the Frost family. Mona, aged thirty-six, was pregnant – heavily so, with the baby due any day. An unexpected baby, a complete surprise: Mona and Wilfred had long since given away the pram, the cradle, the entire paraphernalia of baby-sized baths and tiny clothes. This was a wholly unplanned eventuality, and there was little doubt that the new arrival would create a measure of financial stress: Methodist ministers received a miserly stipend, and

– unless there was family money – consequently, had little option but to learn to live simply, thriftily, and rely in part on the charity of the community in which they were based. And the Frosts had little family money, and so they knew they would simply have to cope. They would cope; Mona's role as the wife of a minister had much to do with coping, and responding to changing circumstances, and she did it well.

Wilfred and Mona Frost had long since forged an excellent partnership. Wilfred was bookish and clever: although he was not notably effervescent in his dealings with his flock, he did possess a certain empathetic way about him that people liked, and an effective air of authority that served him well. He was as old as the century: thirty-nine in the spring of that year – and he was a good preacher, a figure to whom his flock listened with trust, knowing that the Reverend Frost was God's man, and knew God's word. 'Paradine', that unusual and exotic middle name, was an indicator of a family lineage that reached back to seventeenth-century France, when the Huguenot Paradines fled the massacres inflicted on their community by the Catholic French state, and sought refuge in England.

Wilfred's character had been formed, or rather had been shadowed, by the experience of World War One: his two elder brothers had been killed in the course of the conflict. This was a common enough tragedy – indeed, it was devastatingly common across Britain – and in this case, it ensured that the Frost family lobbied the authorities to have the youthful Wilfred, then in training to go to the front himself, excused from active service. At length, the War Office agreed, and Wilfred received his discharge papers in November 1918, on the day the war itself came to an end. Thereafter, he had worked for his father, a busy and prosperous ironmonger in the market town of Halesworth in eastern Suffolk.

Mona – Maud – Frost was also of Suffolk stock. She was born near the village of Darsham, one of the eleven children of a Methodist farming family – and she was kindly, gregarious, broad-minded, with a warmer manner than her husband, and with the common touch, delicacy, tact and diplomatic skills necessary to navigate the often choppy waters of parish life. She had the knack of bringing out the best in people, and expected them to live up to her own high standards. Mona Aldrich and Wilfred Frost married at Halesworth in 1922. Wilfred had been born a Congregationalist, but Mona persuaded him to join the Methodist flock – and eventually, he heard the Lord's call and signed up to train for the ministry. He served out his probationary period at Horsham in Sussex, and then the family moved north to the mill town of Burnley in Lancashire. Jean was born in June 1923, Margaret in May 1925 – and it was Margaret's health that occasioned the family's return to the south. As a child, she contracted a dangerous combination of diphtheria and pneumonia, and her parents were told that her recovery, amid Burnley's egregious air pollution, was unlikely. The family formally requested a transfer: Methodist conference, after meeting with Wilfred in London, at length agreed – and the family moved to Tenterden.

Now, more than a decade later, the two Frost girls were close, though quite unalike in manner and disposition. Jean, her sights already set on university, took after both her parents: her father in her academic leanings, Christian devotion and high-mindedness; her mother in her warmth and exuberance. Margaret was her mother's daughter, with Mona's mild, diplomatic touch and lightness of heart. Her form of Christianity was milder too: she was committed to her faith, but it was not for her the be-all and end-all of life. She had a natural way with children, and in the spring of 1939 was contemplating tentatively a career as a nurse.

And Tenterden was a pleasant place: "a delicious little town", handsome and historic, with its substantial commercial streets and stock of fine old buildings.[3] Its setting in the valley of the river Rother glanced at a long trading and shipping history, before the silting up of local rivers forced the town to look instead for its economic livelihood to its rich Kentish hinterland. Joanna Lumley, who spent her teenage years a few miles away at Rolvenden, remembers it as "very much a working town, all farmers and gumboots".[4] To the north stretches the picturesque Weald, with its woods and views and uplands; to the south, the low-lying Romney

Marsh, with its skyline punctuated by the flint steeples of medieval churches, and its views of the English Channel and distant, white-glimmering cliffs of Dover.

These of course were difficult, fraught times in the wider world: in early April 1939, Mussolini's Italy invaded Albania; it was evident to all now that a greater war was coming to Europe once more; and Tenterden, far from being secure and prosperous in an ostensibly inviolate and profoundly peaceful British countryside, was – like all of south-eastern England – instead, uncomfortably aware of the proximity of the coast, of the narrow waters of the Channel, and of the looming continent on the further shore. Not that there was much to be done about any of these larger geo-political issues: not in the shops and churches and parish halls of Tenterden, not in the Frost household – and especially not when Mona Frost went into labour early on Good Friday, April 7th, 1939. She had left the house well-primed and well-stocked: Jean was tasked with preparing the family's meals for the duration; Margaret put together bouquets of flowers for delivery to the Kenchill Nursing Home outside town; Wilfred went on about his business, as men did in those days. And Mona herself was delivered safely of a baby boy at 10.30am.

It was the gender of this child that lifted the Frosts beyond merely coping. To have a son – at their age, when they had relinquished any such expectations – was a source of the greatest delight to Wilfred and Mona. Years later, Margaret Frost remembered how, if she (in true teenage fashion) wished to aggravate her mother, she would murmur that she had been born in the wrong skin, that she had been born a girl instead of a boy. This was not the case – her mother's distress in the face of teenage needling in itself spoke volumes – but it is certainly true that the lack of a boy child to round out the family had been felt as a lack, an absence, a failure. It was a Frost tradition that the boy of the family be given the Paradine middle name: but Mona and Wilfred had baptised Margaret herself with the name Paradine – a mute but eloquent indicator of their certainty that no further children, and certainly no boy, would be born to them.

And now, fourteen years later, a boy had come along – and suddenly there was a clutch of Paradines in the Frost family. So, the baby was baptised David Paradine – and he was the apple of the family's eye, to be cherished and loved – and coddled in a way that was quite uncharacteristic of his parents. Naturally, his austere father baptised the infant himself – before immediately dabbing the christening water from the babe's brow. It would, after all, never do to have little David catch a chill. Thereafter, the family's life revolved around this infant: an early breakfast before Jean and Margaret departed for their twelve-mile bus journey to school at Ashford, leaving Mona free to devote as much time as possible to the baby; the girls returned at five o'clock to a rapid family tea – and then to the ritual of feeding David, perched as he grew in his high chair. Then three hours of homework for the girls, and bed at nine o'clock. Packed days and early nights – and with an eye always riveted on the baby and his welfare.

*

In some ways, however, this child was born at a profoundly inauspicious moment. David Frost was not yet five months old when the long-expected European conflict began: with Hitler's troops on the move in Poland, Britain and France declared war on Germany. The Frost family was on the beach at Dymchurch on the great shingle peninsula of Dungeness when the news filtered through that war had been declared. Within a year, that same Kent coastline was on the front line of the conflict as German planes flew across the county en route to London; and the Frost household was issued with gas masks and tin helmets. The family became accustomed to the air raids sounding across the town, of hasty dives into the large cellar of the Tenterden manse, the baby jostled up and down the steep steps in a basket. Jean Frost was evacuated briefly to Burford in Oxfordshire; Margaret remained at home, shuttling between Ashford and Tenterden, and ministering to her beloved little brother. Mona coped and Wilfred made the best of it. When the windows of the manse were blacked-out, as was compulsory during the war years, he saved a section of the material and fashioned an apron out of it. "There he would be," remembered Margaret, "doing the potatoes for dinner in this giant, black-out apron."[5]

By the time David Frost was three years old, however, the family had left Tenterden. In 1941, Jean departed to take up a place at Liverpool University – and in 1942, the rest of the family left too. Mona and Wilfred had already spent much longer in Kent than was the general pattern for peripatetic Methodist ministers and their families: three years was the general rule – but Wilfred had been asked by his flock to stay on, and this would become a pattern in his future postings. This move, when it finally came, would be the first of many such for the little boy, the nature of the Methodist ministry ensuring that he saw a good deal of England in his formative years. The family's next posting was north of London, to the town of Kempston on the western outskirts of Bedford. Here, Wilfred became the minister for Kempston's two Methodist churches – and here, the youthful Frost recorded his "earliest childhood memory [...] of Brinklow's, a small general store in Kempston. At approximately the age of two, I was sitting in a pushchair outside the said Brinklow's when I spotted a container of mustard in Mother's basket, which was hanging from the pushchair. I managed to get it open while Mother was inside the shop, and tried to swallow all the mustard down in one giant swig. The taste was horrendous, and to this day I have never been able to touch even a smidgen of mustard."[6] Nor – as many years later his family was of course to reflect ruefully – any other strong flavours. Indeed, as we know, David Frost's taste for dull and bland food, perhaps as a result of this heated early experience, was to become a defining characteristic.

The family remained in Bedfordshire for five years. During this period, Jean – now with a teaching certificate to add to her degree – took up a position at a secondary school in nearby Shefford; and Margaret left home to begin her paediatric nursing studies at Great Ormond Street Hospital in London, demonstrating a Frost steeliness by ministering to tin-helmeted children as German air raids took place outside. David, meanwhile, began his education at the Froebel school at Bedford, and here he blossomed under a creative and liberal educational ethos. Corporal punishment was unknown, games and playing in general encouraged, and Frost had his first taste of performance, as the back end of a dragon in a school performance of *St George and the Dragon*.

He flourished at home too. Margaret and Jean, frequently around the family home at Kempston, were roped into football and cricket matches in the garden. Both games had, even at this early point in his life, become a passion: later, Frost credited his early achievements in literacy and numeracy, not to his Froebel teachers, but to an urgent wish to survey the football results and cricket scores; and even as a small boy, he was able to assemble a multitude of imaginary cricket greats to join him in the back garden at Kempston:

'Who are you now?' the bowlers would ask wearily. As often as possible, my reply would be either 'Bill Edrich' or 'Denis Compton'. I will never forget my first visit to Lord's, which my father somehow arranged. It was the glorious summer of 1947, when Edrich and Compton were clouting the South African bowlers to kingdom come. On the balmy June day, we went to the Test, they put on 370 for the first wicket. It was Bill Edrich who particularly captured my imagination.[7]

At the age of five, he wanted to be a train driver when he grew up; by age seven, this had morphed into a fervent wish to be a football player for Newcastle United, sporting that team's excitingly striped shirts. As for Wilfred's effort in tracking down Test tickets for Lord's: this was of a piece with the parenting that David Frost always experienced. With Jean and Margaret now adults, he was essentially an only child, and all the family's – still relatively slender – resources were channelled in his direction. To go with the Test tickets, Wilfred began to develop an interest in football: he too kicked a ball around the back garden and learned to love the light-heartedness and energy that a late child can bring to a home – though it was Mona who tended to ferry her son to and from matches. With uncharacteristic frivolity, Mona and Wilfred even bought their son comics, which he treasured, storing them on his bookshelves in neat, precise rows. He was spoiled, in other words: spoiled thoroughly, assiduously, with relish and gusto. And the boy's response was to develop a degree of self-confidence, an optimism, a relish for life that would stand him in good stead in the years ahead.

Mona and Wilfred's spoiling of their son did not, of course, interfere with the practice of their faith. David Frost remained first and foremost the son of a Methodist preacher: and this influence formed, alongside the love of his family, the second main plank of his childhood. Mona Frost served her Sunday lunch on a Saturday: she was obliged to do so, for Sundays in the Frost household were dominated exclusively by church, by worship, by God. Sunday morning service was followed by Sunday School, and by another service in the evening. Frost's life was threaded with the lives of missionaries, who came to the church and to the family home with dramatic tales of their labours in Asia and Africa, of the challenges that came with these labours, of diseases such as leprosy observed at first hand.

The principles of Methodism had the effect of setting a highly coloured backdrop to David Frost's childhood – and placed him quite outside the developing secular mainstream of British life. He might at any point watch his father preach persuasively and with passion to his flock; he might observe the strong social and moral tenets of Methodism itself, with its deeply held conviction that every soul was an aspect of God's plan, that every soul was entitled to God's love and grace, that every man, every woman was blessed. He might at any point note his parents' religious convictions played out in their daily lives and their interactions with their parishioners; and see the radical social instincts of Methodism at work around him.

Perhaps most significantly, he might at any time tune into the essential drama of Methodism: its inclination towards passionate evangelising and missionary work (witnessed at first hand through

Jean Frost's role as secretary of the Student Christian movement, which entailed much in the way of outreach and criss-crossing the land), its love of music, and its ability to reach into the fabric of society itself, its schools and hospitals and orphanages, in an effort to embrace the human, both body and soul. The result of these influences – a steady, ardent and unconditional family love combined with a current of profound and ongoing social engagement – are crucial to understanding the development of David Frost's character; and foreshadow many of the events of his later life.

In 1947, Wilfred, Mona and David Frost moved back to Kent. The destination on this occasion was the town of Gillingham, a port and naval base at the mouth of the river Medway. To be sure, Gillingham lacked the picturesque backdrop and architecture of Tenterden and lacked that town's essential prosperity too: it was an earthier place, and the long-established presence of the naval dockyards at Chatham had helped to establish Gillingham as a gritty, workaday sort of town. But there was beauty to behold here too, in the form of the wide, luminous skies above this part of Kent, and the expansive landscapes that stretch on either side of the Thames estuary.

The family moved into a Victorian house on Napier Street, within easy walking distance of the town centre and local parks. Wilfred was minister at Trafalgar Street and Byron Road churches, both of which were also within an easy walk of the family home. Frost himself was enrolled in Barnsole Road school, a few streets away – and the liberal Froebel educational principles of Bedfordshire were now replaced by use of the cane and of corporal punishment in general. For a less grounded child, this might have been a shocking transition: for Frost, not so. He simply got on with things: with his education, his life and his family activities. He settled nicely, in fact, into the local milieu, finding his feet and a focus for his energies in the affairs of the 'Gills': Gillingham Football Club which in 1950 was returned to the Football League, and which became a source of sustained and passionate interest. Once again, Frost's interests became the family's interests. "David at Gillingham was still fond of football," remembers Margaret Frost, "and so my father was still fond of football: they called him the football parson. He had his boy, and he wanted to support him, and he was always off at the matches, and even though he couldn't afford it, he got them both a season ticket."[8]

Jean Frost, meanwhile, was building a life of her own – and its drama once more emphasises the colour which underlay her brother's ostensibly rooted existence in Gillingham. Jean, still devoutly Christian, had met Andrew Pearson while a student at Liverpool. Andrew had been a conscientious objector during the war, and was now freshly qualified as a doctor: he was also a Methodist lay missionary who had been born in China and who, following the completion of his studies, returned there to work in the field. Jean had joined him, and the couple were married at Hankow in eastern China in 1948. Jean's future life emphasises once more the extent to which the Methodist church and a wider Christian faith infuses the story of this family: in 1949, Jean and Andrew had their first child, Michael; but in 1951, they were expelled from China by the Communist authorities and returned to Britain. "We hoped now that they had come home, they would stay home," remembers Margaret Frost. Instead, however, following the birth in the same year of their second child, Roger, Jean and Andrew went overseas once more – this time to Nigeria, where the couple would live and work as Methodist missionaries, teachers and medics for the next thirty-five years.[9] Two further children would follow: Alison, born in 1953; and Bryan in 1955.

For the moment, Jean's adventures affected Frost very little – except to underscore his status as effectively an only child. Only with Jean and Andrew's temporary return from China to Britain and the arrival of Michael did their lives impinge on his own – and this only because at the age of eleven, he was now an uncle: a state of affairs that was sufficiently novel as to make the young Frost briefly a talking point among his peers in Gillingham. Margaret married in these years too: in March 1952 to Kenneth Bull, an engineer from Yorkshire whom she had met at a Methodist guild home at Sidmouth in Devon. "In my memory, it's [David's] first time in long trousers; and there he is standing at the front of the church handing out hymnals; and looking very smart."[10] Margaret's marriage would first take her elsewhere in south-eastern England: to Bromley on the fringes of south-east London; on to the new town of Crawley in Sussex where she and Kenneth helped set up a Methodist chapter in this new community – and then, in the autumn of 1955, to the historic and atmospheric fishing town of Whitby on the north Yorkshire coast, where they settled. Their first child, Nigel, was born in the same year; a daughter, Sally, would follow in 1959. Whitby would in the future provide an important northern focus for the wider Frost family, with summer beach holidays and Christmas seasons spent together in the town's bracing air.

In the autumn of 1950, Frost had entered Gillingham Grammar School. He sailed through the Eleven Plus, a newly introduced and baleful rite of passage for boys and girls up and down the land, and an indicator of their destiny. The examination streamed children once and for all. A successful navigation of the Eleven Plus opened up a wider life and career prospects. Failure to do so limited these possibilities. It was as harsh and as simple as that. The Butler Education Act of 1944 – named for Rab Butler, the Conservative politician who had steered the legislation through parliament in the final months of the wartime national government – had changed and widened the world's possibilities for future generations of British children in ways that are difficult to credit today. The act – which covered England and Wales; a mirror act covering Northern Ireland was passed in 1946 – established for the first time the principle of free education for all, and ensured that the children of David Frost's generation, assuming they overcame the frightful hurdle of the Eleven Plus, could contemplate a grammar-school education – and, by implication, a university degree – without the corollary of financial strain.

It is of course likely enough that Frost would have been streamed towards university regardless of the existence or otherwise of the Butler Act. It was already clear that he was a bright boy, and the son of parents who, though lacking resources, nevertheless knew how the world worked and who held a certain standing in society. The funds would have been found, probably though the workings of the Church, for the appropriate education, and for all that flowed from this. But educational change, free schooling, the widening and stretching of the world before him: these reforms established the context for the life of David Frost, as they did for the lives of thousands of other British children. They set in motion the social alterations and the change of climate that enabled him and others like him to inherit the earth.

Gillingham Grammar was by no means a light-hearted establishment. It was presided over by Headmaster 'Dixie' Dale, a gentleman clad habitually in black academic robes and mortar board and with a fondness for the cane. The school housed its share of the usual characters: violence and deep intellectual frustration was evident in the teaching cohort, and Dale's delight in corporal punishment was imitated by most of the staff. Discipline was harsh, and students learned to expect brutality, though Frost himself escaped the worst of it. He was, for one thing, streamed in the highest, or 'L' class, as a student thought capable of coping with Latin as well as the usual French: his brains and academic ability helped to ease his way through lessons – and so his four years at Gillingham Grammar passed more smoothly than was the case with some of his peers.

His character was formed during his four years at Gillingham. He was a sometimes bumptious boy, quick with language and with jokes; and he could be kindly too, with an eye for justice and fair play. One contemporary and neighbour, Richard Green, recalls being befriended by Frost: Green was in a lower stream, and fraternising between different streams of boys was uncommon at Gillingham Grammar. No matter: Frost ordained – in a way that would not be gainsaid – that the two boys would walk home from school together; and a friendship was born. Green recalls his new friend as assertive, confident, accustomed to getting his own way. He was occasionally outspoken too, even when it did him no good.

And there were plenty of opportunities, in the rough and tumble – and occasionally violent life – of Gillingham Grammar, for all of these characteristics to find expression. Green recalls giving a wrong answer in one class, and being struck across the face by the teacher with such force that a tooth broke. This was par for the course in those days, but Frost stopped the teacher in question the following day and remonstrated forcibly with him, there in a crowded corridor. He handled his milder, nervous Latin master in rather a different manner. The teacher was apt, from sheer nerves, to spit as he spoke, and Frost would ape this salivating, spitting in reply as he answered questions. With another (rather strange) teacher, he altered his tactics once more: a wrong answer led to a choice of punishment – to be sent straight to the Headmaster's study, or to be taken by this teacher into the school photographic lab and spanked in the darkness with a soft slipper. The boys invariably opted for the latter punishment, disturbing though it was – but when it came to Frost's turn to choose, he replied, "Neither, sir." Nothing more was said, the soft slipper remained in its desk drawer – and Frost went unspanked.

He had a measure of financial savvy too; and he was generous with the pennies. He sold off his stock of twelve Biggles books to Richard Green at a rate of sixpence a week, over twenty weeks: "we shook hands on the deal", the first sixpence was handed over and Green was permitted to take the full set of books away with him.[11] He treated Green to glasses of orangeade in the local park on warm summer Saturdays too, refusing to allow his friend ever to pay for the treat. And Frost dealt with a school bully smartly and sharply, brewing up a plan to lure the lad to an isolated spot near the tennis courts in one of Gillingham's parks. He had been promised cigarettes; instead, he was set upon by a crowd of his victims, frogmarched to a nearby toilet block and – superintended by Frost himself – head-dunked into a sink filled with water until he had learned his lesson.

Such exploits ensured his popularity off the pitch; and his sporting prowess won him friends on it. For his years of practice with football and cricket bat were now paying dividends, on the football field at Gillingham Grammar, and on the grass of the Lines, the great expanse on chalky upland on the western edge of the town. His speed, strength and control of the ball earned him attention and praise. One result, in the course of his years at Gillingham, was that he was asked to play with the local Pendragon youth team – and here we glimpse one of the few occasions in which Wilfred Frost denied his son his wishes. For Pendragon played in a Sunday league – and Sundays remained sacrosanct in the Frost household. The young Frost continued his Sunday devotions; and Pendragon was obliged to manage without him.

He chafed only a little, however, under his family's religious tutelage. By 1954, to be sure, the teenage Frost was indeed wondering about the existence of God and querying, even, if He did exist, the extent to which the Lord had much relevance in the life of David Frost of Gillingham. The visit of the American evangelist Billy Graham to Britain in the spring of that year was therefore timely on a personal level, as well as, in wider social terms, an electrifying affair. Graham had already established himself, in that essentially pre-television age, as a pre-eminent and deeply influential evangelist in his native country. He was given to taking part in month-long 'Crusades' in cities across America: such campaigns, beginning in 1947, drew crowds in the tens of thousands who came to listen to Graham's message of the Good News – and, in 1952, plans were formulated to bring his energy to bear on British Christianity. He arrived in the country in March 1954, the eve of David Frost's fifteenth birthday, to a chilly welcome from the mainstream British media and society at large. There was a sense of confusion as to the motives and intentions of this American, here to preach a Christian message in a society essentially unaccustomed to fiery evangelical discourse:

I remember the opening night of our meeting in London in 1954. [...] And the press was all against us. Every newspaper. The church leaders that had brought us there, many of them had deserted us. It had been brought up in Parliament as to whether I should even be allowed to land in Britain or not, and everything seemed against us. I had invited Senator Stuart Symington and another US senator to be my special guests there. And that afternoon, Senator Symington called me on the phone and said, "The American ambassador feels that because of all this bad publicity we should not come. Instead, we're going to have dinner this evening with Sir Anthony Eden", who was then the foreign secretary. And then I was called to my little hotel about a half-hour before the service and they said, "The place is empty. There are four hundred newspaper people taking pictures of all the empty seats." And we had rented the place for three months …[12]

Opinion would soon swing in favour of Graham: the reactionary Archbishop of Canterbury, Geoffrey Fisher ("dreadful Geoffrey Fisher", as Alan Bennett later called him) had been critical of the visit – but ended by himself praying with Graham; and the evangelist was invited to preach to the Queen at Windsor.[13] But certain elements in British society had of course delighted in the visit from the first – among them Wilfred Frost, who invited a member of the Graham entourage to visit Gillingham. Grady Wilson, Graham's second-in-command, came and spoke at a well-attended service – but for David Frost, this was merely the prelude to an infinitely more colourful occasion. He travelled to London with Gillingham Youth Club to attend one of the Crusade meetings at Harringay Arena, a disused greyhound track seating 12,000 – and which Graham filled nightly for the full three months of his visit to Britain. Frost also went with his parents to the closing event of the Crusade: a spectacular event at Wembley on May 22nd, 1954, at which the family were three of the approximately 120,000 people filling the stadium.

These two events, and his general observation of Graham's Crusade, constituted a significant moment in his life. Later, he wrote of the event with a certain characteristic levity that does little to disguise its place in his mind:

Even though it differed little from my father's, Billy Graham's message made a real impression on me that night [at Harringay]. I did not actually 'go forward', but I think that was probably because of self-consciousness as much as lack of conviction (together with a nagging fear that the bus home might not wait for me). I do not want to be melodramatic, to portray Harringay as a Damascus experience. But it was certainly a Harringay experience. I remained happy to be a mischief-maker when it looked like being fun, but somehow there was never any danger any more of my really going off the rails. And religion now engaged me intellectually in a way it had never done before.[14]

*

At the end of that summer, the Frost family moved once more: this time north to the small town of Raunds on the eastern edge of Northamptonshire. The nearest main town was Wellingborough, some ten miles to the south-west, and it was at Wellingborough Grammar that David Frost enrolled at the beginning of September, 1954. The school had a reputation for academic rigour and excellence: and the Frosts were perfectly aware of the fact. They were aware too that, while the education reforms of the 1940s had opened up the world to students like David Frost, they had also created a situation in which examination preparation and examination results mattered more than ever.

The calibre of individual teachers also, therefore, mattered more than ever: and it was here that Frost was particularly blessed. He chose Latin, History and English as his A-Level subjects – and now for a few years his path crossed with that of an inspirational English teacher: Geoff Cooksey, whom Frost in later years remembered with affection and respect. Cultured and politically aware, Cooksey taught his students to be alert to the play of ideology in all that they read, heard, and listened to on the wireless. In late 1956, with the Suez crisis in full swing in Egypt, he urged his charges to buy and read copies of the *Observer*, then in its principled heyday as the main opponent of the conflict; and he organised an outing to the Royal Court Theatre on London's Sloane Square, where a young playwright named John Osborne was electrifying audiences with his new play *Look Back in Anger*.

Frost also took part in dramatic turns of his own. He was a regular in the school play, on one occasion taking the part of Banquo in *Macbeth*. A schoolmate, Brian Clayton, recalls agreeing with Frost that the occasion needed to be jazzed up a little:

We dressed in full gear including false beards and rode on bikes at high speed down the hill […] and burst into Vic Huckle's barber shop. We flourished our swords over the clients' heads inviting them to take a special haircut. We then rode back, did the play and waited for the "call" in the morning. The headmaster, Dick Wrenn, had been informed and asked for an explanation while at the same time finding it difficult to keep a straight face. He asked us not to do it again and then said he wished he had been a fly on the wall.[15]

The world was opening up for Frost, and it is possible at this point to catch a glimpse of the man to come, and of the course of his personal and professional trajectory. He was outgrowing his immediate surroundings, and beginning to inch away from his existing terrain of provincial towns, and school and sporting accomplishments. His ambition was growing apace: it was as yet an unfocused ambition, but it had to do with assessing the possibilities of a wider world and taking advantage of these possibilities as they arose. It is significant, for example, that one of the earliest of these possibilities, glamorous and glittering though it would have appeared to another boy, was turned down easily by Frost, simply because it did not fit with the future he was beginning to sketch in his mind.

Frost's dedication to football had survived the transition to Northamptonshire, so much so that he was spotted in action putting eight balls in the back of the net by a scout for Nottingham Forest ("Hot Frost strikes again," was how a sub-editor on the local newspaper put it) and offered a trial with the club. For a football-mad teenager, this was surely the ultimate accolade – but in an indication of Frost's essential pragmatism as well as of the broad scope of his ambition, he turned the offer down with little or no apparent regret.

It was too risky, it paid too little and it would have tied him down, at the precise moment when such a state of affairs would have been intolerable. "There was no particular financial incentive. Footballers in those days were paid about as badly as Methodist ministers. If, for instance, a great player like Stanley Matthews had ever tried to be paid a pound more than the maximum wage of £15 a week, he would have been suspended for life."[16] And besides, Nottingham Forest was not Newcastle United: "They had very boring shirts."[17]

The truth is, of course, that the Nottingham Forest offer – for all that it has assumed a prominent place in various versions of Frost's life – was never going to be accepted. The inadequate money was the least of its problems. It was not what Mona and Wilfred would have wanted for their son; and rather more significantly, it was simply not what Frost himself wanted – for he had much bigger fish to fry. Wellingborough Grammar was accustomed to sending a couple of students every year up to Cambridge University, fifty miles or so to the east across the flat landscape of East Anglia. And it was on a place at Cambridge that Frost had now set his heart, understanding very well that the university held the key to his future. In December 1956, therefore, he travelled to the city, and sat the entrance examination to study English. His chosen college was Gonville and Caius, with which Wellingborough Grammar had an established connection – and this was his first night ever away from home. "I was not daunted," he remembers, "only excited. In fact, I had to take care not to get too excited as I gazed at King's College and walked along the Backs. I loved everything I saw, and yet I knew I must not get too fond of Cambridge yet – after all, I might not be coming back."[18] Two week later, in January 1957, he heard the welcome news: the college had offered him a state scholarship and a place to read English, beginning in the autumn of 1959.

In the meantime, there was the small matter of National Service in the army – then compulsory – to be worked through. Frost's situation was altered a little when the government ruled that students would now take part in National Service *after* they graduated from university – and while Frost was at Cambridge, National Service was abolished, meaning that he avoided it altogether. The actor Ian McKellen, who would begin his studies at Cambridge in the same week as Frost, calls this blessed reprieve "an extra two years added on to our lives", though he also remembers the sense that he – and presumably Frost and others of their vintage – felt like an overgrown schoolboy when set against the men who were kicking off their Cambridge careers after two years in the army.[19] Even with this change in rules, however, Gonville and Caius could move his place forward by only a year, to the autumn of 1958. Still, he had his coveted Cambridge place, and now, once he completed his stint at Wellingborough, he had a free year and more at his disposal.

This period was spent stimulatingly enough. He taught for several months at local schools, followed by a longer spell at Irthlingborough, a couple of miles from Raunds, at a secondary modern school. Such schools occupied the rung below the grammars on the educational pecking order, and they were the destination of those children who had failed the Eleven Plus. For Frost, swaddled by the grammar system at Gillingham and Wellingborough for the previous seven years, the experience was salutary. He observed the altered range of expectations that worked within the secondary system: local students were expected to leave education at sixteen, were expected to join one of Northamptonshire's constellations of shoe plants or other factories, were expected to remain there for their working life, with limited or no opportunities for expanded earning power or career progression. Such may have been their choice – but for Frost, this seemed scarcely the point:

There was not just a lack of opportunity for those pupils, there were positive barriers to their progress. At the time this seemed to me to be an inequity in the English school system that was in urgent need of reform: but quite soon, as my perspectives altered, I started to see that it was symptomatic of a wider need for reform across society – of attitudes as much as structures.[20]

*

Frost dealt with the discomfiting awareness of his own educational privilege, past, present and – with Cambridge now looming – future in as pragmatic a manner as he knew how. He persuaded two of his Irthlingborough charges – two boys who showed academic promise – to peel away from the secondary system in the only way then possible: by enrolling at the local technical college to sit O-Level examinations, and from there to enter the A-Level system at Wellingborough Grammar, after which university and a choice of profession would be possible. His success in guiding these boys, Frost wrote later, "was one of the most rewarding experiences of my life".

These episodes speak much of the young Frost's own moral universe at this point in his life, and the extent to which his upbringing guided his principles. Not for the first time, he was challenged by the sight of a situation, a pattern, a model, that disturbed his own Methodist-influenced vision of the world encompassing fair play and justice for every man, every woman. In later years, commentators would seek to identify this politics and pin it to a party card, and would react sharply and sometimes dismissively when this proved impossible. In truth, Frost's politics would remain deeply human, deeply humane in focus and they slipped through party lines.

At this time, he also wrote and produced a revue for the local Methodist youth club at Raunds – an experience that whetted his appetite for more, much more, of the same. At the same time, he was digesting as much of the new medium of television as he could. This was, in truth, not very much at all: Mona and Wilfred declined to have a set in the house, and their son was forced to slip across the road at weekends to watch TV in a neighbour's house. He also took to the local Methodist circuit as a lay preacher. Such work was not difficult: indeed, after years observing Wilfred at work, it was something his son could undertake with ease and a certain spiritual comfort. His sermons drew on popular culture in a way that his father, perhaps, could not have managed: one sermon took as its text the lyrics from "Ol' Man River", with its talk of folks tired of living and afraid of dying, and Frost used these sentiments to speak of the wasted lives to be seen throughout society, the wasted instincts and blinkered visions of the world – when the opposite, a world of abundance and opportunity, was just as possible and perhaps even easier to imagine. Frost's words welled from that sense of a common humanity that lies at the heart of Methodism – and it is to his credit that he was able, at this relatively tender age, to put these ideas and images into words. Wilfred and Mona watched some of these sermons: and Wilfred, at any rate, wondered if his son might not do well to follow in his own footsteps and devote himself to the Lord.

But David Frost himself did not see this interlude in such a light. His preaching answered a fundamental need for this busy young man to be always active and challenged – and it answered another need too, one that was assuming a greater significance in his life: the need to perform and to be a focus of attention. It was a wholly satisfying experience, therefore, speaking as it did both to his sacred and profane interests. But there was also implicit tension between these two sides of Frost's life – sacred and profane, spiritual and secular – and this tension would be in evidence for the remainder of his life. Certainly, he never at any point realistically contemplated following his father's footsteps into a career in the Church, and it is ironic that his time on the Methodist preaching circuit, with its element of performance, should in fact foreshadow the breakout into the material life on which he would presently embark at Cambridge.

This hiatus in his life ran its course – and now change caught up with the family as a whole. In 1958, Wilfred and Mona Frost undertook what would prove to be their final move. With Wilfred fifty-eight years old and Mona fifty-five, and in what was presumably part of a careful policy of the Methodist council towards ageing ministers, they were posted south – to their home county of Suffolk. They took over the Methodist manse at Frederick's Road in the centre of Beccles, a small town in the east of the county, and ten or so miles north of Halesworth, where Mona and Wilfred had married thirty-six years before. With regular trips north to Whitby, occasional visits to Britain by Jean and Andrew, five grandchildren to be catered to and a sixth on the way – and all this on top of their Church duties – the couple was as busy as ever, and deeply fulfilled.

David Frost accompanied his parents on this last move south to Suffolk, but this relocation was for him a temporary affair. That autumn of 1958, he stood an inch or so away from being six feet tall; he was slim rather than stocky, fit and healthy, and with features – slightly prominent cheekbones and teeth – that were interesting and characterful, rather than in any way handsome or distinguished. His time on the preaching circuit now stood him in the best of steads, for he could speak confidently in public; indeed, he was bursting with confidence, in a way that marked him out as being a little different to an average grammar-school boy on the edge of university life. He was bursting too with eagerness to see what the future would bring – and with a will to shape that future himself, if he possibly could. He spoke in clear tones, a little high on the male register, with a touch of the nasal; and with no particularly prominent accent – the result of his peripatetic childhood, his education, and his will.

He was not to be underestimated – and now, in late September 1958, he set out for Cambridge seventy miles to the west, to begin his student days. As he entered the dining hall of Gonville and Caius College for his first meal on that first night, he saw tall candles burning in the shadows, a sight that he had never seen in his previous home in the plain manses at Beccles and Raunds and Gillingham; and a potent symbol of what he already knew. He had left home, and his life was about to change for ever – which is not to say that he was preparing to divest himself, as he might have done, of his old life. Later in life, indeed, his friends noticed the extent to which his childhood and upbringing provided the sort of anchoring or grounding that was all the more essential, given the form of the life he would have subsequently.

"The basis on which he was brought up enabled him to enjoy his life but was always subject to a control mechanism," notes the Conservative politician David Mellor, his friend in later life. "For some people, early celebrity and ongoing celebrity would have been profoundly disorienting, but he was never damaged by that. There was an off button, which he knew how to use – except, perhaps, in the matter of travel. He could keep control, in a way that other people in his position would not have been able to do."[21] Joanna Lumley also notes this anchoring effect. "He adored his family and had a profound respect for them. There was no 'side'. The media can't bear middle ground: they like you to either have a silver spoon in your mouth or be a beggar; but his background was steady, fine, kindly, with people who wanted him set fair. It suited his character: he had those qualities already, and his parents merely fanned them. He never cut away his past; he loved it."[22]

*

The first night I spent at Gonville and Caius College, on Saturday, September 27th, 1958, was only the second night I had ever spent away from my parents. I had arrived at five that afternoon, driven by my father from Beccles [...] in his 1935 Singer; and by six I felt I had lived there for years. [...] You felt surrounded by history, and the atmosphere of cloisters and spires gave a sense of the medieval. As for the building next door to us at Caius – King's College Chapel – well, it certainly bore very little resemblance to any chapel that I had ever clapped eyes on.[23]

Now, in the late 1950s, Cambridge University was squaring up to alterations in society. On the surface, the city was unchanged and unchanging under wide East Anglian skies, the mellow limestone and shining Portland stone of college after handsome college asserting a continuity that managed to be both comforting and authoritative. The river Cam, with its punts and bridges, and the wide grassy Backs added further to this idea of calm beauty – and it is not difficult to imagine the nineteen-year-old David Frost as enamoured of Cambridge as generations of students before him had been.

Gonville and Caius College was venerable – founded in 1348 as the fourth oldest of Cambridge's colleges, and generally abbreviated to Caius – and one of the wealthiest in the university. The college, with its five fine courts, tree-lined avenue and three symbolic gates, occupies a prominent location on Trinity Street in central Cambridge; and its scale is attractively intimate and human, especially in comparison with the grandiose buildings and quadrangles of King's College and Trinity College which flank it to the north and south. The college's library – in a familiar family note, but one which was presumably entirely lost on David Frost – is of pale Whitby sandstone. Even today, the college retains something of a traditional air; and certainly it was a traditional-minded place in 1958. Not that David Frost had too much truck with some of these traditions: years later, as he toured the college with his wife Lady Carina, he was able to point out his ground-floor rooms with their French windows – so conveniently placed, as he noted, for slipping home after hours, and for the occasional girlfriend to use as an entrance and surreptitious exit.

But change was coming to Caius, and to Cambridge as a whole. The war years, when a comparative dearth of male students meant that the University's female students came strikingly to prominence, were now a decade and more in the past; and the majority of Cambridge's colleges, including Caius, grimly held to a ban on the admission of women. But the college could not hold modernity wholly at bay; and certainly it could not turn its face against the educational reforms of the 1940s, the consequences of which were now visible in the form of increasing social – if not yet gender – diversity in the student cohort. David Frost entered Cambridge, and Caius, as one of this new wave: a young man from a state school and not a public school; a young man of modest means; and a young man of ambition. It is evident in hindsight that the impact of this combination of ingredients on some of his peers was positively indigestible.

The social changes now under way at Cambridge, of course, simply added a further layer to the wealth of talent already attracted to this small East Anglian city, which was such a magnet for young people of skill and diversity. Neil McKendrick, a young History lecturer at

Caius who had taken up his appointment in the same week as Frost had begun his studies, notes: "[O]ver the last sixty-odd years, I have had the good luck to observe generation after generation of aspiring theatrical talent in Cambridge. Not one of them has come close to comparing successfully with the Frost years. Admittedly, some were attracted from elsewhere, but around 1960 Cambridge seemed to be alive with the gifted and aspiring young, all ferociously competing for attention. Eleanor Bron, John Cleese, Alan Bennett, Jonathan Miller, Peter Cook, Tim Brooke-Taylor, Derek Jacobi, Ian McKellen, Trevor Nunn, Margaret Drabble and many others. It was an impressive constellation of talent. To match them would have been a signal achievement, to surpass them (as some have argued that Frost did) would be truly remarkable. Many have mused over how Cambridge simultaneously came to produce the array of future Tory political stars who came to be known as the Cambridge Mafia. [...] When I asked David Frost how he could explain this remarkable coincidence of the arrival in Cambridge of the future political Establishment and the arrival of the satirists who were to make such a mock of them, he said he could do no better than Peter Cook, who when asked the same question, replied with one word: 'Rationing!'"[24] Frost arrived at university intent on entering these circles of talent and opportunity, and making his mark within them.

With this in mind, there now began a period of frantic activity for Frost – activity which, however, had very little to do with academic exertions, and much more to do with forms of creativity that would serve him well in the longer term, certainly, but that in the short term would come close to spiking his university career before it had really begun. He began to network, before the term was even invented: navigating the frequently tricky social waters of Cambridge and connecting himself with people and to contexts that mattered, or that might possibly matter, that might smooth the path of his future life. So that, while he enlisted for a little while as goalkeeper in the Caius football team, it is evident that sports played less and less of a role in Frost's life, and never again would he enjoy the excellent physical fitness of his adolescent years.

In his first term at Cambridge, he established with Colin Renfrew – later the prominent archaeologist Lord Renfrew – a private and rather pompous-sounding dining club they called The Cabal, which met (by invitation only) once a term for an elaborate meal at the Garden House Hotel. The Cabal, in hindsight, set the tone for the rest of a life in which gastronomic and oenophiliac concerns were constantly present. But it was his membership of two prominent Cambridge societies in particular that set the tone for these next three years of his life. The first was the arts magazine *Granta*: it took him well into the academic year to have a piece accepted by the publication, though he managed it in the end. And the second was Footlights, the university's revue and cabaret society. "He knew everyone: he made a point of knowing everyone who mattered, who was in charge. And he became known himself, in that very small world, as a phenomenon of sorts. 'I make it my business,' he used to say, 'to know people.' He was simply very ambitious in a way that few Cambridge people were."[25]

John Cleese, who arrived at Cambridge in 1960, writes engagingly and with affection of the pleasures of an association with Footlights in particular: after watching a troop of budding young (and mainly Conservative) politicians spar and earn their spurs at the Cambridge Union, it was agreeable to leave them behind and repair instead into the cheery and amusing – albeit highly competitive – ambience of the then brand-new Footlights clubhouse, which "was relaxed and comfortable, with a tiny bar and some lunch tables and sofas, and at one end a small permanent stage with curtains and lights. But what really excited us was that it was plumb in the middle of Cambridge – the perfect place to pass time between lectures or to grab a quick and incredibly cheap lunch."[26]

For Frost, however, there was rather more at stake than cheap lunches. Early in his first term, he auditioned for Footlights membership by means of the so-called "Smoking Concerts" or Smokers: monthly cabaret shows that at that time took place at the Dorothy Ballroom on Hobson Street, a few minutes' walk from Caius. He performed in two shows – and, following the second, was duly elected a Footlights member. "He truly believed," remarks Frost's friend and Cambridge contemporary Peter Chadlington, "that anything in the world was possible if only he could work hard enough. The reason David achieved so much was because he had a clear sense of where he was going and he made the most of everything that happened to him to get himself there."[27]

Acceptance at Footlights was a signal moment for Frost, and an affirmation of this belief in the importance of work and graft in attaining one's desires, and it was in the course of this second Smokers that he performed for the first time alongside a figure who would have a significant impact on his life. In "Novel Reactions", a sketch written by Frost, Peter Cook read from the pages of a novel while Frost acted out the passage. The text called for a series of ever more painful and convoluted actions from Frost: "He bit his lip until the blood came," read Cook – and Frost duly bit his lip for all to see. Cook liked the sketch: whether he much liked Frost has been a moot and much quarrelled-over point.

Peter Cook was then in his second year at Peterhouse College. He had managed to be exempted from National Service on the grounds of his chronic asthma, and this in turn meant that he was a couple of years younger than most of his Cambridge peers. He had the knack of being able to make anyone laugh, to take any subject and discover the humour in it, and to transmit that humour to anyone prepared to listen. As was the case with many comedians, he had fostered the ability to laugh and to make those around him laugh, as compensation for and a defence against a shatteringly lonely childhood: his father was a colonial administrator in Nigeria, and so his parents were usually abroad.

The intervention of the Second World War had made this situation – not at all uncommon at a certain level of British society – chronic: he did not see his mother for the full six years of the conflict, and was instead packed off into a series of boarding schools. "I disliked being away from home," Cook recalled. "That part was horrid. But it started a sort of defence mechanism in me, trying to make people laugh so that they wouldn't hit me. I could make fun of other people and therefore make the person who was about to bully me laugh instead."[28] Cook's first year at Cambridge had passed quietly enough: he had steered clear of Footlights – but success in Peterhouse revue concerts and popularity in his college generally had encouraged him to venture further abroad. Now he met such figures as John Bird, who directed Cook in his first Footlights show, and Eleanor Bron, who featured in the show alongside him. Soon, Cook had Footlights and all of Cambridge at his beck and call. And before too long, he would – while still a student – be writing for the West End, and with an income to match.

Cook's influence at this time was pervasive – and Frost himself was as pervaded by it as anyone else. Ian McKellen, reading English at St Catharine's as Frost was at Caius and now beginning to test his talents in the university's theatrical circles, notes that Frost's voice began to alter to track Cook's own tones: "Certainly, he liked to impersonate: he soon adopted Cook's whine."[29] Tales of Frost's plagiarism, which dogged him for years later, can be traced back to these months at Cambridge in the winter of 1958–59, when he and – as it sometimes seemed – everyone else in those youthful Footlights circles worked and devised within the long shadow cast by Cook's unique talent. "And if he did," McKellen remarks crisply, "that was hardly unusual in comic circles; people always used other people's material."[30] But McKellen (like Frost, a grammar-school boy) does remember that Frost certainly lacked a measure of charm – this was still a lesson he had to learn – and also that he wore his ambition on his sleeve. "I always had a sense that he saw Cambridge as a mere staging post, and that unlike most of the rest of us, he had some kind of a game plan – a well worked-out game plan that would lead to his assuming his rightful place in the world."[31]

Commentators on these Cambridge days have frequently traced history backwards, rereading the story of this period with foreknowledge of Frost's early fame and success. Peter Cook's relationship with Frost is inevitably read through this prism – and with an eye too on the utter difference between the two men, their characters and their backgrounds: the one who endured an essentially parentless life, and who took to comedy as a defence and a shield; and the other whose childhood was sheltered and bolstered by a close family and unconditional love, and who came to comedy as one step in a long and very wide road. And another aspect of this story has to do explicitly with class, in a particularly English manifestation. The Footlights people, writes Harry Thompson, "loathed David Frost, loathed everything about him, from his suburban accent to his silly little bicycle clips".[32]

The language, the references, are immensely telling: they drag in their wake the disdain felt for a middle-class boy, who manifested willingly his brimming confidence and ambition and did not – or rather would not – play by the class rules that might otherwise have hedged him in. Had David Frost been less confident, had he been less buoyed by his upbringing and supported by the stout framework of his Methodist moral universe, had his ambition not clothed him in armour without apparent chink, had an innate canniness not reminded him that there was nothing to gained from falling out with those around him: had these been not present in his life, the disdain of many of his Cambridge peers might have been fatal to his vision and his ambition. As it was, he was able to slough off this disdain, or at least to seem to do so, to act as though it did not exist at all. "He simply handled incidents that he didn't like by behaving as though it didn't happen," says Cleese. "He was amazingly self-confident – and that manifested in all sorts of ways, including this one."[33] It is evident, however, that the scorn he detected at this time did indeed leave scars on David Frost: and that he was in reaction to this experience for the rest of his life.

As his first year at Cambridge came to an end, however, there was one source of distress that certainly could not be sloughed off. Frost had done next to no work towards his English degree – his ostensible reason for being at Cambridge in the first place, though the results of his summer examinations implied that he had quite forgotten this fact. He had arrived at Ian McKellen's rooms at St Catharine's College late one evening, "and said, 'Have you got any notes I could borrow?' I was just about to go to bed and the exam was the following morning, and so off he went with my notes, and stayed up all night and sat the exam the following day."[34] He "gained" – the word is suspect – a Special: a Cambridge euphemism for a grade hovering humiliatingly between Pass and Fail. The college authorities at Caius were furious – as Neil McKendrick recalls: "If he sometimes drove his student friends into a state of justified exasperation and understandable envy, he drove the dons who taught, or tried to teach, him into a state of justified near-frenzy. It was said […] that he studied part-time at Caius – so part-time that some of the Caius English dons wanted to send him down."[35] Furious too was his former Wellingborough headmaster, who in August 1959 wrote a stinging letter to his erstwhile former pupil:

Dear Frost,

I have now had a full report on Caius, and frankly I am disgusted. We did everything we could for you here, and you repay the school by doing your best to queer the pitch for us at a college to which we normally send a number of boys. I chose Caius for you in order to improve your chances, and it looks now as though you will be the first boy of ours to be sent down from Oxford or Cambridge.

I gather that there is a temporary reprieve. As it is not a lack of brains that is your trouble, but lack of common sense, I hope that you will pull yourself out of the mess. If you don't, you will regret it for the rest of your life.

It was a chastening predicament – and was made more so by being parsed and dissected by a gathering of an appalled Frost clan at Margaret Frost's home at Whitby for a summer holiday. "They were going to expel him," remembers Margaret bleakly; but when it became apparent that the university could perhaps be persuaded to be lenient (the "temporary reprieve") towards their golden child, Wilfred, accompanied by Margaret's husband Ken, drove from Yorkshire to Cambridge to plead his son's case, in as eloquent a manner as he knew how.[36] This was deeply humiliating for Frost:

Wilfred was suffering from a debilitating ear infection which made any movement troublesome, and travel in general extremely painful. Frost had the sense that this embassy, and his father's words, saved his place at Cambridge. The truth, however, is that there were voices inside Caius – McKendrick's among them – who were prepared to speak up for what they perceived to be a distinctive (if not academically industrious) young man. "I recall defending the young Frost when his performance was brought up at meetings of Tutors and College Lecturers," says McKendrick. "Having got to know him, I had grown to admire his unremitting positivity, his seemingly inexhaustible stamina, his effortless charm, his theatrical versatility and his vaulting ambition."[37] And the authorities relented: Frost was permitted to go forward into his second year at Caius. "I knew already that I could never repay my debt that I owed my parents, but this was yet one more entry in that ledger."[38]

Frost did train a slightly closer eye on his academic duties – although he never transformed into the resident Caius swot, and his attitude to his studies continued to enrage his tutors. Donald Davie was Frost's director of studies at Caius – and he was the recipient of regular insouciant essays on a variety of topics. One such, on *Hamlet*, opened with the words, "As Hamlet said to Peter Cook ..." and the effect on Davie, a Cambridge don who had devoted his life to serious textual analysis, was infuriating beyond words. But Frost's other work – his grafting at Footlights – began to pay long-term dividends. With Christmas 1959 came a significant professional advance: a first movement into television, and a movement that was in itself modest, but that was weighed down with symbolic importance. Although his experience of television remained relatively limited, David understood well enough that the medium's expansion and confidence was a key and ever-increasing driver of social and cultural change. He also understood that, while television was undoubtedly still in its infancy, it was talent-hungry and its expansion could only gain momentum.

This expansion was for the moment led by the Independent Television (ITV) network, launched in 1955 as a counterweight to the BBC's hitherto unrivalled dominance of British broadcasting. The structure of ITV was relatively original and distinctive: the new legislation that brought it into being envisioned the country carved into numerous regions, each of which played host to a locally managed and locally based ITV station. Each station would provide programmes to the national ITV network, while also remaining firmly rooted within and selling advertising space within its own region: the idea was to achieve a commercial and financial balance between this mass of local television stations, and at the same time to provide a necessary corrective to the dominance of London by fostering programme-making and creativity at centres across the country.

Anglia Television at Norwich held the franchise for East Anglia, including Cambridgeshire. It produced the *Town and Gown* magazine show which focused on life in Cambridge itself – and now the station came to Peter Cook with an idea for a Christmas special edition that would parody the show's regular diet of sensible Cambridge-themed features. Cook anchored the show, surrounded by other Footlights members, and he wrote the script with Frost – a fact which would seem to give the lie to the notion that the latter was seen merely as a talent-light hanger-on. The programme has not survived: its significance lies, perhaps, in the fact that it marks David Frost's first entrance into a television studio. He loved it, loved it from the first, and understood from the first that this was a medium in which he could thrive and which he understood instinctively and completely. "When we walked into the studio," Frost reminisced years later, "I remember thinking, *This is home; this is where I'm meant to be.*"[39] And with this understanding, he stole a march on his peers.

In Frost's remaining eighteen or so months at Cambridge, the scope of his activities and interests continued to broaden. The comedian and environmentalist Bill Oddie recalls his Cambridge baptism, in the autumn of 1960: "I met Frostie in what was virtually my first day at Cambridge. You go along to the Societies Fair – and there was the Footlights – and I remember David was an example of what you could become if you join the Footlights. Although he was still at

Cambridge as a student [...] he was always off somewhere getting something else going. That was his image, of this sort of person who was determined to be successful."[40] In the spring of 1960, Frost had become editor of *Granta*, and quickly displayed a degree of business acumen – within months he had doubled the journal's circulation by a canny combination of cutting the proportion of literary criticism in its pages, and adding to the proportion of humour and articles on film on offer. Advertising rose too, and so did the number of special editions, and the size of the journal in general.

For some of those watching Frost's trajectory, these were yet more vexing indications of success, and it must have seemed that Frost was glorying in their vexation by enjoying "the perks he felt came with his position – the right to order a car to take him around Cambridge, the right to order breakfast to be delivered to his rooms from a local hotel, and the right to charge these indulgences to *Granta*'s account to the tune of thousands of pounds".[41]

In the 1960 summer vacation, he did additional work at Anglia: this time, straight reporting, both in studio and on location. But the station opted not to continue its relationship with this ambitious young student, one executive sniffing that Frost was "not television material". Years later, Frost's friend Greg Dyke remarked that this was "the television equivalent of Decca turning down the Beatles."[42] To this, he added later some freelance work with BBC Norwich – all critical additions to his portfolio. In his final year at Cambridge, he became secretary of Footlights, just in time to see the society move into the new clubhouse described by John Cleese.

And not forgetting the lessons learned previously, he passed his Finals – just barely. With a third-class degree, he did not cover himself with glory, and disappointed his family. Indeed, he came within a whisker of going down from Cambridge with no degree at all: "In Part II of the English Tripos in 1961, fourteen Firsts were awarded, Seventy-five Upper Seconds, seventy-six Lower Seconds and forty Thirds. Of those forty Thirds, David Paradine Frost of Caius was one of the worst, arguably *the* worst." Those judging his fate included the celebrated critic FR Leavis, and CS Lewis, by then already well-known as the author of the *Chronicles of Narnia* – "and they spent an impressive amount of time discussing the appropriate class to put him in. […] Frost's nearly unintelligible handwriting led to the discussions being greatly extended as the examiners conscientiously struggled to decipher his meaning. Some have suggested that Frost had cunningly made his scripts as difficult to read as possible in the hope that the examiners would read more meaning into them than was actually there. Perhaps they were right, because the examiners eventually decided that the scripts just merited a Third Class. Having done so, they turned to [Donald] Davie and asked, 'Did we get it right?' Davie said, 'No. You should have failed him.'"[43]

It was now the summer of 1961 and Frost was now twenty-two years old. The way ahead was clear to him: a move down to London, and a move into London television. With this in his sights, he attended the annual party given by the BBC with the aim of trawling for suitable candidates for its limited number of General Traineeships on offer. These were sought after and competition was consequently intense – but the job description did not appeal. Too managerial, not sufficiently hands-on – and instead, Frost opted to apply for a trainee position at ITV that was roughly equivalent, but rather less structured, more practical and more oriented towards actual programme-making. David was accepted to one of the two positions on offer – and his immediate course was duly set.

CHAPTER 2

"You Can't Do Both"

*"If I'd known I was going to be part of an era, I'd have paid
more attention."*

Millicent Martin

This was an auspicious time for an ambitious young man to make his move on the London scene. The memory of the war years was now fading, rationing had come to an end, and although London continued to be pocked with battle-scarred buildings, and bomb sites and empty spaces colonised only by thickets of buddleia and willow-herb, there was a sense – tentative but tangible, here as in Cambridge – that a new page had been turned. London was not yet beginning to swing, perhaps, but the greyness of the post-war years was now giving way to a renewed world of colour.

London played host to two ITV stations, one broadcasting on weekdays and one at weekends – and Associated Rediffusion, the weekday station to which David had now signed up, had had the kudos of being the first national ITV station to go on air, on the evening of September 22nd, 1955. Its roster of programming, while reflecting an intention to retain a certain benchmark of quality and distinctiveness, was certainly more populist in tone than was the BBC, and for many television viewers this was no bad thing, for it had become a commonplace among the public to grumble at the patrician tones of "Auntie" BBC, which had a perceived habit in the post-war years of handing down morally improving programmes engraved on tablets of stone.

David Frost had now defected to television, but he, Jean and Margaret Frost had been avid listeners to the wireless in the course of the 1950s. The youthful Frost, at home in Gillingham, squabbled with his adult and sophisticated elder sister Jean on her visits home as to which programme to patronise: why, he wondered, would one listen to Jean's Promenade concerts on the Third Programme (the forerunner to Radio Three), which were high-minded and boring – when there was a combination of comedy, modern music and variety shows over on the Light Programme (the forerunner to Radio Two)? Squabbling aside, however, Frost and his family instinctively understood what all listeners to radio understand: that the simple experience of listening brings together a community, a society, in a way that newspapers can never manage. He would come to understand the responsibility that, for the makers of these programmes, went along with this: and understand too that this responsibility applied equally to the new medium of television. "[It] taught me a valuable lesson for when I got to London later: never to forget that the views in the Kempstons, the Gillinghams and further afield were as intrinsic a part of our audience as those close by in the metropolis, and often a good deal hungrier."[44]

Frost was aware that the media landscape was changing, and that even the BBC was quite capable of moving with the times. As early as 1951, BBC radio had begun broadcasting *The Goon Show* on its Home Service (the forerunner of Radio Four). This programme, which made stars of Harry Secombe, Spike Milligan and Peter Sellers, was occasionally surreal, anarchic and satirical; it was, in other words, everything that the BBC and Britain in the early 1950s were not supposed to be. BBC management was frequently left cold by the show, but its popularity protected it from undue interference, and its influence on the next generation of television writers and actors, as afterwards became apparent, was deep and long-lasting. In television, meanwhile, a glance at such innovative programming as *Panorama* (which launched in 1953) gave the lie to any notion that the Corporation was set hopelessly in aspic. And in addition, the BBC was not above making a little mischief when its own interests were at stake: famously, it had cast a pall over Associated Rediffusion's London launch night by choosing to kill off on that same evening a core cast member of its popular rural radio soap, *The Archers*. Yet, even as Grace Archer met her pathetic end trying to save her horse Midnight from a stable fire, Associated Rediffusion was going successfully to air – and the station would remain a vital part of London culture for the next ten years.

Associated Rediffusion was based at Television House, a splendid 1920s-era building at the junction of Aldwych and Kingsway in central London. Television House was home to a clutch of ITV-associated companies; it also housed the listings magazine *TV Times* and Independent Television News (ITN), the official news provider to the whole ITV network. Moreover, it looked across Aldwych at the imposing façade of Bush House, the home at this time of the BBC World Service – the area, then, for some years formed a significant nexus of broadcasting in London. Not that it was all cutting-edge professionalism: rather, an "air of happy improvisation" governed the cramped studios and corridors of Television House as David Frost began his traineeship in the building in August 1961.[45]

Frost's relationship with the company began with orientation sessions that would have irked a less ambitious young graduate: he was treated to tours of the purpose-built studio suites and other facilities; and the mysteries of advertising and features production were explained to him. Frost chafed under this tutelage: he was – as he already understood at Cambridge, before the traineeship had even begun – anxious to get on with the business of actual programme-making. But his first experience was not long in coming: *London Weekend* was a five-minute slot previewing happenings across the capital in the coming weekend, and Frost was given a presenting berth.

His first subjects were not, perhaps, riveting: "Two sporting events that take place tomorrow: the British Karting Championship at Brands Hatch racing circuit, starting at 2. And also on wheels – or more or less – the last stock-car racing of the season at 7.45 at

Harringay." Yet this was a significant moment: he was broadcast-ing this time not across the sparsely populated landscapes of East Anglia, but to London – and there would be more, much more where that came from. And Frost's stint as a trainee at Associated Rediffusion indicates, with the benefit of hindsight, the character of his long career in broadcasting. During his stint at the station, he moved from role to role – in the process, trying each one out for size, and in the process discovering his own strengths and interests.

Soon, for example, he had left *London Weekend* and stock-car racing behind, for a stint as a researcher on *This Week*. This was the station's flagship current affairs show, its reminder to the region that it could rival the BBC in quality, status and serious broadcast-ing, given half a chance. This was an excellent opportunity for Frost to prove himself, and soon he was combining research with off-camera interviews. In an interview with a group of teenage London smokers, for example, Frost enabled these nicotine-addicted young subjects to speak for themselves in a way that was relatively chal-lenging. Contemporary British society remained rigidly stratified by class, with limited social mobility and a dedication to eti-quette and to a herd of sacred cows, from the Royal Family down. Television of this kind allowed viewers access to other versions of life, of childhood, of Britishness to be experienced on the seamy streets of London – albeit one to be viewed from the safety and comfort of one's own three-piece suite; and was designed to capture the attention of the city's middle classes. Frost's interviews for *This Week*, though by no means revolutionary, were fresh and new, according to contemporary standards. Indeed, their element of grittiness was very much in tune with the changing times: by 1961, the so-called Angry Young Men – among them John Osborne, John Braine and at least several female figures, including Shelagh Delaney and Lynne Reid Banks – were already ploughing a furrow through British culture.

And yet the producer of *This Week* was less than thrilled with his young trainee. However fresh Frost's reports were for the pro-gramme, Cyril Bennett was convinced that Frost worked better off-screen: and he made no move to try his young colleague in front of the camera. By April 1962, then, a thwarted Frost shifted sideways once more – this time to the station's Light Entertainment division. The twist was at its height as a dance craze – and now Associated Rediffusion decided to capitalise on this phenomenon by filling a fifteen-minute slot in the schedules with a contest called *Let's Twist to Win*, in which contestants would set about twisting before an independent panel of judges. Frost's job – hardly onerous but gratifyingly visible – was to introduce the show and provide the links to fill the gap between contestants. *Let's Twist to Win* was a success – and was followed by further versions filmed in Paris and on the French Riviera. It was at this time that Frost made a lifelong friend. Judging one episode of *Let's Twist to Win* was a young actor named Michael Caine. "I was sharing a flat with Terence Stamp at the time," recalls Caine, "and he was just on the edge of fame and I wasn't; and he was doing the talk shows and I wasn't; but I'd always tag along to these events for the free drink and the cucumber sandwiches; and one of these places on one of these nights was at Associated Rediffusion, where I found myself asked to sit as a twist judge. This young chap was there as part of the programme; and at the end of the night, I said, 'So, what's your name?' 'David Frost,' he said – and at the end of the night, I said to Terence, 'We'll see more of that chap.' And after that, I'd see David out in London all the time; and in due course we became friends."[46] This association with the as yet little-known Caine developed into something sustained and meaningful: the two men, together with their wives Shakira and Carina, would enjoy a lifelong friendship.

Frost's work on television at this time was, however, only one element in his professional life – for even as his traineeship was kicking off at Television House, Frost was busy moving into the cabaret scene now thriving in London. "I wanted to do television by day," he remarked later, "and other things by night."[47] Already he had signed to the Noel Gay talent agency, re-founded several years earlier by Richard Armitage and now already a powerhouse of talent and connections. Armitage had travelled to Cambridge in June 1961 to see for himself the final Footlights show of the academic year – and, based on what he observed on the night, had invited Frost to join his list. His quarry had other offers: in particular from Donald Langdon at MCA, who also represented Peter Cook. But Frost declined the offer: in a rare glance at the rivalry which would later characterise his relationship with Cook, he notes delicately that his prospective agent's "loyalty would naturally be to Peter. So with no disrespect to Donald, it had to be Richard".[48] Armitage's son Alex underscores the gamble that his father took on signing up Frost:

> He was my father's first comedy client – at a time when satire was new. It was a hell of a thing for my father to do, to take on such a client. He didn't sing, he didn't dance, he didn't play the ukulele, he was just clearly very good at being David Frost – and he was unquenchably enthusiastic about everything. Nobody knew what he did or what he might do – but my father took him on just the same. He took to referring to my father as "my bespectacled Old Etonian manager". Theirs was an enormously close relationship, always – and of course with the result that his astonishingly larger than life character was always part of my life.[49]

Certainly the agency was prepared to put energy into its new client: Diana Crawford, who handled Frost's day-to-day affairs within the agency, remarked, "I'm fairly certain that he'll open the first television station on the moon."[50] And soon, Frost had established cabaret slots in the West End. One was the theatre club at the Royal Court, at that time run by Clement Freud, a grandson of psychoanalyst Sigmund Freud; the other was a cabaret joint called the Blue Angel, off Berkeley Square in Mayfair. And so, while Frost's varied traineeship at Associated Rediffusion undoubtedly helped to sow the seeds of a future career, it is evident in hindsight that it was his engagement at the Blue Angel which provided the first big break. Not everyone was pleased with these developments: Frost's colleagues at Television House watched him juggle his day and night jobs, his television work with his cabaret bookings – and told him, "You can't do both."

But the point was, of course, that he could.

*

> Because I lived in the middle of London, I would buy the listings guide and take in any old thing that happened to catch my eye – and one of those things was the comedy going on at the Royal Court and other venues. One evening I saw David at the Royal Court, and I thought he was great – young, witty, fresh – and after the show I introduced myself and said hi – and after that I would run into him all over the place. I would grab a bite late in the evening, after a Beatles recording session or a gig, and so naturally our paths crossed – at the Royal Court, at the Blue Angel, at Quaglino's restaurant in St James's, where David had a show. I would see him everywhere: we were in similar circumstances, after all, newly arrived in London, with masses in common and part of a very young scene.[51]

Paul McCartney's words encapsulate a flavour of the London *Zeitgeist*. Metropolis though it was, the city was also a village: it was possible to move from venue to venue across the West End, in the process encountering prominent figures in politics and the arts, clustered together in the same clubs and restaurants. "I got to know designers, artists, comedians, producers," McCartney adds, "and all these worlds very easily mingled in the very good club scene that London had going. And it was more than just entertainment: it had a political edge, this scene. And you felt you could run into Kenneth Tynan, Dudley Moore, Harold Pinter, Colin Blakeley, John Mortimer; it was a fabulous scene and a lot of fun. I would just stand there for hours talking about anything, and listening to what these people were saying."[52] This was the intimate London of the time – and David Frost was perfectly at ease in this milieu.

On the stage at the Blue Angel, Frost demonstrated that he had learned enough of the ropes at Cambridge to be able to hold his own in the pitiless environs of the West End. His natural assurance and self-confidence kept the wind in his sails: and soon a week's booking at the club turned into two months. In his autobiography, the comedian Ronnie Corbett – who in the 1950s had had his own extensive cabaret experiences – describes the club scene in contemporary London in vivid and touching terms:

> It was a time when there were lots of night-clubs in London – like Rico Dajou's and the Wardroom, run by Eustace Hoey, and Siggi's, Al Burnett's Stock Club and the Edmundo Ros Club. It was the heyday of a sort of post-war nightlife glamour which might appear unsophisticated by today's standards, but which we found tremendously exciting at the time. They were the sort of places you could go to dine out in an ambience of plush and soft lighting, dance, see a cabaret, or talk to a hostess who would usually try to look interested. Or at least pretend to listen.[53]

To Frost, everything was trotting along very nicely indeed – but not every onlooker was so easily convinced. John Bird, newly down from Cambridge and Frost's companion in a dank, dark, utilitarian and distinctly unluxurious little Pimlico flat, recalls his companion's utter unflappability even in the face of stage adversity:

> He's someone with complete self-belief. He'd come home from the Blue Angel, and I'd ask how it had gone, and he'd say, "Oh, fine," and then he'd describe what to me sounded like a nightmare – some drunk interfering with his act or what have you – but David always saw himself as coming out of any situation triumphantly. And I envied him that.[54]

Bird notes that this self-belief, so aggravating to Frost's Cambridge peers, was terribly vexing to many in London: "I liked him very much – we used to go to football matches together, I thought he was a very decent guy – but not everyone was pleased by this supreme confidence, by this sense that nothing would trouble him, even in extreme circumstances; and many thought that his confidence was misplaced and annoying, and that his success was not based on anything very substantial."[55] And such comments on Frost's unflappability are corroborated by others. Richard Armitage invited the influential BBC producer Bill Cotton to view Frost's set at Quaglino's one night; and the pair had not been in their seats for too many minutes before they realised – in Armitage's case with personal horror and professional mortification – that Frost had lost the audience, that his show was dying on its feet.

> In a dining club, of course, this feeling is emphasised, magnified in this nightmarish way by the chatter, the growing murmur of diners, the clink of cutlery on plates, the tinkle of glasses, clink clink, tinkle tinkle. And then afterwards, David came down to the table. He threw himself down on one those Quaglino's banquettes so that everyone bounced up and down, and he said, "Well, I thought that went *very* well, don't you?" Most people would simply have ended their set and cleared off the stage: but the point is my father taught me that if there's only one person who's paid their tenner and is sitting there enjoying it, then you must carry on – so you carry on. And David knew this: and he carried on – and as far as he was concerned, it was a great show.[56]

The cabaret scene was at this time heavily influenced by a new spirit abroad in the land. *Satire* is of course the catch-all term applied generally; but the word is in itself inadequate to represent the range of creativity – from mild comedy and irony to overt criticism of the prevailing order – that had evolved in the course of the 1950s and in the face of Establishment complacency. The Prime Minister, Harold Macmillan – who had assumed office in January 1957, in the sixth year of a Conservative government – had summed up this complacency in a few famous words: "Indeed, let us be frank about it – most of our people have never had it so good," he told the nation in July 1957, as his administration surveyed a scene of rising employment and increased economic output and material wealth.

The irony was, of course, that this very material wealth acted in part as a catalyst: it encouraged exploration, questioning and, ultimately, dissatisfaction with the status quo.

And there were any number of indicators that the state of the nation had changed for ever. Frost was part of that British generation which experienced the slow but relentless disintegration of the Empire in the years following the war. The disaster of Suez in 1956 had been observed narrowly by Frost's English A-Level class at Wellingborough, and, "[I]t was not so much that we expected our generation to take over the world and suddenly turn it into paradise. It was just that we were being forced to the conclusion that we could scarcely make a worse job of things than the current crew. In the meantime, as we read – and indeed wrote – about everything from Supermac to Blue Streak [Britain's abortive independent nuclear deterrent, cancelled in 1960] and the Aldermaston marches, the frame of reference for our jokes was growing."[57]

Given this context, it is hardly an accident that the likes of *The Goon Show* had already found its target – and there were other, rather different straws in the wind. *Private Eye* magazine – founded in London in 1961 and part-funded by a Peter Cook, who was flush with cash on the back of his critical and commercial success in the West End – also provided an outlet for writing and humour critical of the prevailing order. Cook was also behind the foundation in October 1961 of a new club – "a tiny, smoke-filled, former strip club" on Greek Street in Soho.[58] He named it The Establishment, and it provided a showcase for sharp-edged comedy, featuring the likes of Bird, John Fortune and – a rare woman on this decidedly masculine scene – Eleanor Bron.

Soon, the Establishment and *Private Eye* had joined forces, and the *Observer* was able (rather ungrammatically) to carol:

The satire industry is booming. Following the recent merger of *Private Eye*, the fortnightly lampoon, with The Establishment nightclub in Soho, the club are now preparing to extend their empire. They plan, among other things, to open a New York

44

branch, to produce a *Private Eye* strip-cartoon […] for Christmas; to start a restaurant in London made of converted railway carriages, satirizing British Railways food; and to launch a weekly shilling magazine about entertainment, called *Scene*.[59]

Scene would rapidly go bankrupt, dragging down The Establishment with it – but in the meantime, the club was the place to be seen, with its doormen in the happy position of being able to pocket hefty bribes to secure admission. All of this alternative cultural activity found a market, and this, of course, is the crucial point. Osborne, Braine, Delaney, Cook: these artists were by no means operating in a vacuum, casting their pearls before swine. Rather, there was a hunger, a sharp appetite in British society for newness and for an articulation – in whatever form might come along – of the frustration and social suffocation felt by many.

Frost appeared from time to time on the stage at The Establishment: and his visits to the club and its influence upon him have become the focus of much querulous debate in the years since – in tones which call to mind the anti-Frost grumbling that had lately been heard at Cambridge. Cook's friends complained that here he was throwing a line to Frost – in London as at Cambridge – by welcoming him onto the stage of his club, a place Frost would surely never have occupied on merit, and that Frost repaid him by taking the material he came across at The Establishment and reusing it in his own acts.

To be sure, there was – and there still is – a set of unwritten rules which governs cabaret and, today, stand-up comedy, and the most sacred of these rules forbids the purloining of material belonging to others. It was on this account that Jonathan Miller would christen Frost the "bubonic plagiarist" – a notorious headline that appeared in *Private Eye*. Years later, in a sign of continued affront, Miller would condemn Frost's "grotesque" ambition: a sentiment which, rooted as it is in an implied disdain for those who seek to rise above their ostensible station, is in itself revealing.[60] Joan Bakewell, both an observer of and a participant in the cultural ferment of these years, notes that such opinions were, as at Cambridge, laced with social snobbery: "The public-school types in these circles felt that effort shouldn't show: you should simply arrive and be clever – and so DF's pursuit of his career was seen as very *déclassé*. But they couldn't do anything about it, except not to like him and occasionally be malicious about him: and both of these they did."[61]

Such condemnation certainly titillates – but it also demonstrates a want of understanding as to the mechanics of cabaret. Material, as Ian McKellen noted of Cambridge, was after all used and reused systematically, shifting from stage to stage regardless of the sacred embargoes placed on such a transaction. Bakewell notes the "communality of these years", a quality as well understood by Frost as by those around him; and John Bird, a friend and colleague of Cook, is more specifically dismissive of these grumbles, making the point that "this material by its nature went round and round, from person to person."[62] And these complaints also betray an ongoing essential ignorance of Frost himself and of his purposes. Antony Jay, who would later work closely with Frost, observes that, "What David was really good at was putting on things; he was brilliant at assembling a programme, at knowing what went where."[63]And Neil Shand, also a later collaborator with Frost, underscores the "intense competitiveness" of the comedy circuit, "which generates bitchiness. The rule is never to tell a joke if a comedian is in the room: a) they won't laugh; and b) they will rush to top you. The scene fosters the most intense envy."[64] For David Frost, then, there was no issue. The world and all it contained were at his disposal – and at the disposal of everyone else too, of course – and everything had its use. Of course he would be influenced by the world around him, and all that it contained; this was what the world was for.

Moreover, he made no bones about it: there was no subterfuge. A little later, with his television career kicking off in earnest, Frost would undertake surveying trips to Footlights shows at Cambridge specifically to scout for material, with the consent of the students involved. Using the gifts of the world – regardless of whether they strictly belonged to him – was, to him, simply common sense: and this expansive frame of mind would carry him a very long way.

And, once again, it is only as a result of Frost's future career trajectory that the plagiarism story has come to be remembered at all.

Frost's essential pragmatism prevented him from being seen as a mere satirist – which was fortunate given the limitations implicit in satire itself. It could never change the world – a point conceded by Cook himself. In an ironic and frequently quoted reflection, he noted that his mission was to model it on "those wonderful Berlin cabarets which did so much to stop the rise of Hitler and prevent the outbreak of the Second World War". Griff Rhys Jones remarks that Peter Cook "was haunted, like so many comics, by the inner demon of nihilism" – such an inner demon of nihilism, in sharp contrast, would have been utterly wasting its time attempting to haunt David Frost.[65] Another fundamental difference between the two men is that, while Cook was committed to satire, Frost's connection was a good deal less emotionally fraught: his intention was to probe the terrain, to scope the landscape of satire, while he had the opportunity. When this was done, like any good impresario, he could move on to explore other opportunities. He was by no means a satirist first and foremost. Rather, he had manifold interests, overflowing optimism and self-confidence and unstoppable ambition. Satire merely provided a key – the first on a jangling ring of keys – that enabled this ambition to find expression.

His life in London – in the few scant months he had been in the city – points to this conclusion: he was exploring the opportunities at his disposal, whether on a stage in the Blue Angel, or in an editing suite or behind a camera at Television House. This was his mode of working: the shape and trajectory of his entire career bear out the sense that he was a restless and keen-eyed entrepreneur – and where once he would be trading his Biggles books in the front room of the family home at Gillingham, now he was dealing in broader and more powerful cultural commodities. And more than anything else, he was already a television man – among the first of a new wave who moved smoothly from university into the embrace of this new medium. It is this fact that marks him out as different, as distinctive from Cook and others: he saw the opportunities that television had to offer – and he grasped them with both hands. "Dislike of the man," says Peter Chadlington, "had simply to do with pique that he had got ahead."[66]

*

"Satire in those days was daring in a way that is now hard to comprehend."[67]

David Frost had now come to the attention of Ned Sherrin, a producer on the BBC's *Tonight* show: and this period marks the beginning of a series of relationships critical to Frost's future prospects. Sherrin was eight years older than Frost, but the two men shared certain similarities of outlook. Neither was from a well-off background: Sherrin was of modest Somerset farming stock and had made it via a scholarship to Oxford a few years before Frost went up to Cambridge. Both were from a church-influenced background: Sherrin too could recall Sundays reserved for worship – although he also remembered, ironically, a father with a particular prejudice against Methodist ministers. And Sherrin had, almost by accident, also undertaken his own television apprenticeship at Television House, before migrating to the BBC. There were also, of course, differences between the two, most notably in their private lives: Sherrin was gay and openly so – unusual enough in those days before homosexual law reform, although the BBC provided a relatively benign and tolerant environment. And Frost, liberal by nature and also wholly accustomed to what Hermione Lee has called "the golden glow of homosexuality" which suffused Cambridge life, was unfazed by such knowledge.[68]

Tonight had begun in 1957: it aired on the BBC at teatime, and was invented to fill the Toddlers' Truce slot in which previously – in a quaint, not to say weird conspiracy of silence between "Auntie" and the nation's parents – television screens had gone blank so that parents could feed their children and bundle them off to bed. It was in itself a distinctive, innovative show, informal and relaxed, with an entertaining combination of arts, current affairs and human-interest stories – in other words, the first in a series of such BBC programmes designed to fill this cosy teatime television slot. It was produced by Alasdair Milne – an Oxford contemporary of Sherrin and later, the director general of the BBC – and Donald Baverstock. The two men, as Sherrin remarks, made for "a formidable editorial team".[69] Antony Jay was a fourth element on the *Tonight* team. He had started out on the programme in 1957, before working his way up through the ranks, becoming in the process a television man to his fingertips. Later, he became the co-creator of *Yes, Minister*.

Sherrin was now in the midst of developing a weekend entertainment and satire show for the BBC. The station more or less shut down at 10.30pm on Saturday nights, and Sherrin's task was to create a programme that would extend the schedule a little and, it was hoped, chime with the *Zeitgeist*. There would be a musical element: Sherrin, in fact, took a particular delight in musical interludes, and *Tonight* habitually marked the death of this or that famous crooner by booking actor-singer Millicent Martin to run through a medley of the deceased's most famous songs for the benefit of teatime viewers.

But Sherrin was decidedly hedged in when it came to the airing of racier material, for here, the dead hand of BBC regulations was clamped onto programme-makers' backs. In his history of British satire, Humphrey Carpenter runs amusingly through the items and topics absolutely forbidden from being broadcast in the name of the BBC's Variety department. The bible of such rules, he notes, was a horrid document entitled *BBC Variety Programmes Policy Guide for Writers and Producers*, produced in 1948 and never revised, which banned any portrayal of:

> Lavatories. Effeminacy in men. Immorality of any kind. Suggestive References to – Honeymoon Couples. Chambermaids. Fig leaves. Prostitution. Ladies' Underwear, e.g. winter draws on. Animal habits, e.g. rabbits. Commercial travellers.

It was permitted to take a crack at politicians, the *Guide* went on, "so long as they do sensibly, without undue acidity and above all funnily".[70]

Until this point, the BBC had been fairly chilly about engaging too directly with the likes of Peter Cook and his fellow satirists, in spite of their manifest success. General discussions about a new satire show, featuring Cook and others, had fizzled out; afterwards, it became clear that the Corporation had simply decided that it could create its own satirical strand of programming, without necessarily having Cook take part. Bird recalls a string of meetings with Sherrin and Baverstock, at which the form of such a show was discussed: it would be, essentially, The Establishment transferred to the screen – and Cook was convinced it would work. But try as they might, the BBC could not be made to take the bait.

That the attitude of the Corporation, then, raised hackles is perfectly evident from an excitably written spoof BBC press release published in *Private Eye* in the summer of 1962:

> We're right on the trail of all the latest trends with our forthcoming satirical programme *Saturday is Satire Day* – a sort of expanded, two-hour version of that frightful, that is to say delightful little cartoon satire that [journalist and critic] Bernie Levin's doing for us at the moment on *Tonight*. Absolutely no holds barred, of course, within the framework of the libel laws, good taste, and the producer's sense of humour – we're going to let these young chaps really let their hair down – we're even going to let them take off some of our own programmes ...[71]

Now, therefore, although the BBC was wondering in public about creating just such a programme, there was no reason for *Private Eye* or anyone else to think that Sherrin's current efforts would come to fruition. Yet behind the scenes, things were moving – and Frost would prove to be a direct beneficiary.

Sherrin had visited both The Establishment and Blue Angel (the latter at the prompting of John Bird) on scoping missions. In his visit to the latter, in the autumn of 1961, Sherrin was impressed with what he found: the young Frost could think on his feet, could improvise neatly, could do what was needed to keep a successful show on the road. Yet, Frost and Sherrin would tell rather different versions of that momentous visit to the Blue Angel. The former claimed, in characteristically upbeat tones, that he was performing as usual that night, that the management was pleased with him, and that Sherrin saw the standard show, liked what he saw, and that it all rolled on from there. Sherrin, however, tells a rather more dramatic story: that Frost's show was floundering, and that it took a last-minute intervention from that "formidable old agent and booker, Beatrice Braham" to persuade the club to put his show on that evening.[72]

It is impossible, of course, to come to the truth of the matter but, in the end, Frost performed, Sherrin observed and a connection was formed. Sherrin invited Frost to come and meet with him and Antony Jay for lunch in an Italian restaurant around the corner from the BBC's decrepit Lime Grove studios, in west London, and here, the shape and spirit of the possible new show were discussed. "It ought to stay sharp in my memory," says Antony Jay, "but the truth is that it doesn't. I remember [Frost] seemed a bright young man, and I thought he deserved a chance, and it all went from there."[73] It was a momentous lunch, just the same; and this meeting, on January 9th, 1962, was the first in a series of such discussions which would prove pivotal in Frost's career – for the result, six months later, was a pilot episode of a programme called *That Was the Week That Was*.

The title had been thought up by John Bird, who had in fact also been Sherrin's first choice of anchor and link-man. Frost himself was initially listed as a supporting member of a cast that also included Millicent Martin and Lance Percival, who had acted in revue alongside Bird. It was only when Bird – reluctant to commit to a BBC show that paid peanuts and that might or might not go ahead, lured by the lights of America but having given his word that he would commit to this adventure – opted instead to leave London to front up The Establishment's new venture in Manhattan, that the producers looked elsewhere. And Bird casually suggested his flatmate David Frost, who was in any case a smooth enough fit. Sherrin's intention was that the programme would mimic, as much as reasonably possible, the mood and atmosphere of a late-night club: dark sets, a studio audience, music and a series of tableaux and sketches that would call to mind the cabaret evenings with which Frost was now so familiar. There were any number of other figures on whom Sherrin might have called, but again, now as in the future, Frost's tenacity, persistence and work ethic sealed the deal.

Frost himself quotes Donald Baverstock, on the meaning and function of the infant show: "Late on Saturday night people are more aware of being persons and less of being citizens than at any other time of the week. It is, therefore, the best time to hang contemporary philosophy on the hook in the hall, to relieve the pressure of earnest concern and goodwill which presses down on us throughout the rest of the week. To abandon what Mary McCarthy calls 'The Slow Drip of Cant'."[74] These were weighty opinions weightily expressed and would not, presumably, in themselves have brought the crowds rolling in – but the point was well made: British audiences, it was assumed, were ready to dip their toes into the waters of television satire, to experience the chill for themselves. And so was the BBC – but only squeamishly, only tentatively: everything hinged on the pilots and how they were received inside the hierarchy of the Corporation. And it was evident even before the programme began that its prospects would be touch-and-go. Sherrin's vision was of highly experimental television complete with roving cameras, and with the studio audience, the sets themselves, the booms and microphones and whole paraphernalia of television-making on full view to the viewers at home, rather than being hidden and closeted behind the all-seeing and authoritative camera. This made sense, in that it left the performers free to slip from one role, sketch, song, item into another and then another, all in a matter of seconds, as would be the case in live cabaret. Sherrin was convinced it would work, that it would reach out to audiences in an unprecedented and electrifying manner. Now the job of the pilot was to convince the highest echelons of the BBC.

This pilot was broadcast two days later – and there was nothing polished about it. For one thing, it ran to over two-and-a-half hours without an interval, straining in the process the patience and bladders of the captive studio audience. But, although *That Was the Week That Was* would thrive on a sense of spontaneity and flexibility, some of the programme's key and most recognisable elements were already in place: in particular, an ensemble cast of bright young things armed with talent and a multitude of opinions. Ronnie Corbett describes Frost anchoring the show by "cultivating an amiable snarl and speaking rather through his nose".[75] Among those joining him were figures who would become familiar names in the decades to come: Brian Redhead, who acted as co-anchor for this single pilot, and who would later forge a distinguished career on BBC radio; the *Private Eye* cartoonist Willie Rushton; Bernard Levin (himself previously a *Private Eye* target) whose envisioned role on the programme would be to debate with and skewer various collections of grandees – on this occasion, Conservative Party wives in large hats who later complained that he had turned them into laughing stocks; and Millicent Martin, who provided the music with glittering professional aplomb – before leaving halfway through the show to go on a pre-arranged holiday to Spain.

Also present were Eleanor Bron, John Bird and John Fortune, who squeezed in the pilot before decamping to The Establishment's New York opening. Peter Cook was supposed to join them on the pilot, but he did not appear. He *had* agreed to a request by Frost that a piece the pair had written for *Granta* in 1960, parodying the television coverage of the opening ceremony of the Rome Summer Olympics, now be adapted for the programme. On the day, however, Cook was too angry and frustrated – at his "justifiable sense", as Bird notes, that the BBC had stolen his satire idea – to turn up.[76] This was an example, arguably, of Cook's skewering a television opportunity as it was going a-begging; and another sign that, unlike Frost, he did not properly appreciate the growing power of television. Cook had reason to be angry with the BBC, in other words, but no reason at all to be angry with the cast. Angry he was, however, though this anger was tempered by his sense that the July pilot had been poor, and an instinct that the BBC would now drop the whole project. Cook sailed for New York at the end of the summer, comforted by the thought that David Frost's ambition had, now, surely met an immoveable barrier.

The film of the original pilot has vanished: but enough memories survive of the official BBC reaction to it to make one realise that Peter Cook was not far off the mark. *That Was the Week That Was* only survived due to – Frost's not unconstant companion – smiling fortune. Inside the Corporation, "[I]t was talked of as some sort of blue movie," remarks Sherrin.[77] Certainly, executives were vexed and unimpressed, focusing on the shoddy, amateurish and crass elements on display in the pilot – and especially on the politics on parade. For the pilot, Frost wrote a monologue lampooning the government: delivered by Rushton, it presented a certain Tory minister, a Sir Arthur Trench Foot, who had sat in Cabinet uninterruptedly since 1938. In addition, a heavy-handed complaint by Conservative Central Office at Levin's treatment of its ladies rattled the Corporation; and Grace Wyndham Goldie, the powerful and formidable Head of Television Talks and Current Affairs was certainly no fan of the pro-gramme. But ironically, it was Tory complaints that more than likely saved *That Was the Week That Was*: their strength and volubility had the effect of moving consideration of the show further up the BBC hierarchy, where it reached the desks of executives who grasped the programme's humour, sophistication and potential; and who pos-sessed, in addition, a touchy sense of BBC editorial independence. "So, but for those Conservative ladies and Bernard Levin," Frost remarked later, "[*That Was the Week That Was*] might never have got on the air."[78] As it was, a wedge had been inserted in the body of the Establishment – and a second pilot was ordered.

At this time, David Frost was still – though to be sure, this fact could easily be forgotten in the pell-mell style of his life at this time – in the employ of Associated Rediffusion. His work rate was in itself simply prodigious, young man though he was: he was working day and night – but matters would now come to a head.

The ITV station, hearing of the pilot, immediately offered Frost his own satire programme, plus a four-year contract and – at the time – generous retainer of £3000 per annum for the first year, rising to £6000 in the fourth year, plus a guarantee of £18,000 plus performance fees for all programmes in which he took part. Frost calls this delightful situation a "predicament": he temporised with ITV and explained it all to Sherrin at the BBC – and now the prospect of losing Frost seems to have settled any remaining queasy BBC stomachs.[79] He was offered a considerably smaller sum – £650 – if he would stay with the *That Was the Week That Was* production team until its destiny was decided. It was a gamble, certainly – but Frost did not hesitate. He went with the BBC – and was fired from Associated Rediffusion on the spot. There were no regrets: he was in the environment and in the creative milieu that suited him at this moment – and the episode speaks volumes about Frost's instincts, attuned antennae and willingness to hold his nerve, to take financial chances and play the longest game of all.

Frost in these months attained a deep professional contentment. He now shared an office with Sherrin at Lime Grove: and his time was spent brainstorming, networking, bouncing ideas with writers and performers over long lunches at the Café Royal on Regent Street: and generally revelling in exactly the tenor of life and creative ambience that suited him at this time. Antony Jay recalls the ambience of the time as one calibrated exactly to hothouse the programme's attitudes: "We met over coffee, lunch, drinks and dinner to reinforce our views on the evils of apartheid, nuclear deterrence, capital punishment, the British Empire, big business, advertising, public relations, the Royal Family, the defence budget … it's a wonder we ever got home."[80] But work was fitted in too: within a few months, the shape of the second pilot was a settled thing.

This new pilot went nicely: at any rate, Wyndham Goldie was as pleased as the producers needed her to be – and the show was given a green light; the series would air in October.

*

That was the week that was. It's over, let it go. But what a week it was – On the Stock Exchange the tea shares hit an all-time low.

Millicent Martin sang the opening words of the first edition of *That Was the Week That Was*, which was shot in the BBC's new Television Centre in west London on the night of Saturday November 24th, 1962. Frost woke early that day in the flat in Pimlico he shared with John Bird and Christopher Booker; arrived too early at the studios for rehearsals; rehearsed all day; and by 10.15pm was watching the studio audience file in, ready for the programme to begin broadcasting at 10.50pm. A certain nervous tension, for the most part fended off, hung over the day – and when the programme began, the nerves remained.

This was a young cast, thrown into the deep water of live, spontaneous television – and Millicent Martin recalls the collegiate atmosphere on the show, a sense of mutual support that under the circumstances was absolutely necessary. Blessed with a photographic memory, Martin was able with a certain confidence to perfect songs in next to no time – though, "I was terrified just the same." She recalls too a sense that her fellow cast members were equally terrified: they leafed frantically through their scripts until the instant the camera focused on them, at which point the scripts were dropped onto the floor; by the end of the show, the studio was knee-deep in abandoned drifts of paper. And Martin adds that, in spite of this adrenalin and tension, Frost displayed that same sweetness of temper that would characterise his entire career: he "never forgot his courtesy: he was wonderful in that respect. He was always, always very aware of everyone else, always kind to the people around him: and he never, not ever, lost his temper or threw a tantrum, as a young man in his position might well have learned to do."[81] In time she noted too a certain degree of shyness to his character, hidden behind a showman's persona – "he covered it well" – but perceptible nevertheless when working at close quarters.[82]

But the live element to the programme, Frost was soon to discover, was very much to his taste. He found that night that he preferred the adrenalin "hit" of live television: it sharpened his responses, his instincts, as though the sound stage was a theatre stage – and this preference would remain with him for the whole of his career. It underscored a vital aspect of Frost's public persona: that of performance – of a performer absolutely intent on creating an event.

Frost's first words on the programme were distinctive – and familiar to many in the audience: "There's a one-eyed yellow idol to the north of Kathmandu, with a little Chinese rifle in 'is 'and ..." This rhyme was a reworking of James Milton Hayes's poem *The Green Eye of the Little Yellow God*, which was already an established and favoured target for parody by *The Goon Show* and very many others. In this particular context, Frost's lines were a reflection on Sino-Indian geopolitical tensions in the Himalayas – at this time ongoing and dangerously fraught. They were, in other words, an indication of the interests of the programme – and by implication, of the audience too. They flattered the viewer, simply by taking for granted that the sort of person who would sit down of a Saturday night to watch *That Was the Week That Was* also observed and grasped the intricacies of international politics. And so when Frost remarks, as he does in his autobiography, that his opening lines were nothing special, he is certainly being disingenuous: his reworking of a hackneyed poem demonstrates a certain clever awareness of what audiences would recognise and appreciate as familiar. Nothing too shocking, in other words, to begin with: rather, a form of inside joke to kick the programme off, bring the audience on-side – and keep it there.

For this was a clever programme. To be sure, it was delivered with a certain lack of polish, with much glancing at scripts and into the wrong cameras – but Sherrin and Frost understood that this simply did not matter; if anything, it added to the programme's weight and distinctiveness, to the sense that this was television at the cutting edge. And again, it kept the audience inside the tent, within a shared community. The writing was clever too: Sherrin had now brought Christopher Booker across from *Private Eye* to work on the scripts; and the opening programme's reflections on the week's by-election in North Suffolk, its lampooning of the Army, of nuclear weapons, of the music and public relations industries, and of British sexual hypocrisy – these all provided a statement of purpose, and a manifesto for the future. Some of the material was recycled from the second pilot – including a sketch based on one originally written by Peter Cook; in this version for television, Frost played Cook's part – and imitated Cook's tones.[83] Later, it was acknowledged quietly that this sketch was not, perhaps, Frost's finest moment. Jack Duncan, one of the assistant directors on the show, said Frost's performance in the sketch had done it no favours – and consequences would, in due course, flow.

Out in the country, audiences were absorbing the impact of the new programme. In Whitby, Margaret Frost glowed: "I would never miss a show, not after that night."[84] In Beccles too, Mona and Wilfred were flushed with pride – and a little trepidation at the thought of what their beloved son was getting himself into. And up in Cambridge, John Cleese and others gathered around the new television set installed in the Footlights clubroom. They felt a certain proprietorial interest, of course, given that Frost had already been to visit them and gather ideas and jokes from the Footlights crew:

We were astounded by it. It was unlike any television programme we had ever seen before: funny, raucous and deliberately rough in style. But what took our breath away was its impudence and its brashness, and above all its complete disrespect for the traditional figures of authority. It was a huge and irreversible tidal wave. [...] Retired colonels throughout the land bewailed the End of Civilisation as they knew it; and the programme made David Frost [...] a star. [...] We were startled how little impressed he seemed by what had happened to him. It was as though he thought it the most natural thing in the world. In a rather endearing way I don't think David was ever at all surprised by his success. From then on, we had the thrill of sitting in the clubroom every Saturday night, clustered around the set

in the hope of seeing one of our sketches being performed in *the*
hit show on national television.[85]

And these reactions, of course, make manifest what the young
David Frost had sensed while still a wireless-listening schoolboy
quarrelling with the sister at Gillingham: the idea of a spider web
of citizens out in the country, absorbing what was being offered to
them, as part of a communal experience.

The programme overran into the early hours of Sunday morning;
when it finally ended, the cast headed off to eat and celebrate. They
fetched up at the Casserole restaurant on the King's Road – camp,
daring and home to a gay club in the basement. Here you could
get a plate of beef-and-mango casserole for seven shillings and sixpence: and here they celebrated the broadcast, and anticipated the
following morning's reviews.[86]

"Then a moment of pure joy."[87]

Anyone who similarly has awaited a review, in a state of
nervous dread, will recognise Frost's sensations as he and Ned
Sherrin digested the back page of the following morning's *Sunday
Telegraph*: "Without reservation, *That Was the Week That Was*,
the BBC's first late-night satirical show, is brilliant. It based itself
securely on the week's events, repeating and expanding on its idi-
ocies, invectives and near-libels. It did so with intelligence and
dislike. [...] All of it was uncompromisingly 'in'."[88] The following
day's newspapers similarly glowed with approval of the programme.
Dennis Potter – later, of course, a celebrated television dramatist –
in the *Daily Herald* wrote that "this TV newcomer smiles as she
bites", and the *Daily Mail* named Frost "the first anti-personality
on TV", a comment that of course could read in any number of
ways. ("Do you think that's good?" Frost asked, in what was one of
his exceedingly rare moments of fretfulness.) But audience ratings
were unequivocal: they came in at over three million; and the future
of the show was for the moment secure. Frost was ecstatic.

Later editions were less obviously sensational – but they remained
smart and strong. A scene in the second programme, broadcast

on December 1st, 1962, once more provided another manifesto moment, in the form of an alternative image of the British police to set beside the genial, understanding coppers portrayed in the BBC's long-running drama *Dixon of Dock Green* (1955–76):

> *[Lance Percival enters in policeman's uniform.]*
> Citizen: Good evening.
> Policeman: Evening, sir. *[He beats Roy* [Kinnear] *up.]* Just a routine enquiry, sir.

And so the targets mounted up: the Church of England, God, the government in general, the Bomb, anti-Soviet hysteria, the Catholic Church and the Official Secrets Act, as well as more established ones such as the dire state of post-war British food and catering. All were among the many subjects mocked in front of small audiences on stages in London and elsewhere – but now here they were being pilloried to a television audience. A *mass* television audience: for within weeks, the newspapers were reporting on a new phenomenon – pubs emptying startlingly early on a Saturday night, dates cancelled, friends arranging to meet in front of the box at home. Annabel Goldsmith – then, Annabel Birley, a scion of the aristocratic Londonderry family, and notionally, therefore, one of the programme's Establishment targets – recalls being "riveted" by the show, and thereafter adopting the habit of declining invitations on Saturday night in order to be at home to watch it. "We loved it so much. That was the beginning of David. The real, young, cocky, brilliant David. It was wonderful, and so funny, and so mocking and so full of humour."[89] *That Was the Week That Was* had become, in a few short weeks, an event and a sensation – and the first British television programme ever to have caught the attention of the public and the spirit of the age in such an extraordinary way. Ratings rose exponentially: from three to five million, to seven, to nine – until six weeks into its run, an extraordinary twelve million people were sitting up on a Saturday night to watch the show – and this at a time when television ownership was still far from a universal phenomenon.

This was essentially a *male* show: men wrote it, men performed in it and produced it; Millicent Martin was the solo female in the permanent cast. In this, it was very much part of the satiric mainstream: Elisabeth Luard notes that, "The Establishment [Club] was run by men. *Beyond the Fringe* was an all-male gang cracking all-male jokes. And the lads at *Private Eye* were precisely that: a bunch of lads turning out a grown-up version of a boys' own mag. *TW3* [*That Was the Week That Was*] employed Millicent Martin as resident songbird, but the serious stuff was delivered by the men." In this pre-feminist milieu, Luard notes, "the women were there only because they were wives and girlfriends".[90]

The BBC, with a critical and ratings success on its hands, could now weather any complaints thrown in its direction. But Harold Macmillan kept his head down: when government papers from the period were released in 1992 under the Thirty-Year Rule, they revealed a stern note from the Prime Minister to the office of the Postmaster General, which had called in the scripts of *That Was the Week That Was* in order to check for violations of the censorship and blasphemy laws. The functionaries subsequently went silent – and the archives reveal why: "I hope," Macmillan had written to Reginald Bevins, the Postmaster General at the time, "you will not, repeat not, take any action about 'That Was the Week That Was' without consulting me. It is a good thing to be laughed over – it is better than to be ignored."[91]

But others were less measured: while the back page of the *Daily Telegraph* garlanded the programme, the opinion pages went so far as to devote an agitated leader column to the subject, a sure indication of the extent to which the show was setting teeth on edge:

Satire is an intimate thing between a few gifted artists and small audiences [...] But when it is poured into licensed channels, such as BBC late-night television, it can work like new wine in old bottles. There is, moreover, the temptation, since millions view it, to insert propaganda in the form of satire. This is a reproach that is sure to be levelled against Saturday's programme *That*

Was the Week That Was. For it guyed cardinals, distorted a film of the Prime Minister to a point beyond ridicule [...] And whereas the real satirist, who plays to a keenly critical audience, is kept on his mettle by their reactions, the TV performer, divided from them by the screen, is in danger of lapses of taste.[92]

Later – when the last programme before Christmas satirised the Queen's upcoming festive broadcast to the nation – the newspaper wailed at the "cynical" and "irreligious" material now being habitually churned out by the BBC on Saturday nights. But the *Telegraph*'s letters page demonstrated that even its readers did not always agree. "Why," one correspondent asks acidly, "should speech or writing be enjoyed only by the minority who can either obtain or afford a seat at the Fortune Theatre or a table at The Establishment Club?"[93]

As that bitter winter of 1962–63 began to bite, closing the country down and from Boxing Day 1962 enveloping it in three months of heavy snow and (in London) filthy smog, *That Was the Week That Was* rolled on. It had already crushed one rival, in the form of a short-lived, late-night programme put together for ITV by Associated Rediffusion – and as the run continued in 1963, so David Frost's role began to change. Jack Duncan had taken his reservations about Frost to Sherrin: "I went up to Ned and said, 'I don't want Frost in any more sketches. He's not an actor.' And I never had him in any more sketches – which was good for the programme, because it turned him almost exclusively into the front-man journalist, which it needed. Though Ned let him go on doing monologues ..."[94]

Certainly, Sherrin was watching his protégé narrowly – for to his eye, Frost was something of a curate's egg. He was wholly admirable, in that he had come into his television "in a bound", leaving others trailing in his wake. He looked and sounded the part, with his sharp dark suits, exaggerated quiff, "curious classless" accent, distinctive delivery, quite extraordinary energy and abundant self-confidence. But Sherrin could detect weaknesses in Frost – perhaps more than Frost himself could. He was less nimble in the matter of sketches and humour; he was better as the straight man, the anchor. And Sherrin's observations foreshadow the later television man that Frost would become, the roles in which he would shine and achieve international fame. And yet the comedy writer Neil Shand – with whom Frost would later work in many projects and establish in the process a close personal friendship – is convinced that it was not television but the call of comedy that lay at Frost's heart. "It was what he wanted to shine at more than anything: those stage appearances, cabaret appearances, were more precious to him than anything else with the possible exception of the Nixon apology."[95] But even at the time, it is clear that those watching Frost understood that they were seeing him evolve into an anchor who, instead of relying on authority and gravitas to keep the show on the road, was able to respond to every aspect of a continually changing and morphing show. In that sense, David Frost was indeed indicating that he had moved from the terrain of satire into the exploration of a much wider brief.

Frost had also to deal with criticism that struck closer to home. As audience figures continued to rise and *That Was the Week That Was* became mainstream media fodder, the newspapers cottoned on to the fact that he was the son of a Methodist minister. On January 12th, 1963, the programme had broadcast a long and witty segment titled The Consumer's Guide to Religion, which poked fun at world religions one by one in a way that would make for rather interesting television even today. The Established Church, for example, was pilloried for its supposed woolly attitudes and its ability to be all things to all people:

The attraction of the Church of England lies in its democratic spirit. If you want transubstantiation, you can have transubstantiation. If you don't want transubstantiation, you don't have to have it! You can just walk down the road to another Church of England church and not have it. If you want Mass, you can have Mass. If you want Immaculate Conception, you can have that too. But nobody will force you to have it if you don't want to.

And the Church speaks to you in *English*. Of course, what will happen if we go into the Common Market, God only knows. But we think it'll still be there, speaking to you in *English*. And it's a jolly friendly faith. If you are one, there's no onus on you to make anyone else join; in fact, nobody need ever know. [...] And it's pretty fair on the whole. With some of these productions – Roman Catholicism and Judaism, for instance – you start guilty from the off, but with the C of E, on the whole you start pretty well innocent, and they've got to prove you're guilty. You get eternal life – of course you get eternal life – but there's none of this toffee-nosed nonsense about the only true faith and the chosen people and so on. [...] We have no hesitation proclaiming it the Best Buy.

The result of this was that Wilfred Frost, at home in Beccles, became for some days the focus of press attention, and was quoted widely and inaccurately on the subject of his son's supposedly irreligious attitudes. "David Frost was wrong, says his Clergyman Father," bawled the *Daily Mail*. In fact, he said no such thing, telling the *Beccles and Bungay Journal* a few days later that he was not in possession of the facts, and therefore had no comment to make. Frost himself remarked a few months later that his father had been pounced on using typical Fleet Street tactics, and had managed the best he could under trying circumstances. "He told one journalist he found the piece very witty, another journalist that he found it irreverent, and a third journalist that he had fallen asleep halfway through."[96] In fact, Wilfred was already showing the signs of the ill-health that would presently bring his work to a premature end – but in any case, given the Frost parents' lavish love of and unqualified support for their youngest child, it is very unlikely that either Wilfred or Mona was unduly perturbed by anything their son was up to.

The programme continued to cast its net widely; and to pull in both foreign and domestic fodder. As tensions spiralled ever upwards in the American South, for example, and a nascent Civil Rights movement began to take shape, a 35-year-old white American postal worker, William Moore, was murdered by the side of a highway in Alabama as he was taking part in a solo walk against segregation. The programme responded with a number sung by Millicent Martin and set against the backdrop of a troupe of black-and-white minstrels. Martin extolled the virtues of the South "... where the Mississippi mud/kinda mingles with the blood of the niggers who are hanging from the branches of the tree. I want to go back to Mississippi [...] Where we hate all the darkies and the Catholics and the Jews / Where we welcome any man, who is white and strong and belongs to the Ku Klux Klan ..." And in these same months, the programme took aim at the London's artistic elite as exemplified in the selection process for the Royal Academy's summer show: in his witty cartoon slot, Timothy Birdsall noted that, "We mustn't forget the abstract. We like to have one or two abstracts in it, just to show that we're with it and up with the times; and also to give the Duke of Edinburgh the opportunity of saying something forthright and down to earth. You remember the Duke of Edinburgh? – he's the one who's just like an ordinary person."

The programme finished its run at the end of April 1963, with ratings hitting upwards of ten million: "You're keeping the children up!" said Roy Plomley, the unctuous presenter of *Desert Island Discs*, when Frost appeared on the programme that month; he selected Edith Piaf singing "Non, je ne regrette rien" as his favourite track; and – in a move that might have surprised Donald Davie – the collected works of Chaucer as his desert-island book, teamed with a supply of potato crisps.[97] And it was just at this point, as the team scattered for the summer, that the Profumo scandal kicked off. This political and sexual sensation arguably did more than anything else in these years to undermine public confidence in the British Establishment and governance of the country. Certainly, it symbolised, with eerily good timing, the sudden fragility of the country's elite. "From the time that *Look Back in Anger* appeared in 1957," notes Antony Jay, "the country seemed to be molten, like warm wax: it seemed as though it could assume any

form; and the Establishment ethos melted too and came apart."
Profumo was the culmination of this – and so of course it was great
good luck to be involved with television at that time. "We felt we
could do anything."[98]

Profumo was certainly sensational beyond the dreams of head-
line-writers. It involved prostitution, a government minister and a
Soviet diplomat all moving in elite circles in London and against
the backdrop of Cliveden, the splendid and gracious country
house on the Thames in Buckinghamshire. *That Was the Week
That Was*, in common with *Private Eye* and the media in general,
had long since sniffed the air with regard to this breaking scandal:
by March, facts and claims were being splashed across the front
pages, the government minister John Profumo had been forced to
the Commons to deny the rumours circulating of his liaison with
the call girl Christine Keeler, *Private Eye* was printing detailed
allegations – and this was the cue for the programme to poke a
little fun in this general direction. "The emotion that gripped us all
was cheerful, uncontrollable glee," wrote Jay years later. "It was a
wonderful vindication of all we believed. It proved the essential rot-
tenness of the institution."[99] The scandal rumbled on throughout
the spring of the year, with Profumo eventually resigning in June,
having admitted lying to the Commons. For David Frost, however,
the scandal was rather more about fun than moral shock:

> Thanks to the mood of the nation – a mood in part engendered
> and in part reflected by *TW3* – the Profumo affair was not a
> national disaster waiting to happen, it was more a national joke
> waiting to happen. And the waiting period between the denial in
> March and the denouement which was to come in June simply
> encouraged the jokes, and the rumours, to multiply.[100]

Other parts of his life were also opening up during these months.
On a Saturday night in March 1963, Frost had dropped into the
hospitality room of the music show *Juke Box Jury*, the only other
BBC show to go out live that evening. This was not something he

habitually did. He "had never had either the time or the inclination" to do so, he notes, and David Jacobs, the host of the show, was surprised to see him. Frost, of course, had an agenda: he had heard that the actress Janette Scott was a panellist on that show that evening, and he was determined to meet her. Women had, after all, never held any fears for the young David Frost. "He was never hampered," Joan Bakewell remarks, "by those frosty inhibitions that came with public school types, who only ever lived in prep schools and public schools and the army, and who, when they found a woman, simply didn't know their way around. David, by contrast, grew up with women, and feeling very comfortable with women. And he understood the importance of appearance too. He was very aware of the importance of looking his best, of making an effort – though he had no illusions that he was a heart-throb or especially good-looking. He told me once about this insight he had gained early in his life: that if you ask enough girls to sleep with you, you'd be surprised how many say yes."[101]

Janette Scott was the daughter of the actress Thora Hird, who by 1963 was already a recognisable and established presence on British stage and screen. And the glamorous and beautiful Scott herself, at the age of 24, already had more than a dozen films under her belt: and Frost had worshipped her ever since he dropped into the Carlton cinema at Raunds at the age of seventeen – to be confronted by the sight of Scott passionately kissing her co-star Vernon Gray in *Now and Forever*, prior to eloping with him to Gretna Green. He later confided with embarrassment to Scott that he had written to the Janette Scott Fan Club at Elstree Studios in Hertfordshire. Seven years had passed, but evidently he worshipped her still – and happily for him, the attraction was mutual. Frost and Scott met briefly behind a section of scenery – and obviously hit it off, because Frost contacted her again the very next day. They agreed to dine together that night, meaning that both of them had quietly to cancel their existing dates for the evening. Which was soon done. Supper "was enough for both of us," Frost remembers coyly, and their relationship was a settled thing.[102]

Janette Scott was emerging from a marriage to the Canadian singer and performer Jackie Ray; in addition, a discreet, year-long liaison with Peter Sellers had just come to an end – and now here was someone else appearing in her life at just the right moment. She was just as thrilled. "I was impressed," she remembers. "*TW3* was such a new and exciting show; and all the chattering classes were talking about it; and nothing like it had been on television before." As for the chemistry with Frost: "It was very instant and very mutual and the timing was excellent."[103] Scott's nous in the public eye was a most valuable stabilising influence in Frost's life in this frenetic period.

Indeed, she brought her influence to bear from the off, encouraging Frost, Bird and Booker to move from their disagreeable Pimlico flat which Scott recalls as having "hardly any furniture and was very much what you would expect of student digs: no housework done and no clothes put away. After one visit I encouraged moving. And much to my surprise […] they did" – into a rather more agreeable flat on the King's Road. Scott had herself just bought a house off the King's Road: and while it was being renovated she moved into the flat too. The quartet got along well – and this period established Frost's habit of convening with associates for breakfast meetings: "After a few weeks, I had to start filming *The Beauty Jungle* at Pinewood. This meant getting up at 5.30am every morning, which under normal circumstances was just part of the job: but when you're in an apartment that's full of people having fun and writing scripts and articles and sketches while other people are playing table tennis on a miniature table and cooking at all hours – well, in that environment, getting up early is tough. However, I did it. And because I had to do it, David got up too and that was the start of something that he became known for: the breakfast meetings."[104]

Brown's Hotel on Albermarle Street in Mayfair, Scott adds, was at that time Frost's favourite breakfasting place – the first in a long line of favourites over the years. This pleasant Bohemian phase lasted for some weeks before Scott moved into her new house – and Frost moved in with her. At the same time, she set about refashioning him. She despatched him off to equip himself with a new wardrobe, and – after diplomatic hints got her nowhere – ordered him to find a new hairstyle. Scott was now able to observe at close quarters the ways in which Frost thought and worked – and at first she was startled at the apparent innocence with which he conducted his business. "I really think that at this early point, he didn't have a clue about the world his career was taking him into. He was kind and quick-witted and highly intelligent – but totally unsophisticated about the profession itself. At one point he was cast in a small reporter's role on *The VIPs*, with Elizabeth Taylor and Richard Burton – and when [in February 1963] he turned up at Elstree, he was totally surprised that the sound was recorded at the same time as the film. He loved what he had the good fortune to be doing, but in a way I think it was almost a game and it was this very naiveté that meant he knew no fear and plunged ahead where others would fear to tread."[105]

Scott did not meet Mona and Wilfred for some months. She and Frost met her own parents regularly: they too lived in central London, and Sunday lunches – at which Thora Hird and Frost sparked off each other in delightful fashion – became commonplace. When Scott was eventually taken to Beccles – or rather, when she took Frost, who could at that point not drive – they set off following an edition of *That Was the Week That Was*, arriving in Suffolk in the early hours. Mona greeted them warmly:

[I]n her dressing gown, full of smiles as if we had arrived mid-afternoon for tea. It was freezing – literally – and she took us through the house to the kitchen where she asked me to remove my shoes. We placed them with some other shoes near a cupboard under the stairs, and David explained that his father enjoyed cleaning shoes. Then we walked back through the ice-cold hall, up the ice-cold lino-covered stairs and along the ice-cold lino-covered landing where I was shown my freezing bedroom. [...] I got into bed as quickly as I could and lay there in the dark thinking I would never sleep and never be warm again. After about ten minutes, the total silence of the house was interrupted by some very quiet shuffling and there was David, wrapped in blankets, coming from his own bedroom next door. He threw the blankets on my bed and climbed in with me. After much giggling and a lot of warming-up, we got to sleep.

The following morning – "wearing amazingly clean shoes" – Janette Scott experienced a true Frost Sunday: back-to-back Methodist services in Wilfred's churches. She observed – in an ominous first sign of the illness that was soon to come upon Wilfred – that her host was becoming forgetful: he was repeating sermons and confusing hymns, though at all times the congregations diplomatically pretended not to notice. But Scott also noticed a striking similarity between father and son: at the friendly social mingling which followed each service, she watched as Wilfred worked the congregation, focusing fully on one family group, then another and another, giving each his complete attention, "laughing at their jokes or making one himself, and then using the laugh to move on to the next group. I was fascinated. I had seen David himself do exactly the same thing at large gatherings – and now I realised suddenly that this was a family thing, that he had learned it from his father. His brilliant networking skills – and they were brilliant – echoed what his father had done for years at church fêtes." And she noticed too that it was Mona's "lively, happy spirit" that had transmitted itself to her son. "[Mona] was the nurturer: she had taken on most of the parenting, or so it seemed to me."[106]

*

"My love affair with the States began the moment I landed at Idlewild."

That Was the Week That Was completed its first series in the late spring of 1963. Enough criticism had been voiced towards the end of its first series – of its apparent drive in pursuit of shock value, of its bashing of the Church, the Queen and other targets – for the BBC to once more pause nervously, take stock and order yet another

The Blonde Bombshell: six-month-old David Frost at Tenterden, with Margaret, Jean and Mona Frost, 1939.

ne habit of a lifetime: David Frost aged eight, in the garden f the family home at Kempston, 1947.

Already at home in front of the camera: two-year-old David Frost at Kempston, 1941.

(above) Coming up roses: 15-year-old David Frost with Jean, Wilfred and Mona Frost at Raunds, c.1954.

(left) Family Frost: Margaret and Jean, Mona and Wilfred, and David Frost at Kempston, 1949.

David Frost (rear): the May Ball at Cambridge, 1961. Courtesy of Colin Renfrew

(above) Already at the centre of things: *Frost at the May Ball*, 1961. Courtesy of Colin Renfrew

(left) The Cambridge Graduate, 1961.

On the chaotic set of TW3: Frost, Willie Rushton, Millicent Martin, Roy Kinnear and Lance Percival, 1962.

Fresh-faced: Frost and Paul McCartney,
A Degree of Frost, 1964.

The Frost Report: 'The Class Sketch' with John Cleese, Ronnie Barker, Ronnie Corbett, 1966.

The Boss: David Frost on *The Frost Report*, 1966.

At the head of the table: Frost with Antony Jay (back left) and Neil Shand (front right) on *The Frost Report*, 1966.

On the set of *The Frost Report*, 1966.

The heart of the action: filming
The Frost Report, 1966.

Golden Frost: *The Frost Report* wins the Golden Rose of Montreux (April 1967): (left to right) Sheila Steafel, David Frost, Julie Felix, John Cleese, Jimmy Gilbert, Ronnie Barker and Ronnie Corbett. Getty Images

Interviewing Robert Kennedy at Portland, Oregon, during the Democratic primaries, March 1968.

David Frost sparring with Muhammed Ali ('I really believe all white people are devils') on LWT, 1968.

Full tilt: in New York with Groucho Marx on the set of *The David Frost Show*, 1970.

New technology: David Frost and LWT in glorious technicolor, 1970. Getty Images

pilot before commissioning a second series. In addition, the world outside Television Centre was changing. Frost's comments on the Profumo affair notwithstanding, the scandal was eating away at the coherence and credibility of Macmillan's Conservative government – and of Macmillan himself. These were tempestuous months – but not for Frost, for whom they were simply a pleasant time away from the hothouse environment of studio and live audience

And time away from Britain itself – at least in part. This summer saw Frost spread his wings, and indulge in the foreign travel that until now had been a rarity in his life, most notably visiting Ireland, and the annual television festival at Montreux in Switzerland, where the novelty and anarchy of *That Was the Week That Was* caused the programme to sink like a lead balloon. He also paid visits to his family at Beccles and Whitby, spent the early summer appearing in variety shows in Birmingham, Liverpool and Bristol, and some of the late summer in seaside cabaret at the congenial-if-not-glamorous environs of Bournemouth and Weston-super-Mare. Scott accompanied him to Weston. She had recently wrapped up filming on *The Beauty Jungle* at the resort, "and found it a pleasant place. So we leaped into my Sunbeam Alpine and off we went."[107]

Significantly, as Scott had got to know her new boyfriend, she too had formed the opinion that comedy did not especially suit Frost: "Being funny was one of his weaker talents."[108] But she understood that he was unwilling ever to disengage fully from any current activity, or to turn down an opportunity to appear before the public. Some of this had to do with his reluctance to square up to the notion that he was not a born comedian; it also was undoubtedly part of a process of maintaining his public profile, which was an important, even critical aspect to the job, and an aspect in which Frost was willing and eager to invest. "He lived to work," as Margaret Frost remarks. "He was terribly driven."[109]

But a more significant aspect of this breathless approach to his affairs lay in his chronic restlessness: in an inability – or at any rate an unwillingness – to sit still, to do nothing, to be reflective. He would, perhaps, have thought himself into a disagreeable place thinking about the two intriguingly clashing aspects of his existence: his love of the good life, which was developing apace now he had the financial means to satisfy it – and the austere, religious tones that until this point that underpinned his thinking. These strands competed and clashed – and so he made himself unreflective. He began to hone a knack of being busy, of arriving at the last minute, of creating a nexus of activity around himself – making calls, making notes, never sitting still, never having to be still. It was a tendency that would become more and more engrained for the remainder of his life. Most significantly of all, Frost paid his first visit that summer to the United States. The trip – to New York to see Cook's *Beyond the Fringe* show, still rocking Manhattan ten months into a run at the Golden Theatre on West 45th Street – was in itself momentous. Frost would later be famously well-travelled, but it is clear that in this first visit, he was bowled over by New York and by American culture. It was also, of course, the first interaction with Peter Cook since the success of *That Was the Week That Was* had swept Frost to fame. The encounter between the two men was watched narrowly and recorded – cast in various ways – for posterity.

Cook had been rendered livid by Frost's triumph. "Beside himself with rage," notes Harry Thompson, recording John Bird's observation that "'by the summer of 1963 [Cook] had built up a fearful head of steam about Frost – he absolutely fed on this long-distance resentment of him. [...] You only had to mention the word "Frost", and he would go off into these long paroxysms of vituperation..."[110] Cook was also deeply bitter at what he perceived as Frost's opportunistic streak, at his cheek in using Cook's absence in America to forge for himself a scintillating career in London. This was a peculiar occasion for bile, given that Cook had left London of his own volition to make, if he could, an even greater fortune in America; but it does illustrate once again the anger that persisted for years afterwards at what was taken to be Frost's abundant good luck – but which was in fact extraordinary focus that held him true to his course. "He was steadfast," says Joan Bakewell. "Peter [Cook] had genius – but David had a quality of steadfastness that others simply didn't: *and* he was amiable, and the combination was exceptional."[111]

Frost was delighted with New York: with its verve and vivid life, even in its steaming summer with the city's movers and shakers wisely decamped elsewhere. Expecting famously truculent New York manners, he was enchanted too with the politeness of American shop staff, the first transformational view of the Manhattan skyline – and a weekend staying with Cook and the Fringe crew out on Long Island Sound in Fairfield, Connecticut. John Bird remembers that, "[W]hen Frost suggested he come down and visit us, I was happy for my own sake – but I thought, *Christ, there's going to be this God-awful row*; I really was quite worried that there was going to be this enormous scene. It was, shall we say, a curious, ironic occasion."

Instead, Bird recounts that Cook received the visitor with chilly politeness ("he was, after all, a very well brought-up young man"), and invited him to take a swim.[112] Frost himself cheerfully admits that he could not swim, but was unwilling to admit this in front of the New York crowd – and this being the case, he began to drown instead:

> Realising what was happening, Peter, who was a good swimmer, dived headlong after him as he went down for the third time, and saved his life. John Bird, hearing the commotion, came through and jumped to the conclusion that Peter was actually murdering Frost in the swimming pool. Frost's first utterance on being brought to the surface was: "Super!"

Cook "later insisted that taking the decision to save David was the one sincere regret of his entire life".[113] These remarks were remembered by Frost's friends, who resented their constant repetition over the years, and who were aware of the disagreeable grain of truth that lay at their root.[114]

Near-death experience or not, however, Frost's love affair with America had kicked off in earnest – and he was explicit about the reasons why: "The first-time visitor from London who was always being credited with a 'classless accent' back home, loved the classlessness of New York. You did not need to be there for very long before you got a sense of the invigorating mobility of American society. Anybody could be president..."[115] These words are instructive, for they are as close as he comes to admitting an awareness of the grudge held against him in certain quarters for being of the wrong class and boundlessly ambitious.

*

"The political content of the programme, which has been one of its principal and successful constituents, will clearly be more and more difficult to maintain."

As that summer of 1963 came to an end and the production office at *That Was the Week That Was* began to swing once more into action, a skittish BBC moved to assert its control over the programme. At a press conference, the director of programming, Stuart Hood, told the assembled media that, henceforth, each edition in the new series would run for fifty minutes only; it would no longer be permitted to over-run, as had become standard practice in the previous series. Moreover, its makers would, Hood implied, have to learn not to overstep the mark politically, and learn too to cut the smut.

Frost and Sherrin were taken aback, although they ought not to have been, given the suddenly altered political climate. Harold Macmillan was suffering ill health, and his Conservative government – following that summer of scandal – was now fragile. A general election was due in 1964: indeed, an early election could not be ruled out; and the BBC was keen to do whatever was necessary to protect itself from charges of bias. The charge of smuttiness, on the other hand, was a little less easy to understand: *That Was the Week That Was* enjoyed its fair share of blue humour and enjoyed too exposing the sexual hypocrisy of the times – but in this regard, the programme was not some sort of sexual primer: it was following and not leading a wider cultural trend. Sex was everywhere, and besides, it was unwise for the Corporation to attack one of its own programmes at a press conference, and warn that, "the element of 'smut' will be omitted".

Frost recalls how, on September 22nd, 1963, the opening song of the second series pilot duly punned on a theme of smut: Millicent Martin's song conjured Macmillan tucked up in bed with a "Trollope", and a week later, the series itself kicked off with Martin and Roy Kinnear glancing through the listings in the *Radio Times* and noting that the "bum and po" show was back on air. For the most part, it was a spirited beginning, drawing attention to the failure of Pope Pius XII to protect Jews from the Holocaust, and celebrating the rise of the Beatles. But the spirit of censorship was now and inexorably on the ascendant: the BBC barred the programme from creating a sketch based around the figure of the Lord Chancellor (whose office at this point still ruled on issues of censorship and public decency on the stage), and barred Bernard Levin's slot on the programme from ever featuring government ministers or opposition front-benchers.

Frost's sense was that the programme was performing well enough, in spite of the pressure surrounding it, but it was clear that not everyone shared this opinion – and even Frost himself admits that there were no "humdingers" in these first editions to compare with the parade of them in the first season of the show. And on top of all this, he and his colleagues now suddenly had a prodigious rival on the horizon every Saturday night: ITV began screening *The Avengers*, featuring Honor Blackman as a sexy secret agent with a penchant for tight, shiny black costumes, even shinier black boots and a general love of the "kinky" that appeared suddenly to be shared by a great swathe of the British public.[116]

In the world outside the studio, meanwhile, things were changing: Macmillan stepped down as Prime Minister in October, to be replaced by the aristocrat Alec Douglas-Home; and the BBC became increasingly exercised by the prospect of the looming election. The new Prime Minister renounced his peerage to fight a by-election and take his place in the House of Commons, meaning that for some three weeks the country was led by a man who was a member neither of the Commons nor the Lords. This was constitutionally messy – and in addition, Douglas-Home's manner remained patrician and unmistakably aloof. In the *That Was the Week That Was* production office, the team were aghast at this apparent slide into a hide-bound past.

"We were angry," Frost remembers bluntly, and a speech was prepared for broadcast on October 19th which referred to the new Prime Minister's previous incarnation: that of a close associate of Neville Chamberlain during his infamous meeting with Hitler in 1938, at which German aggression was appeased and Czechoslovakia sacrificed. "You have always drifted with the tide – the tide of appeasement, the tide of Suez [...] you have drifted without understanding and the tide has left you naked and exposed on the shore. The art of statesmanship ... consists as much in foreseeing as in doing. You, my lord, have foreseen nothing." Frost ended the broadcast – which could by no means be called satire any longer, but bile – with a statement on the unappealing choice before the British people, as the election loomed: "On the one hand, Lord Home; on the other, Harold Wilson. Dull Alec versus Smart Alec. Goodnight."

It was a significant moment. *That Was the Week That Was* had extended the bounds of satire on television – but it had now stepped beyond satire into raw politics. And this meant trouble: the BBC's vision was bound up with the principle of political neutrality – and now here was a programme driving a coach and horses through that principle. And so the BBC called a halt to proceedings. It was a significant moment too for Frost personally, for it offered a glimpse of a personal political morality. There was true affront in his signing-off line – and this was something he seldom revealed even as a young man. "David was not on any particular side," says Antony Jay, "partly because he did a certain amount of challenging of right *and* left. One might hear him criticise a certain politician – but I hardly ever heard even this. It was his professional duty to think them all awful. His job was to keep the show on the road, not to sit around opining himself on politics."[117]

He learned his lesson – for this was the end of the programme: Frost acknowledges its death-knell, although it ran on for a further three editions. In the middle of November, however, came the axe: the BBC announced that, with 1964 an election year, *That Was the Week That Was* would end at Christmas, and not run into the New Year as had been planned. Cynics reminded the Corporation that 1964 was always going to be an election year: and that it was strange, therefore, for the BBC to realise this so belatedly. The Labour leader, Harold Wilson ("Smart Alec") announced a touch opportunistically that, "We would very much deplore it if a popular programme were taken off as a result of political pressure." But the deed was done. "It's a compliment," Frost said tartly. "I'm delighted the show is being taken so seriously."[118]

Interestingly, the programme was indeed being taken seriously – and not only in Britain itself. Herman Rush, who worked with Herb Siegel's GAC (General Artists) talent agency, had observed the phenomenal impact of *That Was the Week That Was* – and of Frost himself – during a scouting visit to Britain, and he brought back the germ of an idea to the United States. In November, in the US, and on the back of the initial suggestion by Rush and Siegel, NBC broadcast a pilot of its own version of *That Was the Week That Was*, with Henry Fonda in the anchor role. One senses Frost's pleasure as he reports how the British press described Fonda – "America's David Frost" – this of an actor with decades of experience already behind him. For Frost, the presence of such an established star as Fonda must have appeared as a daunting obstacle to any American aspirations of his own, but as it turned out, time would sweep these obstacles away, very rapidly indeed.

In London, the final editions of the programme were far from usual. On Friday, November 22nd, 1963, President John F. Kennedy was assassinated. The news arrived in London as the cast of *That Was the Week That Was* assembled at the Dorchester Hotel on Park Lane for a television awards ceremony. Janette Scott had just prevailed upon a reluctant Frost to join her on the dance floor "when the strangest wave of whispering swept through that huge ballroom. We stopped dancing and all too soon discovered that Kennedy had been shot at Dallas. Every single head of every television station was in that room – and all, as quickly as they could, left and went to their offices […] David and Ned Sherrin and one or two others came to my house and worked all night on the script of the show due the following day, with the radio on to get the latest news …"[119]

With the original script jettisoned, the following evening's show instead featured a straight tribute to the dead president that over the years has divided opinion. In particular, it was view by some as being deeply sycophantic – but this opinion, written with the benefit of hindsight and with a greater knowledge of Kennedy's complex personality and flawed presidency, do not take into account the raw shock which accompanied the assassination, nor the emotions felt by a wide range of people. Kennedy's White House had after all been the new Camelot, embodying the youth, style and glamour that fitted precisely with the new decade's sense of itself. The pictures of the motorcade at Dallas and of Jacqueline Kennedy's pink, blood-spattered Chanel copy were all the more shocking in the light of the images of the Kennedys – chic, stylish and youthful – that had dominated the previous three years. And so it is scarcely surprising that the cast of *That Was the Week That Was*, with the power of television at its disposal the very next day, should wish to take the opportunity to express something of society's immediate reactions to Kennedy's death – and to do it in as straight a fashion as possible, since any other mode of delivery would clearly have been inappropriate.

Frost opened the show with remarks he and Christopher Booker had put together, and closed it eloquently and in a way that fitted the context of the time:

The reason why the shock was so great, why when one heard the news last night one felt suddenly so empty, was because it was the most unexpected news one could possibly imagine. [T]hat Kennedy should so – well, we just didn't believe in assassination any more. [...] The tragedy of John Kennedy's death is not that the liberal movements of history that he led will cease: it is that their gathering momentum may be lost. That is the aftermath of Dallas, 22 November. It is a time for private thoughts. Good night.

Such delivery, such words, and such a stark contrast to the usual tone and content of the programme ensure that this edition stands out. It has not, perhaps, worn well, nor is it to everyone's taste. Yet it is an exemplar, a powerful testament to the influence of television at the time, and a reflection of the fact that the makers of this programme understood this very well indeed. But it is certainly a reflection of its makers' ambitions too, for it ensured that the programme, and Frost himself, were noticed elsewhere. Indeed, Ned Sherrin, by producing the edition in American format, made doubly certain of this. On the Sunday, it was broadcast on NBC in the United States, was repeated several times on Monday, and on the floor of the Senate several weeks later, Senator Hubert Humphrey noted on behalf of Congress – and by implication the American people – that "it is humbling to know what our friends think and hope. I wish to thank the British Broadcasting Corporation and through them the individuals who wrote and produced the programme. I ask unanimous consent to have the BBC copyright transcript printed in the Congressional Record."[120]

That Was the Week That Was ended for good – after thirteen months and a mere thirty-seven episodes – on December 28th, 1963. The last show, though not without its stings, was on the quiet side. Many of the sharpest and most popular features were re-run, but the cast opted not to go out with a bang. Instead, they drove off in a sports car as the set was dismantled around them. *That Was the Week That Was* had run its course. There was a general sense that like a meteor, it had been destined to gleam exuberantly, but only briefly. It had helped to dissolve the barriers that existed between the various silos and arms of television. It had challenged the BBC as an institution to think of and imagine itself in new ways. It reflected the country's ability to reimagine itself too: the old Establishment were still in place, of course, but they were less trusted, less relied upon, and there was a sense of new possibilities in governance.

The success and popularity of *That Was the Week That Was*, as with *Tonight* and *Panorama* before it, also demonstrated something critical to an understanding of this era: the ability of the new medium of television to reach mass audiences, to infiltrate the popular consciousness in a way – as that correspondent to the *Daily Telegraph* understood just as well as David Frost – West End satire shows and *Private Eye* simply could not manage. There was an audience across the country that was hungry for a programme or programmes to reflect its own secret, transgressive thoughts – and Frost and his colleagues rolled up just in the very nick of time to reflect these thoughts back onto society. And, if the programme – if Frost – managed this in ways that the purists could not approve of; if the programme – if Frost – overran the boundaries deemed acceptable by a fearful and skittish BBC itself; if the programme – if Frost – achieved success by dint of taking some ideas, jokes, satire already doing the rounds of the clubs: well, so be it. It teamed these ideas with its own, original work, and together this work found its target. *That Was the Week That Was* had timed its arrival well. It had earned its place in British culture, and so had its anchor, who had understood early the power of television and worked to establish his place within it.

And now, new horizons were opening up. Four days later, David Frost was on a flight to America.

CHAPTER 3

The Founder of the Feast

I'm always rather minded of a quote from Wordsworth: 'Bliss was it in that dawn to be alive, but to be young was very Heaven.' For that summed up the fantastic feeling of being young at that time. It was a great time to be alive.

David Frost, *Daily Express*, March 4th, 2008

D avid Frost spent the first two months of 1964 in New York. Janette Scott joined him a few days after his arrival in early January. At the airport – in a sign of the glamour and attention that she and Frost at this point commanded – she was obliged to run the gauntlet of press photographers. In an indication of her considerable media experience, this seasoned performer told these photographers composedly that she was off to America "to buy a refill for her mother's pen". This was the beginning of a long phase in Frost's life in which trans-Atlantic travel became an accepted part of his routine, not to say an essential aspect of his marketing as a glittering television star and fully paid-up member of the jet set. Scott would remain in New York with Frost for six weeks. The couple took up residence at the Shoreham Hotel in midtown Manhattan, a block or two from the Museum of Modern Art.

Frost's first job in America was, on paper, relatively modest, but would prove to be a potent launch pad for his future American career. He had gone to the US against the better judgement of his agents, Diana Crawford and Richard Armitage at Noel Gay, who had fretted that the role proposed for him was too minor and would damage his burgeoning career. The role in question was a three-week "guest" spot on the NBC version of *That Was the Week That Was*, which – ironically, since Frost had just days before given voice to the original show's death rattle back in London – was kicking off now following its successful pilot in the previous autumn. Henry Fonda, having steered this pilot, had now been replaced by two light-entertainment veterans, Elliott Reid and Henry Morgan. Reid turned forty-four years old that January and Frost notes that he was "genial" and a "veteran of many light revues". In fact, Elliott was rather more: he was an experienced and established actor in radio and film with a string of movies to his name, and was best known for having starred with Jane Russell and Marilyn Monroe in *Gentlemen Prefer Blondes* (1953). Morgan, who had supported Fonda in the pilot episode, was quite different: a tough New Yorker and rather less urbane than Reid, he had been blacklisted briefly in the anti-Communist purges immediately following the war, before going on to establish a name for himself as a steely satirist in his own right. Certainly, Frost records a definite sense of *froideur* emanating from Morgan and records the memory of feeling "superfluous".

In a less confident man, these sensations might have been discomfiting: Frost, however – embarked steadily now on his great American adventure, not about to allow anyone else's bad vibes to disturb him, and accustomed in any case to the chilly attitudes of other people – merely retuned his antennae, recalibrated his expectations of his fellows and set about carving out a space for himself. The American version of *That Was the Week That Was* was quite a different animal to the youthful, free-flowing creature that had briefly inhabited BBC Television Centre: the average age of the cast was older, for one thing; and – in keeping with the general conservative instincts of the big American networks and the Puritan streak that characterised American culture as a whole – the tone of the entire enterprise was rather more cautious. Ned Sherrin writes quite bluntly that the new producers "proceeded to botch" the show "with wholehearted American thoroughness, enthusiasm and showbiz knowhow. It took American television more than a decade to realise what a potent period late-night Saturday is."[121]

Yet there was an education to be had here. Frost would in particular learn a good deal in those first days in New York about the cultural differences between British and American television. Whereas the former tended towards the collegiate – at least on the set of *That Was the Week That Was* – American attitudes mirrored their society in being a good deal more individualistic and competitive. For Frost, this came down – of course – to his lines. These were supplied by the teams of scriptwriters assigned to the show, and it came as a shock when he realised that the best lines could quite easily be stolen from under his nose. For Frost, there was obvious irony in this situation – having so lately been himself accused of stealing other people's lines with abandon, now he was driven to guarding his own lines against theft. But it was also an opportunity: to cast aside any remaining notions about collegiate attitudes, and toughen himself up. Frost was, after all, never slow to learn, absorb and take what was needful from any situation. As Andrew Marr notes, "He was a great absorber and tucker-away of useful nuggets."[122] Henceforth, he would have his own lines ready, and kept strictly under embargo until called for.

Frost *did* have his allies – chief among them being the show's producer Leland Hayward, Nebraskan-born, sixty-one years old and at this point in his career, something of a legend. Hayward had started out as a talent scout and agent in Hollywood, signing up the likes of Fred Astaire and Ginger Rogers and dating Katharine Hepburn and Greta Garbo into the bargain. He had then moved into production: his had been the original Broadway productions of Rodgers and Hammerstein's *South Pacific* (1949) and *The Sound of Music* (1959). He was a power in his own right, influential and fabulously well-connected, and in fact it was his signature that persuaded NBC to run with what otherwise would have been a difficult sell. Satire was potentially alarming, potentially dangerous; the show needed Hayward, the steadiest of steady hands on the tiller. David Frost was perfectly alert to his colleague's sway and influence – and given this significant presence at the heart of *That Was the Week That Was,* it becomes ever more difficult to quarrel with Frost's decision to work on the show.

The first edition went to air on Friday January 10th, 1964, at 9.30pm – and Frost's tag as the programme's London correspondent explains the Anglo references which peppered his monologue. Alec Douglas-Home earned a mention: this would have been a bad idea had not the low-key British Prime Minister recently earned a degree of notoriety in the United States by supporting a British Leyland deal to sell buses to Fidel Castro's Cuba, much to the chagrin of the State Department and the new president, Lyndon B Johnson. Frost's was a reasonable monologue, a reasonable beginning: nobody stole his lines; and he was noticed. "He was brilliant," remembers Herb Siegel. "The first impression was that this show might be very difficult – and could we get away with an Englishman as host? But we could, and we did. And we stayed good friends for over forty years."[123] Frost and Siegel did indeed remain friends after this happy and successful beginning: twenty years later, indeed, Siegel would become godfather to Frost's second son. Two more shows passed smoothly, and then Hayward signed him for another three. Janette Scott went back to London in mid-February, to be met again by the press and questioned about marriage plans. "David was in America while I was there and I saw a great deal of him. I also saw a lot of other people, including the four Beatles, and I am not marrying them either."[124] Frost himself stayed on for another few weeks in order both to fulfil his commitments to Hayward, and to pursue yet more new leads.

Though abroad, he had remained connected with former colleagues – and sometime adversaries – at the BBC. It was typical of a nervous Corporation that, having dumped his old show so unceremoniously and so recently, it now wanted to explore new avenues with Frost, whose stint in New York naturally ensured renewed currency back home. An outline of a new British-based project began to take shape, then, from afar: a ghost of a programme that, viewed from certain angles, bore something of a resemblance to *That Was the Week That Was*. Frost's main role was to bring in an American element: specifically, the American comics and performers Elaine May and Mike Nichols, who at this point had already achieved fame, success and scintillating reviews as the satiric comedy duo of Nichols and May. They had appeared in the American *That Was the Week That Was* and now, here they were signing up to perform two of their best-known sketches for Frost's new programme for the BBC. This was an exciting phase for Frost: breathless, thrilling, demanding. "Heady days," he remembered. "Taping a *Tonight* show with its new host, Johnny Carson; then returning to Studio 6H for our own rehearsals, where across the hall Johnny's predecessor, the legendary Jack Paar, was taping his Friday night show, which followed *TW3*. Jack Paar's own predecessor, Steve Allen, came and guested with us on *TW3*. He volunteered to help with a warm-up. 'Do they get this show in Des Moines?' shouted a member of the audience. 'They *see* this show in Des Moines,' said [Allen], 'but they don't *get* it."[125]

Two weeks after Janette Scott's departure, Frost himself left New York for London, and a new flurry of activity. The BBC was short of money and low on morale: but notwithstanding such difficulties, plans were far advanced for its second – and Britain's third – national television channel. The new BBC2 was designed to cater not to commercial or a mass audience, but to minorities. It would be the home of arts, religious and ethics programmes and other less mainstream strands, and Frost was commissioned to supply the first religious programme – an interview with Billy Graham – for the new station. And in a sign of his commercial acumen, Frost now had a production company ready and waiting to go: Paradine Productions, which would be a crucial arm of his career for the next five decades. He notes wryly that some of this was new and challenging territory. For such a young man – he turned twenty-five in the spring of 1964 – Frost had already a formidable record in broadcasting, But actually producing a show himself, watching the budget and the money flow; this was new, and, one senses, challenging.

At the same time as the Graham project was taking shape for BBC2, the proposed BBC1 show was also firming up: it would be called *A Degree of Frost*, and after its completion, he had the promise, the lure, of a further two months in New York guesting on the final *That Was the Week That Was* shows of the season. *A Degree of Frost* was designed as a one-off, but it was clear enough that it was yet another pilot or tentative glance into the future by a BBC at once both attracted by and wary of the impact of *That Was the Week That Was* in the previous year. This one-off was a quite different animal. After all, 1964 was a general-election year: this hadn't changed, and the BBC's instincts hadn't changed either, but it showed the Corporation limbering up, a trifle stiffly, for the post-election world. And, taken together with the Billy Graham interview, *A Degree of Frost* enabled its host to demonstrate his ease in a variety of formats.

The programme, then, was spiced by domestic satire and a little gentle fun at the expense of *Reader's Digest*, and given a dash of American glamour with the inclusion of the two Nichols and May sketches, "Wrong House" and "Interview". It's anchor piece was deeply significant, for it was a coup in itself for Frost, but also an indicator of the shape of things still to come. He secured an interview with Paul McCartney, in what was the first solo television slot with the Beatle. It had been suggested in the course of a dinner à trois with McCartney and his then girlfriend Jane Asher at the fashionable Parkes restaurant off London's Brompton Road. One can imagine what Frost, with his fussy, limited, mustard-scarred palate, made of the nouvelle-cuisine-tinged Parkes dishes served up with floral accompaniments. As his son Wilfred Frost noted years later, "Dad certainly loved fine wine and fine restaurants: but it would be wrong to imagine that he loved *fine* food! – he didn't like elaborate food; simple dishes were always what he wanted."[126] But he was certainly at home in such ultra-fashionable surroundings; indeed, he was thoroughly at home having his dinner thus with a Beatle. For this young man, this son of a Methodist preacher, these were becoming normal, everyday surroundings. And besides, restaurants were a necessary part of his life, for he had never learned to cook: between them,

Mona Frost and Gonville and Caius College had very efficiently seen to that.

The friendship between Frost and McCartney was now a settled thing: the latter had come to trust Frost implicitly, and this trust sealed the deal. "I liked his irreverent streak, and was intrigued by it, given his Methodist background. My stereotype was that a churchman's son would not be irreverent – and then, there was David. You could get serious with him – and you could get very jokey. He was very comfortable to be with, he was trustworthy, he understood the importance of trust and privacy. I always felt I could trust him."[127]

This celebrity interview was recorded as live at Television Centre on the evening of April 15th, 1964, and the programme itself was broadcast a month later, on May 18th. Frost's questions to McCartney took for granted a certain kinship between interviewer and interviewee, both in the opening stages of prominent careers. Indeed, the questions reflected his own preoccupations and sense of a professional trajectory:

Frost: When you started as a group, did you expect things to go like this?

McCartney: We used to think of things in stages. Still do, I think. When we first started off, playing in The Cavern [Club, in central Liverpool] and things, I thought first of all, *Let's get a record contract*. We all did. We got a record. Then we said, "Let's get a number one hit." Got one of them. Then we went on. "Let's do it in stages."

Frost: When people ask you, "What's the best thing about being one of the Beatles at this stage?" you usually reply, "The money," as the first quip. But what after that is one of the good things?

McCartney: Being able to do things you enjoy doing. You get a bit of power when you reach a certain stage, in that you can suggest things to people that you want to do. We can turn around to Brian [Epstein, the Beatles' manager] and say, "Could you fix such and such a thing?" like a film and he can say, "I'll

try to fix it, boy." And he does. […] We can now do more things
that we'd like to …[128]

The interview provides no great range of remarkable insights, but
it is distinctive for the kindly and fresh-faced element of the whole
production. Frost's prominent quiff, the two men's dark sixties suits
and thin ties and youthful visages, and McCartney's finger-sucking
and ear-tugging and general fidgeting lend a curious innocence to
the whole. Certainly this is straight interviewing: there is humour
and a degree of joshing, but not a breath of satire to be detected and
certainly no difficult questions. There was instead that feature that
became a Frost trademark: a genuine interest and curiosity in his
guest that transmitted itself to the audience.

McCartney remembers the interview warmly – though he also
recalls one aspect of Frost's technique that he found discomfiting.
"It was good to be interviewed by someone who wasn't digging, who
didn't have a nasty edge, who was genuinely interested. But – and
I never told him this – what always put me off was that I'd be very
comfortable, and chatting away and answering as best I could …
and then [Frost] would look away, and glance at his clipboard for
the next question. And I would go, *Oh shit, I'm not being interesting,
I'm boring, he's bored, the audience must be bored too* – and my head
would go into a spin. It was his way, but it always put me off."[129]

Notwithstanding Frost's technique, however, this interview was
startlingly well judged. It introduced McCartney to a television
audience ravenous to see him; it humanised him by introducing
him on his own, without additional Beatles or Beatles paraphernalia; by keeping proceedings short and sweet, it left the audience
wanting more; and last – but certainly not least – it showcased
yet another Frost to a British audience accustomed principally to
the satirical and occasionally angry young man of late-night 1963
broadcasting. And Frost himself could not have been unaware of
the significance of the interview in his own developing career.

This textured one-off broadcast helped to re-frame Frost once
more in British minds: certainly, it firmed up the prospects of

future work with the BBC which he had been discussing with Ned Sherrin and others. But he was continuing at the same time with his Atlantic juggling game: *A Degree of Frost* safely in the can, he took off once more for New York to fulfil his remaining commitments to Leland Hayward and *That Was the Week That Was*. This was a delightful time to be in Manhattan, and Frost made the most of it. He was now settled in a pleasant serviced apartment on 55th Street, Scott flitted over from Britain, and leisure time was spent enjoying the pleasures of the city. They caught *Hello Dolly!*, now on its opening Broadway season, and getting ready to sweep the boards at that year's Tony awards. Scott recalls walking down "a deserted Avenue of the Americas at three o'clock in the morning with David, Malcolm Muggeridge, Roddy McDowall and Alasdair Milne from the BBC, all of us singing 'Hello Dolly' at the tops of our voices".[130]

There were also trips to Los Angeles: on one occasion, to be lauded for his television work at an A-list brunch laid on by Warren Beatty by the pool (from the edges of which Frost steered clear) in what had once been Merle Oberon's splendid house off Sunset Boulevard. "We were delighted," recalls Scott, "that everyone we spoke to knew of or had seen *TW3* and soon David was networking around the pool with ease and every once in a while I could hear that great laugh of his that let me know that all was well."[131] Raunds and Beccles and Gillingham had never been so far away.

They also slipped into a New York preview of a new movie called *Mary Poppins*, and were taken out to a smoke-filled suburban bar where a young Woody Allen was performing an already-trademarked nervy, neurotic stand-up routine. And Frost spent an agreeable evening at the Winter Garden theatre on Broadway, where a native New Yorker, singer and actor named Barbra Streisand was playing Fanny Brice in a new production. The show was called *Funny Girl*, and Streisand was cutting a swathe along Broadway. She was a mere twenty-one years old when the show opened in March 1964. Frost sometimes underplayed the glamour of those who crossed his path, but there was no chance of doing this with Streisand. Here was a breathless audience member clearly aware that a star was being born in front of his very eyes:

> For sheer artistry, there was nothing to match Barbra Streisand [...] Her sense of comedy could hardly have been bettered. Neither could her acting. And, just as a bonus, her body carried with it an enormous sex appeal. As she arched her back, as her body almost pouted, she was the first all-Semitic Cleopatra. A totally unorthodox, oddly vulnerable beauty ...[132]

Frost was also busy monitoring the difference between British and American culture, and his thoughts on this matter come close, perhaps, to a declaration of his personal *credo*. In his autobiography, he invests a good deal of meaning and a certain emotional intensity in his declaration that ambition is in and of itself a good thing. Years later, he elaborated on this theme, telling the *Observer* that "[Ambition in British terms] means seeking success and doing it for its own sake and *tends* to be a pejorative. Whereas 'ambitious' in American terms means being determined to make the best of whatever abilities you may have been given and do as well as you can, and it's an admirable trait. I would happily plead guilty to being ambitious in the American sense of the word, which links back to my Methodist childhood and the thing about having a *duty* not to waste such time or talents as you've been given."[133] This is an indication that he was perfectly well aware of the critical lens through which he was viewed by his public-school contemporaries at Cambridge and, later, London: the modestly born and raised son of a minister, determined to get on in life, wearing his ambition on his sleeve; and being deplored for it, frequently in disagreeable terms, by his fellows – and sloughing off this criticism to continue his trajectory. As his friend Peter Chadlington notes, "David's success was not an accident. He constantly reinvented himself. He was essentially an entrepreneur where he – personally – was the brand! Success was neither happenstance nor that of a short-lived meteor. He was constantly looking for new opportunities, changing his brand – himself – to adapt to new circumstances as society and the media changed. That was his genius."[134]

Contemporary Britain cut the ground from beneath any sense of ambition. It planted road-blocks, Frost writes bluntly and quite uncharacteristically, in the way of a citizen looking to get on: "Whether the ideological roadblock of taxation so punitive that real capital could sometimes only be made by devious means, or the class-designed roadblock of privilege. The fact that two such inimical embargoes on ambition could co-exist was in itself a commentary on the flaws inherent in British society. […] In Britain, 'ambition' could be, and frequently was, used in a pejorative sense."[135] The same sense of anger can be glimpsed in that fatal edition of *That Was the Week That Was* which tears to shreds the figure of the aristocratic new Prime Minister – but arguably, at no other time does Frost's frustration at the system emerge with such clarity. America, in this context, provided him with new air to breathe. It fostered ambition, and in official American discourse, ambition was a public good, at the well-spring of the Republic, and a sentiment honoured and emphasised in American society.

The American version of *That Was the Week That Was* ended its run in mid-July 1964. It had already been commissioned for another series, to begin in the autumn: and to his delight, Frost had been signed once more to take part. In another foreshadowing of that much-travelled Frost trademark, the *New York Post* remarked that "Frost could become TV's first transatlantic commuter inasmuch as he is scheduled to start a new BBC show in the fall. He recently expressed some doubt over ocean-hopping between shows. 'A doctor friend of mine says he wants to examine me if I try it,' he said. The doctor apparently has a case. 'He's going to commute,' says Hayward." That the *Post* would trouble itself with Frost spoke volumes about his increasing stature on American television. It was a sure indication that his Stateside graft was undoubtedly paying off.

And it was a gift to him, an opportunity to show his adaptability – and at this point, Fortune smiled once more, with producers on both sides of the Atlantic arranging their programmes almost as though specifically to convenience him. At the BBC, Frost's new vehicle was scheduled to go out at weekends, rather than the weekday slots originally envisaged. And at NBC, the new season of *That Was the Week That Was* would air – strangely, as soon became clear – on Tuesday evenings. The *Post* was correct: Frost was going to commute between his shows. Whatever Frost's doctor friend did or did not say, the fact was that this all perfectly possible.

In the meantime, he could look forward to time spent once more with Janette Scott: and to a summer spent in a rather less humid atmosphere than New York. First it was home – or rather, "home" – to Britain for several weeks, to meet with Ned Sherrin and Alasdair Milne who, having protected *That Was the Week That Was* from the BBC hierarchy to the best of his abilities, was now the producer of the new show. Pilots were in preparation, to be ready for the end of August – and so at the beginning of the month, Frost and Scott flew out of London for a holiday. Their destination was a secluded beach resort on Kauai in the Hawaiian archipelago – in Britain in the 1960s an impossibly glamorous holiday destination. A secluded beach resort, so they thought – but it proved not to be so very secluded, as practically the first person they met there was a holidaying journalist, to whom they were incorrectly introduced as a married couple. "'Mr and Mrs Frost, may I introduce Alex Faulkner, head of the *Daily Telegraph* foreign bureau.' […] Luckily, Alex Faulkner was more interested in foreign affairs than domestic affairs, so we got away with it."[136]

*

Back in Britain, the country was now preparing for the general election of October 1964, and the BBC, inevitably, held off advancing plans for Frost's new show until it could assess how the land lay. Frost, in any case, had enough to be getting on with. In early September 1964, he and Janette Scott sailed for New York on the *Queen Mary*. For Frost, the crossing was another childhood fantasy come true: the ship was now approaching the end of her reign as the flagship of the Cunard line, but she still possessed the glamour of her Blue Riband-winning past. In mid-Atlantic, she encountered her sister ship *Queen Elizabeth*, the two liners sounding their horns in salute as they passed. After a few days in New York, they travelled to Washington for a reception at the White House, and here Frost was placed first in the line to meet Lyndon B. Johnson.

Back in New York, the first show of the new season of the American *That Was the Week That Was* was scheduled for September 22nd, and Frost had new team members to meet. Herb Sargent had been enlisted to produce the show; he would later forge an Emmy-winning career, working with such figures as Anne Bancroft and Burt Bacharach; and he and Frost would remain friends into the future. Sargent's girlfriend was Gloria Steinem, then aged thirty and already with a body of significant journalism to her name – but not yet the influential feminist and cultural commentator she would become. As for the Tuesday-evening slot on NBC: this was inauspicious, for the show was now up against *Peyton Place*, the new ABC "continuing drama", in which a good deal of hope and cash had been invested. Yet Frost had reason enough to feel positive about the programme's upcoming run: as far as he was concerned, the quality of the writing and production team spoke for itself.

He assumed now his regular habit of picking up the 11.15 BOAC flight from London to New York, enabling him to arrive at the studios, showered and refreshed, by 4 o'clock that afternoon. Frost thereby invented the eight-day week. Tuesdays would be consumed with preparations for the show, and Wednesdays by flying back to London, ready for work in the grotty environs of Lime Grove on Thursday morning. It was also the beginning of another significant professional – or rather, corporate – relationship: BOAC eventually evolved into British Airways; and Frost's attachment to British Airways was one which would endure for the remainder of his life. Such was Frost's visibility and ubiquitous presence on this particular route that it created its own famous quotation: "I'm sorry, Mr Frost," one apologetic BOAC stewardess told her famous passenger as lunch was served in the first-class cabin, "I'm afraid it's caviar again." Yet, in spite of the seeming glamour of this commute, Frost's life at this point was a frenzy of activity – but he was buoyed by a sense of personal gratification too: for he was now promoted in NBC advertising as its co-host.

But the new season of *That Was the Week That Was* would prove to be singularly ill-starred. The presidential election of 1964 was looming, pitting Lyndon B Johnson against his Republican challenger, Barry Goldwater, and the Republican Party seems, to go by the available evidence, to have had it in for *That Was the Week That Was*. The show's opening night was pulled when the Republican National Committee – as was its right – "pre-empted" or purchased that particular slot to air the American equivalent of a British Party Political Broadcast. For two of the following three weeks, the Republicans once again chose the show's Tuesday evening slot, and were only prevented from claiming a clean four-week sweep because the Democratic Party had already booked an advertising slot on the show's second week. *That Was the Week That Was*, then, went to air belatedly on September 29th, before vanishing again for another fortnight. And there were more cancellations to come: in total, the programme aired only once before the election of November 3rd, 1964.

This was a body blow to the prospects of the series itself once more building up a respectable audience. Upended and drowning in the churning, soapy wake of *Peyton Place* and unable to gather a sense of momentum, the programme struggled from the off. With the benefit of hindsight, however, the programme appears always to have been ill-starred. Ned Sherrin noted its weaknesses in waspish terms:

> It was beautifully American. Rather than expose their own bare studio, they built a set that exactly replicated ours, rendered in pastel shades – they even reproduced the ventilator pipes! And though it was called *That Was the Week That Was,* it went out at 8.30 on a Tuesday, which is quite a short week. And it was much more anodyne, very gentle.[137]

In Britain, meanwhile, Labour scraped a win in the general election, and now the BBC pressed forward with its new show, which had finally been given the rather forced title of *Not So Much a Programme, More a Way of Life*. Frost had a prominent role in the new programme – but he was not the sole anchor, and this decision rankled. He was to share top billing with Willie Rushton (with whom he had worked on the original *That Was the Week That Was*) and the actor and writer PJ Kavanagh. But what sort of show was it to be? Ned Sherrin had been obliged to produce six complete pilots before the series was given a green light by the BBC: a startling fact, but instructive in itself, in that it demonstrated a certain fuzziness about what was needed and what could be delivered. There was an instinctive caution dogging progress too: it could not be too like its predecessor – and it was for this reason that Sherrin was insistent on Frost sharing the stage with other figures.

But Sherrin's original vision, such as it was, did not survive. He records Rushton's remark – genuine or not is impossible to discover – that neither he nor Kavanagh "wanted to be on the programme. So we got elbowed to one side a bit; and in the end we were being paid £80 a show for doing nothing – it was the best job I ever had, except that it was driving me absolutely up the spout."[138]

Frost's memory of the situation is rather different:

Although I was always hugely entertained by the beloved Willie, and liked PJ Kavanagh the moment I met him, I did think that this three-headed monster was a bit of a loony idea. But while Ned [Sherrin] and I discussed everything to the nth degree, that was the one point on which I was somewhat reticent, as I could have been seen to have, shall we say, a certain special interest in the outcome. Which is an interesting comment – and probably a shattering indictment of – my Britishness.[139]

Frost adds tartly that the first edition did not go well, and "having three hosts did not help".

Certainly, the programme had issues. It was too long, too sagging, too unfocused; it ran three nights a week, a beast of a programme that devoured material. The BBC's caution had entered the marrow of the show, rendering it nervous. It tinkered with its material, rather than at any point showing boldness. There was good music and comedy from the likes of Millicent Martin, John Bird and Eleanor Bron, and Frost did what he could to hold the show together. But his sense of time-keeping – in a theme that would continue for the rest of his life – was simply appalling. John Bird recalls that Frost, "would leave it until the very, very last moment to take his place: perhaps this was a piece of flamboyance, perhaps he just wanted to make an entrance, or perhaps he liked to keep people on the edge of their seats. I suspect that he didn't much like the idea of having to sit there for two, three, four minutes waiting to go live, with the adrenalin peaking and then beginning to diminish – and I can certainly understand that."[140]

Eventually, the show got its second wind, and as 1964 came to an end amid an uncomfortable and humiliating climate of a falling pound and emergency financial loans to Britain from the International Monetary Fund, the BBC extended its run through to April 1965. The response of the tabloid press was baleful, and they began increasingly to focus their bile on the programme in general and on Frost in particular. The *Daily Express*, in a series called "The Hate Makers" on public figures the newspaper did not like – it was a long list – blasted Frost as the worst of the lot. "There is," the newspaper remarked, "an excellent maxim on big newspapers. It is: never pick on the little man. Today, however, I must break that maxim. For any obituary of the Hate Makers must begin with the short life and sad decline of David Frost. [...] He has directed a thin spray of hatred and scorn at anyone who dares to disagree with him – and in particular against the ordinary man in the suburbs or in the country marketplace. If the ordinary man is in favour of anything – whether it is patriotism or the Crown or controls on immigration – you can be absolutely certain that Mr Frost will be against them."[141]

In his autobiography, Frost records the extract faithfully – and sets out his argument against the newspaper's remarks. This is an indication in itself of the sting caused by the *Express*'s words, since it was such a fundamental part of Frost's self-image to believe he was able to reach through or bypass the media, the Establishment, the screens placed in front of figures such as himself, and touch the people directly. And in particular, he was certain of his ability to reach out to the man and woman who lived in small towns and suburbs and in the countryside, those to whom the metropolitan media and the movers and shakers paid scant regard. He was, after all, one of these people himself.

Antony Jay recalls the ways in which Frost handled press criticism. "He disliked hostile criticism: it was terribly painful for him, it hurt him. He would sometimes set out his reasons, he would sometimes rebut – but he *never* said anything nasty about or to the press. He understood, unlike many others, that it was never in his interest to take on the press in that way. Love the hater: forgive them – that was his general attitude. It irked his friends, but it proved wise."[142] Certainly, they were few and far between, these broadsides: and soon they vanished altogether. Frost kept his own counsel regarding the media, the journalists – and especially those individuals beyond Fleet Street whose opinions he must have cared about – and in particular, *Private Eye* and its owner, Peter Cook.

The magazine delighted in reporting and opining on what it considered the execrable content of *Not So Much a Programme, More a Way of Life*. Occasionally, it issued gramophone recordings which were attached to its front cover – and one of these featured a sound recording of Cook imitating Frost trying to host the programme as the din behind him increases and increases, so as to suggest a show that is simply beyond control. Much of this, to be sure, stemmed from envy and bile, and had to do with the fact that Cook himself was still not getting any work from the BBC. He was now established in a gracious Georgian house in Hampstead, which rapidly became a focus of fashionable London social life. Yet, Frost had his own show while Cook did not – he had returned from New York "expecting to be enormously well known, and of course nobody knew me from Adam" – and *Private Eye* was a convenient way to express his feelings.[143] Frost sailed on regardless, but it is quite wrong to suggest that the flow of criticism did not jostle and bruise him. It did both: he simply opted not to bare the bruises.

In February 1965, just as – Frost records – the show seemed to have settled into some sort of fragile groove, the end came. A sketch was broadcast featuring a Liverpudlian Catholic woman of Irish extraction, who is asked by her tyrannical priest to account for the fact that she is not pregnant: after all, she has only fifteen or sixteen children and the youngest a full fourteen months old – so is it not time to be with child once more? Or is she secretly on the Pill? It is an amusing enough sketch, and the context of a Catholic Church raging against the newly born permissive society is apt and smart; in addition, it was followed by a long and responsible discussion on the Catholic attitude to contraception.

And yet, this marked the termination of the programme. The matter was raised in the Commons, where David Frost was called upon to apologise to the nation; in the Lords, Lord Longford called the programme "dirty beyond belief"; and the BBC Director General Hugh Greene issued an apology. But Frost himself did not. Yet again, for the second time in quick succession, this was one of those rare moments when he felt an official rebuttal was necessary:

It is a surprise that Lord Longford, whose name has always been rightly associated with liberalism and tolerance, should allow himself to become the spokesman for this kind of pressure group. It is not just that he and his friends are spokesmen for a minority. That we all accept. It is that they are quite possibly spokesmen for a minority of that minority. It is quite clear from the hundreds of letters I have received that, not only did the non-Catholic public welcome the treatment of the subject, but so too did a great many of the Catholics, who said that they felt that their leaders have been trying to stifle public discussion for too long.

Frost's comments had little effect. The *Daily Mail* wondered if he and Sherrin should "be whipped through the streets", and *The Times* called the broadcast "gross". It was, of course, nothing of the sort: and a glance at the context of the time illustrates this. At this point, the Second Vatican Council had been in session for over two years and was coming to an end of its deliberations. It had been convened in the first place to address the unquestionable fact that western society as a whole was moving now unarguably out of step with the institution; and that the Church would need to modernise its practices in order to sustain itself. That *Not So Much a Programme...* had broadcast a skit featuring a downtrodden Irish Catholic mother of fifteen in hock to an unspeakably orthodox priest was nothing out of the ordinary, by the standards of the times. Indeed, Frost's words were in many ways wholly in keeping with the *Zeitgeist*.

A month later, on Friday March 26th, 1965, the programme referred to Alec Douglas-Home – almost in passing – as a "cretin" and an "imbecile"; and the Sunday programme featured a dig at the Duke of Windsor (Edward VIII, the anti-hero of the 1936 abdication crisis which had shaken the British monarchy) without taking into account the fact that his sister, the Princess Royal, had died earlier that day. The press once more complained volubly – and the following day, the BBC announced that the programme would end its run in a fortnight, and would not be coming back. Frost and Ned Sherrin now went their separate ways, with no further ideas ready to be shaped and given life. The BBC made it clear, in fact, that Sherrin could begin moulding a new satirical programme – Hugh Greene, had implied as much when he announced the cancellation of the programme, remarking that "there is room for satire, but I am not sure we have the form right" – but only if Frost was not involved. The result would be *BBC3*, fronted by the older and distinctly un-Frost-like Robert Robinson and broadcast for the first time in the autumn of 1965.

Frost and Sherrin met for breakfast, in the well-heeled surroundings of the Ritz Hotel on Piccadilly on May 17th, 1965.

"This, by now, was Frost's *milieu*," remarks Frost's great friend Ronnie Corbett. "He liked a good *milieu* and a decent cucumber sandwich."[144] It was at this point that the former realised he was being shed. Sherrin outlined the position of the BBC – in his autobiography, he notes that BBC executives "polarised their fear of the late-night monster around a determination to behead it by sacking David. It was unfair, but I was intrigued by the challenge of being without him."[145] For his part, Frost recalls his "shock" at being dumped in such a way. It was agreed that he would ostensibly resign and step back, so as to avoid the sense that he had been pushed. "I had been wondering," Frost remarks, "whether it was time to move on – but it is certainly more pleasant to do that over the pleas and entreaties of your employers."[146] Laconic enough, to be sure, and he adds for good measure that he and Sherrin had outgrown each other: but this is nevertheless one of those moments in his story in which he permits – momentarily – sensations of hurt and pain to be glimpsed.

For Frost, indeed, the fact was that this was an immensely challenging period. The London cancellation was followed by another axe falling: this time in New York, where *That Was the Week That Was*, having come to the end of its run, was pensioned off. NBC announced that the programme would not be returning: it had been vanquished by *Peyton Place*, the vagaries of television scheduling and the ill-will of the Republican National Committee. Frost was fairly sanguine about this blow: it came as no surprise; and the programme would in time be recognised for its influence on later American programming, especially *Rowan and Martin's Laugh-In*, which ran for six years from 1968. Certainly, it enabled the sort of fresh thinking and cross-fertilisation of ideas that had been rather missing in dusty, po-faced, post-war American television. Yet the fact remained: Frost, having so recently been juggling two shows at the same time, was now bereft of a vehicle.

And now, Fate put the boot in by at the same time ending his relationship with Janette Scott, which had run for over two years. Scott and Frost had encountered the American musician Mel Tormé in early February 1965 at the opening of The Cool Elephant, a private jazz club in Mayfair. It was a wildly fashionable joint: "Princess Margaret was at the head of a huge table," remembers Scott, "and the London glitterati had turned out in force."[147] Dudley Moore was something of a resident pianist at the club: on that night, he joined Tormé on stage, and later they were introduced to Scott and Frost, the latter of whom soon vanished, however, to work the room. It is a sign of the smallness of the mingled social London circles in which Frost moved, in fact, that he, Tormé, Scott, her ex-boyfriend Peter Sellers and Sellers' new wife Britt Ekland (as well as Moore and Princess Margaret) were all clustered together that night under the one roof. Relationships on this London scene intertwined very easily indeed – and certainly this was one consistent trope in Frost's life.

Scott, Frost and Tormé met again the following day at Television Centre, by which stage a spark between Scott and Tormé had clearly been struck. This spark flew at a significant moment, for both Scott and Frost were conscious that they had reached a junction in their relationship. She wanted to settle down, to marry and have children; he wanted none of these things, but rather for their relationship to continue as it was. Shortly after this second meeting, Scott flew to South America to attend the Cartagena Film Festival. Tormé, now in the United States, pursued her by telephone, and persuaded her to change her travel plans, and the pair met again shortly afterwards in Los Angeles. Scott remained in the city for three weeks, renting an apartment on Sunset Boulevard, within walking distance of Tormé's home, and the couple tentatively began a relationship.

Frost, back in Britain, was aware of all this, aware too that his relationship with Scott was unravelling with frightening speed – and three weeks after she had arrived in California, he came in search of her:

Early one morning, the doorbell rang. I got out of bed and peeped through the spy hole in the door – and there stood David. I think he was quite relieved that he had found me alone and he immediately wanted to know if I knew what I was doing. I answered in all honesty that I wasn't sure I did, but that the only way for me to find out was to stay for a while …

For Scott, there was a looming awareness that Frost and she had indeed reached the end of the road, and that Frost, besides, was no longer in need of her professionalism and aplomb before the cameras. He had by now acquired the same sort of smooth carapace that grows in the course of a life lived in public. And there was, besides, the understanding that Mel Tormé was rather more her sort of man. Like Scott, he had grown up in show business, knew the ropes, and knew too the value of a low-key life, one lived at least partly in private. "David was on the crest of a sparkling wave that was going to carry him forward for years – but I was ready to move on."[148] Frost was shaking as he left the apartment on Sunset Boulevard, Scott was in tears – but there was a civility in their parting that found expression in an enduring friendship. Frost returned to London, to move out of Janette Scott's house in Chelsea. She and Mel Tormé, meanwhile, were married within the year.

David Frost was, then, bereft both of a personal relationship and of professional vehicles – for now. But the storm of recent television activity, in Britain and in America, would pay dividends, even if for the moment they were unimaginable. He had established something of a name in America, and even more so in Britain itself. And more critical even than this, was the fact that he had learned the ropes – quickly, unthinkingly, he had gained a television education. These turbulent events were even a blessing in disguise, for they obliged Frost to seek new television formats and collaborators in ways that would bear fruit, both personally and professionally, in the years ahead.

*

David Frost was very rapidly back on his feet again – if indeed he had ever been felled. For one thing, a new love interest appeared in his life: the actress Carol Lynley, who was in Britain to shoot the psychological thriller *Bunny Lake Is Missing* alongside Laurence Olivier. Lynley was American and very glamorous: twenty-three years old in 1965, she had previously been a child actress before making the transition to older roles, and was now an established name, with a pair of Golden Globe nominations under her belt. She had also been previously, though briefly, married, and now she took up with Frost, in a relationship that would flicker, now on and now off, for eighteen years. Though it was not without its ups and downs: later that same summer, for example, he took Lynley to experience an occasion quintessentially English: a languorous day of cricket in the form of a Test match at Lord's. Years later, he told Janette Scott that the occasion was ruined thoroughly: "It was not a success because people kept coming up to [Lynley] and saying, 'Oh, Miss Scott, please may I have your autograph?' David thought this very funny."[149] Lynley, one assumes, did not.

Frost writes amusingly of the subterfuge that characterised the beginning of his relationship with Lynley. Otto Preminger, the Austrian-American director of *Bunny Lake Is Missing*, was notoriously exacting of his casts and crew, in particular requiring – as Frost puts it – "his young actresses to live like nuns and get bags of sleep during the period that they had the signal honour of being under his command".[150] Other figures confirm Frost's remarks: Olivier, for example, referred to Preminger as a "bully", and his tantrums were well-known and feared. Now, therefore, Frost and Lynley met discreetly – though as it turned out, not at all discreetly enough: "[O]ne morning on the set, [Preminger] questioned Carol about why the skin on her chin was peeling slightly. 'Sunburn,' she replied quickly. 'Looks more like Frostbite to me,' barked Otto. Carol blushed, and thus was spared one of Otto's legendary temper tantrums. Her open-mouthed amazement at his omniscience was sufficient reward for the great man."[151]

Frost's relationship with Lynley stopped and started – but at this time, he began seeing another woman too, on a rather more steady basis. This was Jenny Logan, a singer and dancer whom Frost had first spotted performing alongside Ronnie Corbett at Danny La

Rue's famous club at Hanover Square in Mayfair. Logan was good-looking, thoughtful, talented – and, since she moved in similar circles, willing to adapt to Frost's frenetic and often nocturnal lifestyle. Logan and Frost maintained a relationship over the next five years: a low-profile relationship for the most part, for they were both protective of their time spent together; blocks of such private time were set aside in such places as the small cottage in the Suffolk countryside outside Beccles that Frost acquired at this point. Logan was able to observe what few others at this point had noticed: that Frost was essentially a *private* man; or rather, that he had a private core to which few were permitted access.

The night that Frost first saw Logan performing at Hanover Square was significant for another reason: this was also the night he saw Ronnie Corbett on stage for the first time. "After the show," recalls Logan, "David came backstage: and we went out – but it was difficult to find anywhere open at three o'clock in the morning, and we ended up having coffee at the Cavendish Hotel, which was the only place open at that time of night. And then he vanished to America for two weeks – and when he came back, we picked up that thread. And it was lovely to be whisked into his life, and to watch him equally at home with my family, or with stars or Royalty, and to see his generosity shine through at all times. One example: I had a son, and David put him through boarding school."[152] Logan met the Frosts, including the "marvellous, formidable" Mona, in whom she, like Janette Scott before her, recognised Frost's zest and vibrant life force.[153]

And Frost had other affairs on the go too – though these were of a more professional nature. He was ruminating, in the course of this quiet professional spell in London, on his next step: to persist in comedy and satire, or to move more definitively into interviews and a more conversational format. There was little sense that he had a particular preference. Following what was an essential pragmatism, Frost's object was to mould programmes that would best suit not simply his own desires, but also the needs and appetite of the moment – and to introduce in the process a sense of novelty.

It was natural, therefore, that he would look to America for inspiration. If *That Was the Week That Was* had been a British idea imported into the United States, Frost's spells in New York had been enough to see that this flow might work both ways. In particular, he was interested in the interviews and conversation strands that characterised American television, and in how these might be adapted to the British screen. This conversational format, however, was something of a slow burner. In the meantime, he returned to comedy and to the BBC, which had lately been so keen to remove him from the scene. On this occasion, however, Frost returned to Light Entertainment, that division of the Corporation that had fostered, broadcast and approved *A Degree of Frost*.

A series of meetings, brokered by Antony Jay, followed during that summer of 1965, and the BBC, once more thawing towards Frost, began the long process of coming on board with the creative process. His recent, temporary travails now forgotten, Frost was able to take delight in a long summer that included the usual round of luncheons, parties and cricket matches; and visits to Ceylon – now Sri Lanka – France and Lebanon. "Lebanon is still basically a Christian country," a Beirut taxi driver told Frost en route to the Casino du Liban. "'That's why you can get all the drink, drugs and women you want.' This was not [...] a definition of Christianity with which my father was familiar."[154]

In this period, Frost was also able to focus on and care for his parents in Beccles. Wilfred, at the age of sixty-five and with his health now in decline, had been obliged to retire early from his ministry. "He was always a diabetic," remembers Margaret Frost, "but now he also began to suffer from a form of dementia too. At that point, David had done *TW3* and had some money behind him, and he was able to buy them a house." The property in question was a bungalow at Ellough Road, in a quiet district on the southern edge of Beccles. "My father didn't really realise," adds Margaret Frost. "That is, he knew about [David's] success with *TW3*, but he wasn't aware David had bought them a house. David was very discreet."[155] In its very discretion, this was an act wholly at odds with his public persona at this time, though it was very much in keeping, as Margaret Frost makes clear, with the generosity of the private Frost.

By the end of August 1965, plans were well developed for the successor to *A Degree of Frost*, and the formal announcement was made late in September. The programme – and certainly nobody could be accused of overweening originality in the naming of these shows – was to be called *The Frost Report*, with James Gilbert producing. It would be live, and it would be broadcast immediately after the nine o'clock news – both factors which militated against anything too spicy. "A move away from the pure satire of *That Was the Week That Was* to something more general," was the impression taken by Ronnie Corbett when he in his turn met Frost at the Ritz to receive an invitation to chip into the show.[156]

Frost assembled a splendidly talented ensemble cast of actors and writers, many members of which would become fixtures in the comedy firmament, both in Britain and abroad, in the years to come. Young writers named Michael Palin and Terry Jones, both fresh from Oxford, worked on the scripts alongside Neil Shand. For Shand, indeed, this experience was the beginning of a substantial body of work he created with Frost, with hundreds of shows broadcast over the next eight years in Britain, Australia and the United States. The music would be supplied by established folk singer Julie Felix, with whom Frost in due course began an affair. "When I first met David [...] I found him suspiciously generous," Palin told the *Sunday Times* forty years later. "I did wonder if that was just because he wanted something out of us. We were just callow youths, but he made a huge effort to invite us to his parties. He saw Terry Jones and me at Edinburgh and then we heard from him to say he immediately wanted us on *The Frost Report*. We were really flattered. His skill was not so much in writing or creating – he was a great showman, a ringmaster. He held it all together. Apart from his skills as a broadcaster and a journalist, he gave the Pythons their first break. [...] Perhaps more than anything he had tremendous confidence and *chutzpah*."[157]

As for the actors: these included the young South African actress Sheila Steafel, the main female presence in the cast. Ronnie Corbett had an established reputation in live theatre, though not yet in television – and he was joined in the cast by Ronnie Barker, who with Corbett later became The Two Ronnies – and in Corbett's emotionally resonant words, Frost's approach was:

> The making of my life: a turning point in my life. And [Frost] was a very, very dear friend, a darling friend; and so many people owe their beginnings to him. He realised that there was a big section of his mind that was excellent at managing, bringing people forward, organising careers. He could work and exercise a chunk of himself in other ways, and he knew this. He knew he could realise the potential of other people as well as his own. He knew he could be a founder of the feast.[158]

Others shared Corbett's stirring sense of a life turning on a pivot. Picking up the Cambridge thread once more, Frost also contacted John Cleese and lured him back from a stint working in America. Cleese relates how Frost telephoned him in the apartment he shared with his partner Connie Booth in New York: again, a call and an offer that would change Cleese's professional life, and even at that moment he was aware of it. And here it was being delivered on the run, for Frost was – inevitably – calling from an airport:

> As usual, he greeted me with great cheeriness and warmth, and after the usual thirty seconds of banter he said he was doing thirteen half-hour sketch shows for the BBC in the New Year, and would I like to be part of it? This extraordinary offer was presented so casually that it felt almost like the natural next development in our relationship. Before the immensity of it had sunk in, I told him I'd love to, and he whinnied, "Oh! They've just called my flight! Got to go! Call me when you get to London. Bye-ee!" – and he was gone. And the next phase of my life had been settled, just like that.[159]

For Cleese, the prospect was daunting: practised as he was on the stage, he was a novice on TV. It was, in fact, the first television he had ever done – and it was also live into the bargain, with no question of a retake. And as it turned out, this was the happiest of meetings: Barker, Corbett and Cleese would go on to star in what would prove to be one of British television's best-remembered sketches.

Cleese recalls Frost's "relaxed and cheerful manner", and notes that "because I knew no more about them than they did about me, we mingled easily without any jockeying for position. It never occurred to me that at least fifteen of this friendly, amusing, low-key group would become major, professional collaborators over the next twenty years."[160] Frost's expansive nature and his openness to the gifts of others: these attributes were key to bringing about the creative sparkle of this new programme – and were the mark of the impresario. This context, then, offers a view of a David Frost who was much more than a producer, an anchor, a comic. He was all of these – and he was something more. "[He] managed the talents of their colleagues," says the television executive Howard Stringer, who became a friend in later years. "He provided opportunities to so many people – I don't know of anyone who could put a show on and open it to people in such an unselfish manner. Acts of kindness – yes; but to take in competing talent in this way, it demonstrates a level of personal security that is matchless. Most competing anchors were worried about themselves, their security, their situation; David just didn't worry. He was oddly secure in a way that is startling – when one considers that he had as much right to be worried about the future, about the next job."[161]

John Cleese adds that Frost was always happy simply to step back and have members of the team focus on their own work: he did not interfere or change or alter other people's scripts or performances. Cleese, however, had the luxury in those days of close quarters and close contacts to observe other aspects to his friend. "He was so light-hearted and sparky – and yet extremely guarded emotionally. I imagined a spectrum of extroversion and introversion, and David completely at the extrovert end – and highly, highly motivated by public attention, with no perceptible change in character regardless of whether he was on television or just going about his daily business. He didn't seem to have any interior life, which I think is why he kept himself so extraordinarily busy; I don't think he liked to sit and contemplate anything. But if there was a very private side of him, I never saw it; hardly anyone did, I think."[162]

But this was still to come: 1965 had run its course – it had begun well enough, dipped horridly, and then raised its game once more; and now, having spent a brief Christmas with his family, Frost returned to London with an idea to kick off 1966.

*

"The episode known as the Frost Breakfast revealed as clearly as any other single event the extent to which, in the course of ten years, television had disoriented the sense of reality in English public life."[163] This was Christopher Booker's opinion of the public event with which Frost chose to kick off his New Year. Frost, unsurprisingly, has a rather different sense of the whole event:

[O]n Monday, 3 January, I had a simple (as I saw it), private (as I organised it), little (as I planned it) idea. The early days of January are often the dog days of the year. The weather is usually pretty depressing, and the bills coming in from Christmas make it even more so. Wouldn't it be a good idea to give a party, mixing up some of the friends I had got to know from varying walks of life? Right now, this week? I settled on breakfast as the time for the party, most of all because of the short notice. I thought that everybody's diaries around lunchtime and in the evenings would probably be full.[164]

In his autobiography, Frost goes on to describe the location of this breakfast party (at the fashionable and luxurious Connaught Hotel in Mayfair); and the food to be served (Ray Parkes's ulanovas, described as a "mouth-watering mixture of sour cream and caviar on a thick but featherweight prawn cracker. The texture was as good as the taste, and vice versa"). He remembers his own remark when challenged by the media: "I'm a great believer in breakfast as an institution," and goes on to delight in the reports which filled the newspapers in the days that followed. "It became a sensation," says Antony Jay, "precisely because David didn't publicise it. So the press became even more excited than they would otherwise have been."[165] Certainly, the media – alerted by Downing Street briefing notes which revealed the presence of the Prime Minister at the event – fed hungrily on the details, and on Frost's *chutzpah* – that word again – at having pulled it off. Frost, however, has nothing at all to add as to why this event was organised in the first place.

Of course, we know why it was organised – and so we know that Frost's précis of the event is breathtakingly, comically and surely deliberately disingenuous. This breakfast was not designed to cheer up guests distracted by the weather and a cascade of Christmas bills onto doormats. Nor was it designed to introduce anyone to Ray Parkes's ulanovas, delicious as they doubtless were. It was to create the ultimate networking event, with David Frost at the centre of all. "Television was so important at that point," Antony Jay adds, "and that's why the people who were invited actually came. Frost meant television – and television was the ultimate medium for self-publicity."[166] Frost's intention, then, was to create a drama, a tableau, a nexus demonstrating power, influence and attention – and this was a phenomenon that Frost would deliberately repeat, in a variety of extravagant forms, for the rest of his life.

And it was a gamble: an extraordinarily audacious one, for it was fraught with the possibility of crippling humiliation. Frost had steel, and a self-confidence that went back to the cradle: although it is also true that the odds were stacked in his favour – not least because he shared Napoleon's splendid and invaluable knack of remembering the name and background of everyone he met, and could therefore rely to a much greater degree than was normal on the loyalty, comradeship and love of those around him. They would, likely as not, rally to his cause – especially given that this cause happened to involve a free breakfast at the Connaught. But this was also a gamble he worked hard to win, as well as one he seems instinctively to understand would pay off.

And on cue, on Friday, January 7th, 1966, at 9.30am, they began to roll up. Wilson – demonstrating the sort of media *nous* that Frost himself possessed – was an early arrival. He was joined by a *Who's Who* of London's media, political and cultural elite: members of the Commons and the Lords, the Bishop of Woolwich, the editor of the *Observer* and the London *Evening Standard*, various BBC and ITV worthies, and countless others. Everyone was there, it seemed, except for Paul McCartney – and he might have come along too, had it been a little later in the day. "I would say to him: 'No, no, no, man, I'm living at the other end of the clock!' So I didn't go, though I was flattered to be asked. I wanted to go but the time aspect was not, not, not good for me."[167] Wilson stayed for a full hour before sweeping back to Downing Street. On his departure, the champagne was opened to speed the remaining guests on their way; and the event was over by 11am.

These figures – these mandarins, knights and moguls – had all responded to Frost's invitation – but why? Christopher Booker had his ideas:

> To appreciate Frost's achievement in gathering together this assemblage of notables, one has only to reflect how, until but a year or two before, the Prime Minister of the day and a cross-section of public figures would have dismissed such an invitation from Frost's equivalent – say, a columnist on a popular Sunday newspaper – as an impertinent stunt. What gave Frost the knowledge that his gamble would come off, was his intuitive sense of television's power to recreate the world on its unreal terms – to reduce everything and everyone, politicians and pop singers, philosophers and journalists, bishops and entertainers, to the same level, as bit players in a universal dream world.[168]

Booker has the Connaught breakfast, therefore, connect neatly into his thesis of a world developing in the Britain of the sixties in which an orchestrated unreality was the order of the day. This thesis is certainly overblown: but Booker does illuminate the newness of those times, the levelling effect of mass media, and the canniness of members of the British Establishment – a new Establishment, as he calls it, though this is open to question – in coming to terms with it.

He is quite wrong, however, in his summation of the organiser of the breakfast as akin to a Sunday newspaper columnist. Frost, in spite of his recent professional travails, was already much more than this: he was a character who, having understood early the critical importance of television, was now asserting his own position in a world increasingly dominated by the medium. Whether one approved or disapproved of the tableau he established – and plenty of people did both – it was undeniable that he had his finger on a cultural pulse. And so did his guests – but it was Frost's presence that was remembered, and not theirs. And this would have consequences both long-term, and short.

Short-term, of course, the affair at the Connaught enhanced Frost's profile – and with the first edition of *The Frost Report* scheduled to air in March, this was surely all to the good. It had been decided that each programme would be themed, with the opening edition focused on Authority. Antony Jay wrote an introductory essay on each week's theme: this would be circulated to actors and scriptwriters. Frost himself used the text as the basis for the monologue which opened each programme, and the writers were guided by Jay's notes and commentary, so that it could be tasted too in the sketches, music and short films which peppered each edition.

The tone was satirical, to be sure, but this was a moderated satire: it was ironic, dry, witty, with an undercurrent of the absurdist and surreal comedy that later flowed through *Monty Python*. It was highly distinctive, in other words, and from the beginning it marked the programme out as original, and at a remove from *That Was the Week That Was*. If this originality has not stood the test of time – the programme can seem tame when viewed today – this was precisely because its legacy was game-changing. *Python* and such later shows as *Not the Nine O'Clock News* sprang directly from the furrow first ploughed in *The Frost Report*.

The reviews identified and praised the programme's subtlety and its canny, exact bite. The *Daily Mirror* delighted in the programme's ability "to separate what we believe is sensible and rational from what we actually do and say"; and the *Financial Times* remarked – presciently, given the pre-Python air of *The Frost Report* – that the programme inspired a pause and a double-take on the part of the viewer.[169] Frost's own response was one of relief. Finger on pulse or no, he absolutely needed a winner at this time – and now he had one. And the programme was a success with the viewers as well as critics – and with one viewer in particular: for in a Catholic boarding school in Berkshire, a long-legged teenager named Carina Fitzalan Howard took to watching *The Frost Report* with a certain rapt attention on the primitive little television in the common room.

It took prodigious, intense levels of work to get *The Frost Report* on air. The cast rehearsed in the unglamorous surroundings of a church hall in Paddington; and Thursdays were consumed by testing and assessing the completed scripts for weaknesses: as Frost noted, a spoken line or gag was potentially very different to a written one, and a sketch might stand or fall on a single weak point. The whole script was tested in such a way – a process which took all day, with the final script delivered to autocue with mere minutes to spare before broadcast. The Friday morning meetings that followed each live Thursday evening broadcast, meanwhile, were equally pivotal: at this time, the cast and crew looked a week ahead in order to sniff out weakness well in advance.

Frost admits that the integrated nature of the programme – everyone was consulted, and many views were taken on board – in this case made for a sharp and successful programme. Forty years later, Frost told the *Daily Express* that "it still seems like some sort of outrageous fantasy to think that *Monty Python's Flying Circus* was spawned on my show; that *The Goodies*' Tim Brooke-Taylor cut his teeth as a writer on *The Frost Report* and that I was working alongside such legends as Denis Norden and Barry Cryer. When I look back on it all, my first reaction is one of sublime gratitude that I was lucky enough to be surrounded by all that talent."[170]

These are generous words – and there does indeed appear to have been a true sense of happiness and collegiality on the show. Frost remembers the game of football that would often close the Friday meeting; Corbett recalls, in rather greater detail, "David, in goal and a natty suit, diving spectacularly all over the place in this rather dirty church hall. Then he would get into a car and go off for lunch with someone grand like Lord Snowdon or Norman St John Stevas or Princess Margaret, covered in dust from the floor."[171]

There were eddies and undercurrents just the same. Collegiality or not, there were no doubts as to who led the programme: Frost, Jay and Gilbert. John Cleese admits the clarifying nature of this arrangement – the chain of command was obvious to all – but there are ghosts of earlier criticisms as he describes Frost's role. *The Frost Report* scripts were credited to Frost "and" the other writers: "The general public," Cleese goes on, "must have wondered why so many of these so-called 'writers' were needed to fill in the occasional gap in what David had crafted. Those closer to the programme would sometimes speculate whether there was any single word which David could have been said in any meaningful sense to have 'written'. [...] David was endearingly shameless in matters such as these..."[172]

Frost would not, of course, hang around the rehearsal room – "essentially he left things to us, trusting our talent. This is a rare quality" – and so Cleese, Barker, Corbett and others were left to get on with it.[173] Corbett adds that they "would not see David until the day of the programme, then he would come in with a great armful of papers, with jokes written all over them in thick felt-tip pen" – a form of working which he patented in the years ahead. Corbett remarks feelingly that "it was a bit alarming for all of us, assembling the show in the scramble of the last couple of hours and then going out live, but I think it was most alarming for John Cleese, who didn't have any experience of learning lines up to the last minute".[174]

Cleese spent long periods in advance of broadcast in the lavatory. For Frost, by contrast, it was meat and drink: he took such last-gasp creativity wholly in his stride and relished it, loving as he always did the kick of adrenalin that accompanied any live television.

The theme for one of the opening shows – that of April 7th, 1966 – was Class: and this episode introduced the sketch which has made *The Frost Report* famous in posterity. Corbett, Barker and Cleese were the performers, with John Law and Marty Feldman the script-writers of The Class Sketch, which deployed the relative height of the actors – Cleese was extremely tall and Corbett extremely short – together with a spare, stripped-back script. The programme had often used the disparity in the heights of Corbett, Barker and Cleese to make a comic point: but this time, viewed through the prism of the British class system, the result was remarkable.

In the sketch, Cleese (in suit and bowler, with tightly furled umbrella) represents the upper class – he stands beside Barker, who (sporting a trilby) represents the middle class; and Corbett (in flat cap) the proletariat. The words are delivered slowly and with the sort of absurd formality that would later become a Python trademark:

JC: I look down on him [nods at Barker] because I am upper class.

RB: I look up to him [nods at Cleese] because he is upper class. But I look down on him [nods at Corbett] because he is lower class. I am middle class.

RC: I know my place. I look up to them both, but I don't look up to him [Barker] as much as I look up to him [Cleese] 'cos he has got innate breeding.

JC: I have got innate breeding, but I have not got any money. So sometimes I look up to him. [He bends in the direction of Barker.]

RB: I still look up to him [nods at Cleese] because, although I have money, I am vulgar. But I am not as vulgar as him [nods at Corbett] so I still look down on him.

RC: I know my place …

The Class Sketch provides another one of those occasional opportunities for Frost to opine with more than his usual frankness on the nature of class – its absurdity, its tenacity, its hypocrisy – in modern Britain. "If a lower-class man pinned someone against a brick wall and beat the living daylights out of him," he remarks of the relationship between class and crime, "it was called assault and battery. If an upper-class man did it, it was called the Eton Wall Game. As an Essex magistrate had said when dismissing a charge of assault brought by a woman against her husband, 'It is not unreasonable, in a certain class, for a woman to have her face smacked from time to time, and to be punched about. It is the normal wear and tear of their married life.'"[175]

Frost goes on in this vein for some time, underlining his opinion that class, hypocrisy and the law were linked inextricably. He may not have written the sketches in question – still, *The Frost Report*, one senses, provided an arena in which to air opinions without any fear of their being pulled by the BBC. And yet, he repeats Peter Cook's sense that any form of criticism – be it in the shape of humour, satire, irony or blunt commentary – would find in the end no purchase on the glassy surface of the British class system: "Behind the turbulence, the citadels of entrenched power and influence were not really in any imminent danger of falling like dominoes to the insurgents."[176]

*

The Frost Report ended its opening run in June 1966 – Frost, in another recreation of the networking extravaganza that was the Connaught breakfast, threw a party at Battersea funfair to mark the occasion – and the BBC immediately commissioned a new series, to begin the following year. In the meantime, there was another summer for Frost to enjoy. London was officially Swinging now, because the cover of *Time* magazine had said so, and Frost duly swung with his surroundings, from lunches to clubs to summer parties, and trips to Whitby and Beccles. But he never stopped working: and the sweep of his activities that summer provide an instructive and almost mesmerising sense of this man's energy and range of interests.

Engagements included a summer radio show on the BBC Light Programme (it would be renamed Radio Two in the following year), which provided another opportunity for Frost to surround himself with his comic friends, this time in a fresh medium – and to poke fun in the process at BBC *mores*. To these activities, Frost added various overseas flits. He went out to Ibiza – in those days cheap, relatively quiet and unfashionable – where John Cleese and Graham Chapman were spending the summer. Here we catch a glimpse of a Frost – still only twenty-seven – losing his battle to stay in good physical shape. "He went into the water in his bathing trunks for a paddle: we knew he took no exercise – but still we were struck by how plump he was for a young man. Even then he was neglecting himself physically – and I think he always did."[177] Frost also went to the French Riviera to visit Winston Churchill's son Randolph, who was writing a biography of his late father. The scene was La Capponcina, the elegant villa acquired by Lord Beaverbrook on Cap d'Ail, across the bay from Monte Carlo, and Churchill and Frost were meditating on the possibility of Richard Burton narrating a series of films based on the book. Burton, of course, had form in this area: he had already narrated *The Valiant Years*, a successful documentary series made for ABC in the United States and broadcast in 1960; and the idea also provided an opening for Frost to fly to Rome for a rendezvous with Burton and Elizabeth Taylor. Nothing came of this notion, but it emphasised the range of Frost's connections even now, still relatively early in his career.

It was, then, a manic summer: and a glance at his itinerary underscores the sense in which the idea of free or down time did not appreciably exist in Frost's mind. He was always working, always scouting – and in this case, always keeping an eye on his connections, whether actual or potential. "I can see my mother sitting there," remembers Margaret Frost, "and saying, 'You don't need to work so hard, you can slow down,' and I said the same thing. But he couldn't, he just couldn't. He wouldn't have stopped, not even if a doctor had told him to."[178]

Nor would he stop detecting opportunities. As London swung, so Frost succeeded in selling to ABC in the United States an idea for a television special from the now-officially fashionable British capital. This new programme would, once more, come with the Frost imprimatur attached firmly: *David Frost's Night Out in London* would explore the nocturnal city through the prism of a selection of the capital's entertainers and show business stars, including Lulu and Danny la Rue, whose club on Hanover Square Frost liked to frequent. But a selection of A-listers was also needed to satisfy ABC: "Laurence Olivier, Peter O'Toole, Albert Finney, Peter Sellers, Sean Connery and Peter Ustinov. I got Peter Sellers, who kindly agreed to do a wine-tasting sketch for me, but Sean Connery, Peter Ustinov and Peter O'Toole and Albert Finney were all unavailable ..."[179]

Frost was obliged to go to great lengths to pin down the necessary figures: first, discovering that Olivier and Finney would be appearing at an upcoming benefit evening at the Royal Court theatre on Sloane Square, he ensured that Paradine rapidly negotiated the rights to film the dress rehearsal and even more rapidly installed cameras in the theatre, before flooding the area with free tickets to ensure a decent audience. This was exactly the sort of episode that caused some people to admire Frost and others to loathe him: it showcased the self-confidence that drove him ever onwards, and the assertiveness which would well-nigh ensure success. And the show *was* a success. For one thing, the Royal Court film was of much interest in its own right, for it captured not only Finney and Olivier in action, but other substantial figures – Lynn Redgrave, Noël Coward, John Gielgud. The US reviewers were delighted – even if for some, Danny La Rue was a step too far: "... the disgusting entertainment: Danny La Rue is a British (sic) female impersonator. There is just one word for his performance, and you don't have to grope for it. The word is 'vulgar'. Some may argue that La Rue, who describes himself as a man, has the ability to look and act just like a woman. That may be a problem for him and his doctor to figure out."[180]

But this frenzy of summer entertainment, all-consuming though it appeared, was in fact a mere sideshow. Another opportunity was now presenting itself: highly significant, in that it provided an opportunity for Frost to showcase yet another side of his television persona. The opportunity came from Associated Rediffusion – Frost's erstwhile ITV employer a mere three years before – which stepped in to offer a new show to fill the intervening months. This – and once more the nomenclature left something to be desired – was to be called *The Frost Programme*: a new three-times-a-week series beginning at the end of September 1966 and described as "a mixture of humour, people, comment and entertainment". This sounded disagreeably like the ill-fated *Not So Much a Programme...*, even if Frost appeared not at all daunted by this obvious comparison.

There were other similarities, notably in the Frost monologue – occasionally, Cleese would step in – that would open the show; there were also occasional dialogues with Cleese. But there was novelty in *The Frost Programme* too – especially in the role of the studio audience. While live television in front of a captive audience was of course nothing new to Frost or to British television in general, the television law of the fourth wall had remained largely intact: the live audience had watched proceedings, sometimes responsively, sometimes as though on the other side of an invisible membrane. This worked well, according to the forms and expectations of the time, but this new programme opted to do it rather differently: now the audience would help to craft and form the programme itself.

Frost credits Antony Jay with tabling this innovation, though he also notes the general sense detectable at the planning meetings in the summer of 1966 that *something* needed to be done to stir up live television, "that: [...] London's drawing power for personalities was not being exploited in television, that there ought to be a sophisticated and cosmopolitan catchment area for the right interviewer, doing the right interviews [...] current affairs lacked an animal contact with the real world. [...] television followed newspapers too slavishly, and should seek out news for itself."[181]

Frost himself was of the opinion that the people – the politicians and power-brokers – who appeared on television ought to be pressed and challenged more, and obliged to account for themselves rather more clearly than was the general rule at the time; and that television had – again in a reflection of his sense that television, radio and their audiences at their best formed a single, contiguous whole – a duty to reflect and give voice to the opinions of its viewers. Some of his previous work had of course accomplished a degree of this: but satire, for all that it pressed and challenged politics and politicians, did so indirectly. These power-brokers were seldom eyeball-to-eyeball with their tormentors.

And so the live, engaged studio audience came to form a central aspect of the show. Again, there is nothing remarkable today about such a television staple – and again, this is partly as a result of the pioneering work accomplished by early television, and by the likes of *The Frost Programme*. Rediffusion was perhaps a little queasy at the thought of what might happen when such an audience was let loose on a programme and its guests; and even Frost remembers a glimmer of a glimmer of doubt: "I could sense that this sort of participating audience would demand more of me and my guests than was the custom. This arena was suddenly that much bigger, and we were a little more naked in it ..." But he ends with a most Frost-like return to a crisp accentuation of the positive: "the risks were well worth taking. We decided to dive in at the deep end."[182]

And it was a gamble that paid off. This was good television: not only sharply argued and smartly put together, but informal and spontaneous – and in touch therefore, with the times and the new expectations of more demanding television audiences. Some issues presented themselves: the show was not available in all ITV regions. John Cleese, for example, recalls that his parents in Somerset were unable to see it, and, wondering if their son even *had* a job, suggested he apply for one at Marks and Spencer – later an application form arrived in the post. And the earlier programmes were formed by the inability of Frost to attract a big name: significant politicians and public figures knew enough about his past to be shy of this latest incarnation.

Yet these early shows, though they did not set the world alight, nevertheless found their groove. Frost speaks of a theme of "activism" running through *The Frost Programme*, an a allusion that speaks to that thread of morality that runs through his television work. One such "activist" edition of the show dwelt on the disturbing case of Timothy Evans, hanged in 1950 for the murder of his infant daughter – a murder, it had become increasingly clear, thanks in part to work on the case by the journalist Ludovic Kennedy – he could not have committed.

There were confrontational set-pieces, but these – familiar as they would later become – were not the programme's strongest suit. *The Frost Programme* is instead best remembered for the interviews – long, detailed – that Frost began to handle. "What a remarkably fine interviewer he was," writes Cleese. "Sharp, agile and yet empathetic, he could get people to say more than they had planned, which paradoxically often rebounded to their credit, and he could also forensically take apart a weak case."[183] Some of his interviews were relatively low-key but impressive set-pieces: long, detailed features, for example, on the meaning and importance of poetry and featuring John Betjeman, who within a few years would be Poet Laureate; other editions aired discussions of Vietnam and the Congo.

One long meditation on the meaning of Christianity with Michael Ramsey, the then Archbishop of Canterbury, drew much attention. Ramsey's theology stemmed from an Anglo-Catholic background: broadminded, communicative and ecumenically minded, he was a sharp interviewee; and he and his host – who was once more, as a result of his upbringing, essentially on home ground – were able to cover a range of issues impressively and to debate questions of morality with care and sensitivity. Such an interview helped to move him decisively away from the rough-around-the-edges culture and sets of *That Was the Week That Was*.

And there were real coups, as in the case of the interview of Ian Smith, the Rhodesian Prime Minister. In November, 1965, Rhodesia had unilaterally declared independence and established a white minority state in what was still formally a British colony. Smith was now leading a country in confrontation with Britain: the *Sun* noted helpfully that "he could be arrested on a charge of treason because he is technically in rebellion against the Queen". The programme, however, issued an invitation to Smith just the same: to be interviewed on *The Frost Programme*, and to be interviewed in London. Ultimately, the interview was conducted by Frost from a cubicle at Television House; with Smith answering them over a – sometimes, very crackling – line from the Rhodesian capital, Salisbury.

Viewed in retrospect, this was certainly an unusual set-up for Frost, whose career was thriving and would continue to thrive on face-to-face interactions. But there was nothing else for it: Smith's presence in London was, in spite of Rediffusion invitations and Rhodesian posturing, neither desirable nor possible – even, as Frost notes drolly, had he been able to guarantee Smith "Claridge's, rather than the Tower of London". The film and audio were later spliced together for broadcast: the result might have been a little messy – but ultimately, it worked.

Paul McCartney recalls watching the interview "with my heart in my mouth. I could see it was genuinely significant television. All the people I knew, presumably all the people I knew, were against apartheid, and we watched with bated breath to see what questions he would ask and what answers he was given. And I saw him getting inside Smith's head: here was David talking to the person who symbolised apartheid, and it elevated David into someone who was internationally significant."[184] The success of the interview in part this simply had to do with the material. Smith was a slippery creature who, in the course of the interview, excelled in sardonic asides regarding his dealings with Harold Wilson and his government; in addition to which, his arguments concerning Rhodesia's majority African population – his mentions of their thatched living conditions and his claims concerning their tendency to burn baby-filled houses – retain, even today, the power to shock and unsettle.

And it was grounded too in Frost's style, which managed to be both measured and polite but also stubborn, rather like a dog with a bone. How soon, Frost asked, before majority rule could be envisaged in Rhodesia?

Smith: This is very difficult to determine, I think you will find people in Rhodesia, people who claim to be knowledgeable in these affairs, who would give you times varying from five years to fifty years. So you pay your money and you take your choice.

Frost: Thank you. But what would you say was the minimum period before African majority government *you* would be happy about?

Smith: Well, there are so many imponderables; I don't think one can very accurately prognosticate. It depends on how the African is going to develop in the future, how he is going to accept the opportunities that are put before him. We find at the moment the African is not interested in our democratic system. […]

Frost: How would you define a democratic system, Mr Smith?

Smith: I would say it is the sort of government we have in Rhodesia and the same as you have in Britain, where you have democratic elections that return members of parliament. All of this is foreign to the African tribesman who works through the system of the headman and the chief …

The programme lasted almost an hour, and by its end, it was reasonable to assume that the television viewer would have found Smith's arguments verging on the fantastical, and Smith himself preposterous. (Certainly, the show of hands on the matter of sanctions against Rhodesia was very much in favour of their application.) And this was achieved by means of mild-but-persistent questioning, delivered without aggression.

And there were further show-stopping moments to come. The most celebrated of these came at the conclusion of the show's first series, in late January 1967, when Frost interviewed Emil Savundra, the owner of the Fire, Auto and Marine insurance corporation. Savundra was a shady creature: he had siphoned off several hundred thousand pounds from his company, which had duly collapsed – and Savundra had skipped off to Switzerland just as investigations were getting under way. As a result, he had become a celebrity, albeit of a strange and deeply unpleasant kind – and the whole interview foreshadows the more mainstream celebrity interviews in which Frost excelled.

Not that *The Frost Programme* was alone in its interest in this crook: so were the government, the *Mirror* and the *Daily Mail*, as well as the Insight investigative unit on the *Sunday Times*, which opened its files to Frost's researchers in order to put the programme together. Government officials claimed later that the state was on the verge of moving against Savundra, but the press disagreed. Investigations against him had been rumbling in the background for months, and journalists who worked on the case had no particular reason to believe that any action at all was imminent. Whatever the truth of the matter, Frost's interview would change completely the dynamic of the case.

The surprise, of course, was that Savundra was willing to appear on the show in the first place – he could not possibly gain anything from the experience, and he, better than anyone, knew that the current scandal was but the tip of the iceberg, for Savundra had a shady embezzling past going back at least to the 1950s. It seems that his extreme egoism and arrogance, coupled with a desire to joust with – and, presumably, topple – the famous Frost lay at the root of this otherwise incomprehensible decision. The result was a classic slice of television. As Ronnie Corbett remarks, "Wielding his trusty clipboard of truth, David was at his most indignantly probing while Savundra was at his most infuriatingly insouciant."[185] Certainly, this was a rather different Frost to the one who had quizzed the Prime Minister of Rhodesia. The substance of the interview, his tone, bearing, manner were noticeably more sharp, a sense of moral indignation was closer to the surface as he took on his shiny-faced interviewee. This was a world away from Footlights and the Blue Angel: if anything, it was closer in tone to some of the more raw moments of *That Was the Week That Was* – and this time, the texture of the programme suited this indignation, and the studio audience, which was composed in part of Savundra's victims, was voluble and behind him all the way.

Frost notes that the interview would be, if he had anything to do with it, focused on issues of morality: "I thought that the interview should drive towards one end in particular: Savundra's own sense of moral responsibility for the consequences of his actions. We needed first-person evidence of that, and we therefore asked along, as members of the audience, some ten or twelve victims of his swindles, people left without any settlement for life insurance claims."[186] The interview, in fact, makes for excruciating viewing – from its very opening seconds, in which Savundra introduces a blatant plug for an upcoming book he has written. Before too many more moments have passed, he has referred to the audience – which are, after all, no more than a few yards from the dais on which Frost and Savundra are perched – as "peasants", and refused to answer their questions. There is even a sense – passing but very real – that Frost himself is perplexed, unsure how to deal with the sociopath seated opposite him. When he does marshal his forces, however, he does indeed introduce issues of public and private morality, Savundra's own Catholic religion, and the impact of his actions on men and women unknown to him. "Let me ask you just one question. You can look at these people here – widows, widowers, whoever they are – and you can feel, 'I have no legal responsibility'? [...] And you can say, 'I've signed a piece of paper and I have no moral responsibility either'?"[187] The result – amorality on parade – is striking and shocking.

The episode concluded in a manner that ensured its notoriety. Rather than engage his ghastly guest in the fashion that was even then expected – anodyne conversation unheard by the viewers as the studio lights dimmed – Frost says his goodnights to camera, and walks off the stage: the audience applauds and calls out its bravos to "Frostie", with Savundra left lurking for a gaping instant in full view of the camera. "On this occasion," Frost writes, "I felt I could not stand the hypocrisy [...] I did not want anyone to think that my feelings ceased when the programme ceased. I was still angry. On the spur of the moment, I simply strode off the set."[188]

This was showmanship, at least in part. Frost was a television man to his fingertips, and a performer; he understood what did and did not work. Yet there was much more to this programme than showmanship. In this edition – as again and again in the first season – The Frost Programme dwelt to a surprising extent on issues of morality: this was something that, in spite of his demeanour and ocean-hopping lifestyle, exercised Frost and struck chords in his Methodist-influenced psyche. If this swift exiting of the stage in the face of Savundra's amorality, then, was what his audience would *wish* to see, it was also what Frost himself would *wish* to do. There is no contradiction between the two: in its own way, indeed, it was a very human situation, and it exemplifies the multifaceted nature of the man.

A week later, in early February, 1967, Savundra was arrested – and the following year imprisoned for fraud. The trial was characterised by bitter exchanges between defence and prosecution, and much in the way of commentary by the press on the subject of trial by media. Frost mounts a stout defence of the programme's tactics, making the point that television was less hidebound than the press in the matter of allegations and the machinery of law: and so The Frost Programme enjoyed the kind of freedom and power of which the newspapers could only dream. What could be better than deploying this latitude and freedom against a con artist – and in full view of his victims, to boot?

Certainly, the public had no gripe against such methods. Savundra did, and his appeal against his conviction rested in part on the complaint that The Frost Programme had proved prejudicial to a fair trial. The appeal was thrown out, but not before the judge called the programme "deplorable". Again, Frost was sufficiently stung to write to *The Times* with a broadside against the judge in question, his methods and his grasp of the facts, noting: "[W]e are all concerned about individual rights in Britain today, but one of the most precious of the rights that the public has is the simplest one of hearing the truth whenever and wherever it is available."

And he added another line, equally freighted with intention. "Television has shown that it has a real part to play in seeking the truth about matters of public concern, and to remove television from this role seems to be doing both public and individual a positive disservice." Frost, then, was placing television centre-stage – not for the first time in his career. And his words, in hindsight, seem pregnant with meaning, for now, as 1967 got into its stride, his devotion to the medium was about to lead him into altogether new and wider territories.

CHAPTER 4

A Firing Boy

"David loved being recognised, loved being famous, but he was essentially a humble man who treated everyone with respect, with care, and essentially with love."

Peter Chadlington

David Frost was now established in his new London home. This was a very substantial house on Egerton Crescent – one on a terrace of handsome white-stuccoed townhouses overlooking a private and manicured park, a stone's throw from the Victoria & Albert Museum in South Kensington. Today this area ranks among the most expensive neighbourhoods in London. It was rather less glittering in the late 1960s: one could still readily enough land a bed-sitting room to rent in these splendid streets, with a miserly gas-scented heater fed with pennies – yet the fact that Frost was able to acquire such a piece of London real estate at this point in his life illustrates the startling progress of his career and earning power.

Frost shared Egerton Crescent with Luisa – Lulu – Carmo, his energetic Portuguese housekeeper, who with her son occupied the property's basement apartment. Luisa was short, busty, immensely energetic and an excellent cook: she cared for the house, which its owner would doubtless otherwise have treated as a glorified student digs or hotel room, to be slept in at night and abandoned in the morning. She cared for Frost too, taking his chaotic timetable and immensely long working days in her stride, and she helped organise the dinners and parties which now began to form an essential part of Frost's life and work. Theirs was a close, warm relationship, and she rapidly became invaluable. "[She] had a way with crispy baked potato skins; David couldn't get enough of them. And she knew how to bundle one girlfriend out of the back door before opening the front door to a second girlfriend. She knew it all."[189] The house on Egerton Crescent provided Frost with a focus, a base, a sense of stability that until this time had been lacking: it was a place he could take for granted, and that freed up additional energies to be channelled into his social life and career. And there were other anchors, in addition to Jenny Logan and Lulu Carmo: in particular, his driver Bob Lambert, his personal assistant Joan Pugh, and the film producer Michael Deakin, one or more of whom were generally with Frost as he careered about London and the world.

Pugh had first met Frost when she worked in the studios at Associated Rediffusion before joining his personal staff: she would work alongside him for eight years, and she recalls "the fun of those years: we had to work very hard and put in tremendously long days, but [Frost] was never cross, never scolding, never fussing, never anything other than supportive, even when mistakes were made. The group of us – we made a terrific team. In my memory, we spent the whole day giggling and laughing."[190] Pugh was folded into Frost's family life: she took, for example, to going to Arsenal football matches with Mona Frost ("Oh, she was crazy about football") when she visited London.[191] They became adept at avoiding the press – though there was at that time a mutual respect between the two camps. "He really was followed everywhere. One cold winter day, the cameramen were huddled outside, and David wasn't planning on going anywhere, so he asked me to go out with a tray of brandy for everyone instead; and I went out of the front door and these people appeared from the bushes, arrived from everywhere for their brandy."[192]

His agent Richard Armitage was another indispensable figure in his life. Richard's son, Alex, nine years old in 1969, recalled Frost as occupying a significant space in his life. Alex would visit the house on Egerton Crescent with his father, to be petted by Luisa and made much of by Frost himself, and he was aware even as a child of Frost's ability to listen, and focus, and make one feel at the centre of his universe. He was present too to watch Frost's appalling timekeeping, and in particular, his unwillingness ever to arrive at an airport until minutes before his flight was due to leave. His staff regularly called ahead – a possibility in those days – to request that this or that flight be held for a few minutes until Frost made his last-minute arrival. Armitage recalls one mortifying experience in lurid detail: "Luisa was watching the clock, was chasing David out of the front door and into the car; my father and I were going along for the ride to the airport too. We were racing down the motorway when I – I was always prone to travel sickness – suddenly realised I was about to be sick. So I lunged for the window, wound it down and vomited out onto the carriageway, out of the window of David's pale-blue Bentley. He didn't turn a hair."[193]

Frost's son Wilfred adds that his father's last-minute travel habits certainly did not diminish with age. "[He] would always want to leave very little time in order to make a flight. And he would always insist on at least a brief visit to the BA First Class lounge. Whenever we reached the lounge, he would do a wine tasting. He would line up six or so glasses on the table and pour a generous taster out of each of the wines on offer. He would say that this was a 'tasting' and not a 'drinking' – and thus whatever time of day the flight was, this was justifiable! There would be someone from BA Special Services to meet us at the airport and make sure we slipped past security and so on – but despite this, it always felt like the slowest process in the world, leaving home to board a plane with Dad."[194]

Frost's social life remained as frenetic as ever. Joanna Lumley, then a young actress and fresh on the London scene, recalls attending a party given by Peter Cook at his Georgian home on Church Row in Hampstead, and glimpsing Frost, a celebrity in a room thronged with celebrities: "I felt like a stamp collector, collecting these personalities as one might collect stamps, standing in the middle of a crowd of famous people, of which I certainly was not one, and wondering why I had been asked, and what on earth I was doing there."[195] As for his career, this remained firmly on the boil. He was still only twenty-seven years old.

*

Early in January 1967, Frost was at a staff party at Associated Rediffusion's headquarters at Television House in central London. Less than six years previously, a short-tempered Frost had trailed his elders around these same studios as a fresh-faced, ambitious young Cambridge graduate. Now, he was the party's star attendee – which in this case meant he was given the honour that evening of drawing the winning raffle tickets from the tombola. He made a joke as he did so. There was an extra prize this evening, Frost told the audience, and the winner would receive the ITV television franchise for Yorkshire.

A mysterious crack to anyone not wholly steeped in television politics, but the crowd in the room at Television House appreciated the in-joke. For the Independent Television Authority (ITA) was gearing up to award new television licences to ITV regions up and down the country. The process was the talk of the television world; the franchises were potentially enormously lucrative – a "licence to print money", as the variously attributed saying had it – and now, for the first time, Yorkshire was to have its own television station. Yorkshire, then, was "the preferred target for would-be new franchise holders. That had never been stated publicly, but was taken as a given by consortium-builders all over the country."[196] And Frost himself had given the upcoming process a good deal of thought.

And yet, as Frost fished around that evening in the tombola, it was not a Yorkshire winning ticket that he had in his sights. Rather, he was turning over in his – always commercially astute and profoundly organised – mind the possibilities afforded by the London weekend television market, the franchise for which he believed might well be snatched. He knew that his American connections would, frankly, pay rather more attention to what was being filmed in London than in Leeds: the one arena would help to create possibilities in the other. And crucially, Frost had the vision to see that mere financial rewards were only part of a potentially much greater whole, that by controlling part of the London television market now, he and Paradine Productions, and the network of contacts he had built up so carefully over the last six years, would be in a prime position to influence the future too, to leave a mark on whatever form this future took.

Frost believed that television production and programming in general were due a cultural renewal, that the iconoclasm of the sixties, much as it had profited him personally and in terms of reputation, had still not been reflected adequately on the screen, that standards were lower than they might have been, and that television talent and potential talent were getting a good deal less of a look-in than ought to be the case. His idea was to instigate the next wave of a cultural change on TV, to create from scratch the station that would make this change manifest, and of course also to be in the driving seat as the station advanced, and to hold shares in its future.

A quick glance at the course of Frost's professional life since his arrival in London demonstrates that this was a natural, organic next step. He had, after all, already shown his proficiency as a television manager, adept at getting things done and bringing disparate individuals together to create a talented team; he had shown too his ability to create, in Paradine, a television production company under his own control. He had repeatedly demonstrated his ability in front of the cameras, to stirring effect. In January 1967, there were few names in Britain as well-known as that of David Frost, and now these ripples could be detected in America too. Indeed, the one fed the other, now and in the future. As he established a reputation in America as a networker and a friend to business and cultural leaders and to royalty, so American attentions were increasingly fixed and held, and this valuable energy flowed in the opposite direction too. He understood business and money, and could direct its flow – and he could navigate the networks of the great and the good. And so now he wanted to explore the possibility of controlling London's weekend franchise, though crucially, this was only one in a number of stepping stones placed by Frost in these years, each designed to move him forward.

"The clue to David," remarks Antony Jay, "is that he was really an impresario rather than a personality." And now here was the ultimate opportunity for Frost to prove that this was indeed the case.[197] He was, of course, under no illusions as to the difficulties he would face. Any consortium of which he was a member would need immense amounts of cash, for one thing; and they would inevitably begin the process as underdogs squaring up to the established power of the incumbent. Yet there were advantages – or potential advantages – too. In those days, the ITV franchise round was not yet wholly to do with cash, and how much the exchequer would wring out of the bidders. Rather, it was a beauty contest, to do with business plans, to be sure, but also to do with ideas, with the vision set out by each bidder and how these clustered visions, or lack thereof, were digested inside the ITA. This meant that the results of the process were incalculable – who knew how the mandarins gathered around the table at the ITA would react to this vision, or that one? Certainly Frost could not know – but it also meant that there was all to play for. This was a gamble, and David Frost enjoyed gambles.

And so began, in the course of the next few days, an intriguing round of conversations with key figures in the worlds of culture and television, including Sir Peter Hall, then the director of the Royal Shakespeare Company; Humphrey Burton, head of music and arts at the BBC; Michael Peacock, controller of BBC1; Alastair Burnet, editor of *The Economist*; and others. And he was pleased, or reasonably so, with what he discovered: not everyone was wholly supportive, but there was sufficient positivity in the air to encourage him forward.

This process of gauging, recruiting, enlisting the individuals and the wealth necessary to mount a bid on the London weekend franchise, continued throughout the first half of 1967. Through the process, Frost maintained a focus on what had initially interested him: in building a bid that emphasised the virtues of creativity and public-service broadcasting over what he perceived to be a dominant structure of top-heavy management. And on the last day of January 1967, he set off for the ITA itself, to probe what that organisation did and did not want to see happen in the upcoming franchise round.

And the news that day was good. The regulator, under the aegis of Lord Hill – Charles Hill, who himself had built a career as a post-war Conservative government minister and prominent critic of the BBC – intimated that it would certainly not be averse to a few changes in broadcasting, both in London and across the country. Television needed more material like *The Frost Programme*: it had, Hill implied, a job of work to do, and Frost understood he was pushing at an open door.

The deadline for ITV applications was mid-April 1967. Frost and his consortium had two months to reach the £6 million threshold fixed by the ITA. A frantic period followed, filled with meetings with investors, potential investors, financiers of various stripe, with – crucially – the Samuel Montagu merchant bank coordinating all matters financial. It was at this time that he first met Michael Rosenberg, then a middling member of the Samuel Montagu hierarchy. "We were the same age," Rosenberg remembers. "I was wearing short trousers – well, almost. We had the same sense of humour, and those similarities meant that he spoke to me more than any of the others."[198] This was the beginning of one of the most significant friendships of Frost's life.

By early April, the components had coalesced. The finances were in place, and the creative element – the character of the programmes to be made and their cost, the ethos of the proposed station – were set out. The group had a tentative name, the London Weekend Consortium, and bold plans for a £2.5 million studio complex in central London. There would be an emphasis on quality, on smart comedy, children's programming, adult education, drama and the arts in general, as well as upmarket current affairs strands, and investment in the new technology of colour television. Frost himself – for the first time in his career – now agreed to contract himself exclusively to ITV (in the UK) for three years. He would present *The Frost Programme* on all three weekend nights: *Frost on Friday* would focus on current affairs; *Frost on Saturday* on chat;

and *Frost on Sunday* on entertainment. The document also set out a manifesto of sorts, a call to the banner of quality television:

> The first, and inherent, principle of the Company's programme philosophy is a respect for the creative talents – for those who, within sound and decent commercial disciplines, will conceive and make television programmes. The second is respect for those who watch them, the audience. This means quite simply the belief that no audience is either mass or minority but a changing formation of groups responding to what is familiar, and what is unknown, with differing interests and tastes, each with a right to be served. [...] We believe that the commercial viability is strengthened by evidence of an active, perceptive and participating audience. [...] Independent television has the capacity to be as complete a public service as the BBC, by being able to deploy the output of a variety of companies, each with its own character, to make a comprehensive and balanced whole. [...] The cardinal principle of our programming philosophy for weekend television is that no single group of viewers, even if it be the majority, should be served to the exclusion of all other groups; no single area or type of television programming, even if it be the most widely acceptable to the majority, should be permitted to predominate; no one aspect of our culture emphasised or over-emphasised while others are neglected; no one single standard prevail.[199]

This was the language of Everyman. These words, though written in committee and of course pitched squarely at the ITA, at Lord Hill, and at what the consortium understood its wishes to be, also reflect Frost's own personal opinions too, to a striking extent. They reflect his views, the result of Methodist nurture as well as nature, and honed in the course of a childhood listening to the wireless, squabbling over channel settings with his sister Jean at Gillingham, and reflecting on the reach and function of broadcasting to a wider community and to every possible member of it. He might as well have written every word of the document himself, so fully did it tally with a personal sense of what broadcasting could mean, both commercially and morally. And now the die was cast. Joan Pugh was called upon to type up the bid document, which was sent off to the ITA on April 14th, 1967 – and a couple of weeks later, in early May, the group was called for interview.

*

Consuming though the bidding process had become, there were naturally other irons in the fire too, and in late April, David Frost took off for Switzerland, and the Montreux Television Festival, where the annual competition for the prestigious Golden Rose was taking place. His previous outing to the festival had been singularly ill-starred, but there was reason to believe that a special episode of *The Frost Report*, compiled by the BBC to launch the new series of the programme, would on this occasion fare rather better. It would be something of a humiliation to traipse all the way to Switzerland in the expectation of winning, and then not win, especially with Europe's media gathered to record the event. Yet, Frost and Jimmy Gilbert, his producer on the show, decided to risk it. They arrived at Montreux early on the morning of Friday, April 21st to the news that *The Frost Report* had indeed won the Golden Rose, as well as the Critics' Prize.

The news helped to cancel out the previous Montreux disap-pointment in the most delightful way possible, in addition to which, Frost could not be unaware that the ITA, considering the London Weekend Consortium application at that very moment, was watching beadily from London. And later that evening at the awards ceremony, Frost demonstrated that his habit, his compul-sion always to be prepared, was as strong and fervent as ever:

I managed to say thank you in all the languages represented at the festival. Well, it wasn't actually quite as casual as that sounds. I had taken the precaution of doing a little research before I left London, just in case ... But I had delayed committing them to memory until I was absolutely sure it was necessary ...[200]

In early May, buoyed by this success, Frost and his partners arrived at the ITA for their interview which went smoothly, and a month later, on June 10th, 1967, the good news came through: the ITA had approved the London Weekend Consortium's bid, with only minor stipulations. Frost and his party repaired (inevitably) to the Ritz for lunch – but "by the middle of the afternoon, the first dizzy flush had dissipated, and gradually we became almost overawed by the scale of the undertaking. That was just as well. From that moment, we had little more than a year in which to build, virtually from scratch, a company that would ultimately employ more than a thousand people [...] and endeavour to live up to its very ambitious plans."[201]

The consortium settled at last on a name: London Weekend Television (LWT) – and set about planning the development of modern studios on the South Bank of the Thames. And as for Frost himself, he remarks that LWT "just seemed like the logical thing to do".[202] And this was the case: his appetite for wide horizons, mocked and vilified though it had been in the dining halls of Cambridge and clubs of Soho, was native to him, an intrinsic part of his personality – and had been sharpened further on the streets of Manhattan, where ambition in all its forms was celebrated unequivocally. His assiduous networking rendered achievable what might have been a dream or a theory, had made it possible to access the funds required and to know the individuals who could make it happen. His own production company, Paradine, had provided him with further learning opportunities, and all this, combined with a sense of moral purpose, essentially made the world his oyster:

I approached it with a sort of optimistic innocence and a youthful determination never to limit my horizons, or my options. And there was the sheer excitement of the challenge and the chase. There were no age restrictions or other barriers in this particular race – unless they were self-imposed, or you allowed them to be imposed by school or society. If the odds appeared to be against you, you forgot the odds.[203]

Such a mission statement is notable not least for being so very open to political interpretation. In narrow party terms, it could – then and now – have been lifted and applied to both a Labour and a Conservative agenda; and to any number of others. It encapsulated Frost's own ability to reach out across such divisions, and into a wider society where such notions might be welcome.

For Frost, now was the moment for Paradine Productions to come into its own. With its owner now in a position of even greater influence, the company was able to pitch ideas at ITV – something that in those days of broadcasting monoliths, was extremely rare. Independent production companies were viewed coldly, to be stamped out where possible; very few of them existed. That Paradine not only existed but was flourishing, had everything to do with Frost's own commercial canniness, his ability to exert a measure of control and independence in driving his own career – and to forget those disagreeable few months in 1961 when he had been a powerless trainee producer wandering the corridors of Television House.

Naturally, he remained aware of the pitfalls – there was no larger organisation waiting in the wings to coddle one in the event of a critical or commercial disaster, and no financial reserves to dip into when a programme failed. But for all this, Frost understood the delights of independence: "The sheer diversity of switching from producer to fund-raiser to executive to author to salesman to consultant to editor is a pretty healthy insurance against boredom setting in, or the adrenalin ceasing to pump."[204] He understood that the rewards of commercial freedom were potentially great too, and now he had the opportunity to put this understanding to the test. He himself was contracted to ITV, but – and this was crucial – his Paradine production company remained free to go into the marketplace as it saw fit.

Frost soon began to explore these new commercial possibilities. He had already approached a bluff young Yorkshireman named Michael Parkinson who was establishing his own reputation in television, and had persuaded him to join and invest in LWT, and to oversee sports documentaries on the channel. "Now, this was a field," Parkinson remarks, "I really knew bugger all about. But happily I was able to hand all those difficult responsibilities over to others – and David and I had a very jolly relationship".[205] Ronnie Corbett, Ronnie Barker and John Cleese, meanwhile, had now signed exclusively to Paradine: "For years," Corbett remembers, "Ron [Barker] and I were joined at the hip to Paradine: shows, sitcoms, you name it. We were eager beavers, and we knew we were on to a good thing. Sometimes I regret not taking my destiny into our own hands, forming our own production vehicle – but we knew even then that it wasn't really our sort of thing; and besides, David was a super manager. He was our bond with the business."[206] Frost agreed with Corbett and Barker that the two – who, even before the advent of *The Two Ronnies*, were connected closely in the minds of the public – would work together on programmes; but he also contracted that Paradine would create separate vehicles for their talent. This was crucial: both Corbett and Barker had individual as well as collective ambitions, and it is a sign of Frost's acumen and sensitivity that he recognised this, and embraced it as an opportunity.

He acted as executive producer for Paradine on a new situation comedy for Corbett, *No, That's Me Over Here*, which he sold to ITV. Corbett's wife was played by Rosemary Leach, then carving out her own distinguished career in British film and television. It was scripted soon-to-be-Pythons Eric Idle and Graham Chapman: the latter had recently come out as gay, and was drinking heavily and behaving in generally very erratically – but the first scripts survived these choppy waters, and the programme ran for three years. For Ronnie Barker, Paradine produced *The Ronnie Barker Playhouse*, a series of six half-hour comedy shows which was also sold to ITV for broadcast in 1968. And for John Cleese, Paradine produced for ITV a Footlights-flavoured satirical vehicle called *At Last the 1948 Show*, which ran from 1967 to 1968 on ITV and which was, in hindsight, another significant precursor to the surreal flavour of Monty Python. All three were moderately successful – indeed, *At Last the 1948 Show* established a cult following, though it is clear from its all-too-frequent shifts within the ITV schedule that programmers hardly knew what to make of its humour – and helped to establish Paradine and Frost himself as producers of original television.

There was to be a coda to this story of Paradine and its rising fortunes. In 1969, *Private Eye* published allegations that Frost had abused his status as a founder of LWT to secure contracts for Paradine programming on the network. Journalists on Granada Television's *World in Action* show – at the time considered the best and most courageous investigative journalism unit in Britain – decided to follow up on these allegations. The programme's editor, a young John Birt, focused *World in Action*'s resources on the story, framing it around a fly-on-the-wall documentary detailing a week in the life of Frost himself. The programme was, by and large, ill-disposed towards Frost, seeing him as a courageous young satirist who had now become an establishment patsy, and Birt secured interviews with former LWT staffers who claimed that Frost had indeed abused his position. There was, however, one problem: they no longer had the documents that would, they claimed, substantiate such comments. Birt's crew continued to shadow Frost as he carried out his manic work schedule on either side of the Atlantic, and it proved a chastening experience:

> While the fly on the wall filming was entertaining, it did not reveal the story we had set out to tell. David and his team came over as serious-minded and professional; and they were convincing about the journalistic bona fides. I interviewed him in the Algonquin Hotel in New York and put to him the allegations of journalistic impropriety, which he vigorously denied. We had no evidence to sustain them, so the interview fell flat.[207]

It was an embarrassment to the programme, the more so when Frost, back in London, opened his files to *World in Action* researchers who were able to trace legitimate audit trails between Paradine and LWT. The programme was never shown.

More than twenty years later, the allegations resurfaced in the House of Commons: an Early Day Motion called on Birt to explain the connection between his abortive, never-aired edition of *World in Action*, and the course of his subsequent career, especially his move to LWT in 1972 as Frost's producer. Birt, by now Director General designate of the BBC, threatened to sue if any such (entirely false) intimations were ever repeated outside the House. But for Joan Pugh, the experience was entertaining: "They wanted to knock David, but we just laughed: it didn't bother us at all. And amazingly, David didn't seem cross about it all. He knew there was nothing to be found – and in a way, I think he saw it as flattering that they wanted to knock him down in the first place; and amusing that there was no knocking to be had."[208]

*

The new season of *The Frost Programme* began in late September 1967. A high point of the series came in mid-November, when Frost interviewed Sir Oswald Mosley, the economist and politician who in the 1930s had been the focus of black-shirted fascist sentiment in Britain. In 1966, Mosley had chanced a political comeback, contesting (unsuccessfully) a London constituency in the general election of that year. His political career was now definitively over, but he was continuing his attempt at an intellectual comeback, using as his springboard the economic difficulties, eddying cultural tides and general political disenchantment of the time. He also had revisionist memoirs to publicise, and, with the war and the Holocaust now two decades in the past, he had in fact received a degree of polite public attention, though more so in America than in Britain where, as Frost remarks, memories were longer, "particularly of what Mosley thugs had done to Jews and Jewish property in London's East End before the war".[209]

Frost was low-key on the night. Dark-suited and neat with a trim, quiff-less haircut, he cut a sober figure. There was every reason to think that the interview might become incendiary: the audience was filled with individuals who remembered the pre-war era and Mosley's actions and speeches in the course of those years; and Mosley himself was persistent in his claim that current economic and political difficulties were akin to those that had appeared in the run-up to the war – fiscal challenges, and a disenchantment with parliamentary politics, and indeed politics in general. Frost challenged his guest repeatedly on his anti-Semitism, capping Mosley's assertion that he was not at all an anti-Semite by quoting back at him speech after inflammatory speech and screening a particularly gripping piece of newsreel showing Mosley flourish the Nazi salute, proving yet again the virtues of careful preparation. A member of the audience added the contents of a telegram sent in 1935 by Mosley to Hitler's lieutenant Julius Streicher, thanking him for German support: "I greatly esteem your message in the midst of our hard struggle. The forces of Jewish corruption must be overcome in all great countries before the future of Europe can be made secure in justice and peace. Our struggle is hard but our victory is certain."

The programme is gripping, though not for the words, rhetoric and denials of Mosley, which were wholly to be expected, and not even for the bitter invective between guest and audience, which laced long sections of the interview. Rather, this edition pivots on Frost's strategy of gradually steering the interview away from audience participation in the interests of having Mosley's unchanged politics aired thoroughly and exposed. It benefitted too from Frost's comparative absence of ego: there was no grandstanding, no flights of dramatic fancy, no excessive wordiness in his conduct of the interview. Instead, he accumulated – slowly, gradually, patiently – evidence against Mosley, and enabled him to hang himself. This was forensic interviewing, the better for Frost's own subtle pacing. The key moment came when Mosley declaimed that the war itself had been produced by Jewish interests, and that the continent's Jews had only themselves to blame for the resulting catastrophe of the Holocaust. The interview ended with audience laughter. Mosley had disgraced himself utterly – a "joke figure", as Frost put it, with his guest's tentative steps towards a new respectability once more stopped in its tracks. The edition demonstrated once more the virtues of the long interview format and the adroitness of Frost in particular at getting the very best out of it.

But grief was looming now for Frost and his family. On November 16th, 1967, the day after the Mosley interview, Wilfred Frost suffered a cerebral haemorrhage. His decline, all too evident in the course of the previous four or five years, had accelerated throughout that autumn, and now it was evident to all that he had only days to live. After hosting *The Frost Programme* as normal the following evening, Frost took the road to the house on Ellough Road in Beccles that he had bought for his parents several years earlier. Margaret was already there; so too was Jean – home from Africa and staying at her British base in nearby Bury St Edmunds. Wilfred's condition did not change the following day, but at 9.15am on Sunday, November 19th, he suffered another haemorrhage and died. He was sixty-seven years old.

"I was staying in Ellough Road at the time," remembers Margaret Frost, "and sharing a room with my mother, while the nurse sat with my father. Jean had gone back early that morning, and David had left for London." Frost, in fact, had undertaken to be in London that same day to launch Oxfam's 1967 Christmas Appeal – he had spent part of the previous summer in India, observing the work of the organisation on the subcontinent. He had returned to the capital with Mona's blessing: both mother and son recognised that this was exactly the sort of endeavour that Wilfred himself would have supported. "David did a lot of extra things like that," says Margaret, "and he didn't like to refuse people; and it was a job trying to find him that day."[210]

Wilfred Frost was buried at Beccles the following Thursday, November 23rd, 1967; and the Frost family and circle of friends gathered for a lunch later that day to honour his life. The obituaries were warmly appreciative of Wilfred's power as a preacher as well as his practical skills as an administrator and fundraiser.

*

A month before Wilfred's death, Frost had hosted lunch for a group of American television executives visiting London on what would today be called a "scoping" mission. The meeting had taken place at the Royal Garden Hotel on the edge of Kensington Gardens, a favourite place for Frost, who could frequently be seen haunting the hotel's top-floor restaurant. ("Where other people were anxious to be seen in the newest bistro or the latest *le hot spot*," Joanna Lumley remarks, "David loved good hotel dining rooms. In those days, it marked him out as exotically and wonderfully trans-Atlantic".[211]) Frost's stock remained high in America, and now he took to the stage to speak on the subject of "To England – and America – with love", which enabled him to talk about and showcase to excellent and career-boosting effect his interviewing experiences on both sides of the Atlantic.

Among those present that day were representatives of the influential Westinghouse company which broadcast syndicated programming across its own network of television stations throughout the United States – and this autumn meeting in Kensington ranks as one more crucial pivot in Frost's career. Before the group left London, Westinghouse executives had floated the possibility of Frost fronting programmes for the company. In December, there was a lunch at Egerton Crescent when details were chewed over along with Luisa's lamb chops – and by January 1968, a deal began to cohere. The idea was that Frost would present several programmes designed to introduce British talent to an American audience, in addition to which he would focus one programme on the upcoming 1968 presidential election. LWT was still in development, with a launch date in mind in the autumn of the year, and once *The Frost Programme* ended in February, there would be little to prevent its host from pursuing other American leads.

Frost would enter an American political drama more fraught and dramatic than it had been for many years. Lyndon B Johnson was coming to the end of his first full term in the White House. It was surely a foregone conclusion that he would seek the Democratic nomination to run for a second term, but this election year was complicated both by a violent and race-inflected domestic scene, and by the disastrous war in Vietnam. Johnson had steadily escalated American involvement in the conflict. Without ever formally

144

declaring war on North Vietnam, he had committed ground forces – half a million by the beginning of 1968 – becoming in the process inextricably linked in the public mind with Vietnam and the horror unfolding there.

For by early 1968, it was apparent to all that the war against North Vietnam could not be won easily, and increasingly evident to many that it could not be won at all, and the draft and the sight on the evening news of ever increasing numbers of repatriated dead soldiers was creating a swelling anti-war mood in the cities and campuses of America. Sections of the Democratic Party were now swinging decisively against the incumbent president. In late 1967, Robert Kennedy – the junior senator from New York and younger brother of the assassinated John F Kennedy – had declined to run against Johnson. But by February 1968, a challenger to the incumbent president had stepped out of this Kennedy-shaped void in the form of Eugene McCarthy, the junior senator from Minnesota, running squarely on a peace ticket. It was certain now that the president's nomination would not go undisputed, with the upcoming primary in the state of New Hampshire the first electoral battleground. On the Republican side, meanwhile, there were any number of candidates – including former Vice President Richard Nixon and the governor of California, Ronald Reagan – jockeying to snatch the White House from the Democrats.

Into this crowded, tempestuous and confused field arrived the fresh-faced David Frost, eager to make his mark, and fully aware that the timing was exactly right for him to do so. The Westinghouse programme – to be styled *The Next President* – was pitched as relatively soft television, courteously probing, definitely non-confrontational, comprising short, timely and considered portraits of the candidates. Frost would focus on each in turn, in essence introducing him – there were no women – to the electorate and providing an opportunity for comparisons and checks. Frost had several points in his favour. He had a track record now on American television, of course – but he also had a quality of fresh-ness. Here was a young British personality with no manifest agenda beyond establishing televisual clarity, and certainly no political axe to grind. "I wanted to talk with the candidates about their personal philosophies, and what made them tick," remarks Frost.[212] This was television intent on capturing a wide sweep of Middle America.

The deal between Frost and Westinghouse was soon done, and the former began to plan on spending February and March in the United States to begin work on lining up the presidential interviews. It would soon become clear that Frost once more had a fair wind behind him. Anyone could see that the early stages of this presidential race were even more fraught and significant than usual – but nobody could foresee how the picture would alter, shockingly and dramatically, in the coming months.

Frost kicked off his interviews by meeting with McCarthy in Manchester, New Hampshire, on March 12th, 1968. This was the day of the primary itself, and by the times the polls closed, it had become apparent that McCarthy had run Johnson very close indeed, and in the process had significantly weakened the president. Kennedy, sensing his opportunity, now reversed his decision and declared his candidacy on March 16th, and by the end of March, Johnson shocked Americans by declaring that he would not seek re-election: "I shall not seek, and I will not accept, the nomination of my party for another term as your president." Frost could now cross Johnson off his list – but he had to add Kennedy, and to embark on what was a familiarly frantic round of travel, criss-crossing America in order to interview candidate after candidate.

Some of the nine completed interviews which constitute *The Next President* are forgettable – largely because the candidatures themselves failed, and the names of the candidates have as a result receded into history. And conversely, several of Frost's interviews – Robert Kennedy for the Democrats, the former Alabama Democrat and now independent candidate George Wallace, and Ronald Reagan and Richard Nixon for the Republicans – remain absorbing as a result of how subsequent events unfolded. It may be unwise to view history through a prism of hindsight – but it can be irresistible too, and certainly these four interviews, conducted over several days in the latter half of March 1968, make for viewing by turns fascinating and chilling.

Take Frost's interview with Reagan, the genial and conservative former Democrat-turned-Republican and film actor-turned-governor of California, conducted at Sacramento on March 21st. Frost remarked drily that, "At that stage Reagan was a complete outsider, and the conventional wisdom was that he had no chance of ever becoming president."[213] Reagan said little that seemed intrinsically gripping: he was folksy in his image and delivery in a way that would presently become all too familiar, describing how he liked to shoot "varmints" from time to time on his ranch. He pitched his message squarely at those segments of American society alarmed by the ethnic tension, city riots and campus demonstrations of this period, smoothly conflating campus demonstrations with muggings and street crime; and he conjured up a vision of his ideal America guided by paternalistic notions of discipline, moral rigour and good example:

I believe that the disturbances on the campus are not the result of too much discipline. I think they are like the small child stomping his feet and what he really wants is a parent to take him in hand and shake him and let him know what the guidelines are, and I think that our younger generation today would like to have someone, namely the older generation, set some guidelines and some rules and say, "Here, this is the framework. This is the pattern. You stay within the pattern."[214]

The interview with Reagan, however, provides – in hindsight – a broader cultural and economic manifesto, and one that in the following years would come into its own and find expression in the Reagan White House of 1981–89. It offers a ghostly projection into a future when individualism and free-market economics were unquestionably in the ascendancy, and figure-headed by Reagan himself:

DF: This is a tremendously big question. What would you say at root that people are on earth for?

RR: Well, of course, the biologist would say that like all breeds of animals, the basic instinct to reproduce our kind, but I believe it's inherent in the concept that created this country – and it's in the Judeo-Christian religion – that man is for individual fulfilment; our religion is based on the idea not of any mass movement, but of individual salvation. Each man must find his own salvation; I would think that our national purpose in this country – and we've lost sight of it too much in the last three decades – is to free, to the limit possible within law and order, every man to be what God intended him to be.

The following day, Frost and his team flew back east for a date in New York with Nixon, the former vice president under Eisenhower who had scored an overwhelming victory in New Hampshire, and who was seen now as the Republican frontrunner. Once more, future events cast with hindsight a shadow over proceedings, and this shadow is evident at the very beginning of the interview. Frost's initial queries were to do with the nature and character of the country: questions formed with the intention of enabling the candidate to establish a personal and electorally appealing vision of America. Nixon's reply was to note a vein of "what I would call a rather hopeless idealism" running through American life, an idealism that, as would soon become all too apparent, Nixon himself did not share.

But the former vice president managed the interview fairly well. The personal darkness and sense of incipient paranoia that characterised both the early Nixon and the Nixon to come were held largely in check in the course of his dealings with Frost that day in New York. He pitched his thoughts on Communism neatly at his prospective voters, and – presumably in the awareness that he could count on few black votes – indulged some musings on the British colonial project ("I'm not one of those who believes that colonialism was an unmitigated evil"). He even managed a touch of irony:

DF: Is there any episode you'd like to rewrite?

RN: Oh, I suppose the answer which comes first to mind is the campaign of 1960. Should I or should I not have debated with John Kennedy on television? And if I did debate him, then perhaps I should have had, as some people have said, a better makeup man and the rest ...

There is a distinct sense, however, of the other Nixon – what might be called the real Nixon – just about held in check. For even in the course of a relatively light and sunny interview – for there was nothing unduly challenging about it – he still managed to glance at what he clearly perceived to be media persecution, past and present: as Frost remarked, "You still did not feel that [Nixon] had conquered his obsession – later called paranoia – about his opponents and the press. You felt that it remained there just below the surface ..."[215]

The following day, Frost and his team were established in the gubernatorial mansion at Montgomery, ready to interview Wallace, whose policies against desegregation had helped to stoke up tension across the American South. The interview was a tense affair, Frost attempting to focus on issues of race and Wallace, with increasing irritation, declaring he would not get into the specifics of the various pronouncements on race that he had made over the years, before going on to elaborate a little more his theories on the separation of the races. Would Wallace, wondered Frost, permit his daughter to marry a Negro? "I don't believe in intermarriages of Negro and white – I'm candid and honest about it. I don't think it's good for either race. I think the races ought to remain intact. I think God made one race, he made another race, and that it ought to that way."

Frost's technique in this revealing interview was that of the gadfly, one small, biting question following another and another. "You made the point it's not good for either race. Why is it? [...] The reasons aren't obvious." Wallace became angrier and angrier and more and more frustrated and churlish: "I'm not going to give you any [reasons]. I don't have to give reasons for it. […] I'm not going to discuss it any further." Frost led his guest deeper into the thickets of his policies, moving from race to the dangers of "the Communist menace" that Wallace detected in America. Wallace would carry five Southern states in the election, but would fail to break out of his core electoral territory.[216]

The most absorbing of this series of interviews was that conducted with Robert Kennedy, in Portland, Oregon, on March 25th. Kennedy's campaign remained in its infancy, the bulk of the primary season still to come. He was lagging behind his rivals in organisation and fundraising, and he had yet to fully establish what would become a distinctive campaign bringing him on the stump to violence-scarred street corners in some of the most disturbed neighbourhoods in America. But he already possessed his own measure of Kennedy charisma, and his message of social justice, increased spending, continued ethnic desegregation and hope was pitched at America's disaffected youth and disadvantaged minorities in a way that set him apart.

Frost's interview allowed Kennedy to expand on this theme of hope and of communality. Kennedy spoke the language of patriotism, but a version of patriotism viewed through a prism of ethics, and with an eye always on the shadow of Vietnam:

DF: Do you believe in the principle, 'My country, right or wrong'?

RK: No, I think one has this affection or feeling for his country, but I think of what Camus said during the war of Algeria, that my criticism comes because I want to love my country in justice, and I think that's what we want. We want to have this affection and feeling for our country in justice.

In what cannot but be read as a glance into the near future, Frost questioned Kennedy on his perceived recklessness, his willingness to go into tough neighbourhoods, to speak frankly, to challenge his listeners in ways that were frequently less than agreeable.

DF: You're often pictured in the open air. Some people write about you as if you're reckless and—

RK: Ruthless?

DF: No, well – ruthless too. We'll come to ruthless, but I was only saying reckless! You just heard ruthless.

RK: Oh, that's what I hear so much.

DF: No, reckless in the sense of all the physical things you do. [...] Are you sometimes reckless?

RK: No, I don't think I'm reckless.

DF: But you like physical risk, don't you?

RK: Well, I enjoy doing some of those kinds of things. Edith Hamilton wrote that men are not made for safe havens. That's part of a human being's life, or a man's life.[217]

Most strikingly, the interview enabled Kennedy to set out his political stall with considerable eloquence, and – replying to the same question that Frost had put to Reagan – in a way that provides a sharp contrast with the latter's message of individualism.

DF: What would you say, at root, that people are on earth for?

RK: I think you'd probably break it down to people who have some advantages and those who are just trying to survive and have their families survive. If you have enough to eat, for instance, I think basically it's to make a contribution to some of us who are less well off. "I complained because I had no shoes until I met a man who had no feet." You can always find someone who has a more difficult time than you do, who suffered more, and has faced some more difficult time one way or another. If you've made some contribution to someone else, to improve their life and make their life a little bit more liveable, a little bit more happy, I think that's what you should be doing.[218]

Kennedy's assassination, at the hands of the Palestinian-Jordanian immigrant Sirhan Sirhan at the Ambassador Hotel at Los Angeles on June 5th, ended violently the alternative meliorist future on which he was setting out, but there is no doubting the impact of the interview and of Kennedy's manifest charisma on Frost himself. Twenty-one years later, Frost was briefly an anchor on *Inside Edition*, a syndicated news programme in the United States. He had signed to the show much against the better judgement of Lady Carina Frost, by then his wife of six years, and it soon became apparent that Carina and other hesitant confidantes had judged wisely. Frost's first assignment was an interview with Sirhan, at that time incarcerated in the high-security prison at Soledad, California. The assignation was deeply uncomfortable for Frost, who was friends with Robert Kennedy's widow, Ethel, and he remembered it "as the most demanding emotionally" he had ever experienced. "When I interviewed Kennedy, it was the first time I was really aware of somebody who encapsulated the whole thing about the mysterious substance called charisma. [...] I found that [interview] definitely the most demanding because I was thinking about and remembering Robert Kennedy – there were memories of the man I admired and then here was the man who had ended his life."[219]

The interview – which angered the Kennedy family – was Sirhan's first. He expressed his regret for the murder, sketched the context against which he found himself at the Ambassador Hotel that evening, claimed that he had never set out to assassinate Kennedy, and had been drunk, agitated and crazed, and infuriated at the sight of a poster advertising a Jewish festival taking place in Los Angeles at that time. Frost's technique at this time is carefully paced, poised. He interjects and directs only occasionally – though at one point he sharply dismisses Sirhan's comparison of Kennedy with Hitler – and in general leaves the space free for Sirhan himself to explain the incoherence and coincidences that fill his narrative. It is a glimpse of a technique that Frost was then honing: to enable his subject to speak, and to provide them, if they would, with the rope to hang themselves, if they were minded to do so. Certainly,

Sirhan was a deeply unconvincing interviewee, and remained seemingly unaware of the enormity of his crime. At the time of writing, he remains in incarceration in California.

Thirty-five years later, when the Frost family was called upon to design David Frost's memorial service at Westminster Abbey, it was his reflections on Robert Kennedy that came to mind, and that were printed in the Order of Service. Frost remembered Kennedy's words – and in so do doing, he had set out much of his own philosophy too:

> My father often used to talk about that old proverb, "Even a stopped clock is right twice a day." In other words, everybody you meet has something to teach you – if you take the trouble to find it. The most unlikely person can enlighten your life. That's tremendously important for the self-worth of the people you meet, as well as your own. [...] There are all sorts of ways in which we're not equal, but we are all equal in what we can strive for. When I interviewed Senator Robert Kennedy back in 1968 – the last interview he gave before his assassination [...] Kennedy spoke a lot about making a contribution. He used to say, "For if we do not do this, then who will do this?" It's so simple – if you have a talent, you have your duty to use it to the full. Making a contribution and making a difference – they should be linked – is not only something that famous people can do, or that dead politicians can be quoted on. It is something that everyone can do in their own lives.[220]

Several years later, this theme of duty and service was invoked again, this time in an interview Frost secured in 1971 with Rose Kennedy, the mother of John F Kennedy and Robert Kennedy, and the family's elusive and enigmatic matriarch. The interview was conducted at the Kennedy compound at Hyannis, shortly after Rose Kennedy's eightieth birthday: and Frost took her through the chaptered tragedies of Kennedy family history, including the deaths of four of her children, her husband's womanising and unsavoury business practices and other connections. What had sustained Rose Kennedy through such a family history? After a long silence, she gestured at the painting on her wall: she was sustained by the intercession of the Virgin Mary, who had not had the easiest of times either, and who helped Rose maintain her focus on duty, and on service. Frost, showing early signs of that technique he would later come to master, was wise enough to allow the interview to end on a long and deeply expressive period of silence.

As for *The Next President*, the programme so painstakingly put together was aired in the last week of May across America. Following the death of Kennedy, television in New York aired the full, unedited reel of the interview. It was then picked up and rebroadcast elsewhere. And, as was the case with the first Kennedy assassination, so Frost's response to the second murder further raised his profile in America. This meant in turn that, when Westinghouse lost its chief talk show anchor Merv Griffin to CBS that same year, David Frost would be in pole position in the race to succeed him.

*

LWT went on air for the first time during the dog days of a London summer, on Friday August 2nd, 1968. There had been sufficient time, as the new channel established itself and began the process of planning for the future, for the BBC to firm up its weekend response; plenty of time too for the critics to sharpen their knives, and pick apart LWT's high aspirations. The management and programme-makers, including Frost, were perfectly aware of the challenges to come, but nobody could prepare adequately for the firestorm of criticism faced by the channel in its infancy.

Frost on Friday – billed as the toughest-minded of David Frost's three weekend shows, and the one most dedicated to current affairs – went on air for the first time that night. It began with an energetic political scrap between left and right; the following day, the show business-oriented chat show *Frost on Saturday* dedicated the whole of its slot to an interview with Bob Hope; while the variety-show-format *Frost on Sunday*, breaking a union strike to get on air, relied on such trusted favourites as Ronnies Barker and Corbett to produce the necessary sketches. It was a reasonable beginning, though relatively predictable and by no means thoroughly sparkling – and this low-key debut was complicated further by a hardening of the strike, causing the second and third weekends of broadcasting to come entirely to a halt. An ill-starred launch, then, for LWT, though the strike did eventually end and a sense of equilibrium was restored. In the course of the next few weeks Frost managed to engage a number of key guests – these included John Lennon and Yoko Ono, the Beatles and Moshe Dayan, the Israeli defence minister, granting his first interview since the 1967 war a little over a year previously.

The interview with Dayan in particular showed the sweep and scale of Frost's interests, his ability to master any number of briefs, and his ambition to make his programmes required viewing. Frost flew to Tel Aviv in early August, and the session with Dayan, as well as covering the expected intricacies of the recent war in detail, contained an unexpected level of emotional intelligence that was typical of Frost. He led Dayan onto the terrain of war as a moral or immoral act, on its impact on the human soul, on its paradoxical quality as a vessel containing both virtue and depravity: territory that might not have been the natural habitat of a military leader and politician, but that Dayan turned out to be more than happy to explore with his host:

It is the most exciting and dramatic thing in life, is war. It is probably the most hateful and inhuman thing, but war is the most exciting drama that can exist. [...] I think that war as such is probably the most inhuman act that people have invented ... but within the framework of war you find individuals doing the most heroic acts and the most human acts, like trying to save the other fellow, though you know you are risking your own life, and probably you are losing your whole life.

And later in the interview, Frost touched on the frightful intractability of the Arab-Israeli conflict: "In a sense, do you feel that the Arabs have a case for feeling the way they do?" Dayan replied most straightforwardly: "If I were an Arab, I probably would have thought the same way."[221]

Back in London, in early September, "quite suddenly, all hell broke loose".[222] Lew Grade, the chairman of ATV – the London weekend channel dislodged by LWT – chaired a meeting of the ITV network, at which it was decided that the weekend schedules must be thoroughly shaken up. Frost's weekend programmes were shifted to less prominent slots; some of the ITV companies declined to continue broadcasting them at all. These were by any judgement commercially odd decisions. LWT had got off to a rocky beginning, to be sure, but most of its problems had not even been of the channel's own making, and the initial ratings – insofar as they even existed after a couple of weeks of broadcasting – were holding up well enough. It seems evident that the reasoning was grounded in pique at the fact that LWT existed at all, and that its very existence implied criticism of the ITV old guard that it arrived to supplant. This pique was given added fire by a very large degree of personal animus – and by Grade's loathing for Frost in particular. At that September meeting, he was quoted as telling the assembled executives that, "I got where I am by knowing what I hate, and I know I hate David Frost."[223] Grade later denied he had said any such thing, but the damage had been done. Such quotations do not die easily, and sometimes they do not die at all.

This particular rumble cooled in the end, and LWT was able to carry on in much the same way. But only after a fashion: the company continued to have a strained relationship with the powerbrokers on the broader ITV network – and increasingly this dysfunctional relationship came to infect the internal workings of LWT itself in a manner which would take some months to become manifest. For Frost, there was a focused season of programming to keep him occupied – and the channel's output in general, and his work in particular, was diverse and often impressive: television which proved its worth, both in terms of entertainment and social value. It is only fair to add that he demonstrated at this time another facet of his personality. Driving drunkenly home from a dinner party in the company of his friend David Niven (the son of the Oscar-winning actor, and himself a significant figure in the world of film production), he ran his Bentley through the expensive windows of Fenwick's store on London's Bond Street – and in those pre-CCT days, left the scene scot-free.

In early January 1969, as his trio of programmes were coming to the end of their present run, a significant opportunity presented itself for Frost to tap directly into a national issue. His joust with Enoch Powell came in the aftermath of months of controversy involving the maverick Conservative politician, who had moved in the course of the 1960s steadily towards a hard-line stance on immigration into Britain. By 1965, he was advocating the forced repatriation of "unassimilable" immigrants; and by 1967, he was speaking against the policy of permitting the dependent relations of Commonwealth immigrants to settle in Britain. Then, in April 1968, he gave his infamous "Rivers of Blood' speech at Birmingham, which electrified the race debate in Britain: "As I look ahead, I am filled with foreboding. Like the Roman, I seem to see 'the River Tiber foaming with much blood'."

The speech led to his expulsion from the Shadow Cabinet – but it won him a degree of popular support, and after a good deal of negotiations, Powell agreed to appear on Frost's show. "I don't see it as a contest," Frost told his guest after the – in this case decidedly inappropriate – jaunty opening theme music died away, "but there are one or two areas of your mind I find a slight enigma." As introductions went, this was something of a polite challenge, and Frost went on to question the source of Powell's most eye-catching claim: that a white woman had had excrement pushed through her letterbox by black immigrants. Was this story – widely circulated, and essentially seeking to capture in symbolic form why immigration was undesirable – genuine?

EP: I haven't the slightest doubt it was, but may I—

DF: But have you – did you check it at all?

EP: I haven't the slightest doubt, and I verified the source from which I had that information. Now—

DF: Did you verify the story?

EP: I verified the source, and I haven't the slightest doubt that it is—

DF: But what do you mean, you verified the source?

EP: —that it is true as it is typical.

DF: But it's not typical. I mean, I'm not saying it hasn't happened—

EP: Ah, well now—

DF: I'm not saying – you say it's typical.

EP: Yes, I do.

DF: You see, you keep using words like 'typical', as though there's millions of piles of excrement dropping through letter-boxes up and down our green and pleasant land. I said, 'Did you check the story?' and you said you verified the source.

EP: Yes, indeed. And—

DF: But if I say, "Did you check the story?" the answer to that question is, "No. Not, I verified the source." Because …

The exchange is excruciating, even though Powell gave no hint of such feelings himself. By the time Frost had concluded this line of questioning, it was evident enough that this woman was apocryphal, and his flourishing of her spectral figure typical enough of Powell's tendency to spin and manipulate figures and statistics. These were indeed habits typical enough of politicians in general, but Powell's political interests ensured that all too many of these remarks were incendiary.

This edition of *Frost on Friday* was permitted to long overrun its allocated slot. Frost and Powell ranged widely over various race-related issues, and Frost's lines of questioning remained striking in their focus and intensity. He implied that Powell's aims were to exploit the fear and ignorance engendered by the relatively new phenomenon of mass immigration into the country, when patient and careful education might provide the answers, and suggested that Powell's presentation of a range of figures had the same inten-tion of stoking fears. The long shadowy twilight of Powell's future political career demonstrates that he made no breakthrough, then or later, as a result of his incendiary language.

There is no doubt that this edition of *Frost on Friday* was a valuable and timely programme, and acted as an exemplar of LWT's vision of a blend of commercial and public-service broadcasting. Frost signalled this achievement, and celebrated the end of his first broadcasting season on LWT, in the fashion of a showman: he organised another dramatic networking event in the form of a party and indoor fun fair at Alexandra Palace in north London, the so-called "People's Palace" built by the Victorians as an education-cum-entertainment centre, and later the first home of the BBC. The history and high-minded origins of "Ally Pally" were part of its symbolic attraction at this time for Frost: his party – expensive, large and spirited as it was – was also designed as a riposte to Lew Grade and those of his ilk who had attempted his programming hijack the previous September. "I reckoned," Frost remarked, "that nobody would spend $5000 celebrating a flop, and that the subliminal message would get through."[224]

And doubtless it did. There were dodgems, and fish and chips, and hula hoops, and the Establishment gathered in force: bishops, newspaper editors, commentators and peers of the realm – though "no-one", as the *Glasgow Herald* put it cattily, "spotted Enoch Powell among the guests". But Frost was not to know, as the dodgems got going that day at Ally Pally, that the most tempestuous days for LWT were yet to come.

*

I began to get concerned about the way the LWT contract might look to Westinghouse and the Westinghouse contract to LWT. Although I was confident I could do five weekly shows in New York and three in London, I did realise that this was somewhat unorthodox.

That same month, as Enoch Powell was settling himself tidily in his chair in the *Frost on Friday* studio, Westinghouse was ready to bring Frost on board as one its new stars, with a talk show all of his own. There was indeed one little matter for Frost to overcome, for he remained contracted to the infant LWT for no fewer than three shows per week, as well as board and other responsibilities. In many minds, this would surely have counted as a full-time job – but Frost had other ideas. After a lightning visit to Florida, to firm up the details of the American side of things, it was decided that Frost would record his five weekly shows in New York over three days, leaving the second half of the week for his London activities – and he flew back to Britain to settle his business there. Here he was on home ground, and so, surely, his British colleagues would be thoroughly accommodating.

In fact, they were not. It took much in the way of horse-trading before matters were settled and timetables drawn up, and it was early February 1969 before the American announcements could be made – that David Frost had been signed to replace Merv Griffin, and that *The David Frost Show* would soon air five nights a week. Delays and fussing notwithstanding, this was an extraordinary coup for Frost – the greatest of his career to date. His starting salary of $350,000 was impressive, and the newspapers duly had a field day. And his potential exposure on the lucrative American market, week after week for months on end, was greater than anything he had experienced before.

His *potential* exposure. Westinghouse's Group W was not one of the great American networks with which Frost was now familiar. It built its business on syndication, on the sale and distribution of individual programmes to the small local television stations that proliferated in the United States, and that set it apart from the British television market; 140 such stations had bought the Merv Griffin show, but none of these was under any contractual obligation to take this new, Brit-fronted programme. Westinghouse was, in other words, taking a substantial punt on Frost. His new talk show needed to be distributed across America, needed to pull in steady revenues, needed to sustain itself and to sell advertising. These were challenges, to be sure, but they were challenges that many of Frost's rivals and contemporaries would have killed to face. "He was so utterly focused and bursting with energy: a firing boy," remembers Joanna Lumley, "and we were all watching, agog."[225]

A typically frenetic period now kicked off, and always with a counterpoint of the looming first season of *The David Frost Show*. Frost remained congenitally unable to switch off or relax. Although he understood perfectly well the long, relentless phase of work and travel now stretching ahead of him, he opted to begin his summer with a long-haul flight to Kenya with Jenny Logan, stopping off for good measure in Nigeria on the way home to visit his sister Jean and her husband Andrew. Then he went to Austria with Logan for a long weekend, travelling by private plane. Frost understood – and so did Logan – that their relationship would most likely not endure the thundering schedule that Frost had now set himself: this was their last flourish – and, although she appeared on the scene in New York, they would soon go their separate ways. "I think at that point he was beginning to outgrow Britain. It was time to move on, and I understood that. Sometimes this is what you have to do for the people you love."[226]

In April 1969, Frost turned thirty years of age, and to celebrate the event, Logan, Luisa Carmo, Joan Pugh and Bob Lambert threw a surprise party at the house on Egerton Crescent, with Ronnie Corbett charged with keeping Frost out of the way until preparations were complete. And later in the month, David Frost was established in New York, initially at offices at the Commodore Hotel. He began to gather his own team, at the heart of which were Peter Baker, who had worked on *The Frost Report*, and his long-time collaborator Neil Shand, with Joan Pugh making monthly shuttle visits from London. "I would spend my time in New York travelling everywhere with him," Pugh recalls, "because travel time doubled as letter-writing time. We could get enormous amounts of work done on the move. And then, after a session of intense work, he would throw me the keys of his car, and tell me to go off sightseeing."[227] And Shand recalls the energy of those first days in New York, and the atmosphere established from the outset. Frost "would never walk if he could take a taxi, he would never take a taxi if he could take a limo, he would never take a limo if he could take a chopper".[228]

The early summer would now be spent largely in New York and the Hamptons. Frost did, however, return to Britain for various engagements. One of these involved a visit to Wales to record an interview at Aberystwyth with Prince Charles on the eve of his investiture at Caernarfon Castle as Prince of Wales. Reflecting on his role-to-be with Frost, the prince reflected, "I'm sort of stuck." Thirty-six years later, he recalls "feeling somewhat alarmed at the prospect of being grilled by the fearsomely satirical presenter of *That Was the Week That Was*".[229] Frost was also in London for a televised guided tour of Downing Street in the company of the Prime Minister Harold Wilson and his wife Mary (Pugh remembers waiting with Frost in the private Prime Ministerial apartment at the top of Downing Street; and laughing like schoolchildren); and to tape segments for the *David Frost Show* featuring John Lennon and Yoko Ono, the Rolling Stones and other British talent. The pace was frantic, but Frost's intention was to stockpile material against the even more punishing schedule still to come.

Then, in mid-June, the production team moved into the programme's home at the Little Theatre in midtown Manhattan, close by Times Square. The theatre – later renamed the Helen Hayes Theater – was the smallest of the Broadway venues: it seated fewer than six hundred people; and had seen much action in the course of the 1960s as a radio and then a television venue. It had its disadvantages: the stage was higher than the stalls, which was a design that Frost found disagreeable; and the stage was also rather too large to lend itself to the intimate chat format that Frost and his colleagues had in mind. Canny design took care of these issues: a soon-to-be-familiar set was born, with two chairs fenced in by a low wall that embraced the interview area and provided additional seating as needed, while excluding the acreage of the stage on the far side.

By the time the first pilot was scheduled, in the second half of June 1969, the show had been bought by thirty-seven stations. This was a long way short of Griffin's final total of 140, but respect-able in itself, and Westinghouse was reasonably pleased with these commercial beginnings. Frost and his team, however, were under no illusions: the success or otherwise of *The David Frost Show* depended squarely on the programmes put together, day after day, and on the diet presented to the large American audiences avail-able. The first show was scheduled for broadcast in early July 1969. This meant that the programme had to be recorded a week before, to allow for the tape – in those pre-digital days – to be flown to Group W's offices at Pittsburgh for duplication and distribution to local stations across America. This process, desperately cumber-some today, was of course then simply standard practice, and could take a week or more from beginning to end. And as the team was fully aware, it also meant that *The David Frost Show* could never be synched to the latest news: instead, the programme had the option of either making the news, or ignoring it altogether. In its three years of existence, the show did both.

The pilot passed in rowdy fashion. It set up a meeting between representatives of the Women's Liberation Movement (WLM) and the anthropologist Lionel Tiger, whose book dealt with the issue of male bonding. The two sides clashed rather than engaged in dialogue, but the programme-makers had tested their systems, and found them good to go. And in the meantime, Frost's work in the early summer meant that a clutch of good films were ready to be broadcast in the first edition of the show. Frost taped opening and closing segments before the audience at the Little Theatre. Meanwhile, the films of the Prince of Wales at Aberystwyth – absorbing to American audiences who were hungry for such royal stories, and impressed at Frost's ability to net them – and of the WLM and the Rolling Stones would keep the programme textured and fluid. The crucial element, however, was Frost's guest that evening in the theatre: the black Baptist preacher and Congressman Adam Clayton Powell.

Powell had a reputation for controversy. First elected in 1945, he had been closely involved in shepherding through Congress a number of John F Kennedy's anti-poverty and other social bills. In 1967, however, he had been expelled from the House for alleged misuse of funds, and by this stage, his lavish lifestyle and frequent and prolonged sojourns on the island of Bimini in the Bahamas was raising eyebrows. The Supreme Court had recently ordered his reappointment to the House, however, and he was continuing to pile up enormous majorities in his Harlem Congressional district. He remained a figure to be reckoned with in the black community, in other words, and having such a polarising, passionate figure on the first edition of the show demonstrated not only a sharp eye for potential drama on the part of Frost and his production team, but also a willingness to take a chance on the audience, by no means all of whom would find Powell a congenial character.

And there was yet another significant element to Powell's appearance on the show, though this would not become apparent until several minutes had ticked by. Powell enumerated the various political and moral scandals of the age, and set them against the scandals as seen by the mainstream media: principally black crime in its various manifestations, which to Powell was beside the point when set against the vast conspiracies which threatened American life and civilisation:

Law and order is: who killed Medgar Evers, the President of the NAACP [National Association for the Advancement of Colored People] in Mississippi? Who killed – and it will never come out in your lifetime – my beloved friend Jack Kennedy? The truth has not come out yet. Who killed Martin Luther King? Where did [his assassin James Earl] Ray get the money from? *Time* magazine asked that two weeks in a row. Who killed Bobby Kennedy? That's law and order. [...] I know some of the truth. That's why they might get me next. They don't know what the truth is. I have about ten people that know it and they have it in safe deposit boxes. [...] Jackie Kennedy's testimony. One half of her testimony was cut out of the Warren Commission's Report. [...] *Go along, baby. Go along, sweetheart. Daddy loves you.* The deputy sheriff of Dallas, sixteen points he made in his testimony. Cut out. The coroner that performed the autopsy on President Jack Kennedy's body at Bethesda United States Navy Medical Center went home that night and burned up his notes in the fireplace [...] I have facts, I have facts ...[230]

Such a tempestuous interview must stand or fall on the conduct of the person leading it, and in this case, where it might have toppled into pure pantomime, Frost showed his mettle. By turns stepping back and coming forward, the host gave his guest all the space in the world to expand on his views, understanding, reasonably enough, that conspiracy theories, and especially conspiracy theories evoking the names of the Kennedys and Martin Luther King, commanded attention and audiences. But Frost did not let Powell off the hook on the fraught issue of his personal finances:

ACP: My salary is five hundred and seventy-five dollars a month, with no fringe benefits.

DF: No fringe benefits?

ACP: Nope.

DF: None at all?

ACP: I will not allow them. They want to give me a car, they want to give me a house, they want to do this, they want to do that. Nope.

DF: Just a little old island.

The audience at the Little Theatre that night – and Frost's production team – were electrified by the interview, and not merely because it had been a considerable tussle between the two men, but because of its thirty-nine-minute length. The long-form interview was certainly not popular in television circles: executives fought shy of a form that, it was generally feared, might possibly demand more from the audience than it was prepared to give. In this case, Frost demonstrated the possibilities inherent in an interview that went beyond the usual hasty eight or nine minutes. The audience would go along, given half a chance, and the advertisers would therefore go along too, and everyone would be happy. The first reviews were excellent: "Amid the torrents of trivia that flow from television's nightly talk shows, the new David Frost dialogues are like rare beefsteak in a marshmallow sundae world" – and it was as good a beginning as could be hoped for.[231] It proved that this newcomer and his team could indeed bring something new, in the form of space for expression, together with a measure of confrontation and excitement, to what was too often a staid chat-show format.

For Neil Shand, this was the beginning of a long, electric period during which he and Frost lived in each other's pockets. They now took up residence at the Plaza, the luxury hotel on Fifth Avenue at Central Park South. Amazingly, this became their New York home, and the operations base for Paradine for the duration of *The David Frost Show*. As Shand recalls, this base was very much of a piece with Frost's overall approach to life and lifestyle: "Only David would have done it. If you were close to David, you really did live very well: dining twice or three times a week at the Oak Room [restaurant] in the Plaza; our wine of choice was Château Latour as standard: wine that now costs thousands of pounds; and we took it totally in our stride."[232] And Shand had the opportunity to note aspects of Frost that others too would detect later, in particular his need for privacy, for an inviolable space at the centre of himself. "The surprise was that he was actually not a master of small talk, unless one was talking deals. In private, he didn't ask too many questions, I think because he didn't want to create a space in which questions might come back at him."

For the most part, then, it was shop talk and work, and there was a good deal of both. Here too Shand noted Frost's idiosyncrasies, most notably in the matter of his shocking timekeeping, even when it came to recording his show. "He was *never* on time for recording. We used to take bets on how late he would be: sometimes a half-hour late; usually twenty minutes, which was awful,

h Prince Charles at Aberystwyth, on the eve of his investiture as Prince of Wales, 1969. Getty Images

king the tour of Downing Street with Harold Wilson, 1969.

'Right on, David: you're doing your thing': in New York with Sammy Davis Jr on *The David Frost Show*, 1970.

In the field for Oxfam: Bihar, India, 1967.

The David Frost Show with Richard Burton, 1972. The frequent presence of Burton, Elizabeth Taylor and a constellation of other A-listers exemplify the show's pulling power.

With the Two Ronnies.

With Nixon and Jimmy Goldsmith inside the house at Monarch Bay, CA, in which the Frost-Nixon interviews were filmed, 1977.

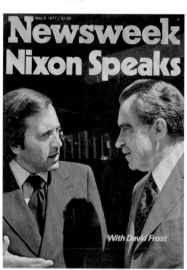

The front cover: David Frost and Richard Nixon pose outside the house at Monarch Bay, 1977.

Seventies-style: Frost and Nixon inside the Monarch Bay house, 1977. Getty Images

otball and travel: two Frost favourites, c.1977.

e fourth man: David Frost on tour with The Bee Gees, 1979.

Wedding bells: David Frost and Lady Carina Fitzalan Howard at Chelsea Registry Office, 1983.

Honeymoon selfie: David and Carina Frost at the Cipriani, Venice, 1983.

oud parents: birth of Miles Frost, 1984, outside the Lindo Wing at St Mary's Hospital in London.

Richard Bernstein's wedding present to David and Carina Frost, 1984.

Meeting the Queen at the Royal Variety Performance, London Palladium, 1989.

Fundraising for Wellbeing of Women: David Frost with the Princess of Wales at the Melrose Hotel, New York, 1988.

because the tapes had to be rushed to Pittsburgh afterwards. One evening, we had Robert Mitchum on the show; and there we all were – Mitchum, and crew, and audience all waiting for David. And finally, Mitchum strode out onto the stage, and said, 'Well, guys, *I'm* here.'" Shand also noted Frost's apparent physical transformation in the moment before he stepped onto the stage: "Suddenly, he would look completely different from the man I'd seen in his office five minutes previously. He was a perfect television performer. Though he could be quite naughty with guests, and especially comedians. They would tell a gag; the audience would laugh – but David would say, 'Tell us another one.' And there would be a pause, and the comedian would sometimes blink, but of course they'd have to come up with another one, right there and then."[233] And there were other episodes too that were more thoroughly alarming, such as the one in 1972 in which the helicopter in which Shand and Frost were flying from Long Island to Manhattan cut out above Seventh Avenue and 58th Street and, driven now only by its own velocity, ditched into Central Park, falling like a stone for the final twenty feet. Frost and Shand came out of the crash unscathed, hailed a taxi to take them to the Little Theatre, did that evening's show, and took another helicopter back out to Long Island that same evening.

As the first season of *The David Frost Show* rolled on – there would be three in all, the programme ending in 1972 – so ratings rose and reviews for the most part were positive. Frost and his producers took a chance with a ninety-minute format. The first guest to be interrogated for a full programme was Peter Ustinov, in December 1969, and once more the gamble proved its worth and was adopted. Media interest in general rose too. The US television critic and observer Ray Richmond remarks that, "Americans are fairly fascinated by a British accent. People here in general automatically bestow a certain intellectual heft on someone who's a Brit. They assume they have a greater intelligence than the average American, and certainly Frost benefitted from that, being really the first Brit to come over and take to the airwaves. And in his case it was true: his competition by and large wasn't in the same league intellectually. Frost seemed cut from a different cloth."[234] Piers Morgan – who years later would sample an American career of his own – remarks that Frost "was a real trail-blazer in America. He had an easy British charm which was a great gift: first, in persuading people to do his show; and then extracting from them all this remarkable information. He invested in incredibly thorough research, mixed it with ready charm and an ability to guide his interviewee into a place where they felt safe, so that they would say anything."[235]

In a long, favourable profile in *Look* magazine in March 1970, Frost was described as "The Inter-Continental Man", an "Englishman dazzling them on American TV" – and was photographed in London at the wheel of his car ("a blue Bentley Continental convertible, with phone and white leather seats, cost $27,600") driving past the Houses of Parliament with one hand on an ultra-modern car telephone.

The New York Times was one exception to this flow of praise. In a long and very often snippy survey of Frost's life and work ("He's no singer, no comedian, no sex symbol: What Makes David Frost Talk?") from a November 1969 edition, the newspaper grumbled that Frost could not sing "at all", did not have a pleasant voice, could do not do comedy "and does not remotely approach being a sex symbol". Even his eyes were the wrong colour, the article went on, warming to its theme. He was "sallow and slope-shouldered and so nearly concave-chested that he seems likely to be giving off tuberculosis germs. His face is long – too long in the jaw – and his hair is thin. His limbs are thin, too, but at the same time he is ample at the midriff. And while it is reported that he was a fine soccer player as a teenager in the English midlands, it is hard to imagine him with the strength even to take a good kick at the ball." And he gushed too much: he gushed to his guests, gushed to his production staff, and gushed even to his sister Jean and her husband Andrew Pearson, a glimpse of whom we are given, dropping into the studio in the course of a New York visit.

Even this long, irked piece of writing, however, settled in the end on a Frost virtue:

Sometimes, the Frost knack for getting what a guest is really thinking is made clearest when the person has been shuffled from one talk show to another in a given week to publicize a new book or movie. For example, first-time actress Anjelica Huston, daughter of the director John Huston, appeared to be uncomfortable while doing the circuit with Assaf Dayan to plug their movie *A Walk with Love and Death*. But it was not long into the Frost interview before she unburdened herself of what she seemed to have been thinking during the rest of the week about her time on camera, something even her co-star did not know:

DF: Do you think of him [John Huston] as the director or your father?

AJ: Yes, obviously, it's my father, but also John Huston. I feel actually that I ought to say now that I don't really think I've done him justice in the film and that I'm very sorry about it. I mean, it's a personal thing, and I feel it's awful. There are so many young girls waiting for the opportunity – dying. They kill themselves to get into acting and to get into a movie, not only a movie just by any director, but a movie by John Huston. I was handed it on a plate, and I felt really bad about that today ... It really shocks me to look at myself two years ago and see that I went into it without any preparation that I should have had. I just wasn't prepared, and I shouldn't have been that selfish to take it, I don't think.

DF: I think you're magnificently honest about what you feel ...[236]

*

Frost's success in America is all the more remarkable when one remembers its context: the endless BOAC flights between London and New York, enjoyable but undoubtedly gruelling over a long period of time; and in particular the nature of much of his London life in this period. If Frost had imagined that his ostentatious party at Alexandra Palace would see off LWT's critics at this time, he would very rapidly come to see that he was quite mistaken.

Criticism of the new station, of its programming, its ratings and its advertising revenues mounted throughout 1969, and with Frost himself in town only for a day or two at a time, there was little he could do to ameliorate the situation. Sliding ratings began to cause unease across the ITV network, and in time, this unease slipped into something like corporate panic.

Popular programming began to be pulled from the weekend and slotted in during the week instead, and this, combined with a strongly populist response from the BBC, weakened LWT steadily and inexorably. As the months drifted by, a downward spiral in terms of audiences and morale gathered pace. LWT executives were also cruelly aware that a particular spotlight was on their station, not merely because ITV itself seemed to regard its own station with a jaundiced eye, but also because the British press was concentrated in London. Put simply, LWT was there to be scrutinised and criticised by a voluble Fleet Street in a way that its regional sister stations were not. By September 1969, LWT investors themselves panicked, and sacked its chairman, Michael Peacock. Half of the board of the station resigned in protest. Now LWT was left rudderless and in a state of utter disarray.

It was at this point that Frost invited a young Australian businessman to appear on his show. Rupert Murdoch, born in Melbourne and thirty-eight years old in the autumn of 1969, had spent the 1950s and 1960s slowly assembling a newspaper conglomeration in Australia and New Zealand, and in 1969 made his move on the British market by buying up the mass-market *News of the World*. In August, the newspaper began serialising the rewritten memoirs of Christine Keeler, the figure at the heart of the Profumo affair six years previously. The newspaper had, in 1964, already published Keeler's original memoirs, and there was a sense in some quarters that this now constituted overkill, that John Profumo had been dragged over the coals quite enough for one lifetime, and ought now to be left in peace to rebuild his life. Murdoch, relatively fresh to the British scene, appeared surprised at this response. After all, the circulation at the *News of the World* remained rudely healthy;

in fact, it climbed another 300,000 copies during the serialisation to well over six million a week, indicating that there remained an appetite for further spiced Profumo titbits.

The interview between Frost and Murdoch is in hindsight an intriguing match. The host, wholly aware of local mores, was at the top of his game; his guest was already a powerful media mogul, certainly, but one who was fresh on the British scene, and clearly was still not completely attuned to local rhythms. And so Frost had the upper hand from the off. Murdoch was on the defensive in a way that was rarely seen in later years. He was forced to defend and defend again his decision to publish Keeler's memoirs in the public interest, and then explain again and again how that public interest could be defined. For Frost chose his terrain well, focusing on this issue throughout what became a public mauling of Murdoch, who at the end of the interview walked out of the studio in a rage.

The interview came at a significant moment in British cultural life. Frost – ironically – approached the case from a distinctly patrician angle. It was not for Murdoch or anyone else to define, or to redefine, the public interest. For Murdoch, however, the publication of the Keeler memoirs signalled an intention to disregard such attitudes, and to redefine the terrain in relative terms. In such a context, the public interest would henceforth be what he, and his newspapers, and anyone else, decided it would be. Keeler's rehashed memoirs might have been slipshod and not worth the paper they were written on, but if there was a public appetite for them, then this was the material point. And it is disconcerting to read the transcripts of this interview years later, to see Frost take what can only be regarded as an Establishment line, and to more than articulate a patronising tone towards Murdoch, this Australian who remained essentially an unknown quantity. In that sense, this interview did not come close to achieving public service quality. As John O'Loan, who worked with both Frost and Murdoch over many years, puts it drily, it was "all part of Rupert's 'Big Welcome to Britain'".[237]

Murdoch's power and influence would only wax after this encounter. The following year, he bought the *Sun*, and rapidly turned it into both a profit-making machine and a political powerbroker of extraordinary potency and efficiency. In time too, he became a hate figure on the British Left, and never again did he permit himself to be used as a punch bag, by David Frost or anyone else. And Frost – again with the benefit of hindsight – might have done better to pull in his horns, for Murdoch's parting vow to defenestrate Frost by buying up the troubled LWT was soon – partly at least – put into action. By 1971, he had amassed more than one-third of the station's shares, had become its chair, and was increasingly guiding programming and advertising policy, though he never managed to ditch Frost himself.

It took the intervention of the ITC – the successor to the ITA – to prevent a full Murdoch takeover. Citing foreign and cross-media ownership rules, the regulator forced Murdoch to relinquish the chair, and John Freeman – Frost's old friend from the station's infancy – took over. Frost was still a major shareholder in the company, and was instrumental both in the Freeman move, and in lobbying the ITC to toe its own policy line. As for Murdoch, he was livid. He had, after all, essentially saved the company from bankruptcy and set it on a new footing, and here he was, being booted out (as he saw it) by a media establishment he had come to revile.

The clash between Frost and Murdoch has gone down in media history, but too much has been made of the notion of lasting animus between the two. These were both deeply practical men, with a good deal more in common – in terms both of backgrounds and temperament – than has sometimes been recognised. Certainly, Murdoch was more than happy to employ Frost in the years to come – in Australia in the 1970s, and years later in Britain itself.

*

Amid this television life, this life on screen, the flesh-and-blood Frost appears distant: his personality projected rather than identifiable or immediate in human terms; his show and his image dazzling; the private Frost diminishing into the shadows. But he did exist and persist. It was at this time, for example, that he began smoking cigars, a habit he adopted to control his weight ("my courtship with cigars was a dessert substitute") and which would in time become one of his trademarks.[238] His fondness for food meant that before long he was eating as much as he ever did, while continuing with his cigar habit. His personal assistants had to become accustomed ("not very ladylike") to smelling of cigars themselves.[239] "I like the chunkier, smaller cigars," he told his interviewer from *Cigar Aficionado* years later. "And I always take tubed cigars with me whenever I travel. They're easier to carry than a humidor and they keep the cigars well enough. [...] I always use a humidor at home. But I like the convenience. The trick is to ration the cigars so I light up the last one on the way to the airport for the flight home."[240]

And there are other glimpses. Richard Armitage's son Alex recalls suffering a serious accident in 1970, when he was twelve years old, and Frost, in the course of a flying visit to Britain, driving up "to sit by my bedside in hospital at Epping: very kind of him, and making me feel at the centre of his universe, and typical of the man."[241] Other traces can be found, ironically, sometimes in the very articles that seem to champion the public figure at the expense of the private man. In the *Look* article of March 1970, the widowed Mona Frost is photographed in a turquoise coat standing proudly beside her son as he gazes at a new waxwork model of himself, soon to go on display at Madame Tussauds in London. "Can you believe you gave birth to that?" Frost asks. "Mum's as outgoing and energetic as her son, and his most unabashed admirer."

Jenny Logan is mentioned, but so too is Bernadette Carey, a "deliciously beautiful black *Vogue* editor", who, the magazine adds, "carefully avoids talking about him, explaining that 'a documented relationship makes for a less flexible future'". Frost, in fact, had been seen out on the town with Carey since the summer of 1968, when they met at "at a very fashionable party in the Hamptons. He was very bright, very nice, very charming. We spent the evening talking and he took me to the train station. [...] I didn't look too bad and I had a fairly decent wardrobe, which David liked. He knew everyone.

We used to go for lots of nice dinners with people such as Jackie and Ari Onassis. David was very fond of Ari. He bought me a gold watch from Tiffany's store, and a gold bracelet with turquoise stones."[242]

*

Sir David Frost in my opinion was the best television interviewer I knew. He stands alone.

Barbara Walters[243]

As *The David Frost Show* continued its run, so its host burnished his various interviewing skills. Joanna Lumley recalls watching Frost throughout his career and observing his ability to hold a silence for that crucial handful of beats that can open up an interview, and an interviewee, or that, as in the case of Rose Kennedy, simply tells its own story. "He understood the importance of silence. Human nature abhors silence, and so people go on and fill it. They jump into that silence, regardless of how much media training they undergo, and keep on going and going, and he understood the power of that. They would volunteer information quite often, but he never made them do it. He never forced people into corners; they went there themselves."[244] This was an ability honed in these early, pressurised editions of *The David Frost Show*, when his guests – in an age when media training was rather less all-pervasive – were fully aware of the acres of airtime to be filled; and rather more anxious than their host, it sometimes seemed, to fill them with words. "You just shut up," as Frost put it bluntly, "and sit back and see what might happen."

Silence, and the ability to hold the line, had all manner of beneficial side effects:

Silence can be equally golden in a one-on-one interview. Again, the interviewer's role is predictive. You can be confronted with one of two kinds of silence. There is the fruitful silence, where you sense that if you allow the pause to continue, the guest could have something more to say, maybe something of a deeper nature.

The other silence is the embarrassing silence, where the guest has simply clean forgotten what on earth he or she was about to say. That pause has got to be filled as quickly as possible, because otherwise each second that passes will feel like an eternity. How do you know which silence is which? It's just instinct – you don't really know for sure, but you feel the nuance in the conversation that you should be responding to, and you go for it.[245]

But there were other strategies in play, and Frost tried his hand at these too. He was never beneath trying flattery to get his way, as in the case of J. Edgar Hoover, the long-serving (forty-four years and counting by 1969) and periodically controversial director of the FBI, whom Frost was desperate to interview. On May 5th, well before the show began to air, Frost had written to Hoover:

Dear Mr Hoover:
I am writing as a long time admirer of yours to ask if you would consider taking part in a special conversation for television.

Let me explain a little why I have the timerity [sic] to ask such a question. In July of this year I am beginning a series of programs for Westinghouse which will take over from the current Merv Griffin Show. However, the form of conversation program which I do is somewhat different in formula to Mr Griffin. In this country in the past year, I have done two special talk programs, one called *The Next President*, with all the Presidential candidates, and the other with Noël Coward, which I think demonstrates the sort of relaxed, intelligent conversation in which I am interested. [...] There are many subjects on which I would love to have the privilege of talking with you, and on which the American people – and television viewers throughout the world – would love to hear you, whether it is about your own personal philosophy in general, or indeed, your feelings and perceptions about the way in which, in an age of increasing permissiveness, you feel society is moving. Of course, the conversation would take place at your convenience, though in the most perfect of all worlds, I would love it for us to be possible to talk between now and the beginning of July, as that is when the series begins and I can think of no one more appropriate and worthwhile way to begin it. In the meantime, I would be more than happy to come to Washington to discuss what I have in mind with you, or with your associates. With best regards,

Yours sincerely,

David Frost

A couple of weeks passed, and then Hoover declined the invitation, firmly ("While I wish I could give you a more favourable response, the pressure of my official duties and the number of similar requests have made it necessary to decline all such proposals."). One can only conjecture as to whether the profoundly controlling Hoover gave even a moment's thought to Frost's invitation. It is highly likely that he did not, given that a very short consideration of Frost's profile would have demonstrated that anything might happen in the course of such a television slot, from the easiest form of soft questioning to a Savundra-esque pummelling, or even an attempt to poke fun at this all-powerful functionary. (And, given the rumours of Hoover's secret homosexuality that had been swirling around Washington since at least the 1940s, Frost perhaps made a wrong move with his mention of Noël Coward.)

Frost's letter, and Hoover's terse reply, touched off a flurry of internal FBI correspondence which, declassified years later, reveals the extent to which this Englishman had caught the attention of the Bureau and its director. Frost's initial letter was marked with an addendum, dated a week before Hoover's reply, stating that, "Mr Frost is not identifiable in Bufiles. We have enjoyed cordial relations with the Westinghouse Broadcasting Company." Further internal correspondence reveals that interest in Frost was sustained. In mid-July, the FBI noted that Frost was scheduled to discuss the topic of wire-tapping and had solicited an appearance by former Attorney-General Ramsay Clark: "As a matter of information, the program was monitored and the subject of wire-tapping was never discussed nor did Ramsay Clark appear." Later still in July, the FBI reported that producers had been in touch with the Bureau seeking "a knowledgeable individual concerning the Mafia" to appear on the show; and were advised that, "the FBI would not be able to be of assistance [...] in this matter".

By December 8th, the FBI was seeking discreet checks on Frost, "who makes practice of having controversial guests on his program, professes to be of English background, indicating he has appeared extensively on television in Great Britain. You are requested to conduct an extremely discreet check re: Frost and advise Bureau." Four days later, the check came back clean, though grumbling that their British quarry had a taste for guests such as "John Kenneth Galbraith, who was critical of the director and the Bureau". But, "A search of biographic reference and other appropriate material in the Bureau Library failed to reflect any additional information regarding Frost." The memos detailed Frost's frenetic work and travel schedule, and remarked that he had moved to America because he had "pretty well used up the English television audience" and that he was "an excellent businessman who, at age of 30, is probably a millionaire". By the early days of 1970, the Bureau was reporting glumly that, "Since regular monitoring of this program has proved to be entirely non-productive over a period of time, it is felt that this daily monitoring should cease."

In fact, the contents of this once-classified dossier reveal that FBI interest in Frost and his programme certainly did not end in that first week of 1970. Rather, they remained sharp and sustained, and couched in language notable for its flavour of tense paranoia: the presence of certain guests painstakingly noted, assumptions made, queries raised and answered. Other letters, addressed to Hoover himself by members of the public, complaining at "the continual hogging of the television screen by extreme left-wing elements, downright subversives, people even convicted of doing offensives, perverts and other unedifying types. [...] Many of these shows drip poison in giving the impression that Vice and corruption are normal and all that is decent is to be continually mocked and derided." In the process, the dossier helps to locate *The David Frost Show* within the complex cultural and political context of America at the beginning of the 1970s.

For, although the programme did not "drip poison", it did indeed feature regular discussion on surveillance and phone-tapping and organised crime, and such guests as Gore Vidal and Joan Baez who were likely to capture the attention of Hoover and who were prepared to voice their views on political corruption and on Vietnam and the anti-war movement, on the mass of campaigns and ideas that define the era. Although it was hardly the intention of FBI operatives, the content of their work holds a mirror up to the spirit of the age in America in a way that makes for truly absorbing reading, in much the way as *The David Frost Show* absorbed the attention of America at this time.

And perhaps Hoover was on the button in his suspicions as to what David Frost might have had in store for him. Late in 1970, the former Attorney General Ramsay Clark did finally appear on the show, and much of the programme consisted of a wide-ranging attack by Clark on the FBI director's grip on the Bureau and on power in Washington in general, on his hold over successive attorneys general and even presidents, on the dossiers Hoover was purported to maintain on the private lives of leading American politicians for the purposes of blackmail and in order to maintain his own position. "Clark stated," one memo notes in painted terms, "even though Mr HOOVER was legally subordinate to the Attorney General, in actuality Mr HOOVER has considerably more power and influence, and no Attorney General could ever remove him without the complete support of the President. He added even a President could hesitate to take on such a task due to the great public support Mr HOOVER enjoys. [...] Then Mr FROST asked what his principal criticisms were of Mr HOOVER. CLARK replied since 1965 the organisation had lacked any personnel who would offer criticism of its operation [...] The Bureau lacks self-criticism." It is impossible to know what Frost might have intended for Hoover's appearance on his programme: he left no notes, and confided to nobody any intended plans. But it seems unlikely that he would allow such a prominent figure to pass through the Little Theatre unscathed, and it is reasonable to suppose that he planned something of a television spectacular: a scalp, and his greatest one to date.

Not that *The David Frost Show* was produced by a nest of Communist vipers. Far from it. It was a talk show first and foremost, and it attracted the best. A regular roster of top stars – Richard Burton, Elizabeth Taylor, Groucho Marx, Truman Capote; the list was endless – demonstrated amply the show's pulling power. Neil Shand recalls a visit made with Frost to Reno to interview the young Muhammad Ali, during which he watched his friend's extraordinary facility with names and faces: "We arrived at the little local Reno TV station where we were due to record the interview, and David saw the lighting technician, and there was this delighted greeting: 'John', or 'Sam', or whatever his name was. He had met him once before, ages before, and remembered his name and everything about him – and, 'How are you? Super, super!' And of course the upshot was that he was lit brilliantly for the duration of the interview."[246] Drifts of letters addressed to Frost survive from this period, and they demonstrate that guests on the show understood its power. Spiro Agnew, the vice president in the Nixon White House, seemed to agree. He was a guest on two of Frost's shows, and appeared to harbour no Hoover-inflected fears for his political health. In a telegram of February 1971, Agnew wrote that, "David Frost has brought the art of conversation and interviewing to a high level in American television, and his popularity attests that the public has found his program to be informative, entertaining and refreshingly different. As one who appeared on two of his 90 minute programs this past year, I personally appreciate his rare qualities as an interviewer. He is intelligent, perceptive, understanding and fair in his questioning of guests, whatever their philosophical persuasion. This citizen of two continents has made a solid contribution to American as well as British culture and to our long lasting friendship."

And there were many other glowing letters from many other guests: Coretta Scott King, the widow of the assassinated Martin Luther King, who wrote that, "The experience of late September and early October were extremely meaningful to me"; Erich Segal, the author of *Love Story* (the tear-jerking and phenomenally popular romantic film of 1970) and Ali MacGraw, its star; the multi-award-winning composer Richard Rodgers; the editor of *Cosmopolitan*, Helen Gurley Brown; Frost's ex-girlfriend Janette Scott and her husband Mel Tormé; and sundry politicians, including Hubert Humphrey, George McGovern and Barry Goldwater.[247] Frost's old friend Michael Caine – now in the big time following a string of roles in such films as *Zulu* (1964) and *The Ipcress File* (1965) – also appeared on the show, though his appearance was decidedly singular: "I was in New York and I said I'd do an interview, and I went along to the recording, and David stood on the stage and began, 'Good evening, ladies and gentlemen,' and then suddenly his tooth fell out and bounced on the stage, and I had to sit backstage with him until the dentist arrived and stuck it back it in."[248] There were also graceful letters from such viewers as Frost's rival Barbara Walters at NBC, who wrote "my first fan letter to congratulate on you winning your Emmy. It is much deserved, and you make all of us who are on television talk shows prouder of our work."[249]

And there was the screen legend, Joan Crawford, who appeared on the show early in January 1970. Crawford was poised and regal, and she charmed her host effortlessly. Frost wriggled and rotated his seat in pleasure; and the interview delights – in retrospect and Crawford's shocking pink gown, matching turban and occasionally blue language notwithstanding – for its odd quality of homespun innocence. "Thank you very much," she wrote to him after the show, "for being so wonderful to me during my guest appearance on your show. It was a joy indeed to meet you and a delight to work with you." Frost clearly took the time to invest further in the relationship, for a second ecstatic letter arrived a month later. "How kind of you to send me such an exquisite arrangement of pink tulips, yellow and orange zinnias, and luscious yellow spider chrysanthemums. I continue to enjoy their beauty each day. [...] By the way – the letters about 'our' show are still pouring in! Bless you." And a third, in June 1970, to seal the relationship: "David dear, My congratulations to you upon winning the Emmy. Your show is indeed the best variety show on television, and you so well deserve the award. Bless you, and thank you for all your brilliant entertainment."[250] Given such a roster of guests, it was little wonder that *Look* magazine could remark that, "If the Pope ever agrees to an interview, it will not be because David made the contact through a cardinal. He will have phoned His Holiness direct."[251]

But there were other failures to add to that of Hoover. There was Barbra Streisand's 1971 appearance at the Little Theatre, a segment which once again (a sure sign of star-struck excitement even in as seasoned an individual as Frost now was) had her host wriggling and twirling in his seat. Streisand was utterly charming, but the interview subsequently never aired on television, the result of her network contract which precluded her from appearing on a syndicated show. "I am sorry," says a cable from February 1971 which manages to be both sorrowful and scolding, "that there has been no resolution up to this writing towards the solution which would allow your programme to use the interview tape which Barbara [sic] Streisand did with you. Unfortunately, no use whatsoever can be made of this tape ..." A solution was never discovered – and the Streisand interview was never shown.

A variety of letters from the White House itself, meanwhile, reveal repeated attempts to lure President Richard Nixon into the studio, attempts always rebuffed, though always in pleasant terms. Frost was invited to act as compere at the White House's Christmas entertainment in 1969. Mona Frost was there too, seated between Nixon and his attorney general at dinner, and she let the two men know that, "she'd had to give up a practice session with the Women's Fellowship choir to be there".[252] Neil Shand, however, recalls a postscript, chilling in hindsight, to this ostensibly jolly Yuletide occasion. Twenty-four hours after the engagement, the Washington newspapers were reporting that the president was upset at a Vietnam joke delivered by Frost on the night; and for seventy-two hours afterwards, Frost was anxiously checking that his work visa was not now in danger of being revoked. In any case, the president never returned the favour by appearing on *The David Frost Show*, and when the show came to an end in the summer of 1972, having won a second Emmy along the way, it seemed that Frost had missed his chance to interview this most bankable of guests.

But it was not so. On the night of June 17th, 1972, a month before *The David Frost Show* aired for the final time in New York, there was a burglary at the Democratic National Committee headquarters in the Watergate office complex in downtown Washington. The burglary touched off a chain of events that would fell a president – and impact profoundly on many other lives and careers, not least those of David Frost himself.

CHAPTER 5

The King Hit

*"He erected a wall to stop other people from gazing into his heart,
and probably also to stop himself from gazing into his heart."*

David Frost, of Richard Nixon

*"[Nixon and Frost] are remarkably similar. [...] At a level too
deep for speech, they understand each other well."*

Clive James

I n the summer of 1972, *The David Frost Show* was cancelled in
America. In the end, and in spite of its quality and its double
Emmy triumph, the fate of the show simply came down to
the issue of money: the programme had not syndicated as well
as it needed to do in order to turn the required profit for its
Westinghouse producers. Frost had always appreciated the flexibility and cut-and-thrust of the American television market. It was
infinitely freer and more fluid than was the case in Britain, and it
was an easier matter to take an idea or concept to the marketplace
and set out to raise the money to make it happen, but the down-
side of this system was an industry considerably more red in tooth
and claw than was the case at home. Success was measurable and
attainable, but so was failure, and against the power and reach of
the three giant American networks, the syndicated model would
always face considerable challenges.

Put simply, *The David Frost Show* had not been taken by enough
local television stations to ensure the profits that Westinghouse
wanted and needed. Quality was no defence against this raw fact.
Frost had never connected with the big networks in order to land a

berth with one of them. The critic Ray Richmond notes that, "What distinguished him also distanced him, from the executives and the culture of the business: he was too clever, too different, at a time when homogeneity was prized at a certain level at the networks. He didn't play nice in a way that he would have needed to in order to get ahead."[253] And for Neil Shand, it had become clear that the absence of network backing in the end would kill the show: "Our Englishness and relative sophistication worked well on the East Coast and the West Coast and in Chicago – but in Oshkosh, Illinois, and Turkey Scratch, Iowa? – less so. English and British presenters tend to last around three years in the American market even today. But we had an excellent product, and I sometimes think that if *The David Frost Show* had had network backing, it would still be on air today."[254]

Peter Chadlington – later a close friend, but in 1972 still a mere acquaintance from their days at Cambridge – recalls the point at which Frost's show was axed:

I was travelling home from the United States on business, and coming into Kennedy airport in a car, with David in front of me in another car. This was normal enough: because David travelled so much, there was always a good chance that I'd spot him on this trip or that trip. But on this day, the word had gone out that he'd just been sacked from American TV, and the press was everywhere. And I watched: he gets out of his car, and I think he looks terrible, white, terribly tired; even as a young man he always walked in a shuffle, as if he was much older than his years. And then he sees the media scrum, and he straightens up, and as I get out of my car, I hear his voice booming out: "No, no, no, no, this is a great opportunity, we're going to forge ahead from here." After a few minutes, the media disappears, and the sag and the old shuffle come back. Michael Parkinson always said that when the lights came on, he became a different personality. He said he would straighten up when he opened the fridge and as the light came on, he would say: "Hello, good evening and welcome." And I saw him do this that day at Kennedy.[255]

The scene witnessed by Chadlington was classic Frost, but there is little doubt that the axing of his chat show, though not unexpected, was a blow. It did not mean in itself the disintegration of his American career: his stock, his visibility remained high; his contacts book remained filled to bursting; he retained close friends, advocates and allies in the American television industry; his professional successes in Britain and America remained mutually enriching. And besides all these, nobody knew better than David Frost the possibilities inherent in reinventions. In addition to all of this, he continued to have other strings to his blow. Not for nothing had he thundered backwards and forward across the Atlantic all those years. For his career in Britain remained extant, a cushion on which to fall back while he recalculated his position in America.

Late in 1971, and sensing, perhaps, that the stars were no longer in alignment for *The David Frost Show*, Frost had approached a former adversary with a business deal. The adversary was John Birt, the editor of Granada Television's *World in Action*, and the figure with whom Frost had had such unhappy dealings two years previously. Birt was utterly surprised. Although the two men had not fallen out over the abortive *World in Action* programme – Frost did not fall out with anyone – neither had they parted as close friends, and for Birt there was no reason to suppose that their lives would come together again in any significant way. But now here was Frost, tabling a specific proposal that would involve the two men working together. Specifically, Frost asked Birt to produce the new series of *The Frost Programme* for LWT. The station would also appoint Birt to direct other programmes, and a hefty pay rise was on the table. The offer was tempting for all these reasons, and also because Birt was living in London but commuting to Granada's studios in Manchester, a situation which was tiring, time-consuming and vexing. So Birt accepted the job. This new relationship between Birt and Frost said a great deal about the latter's essential pragmatism and also about his critical acumen. Birt was an exacting and talented producer, and Frost understood the possibilities inherent in a professional relationship with him. This new partnership, emerging from such an unpromising context, would prove to be absolutely pivotal in the latter's career, for years to come.

The two men began work in the first week of January 1972, and almost at once were pitched into a rapidly moving international news story. At this same time, the new state of Bangladesh came into existence following months of bitter and bloody conflict with Pakistan. As one of the conditions of the ceasefire, the government of Pakistan undertook to release the Bangladeshi leader, Sheikh Mujibur Rahman, but instead of delivering him to the infant state of Bangladesh, the Pakistani authorities flew him to London, where he holed up in a luxurious suite at Claridge's Hotel in Mayfair. This was as good as home turf for Frost. Claridge's had long been a favourite haunt, and now he set off for the hotel, slipped through the security cordon, wangled his way up to the suite, and had Rahman agree to his proposal for an interview, his first as Bangladeshi head of state. The catch was that the interview would have to take place on Bangladeshi soil: and so now Frost and Birt flew east to record the interview, which proved to be a good old-fashioned journalistic scoop.

These first weeks of the year passed in a blur for Frost and his new producer. From Bangladesh, they went to the Rhondda Valley in South Wales to cover the ongoing miners' strike. Britain was set to introduce rolling power outages and a three-day week as a means of coping with fuel shortages; a state of emergency would be introduced before the miners went back to work in mid-February, but the novel decision of Frost and Birt to interview the miners in their own social club brought a sharpness and immediacy to proceedings. From the Rhondda, the two men and their crew travelled on to cover the shocking aftermath of the Bloody Sunday killings in Derry and to explain – or attempt to do so – to a British audience the situation in a Northern Ireland that seemed now on the brink of civil war. And from Northern Ireland it was on to Rhodesia for an interview with Ian Smith, still firmly in place as prime minister of what remained in theory a renegade colony of the British Empire.

This series of events, this pell-mell activity across the globe, was of course a cake-walk for Frost. Extraordinarily, he was continuing to record the final season of *The David Frost Show* in New York throughout the month – and January also saw him taken by surprise in London during a visit to Quaglino's. The surprise was delivered by Eamonn Andrews, the urbane host of *This Is Your Life*: this episode of the programme, complete with its big, red book, brought together Mona, Jean and Margaret Frost, along with a lengthy roster of Frost associates, including Richard Armitage, John Cleese, Ronnie Corbett, Fenella Fielding, Luisa Carmo, Bob Lambert and Joan Pugh. Sammy Davis Jr – who had submitted to no fewer than three ninety-minute interviews for *The David Frost Show* – recorded a tribute from the United States: he remarked that "I've never met a kinder, more generous man in my life. [...] Right on, David: you're doing your thing."

This Is Your Life was, of course, a mere interlude in a hectic schedule. Birt records his own sense of disorientation and giddiness, the result of a chronic lack of sleep, jet lag and repeated doses of adrenalin flooding his system. He also recalls his observations of Frost's energy and dedication to the principle of connection, to the idea of producing the sort of television that would form a finely spun web among its viewers:

> Over those hectic months, David and I combined to produce a series which created a real stir, which chimed week after week with the big stories of the moment, and was required and compulsive viewing. Working with David was a tonic for me – he and I had much in common, particularly a willingness to take on a challenge and to blast through to a result – but he raised my game. He boosted my confidence, gave me powerful encouragement to follow my instincts. I learnt from him in other ways. He had a great television and journalistic brain. He could master a brief quickly and focus on what mattered: the key facts that sharpened an issue, that would engage an audience.[256]

Birt also provides a touching personal glimpse of Frost in this creatively and commercially successful period. He describes his colleague in generous terms, drawing attention to his relentlessly sunny optimism and loyalty to his team. He was "lively and beguiling company, acute and well informed, with a ready wit and an unexpectedly fanciful, surreal streak of silliness. He had the gift of intimacy, of making any companion feel special. [...] He wanted the good, well-meaning guys from every party to be in his gang."[257]

He had, as Birt notes, his own particular methods. In particular, Birt remembers Frost's fondness for large buff manila folders and thick felt-tip pens, quantities of both of which filled his offices, his briefcases, the back of his various cars. Ronnie Corbett records an early glimpse of these folders on the set of *The Frost Report*, and now these same folders, sometimes glimpsed entirely blank, sometimes scrawled over in a way that seemed to defy clarity, were an essential accessory and tool in Frost's interviewing armoury. "Every square inch" of these manila folders, notes Birt, was "crowded with information laid out chaotically and to any other reader, incomprehensibly."

The manila folder, indeed, formed a consistent thread running through his career: and many other observers noted the same method at work. Years later, his long-time producer Trevor Poots saw the arrival of the manila folders on the scene as signifying the final move in a long process of preparation. "He would ask me and the researchers to amass a lot of questions, and he would take these questions and select those which would fit the strategy he had instinctively put together. He would write these questions in black felt-tip pen on the back of the manila folder, and use them as a template, set out in little sections."[258] Frequently, the process would culminate with all the questions revised, retouched, written out afresh last thing at night or early in the morning, and all done rather gingerly, for fear of (all-too-frequent) coffee spillage. Such a system – unappealing to one sort of structured mind – functioned as a sort of stream of consciousness, an impressive indication of Frost's ability for most of his career to maintain a three-dimensional grasp of the interview even as it was unfolding before him.

For John O'Loan, who worked with Frost in Britain and over-seas, there was "never anything in this manila folder that he carried with him everywhere. I used to think it was a prop. But then I realised that he needed it to guide an interview. He would write a series of random thoughts in a heavy pen all over the folder, as though they were speech bubbles, and then he would connect them up in the course of the interview, creating a route to the king hit. He was developing the shape of the interview as the interview was going. It was a completely non-linear approach as a way of getting his subject to the point, and it was a very challenging way of con-ducting an interview, but the point was that it worked for him."[259] And the Duke of York – a friend in later life – makes the wry point that, while it pays for an interviewee to be able to read the inter-viewer's handwriting upside-down, "there was absolutely no point trying to read David's handwriting scrawled all over his folders; it was simply impossible".[260]

*

The Frost Programme ended on LWT in 1972, and it was at this point, in the period following this pensioning-off of his established vehicles in both Britain and America, that a form of fragmenta-tion creeps into the career of David Frost. He continued to appear on screen in Britain, but he was less visible and certainly he no longer held his position at the centre of British broadcasting. This was a change that had become manifest seemingly overnight. He had been overexposed, and – the late success of the Birt-piloted *Frost Programme* notwithstanding – his position at the centre of a trouble-racked LWT had damaged his professional credibility. Though he was no loser, he had lost some of his golden sheen.

There was trouble in his personal life too. Frost and Bernadette Carey had stepped out together until the summer of 1970, but, in early June of that year, during a visit to California, they had taken in a show at the Now Grove – the newly named Cocoanut Grove club – at the Ambassador Hotel on Wilshire Boulevard, the very hotel in the kitchens of which Robert Kennedy had been assassinated two years previously. On stage that night was Diahann Carroll, thirty-four years old, strikingly tall and beautiful and one of the foremost black American stars of the period. Carroll had had her own Golden Globe-winning sitcom, *Julia*, for the last two years, and in the summer break before the third season got underway, she had begun revisiting the singing talent that had earned her a Tony award for a Broadway production of *No Strings* in 1962.

Frost and Carroll hit it off instantly, and with their respective dates, went on to Bumbles nightclub. An exchange of phone numbers was clearly impossible, and so, back in New York, Frost decided to have Carroll invited on to *The David Frost Show* instead, as the best way to see her again. A few weeks later, the show's fixer, Bob Carman appeared in the office in a state of excitement and perplexity. "It's amazing! Diahann Carroll never does talk shows – she just turned down the *Tonight* show – but her manager has just called to say she's coming to New York next week and says she'd like to do our show!" Frost, though certainly gleeful, was less perplexed.

An extraordinary couple of weeks now began. In early June, Carey accompanied Frost to the Emmy awards in Los Angeles, which were hosted that year by Frost himself. This was the year that *The David Frost Show* won its first Emmy – the first syndicated show ever to win an Emmy, and a notable triumph for Frost and Westinghouse. And four days later, Carroll turned up at the Little Theatre to record her appearance on the show. "I can see my face," Carroll recalls, "and I can see what I wore: a ridiculous harem outfit, made by some tremendously successful designer; it was unusual and lovely. And David flirted with me all the way through the show. like high-school flirting. It was very sweet, and as happened when anyone flirted with me, I turned into a two-year-old. And of course Americans simply don't know how to behave themselves when they hear an English accent. *And* he was very intelligent and so personable. He had a sensuality about him."[261] They dined together after the show at Orsini's in midtown Manhattan. The following afternoon, Frost returned to London for an overnight stay and a photocall with his family to celebrate his newly announced

OBE, and the day after that, he returned to New York for a Saturday dinner with Carroll.

> We did not want to be spotted at this early stage of our relationship and decided to go to Le Pavillon, confident that the restaurant would be full of out-of-towners, as New Yorkers would be out in the Hamptons for the weekend. But our attempt at privacy was not to prevail. As we entered the restaurant, at the first table we were greeted by Joan Rivers and Rex Reed, one of New York's leading gossip columnists. Two or three tables further on, we were greeted by two of Diahann's greatest friends, Harry and Julie Belafonte who were dining with Bill Cosby, which meant that both the Jewish community and the black community were already in the know. So much for discretion …[262]

Frost was surely being disingenuous. Had he and Carroll truly been seeking discretion, they would not have chosen to dine at an upmarket French restaurant just off Fifth Avenue, regardless of the season. "Without a doubt," adds Carroll, "I felt as though something was going to happen. But becoming involved with someone always frightened me. I have always been that way, my entire life, and even with or especially with someone as charming as David. This sensation went away in time because he made sure that it did, and I was so grateful that he took his time, and allowed me to take my time. I over-analyse everything, as David reminded me."[263] And so a new relationship was forged, and Bernadette Carey was swept away by an infinitely more glamorous newcomer. Frost's relationship with Carroll was intense and mutually fulfilling, though not without its challenges. She rapidly learned, for example, to afford Frost the privacy and space he needed: "There was a piece of his inner life that he showed to no-one. I learned very early on that that is a part of him; and in order for him to be whole and to function the way he did, that it must stay that way. The reading, the walking, the thinking: that was his privacy, and one had to respect that."[264] Besides which, Carroll herself needed the relationship to function in a certain way too, especially in the matter of their respective professional lives: "I was very, very involved in my own work. In theory he was an enormous intrusion into my work; that was how I thought I *ought* to feel. So there was joy, and fear, and 'delight-fulness' and wonderful learning, and feeling angry with myself at how much I enjoyed it – all those things. It was complex, as all good relationships are. And I found a balance. My work and his work continued regardless, and we created a balanced space between the two."[265]

Carroll was introduced to Frost's wider circle. To Joan Pugh, "she was lovely, we all adored her, charming and great fun, very sensible, with a good head on her shoulders. I was in New York one weekend, and David rang Diahann and said, 'Oh, Joan's in town, can she come and meet you?' And Diahann said, 'Oh, bring her down, bring her down,' and I ended up staying in her apartment for a few days."[266]

During a visit to London, Michael Deakin was entrusted with smuggling Carroll across London in the back of a transit van, in order to avoid the attentions of the paparazzi. She took it all in her stride, it seems, considering it something of a hoot. And Neil Shand recalls being invited to dine with Carroll and Frost in Manhattan, but Frost was late, and while they waited for him, Shand and Carroll fell to discussing music. "I mentioned that I had loved 'The Sweetest Sounds', a song from Richard Rodgers's musical *No Strings*, and of course Diahann had starred in the original Broadway production in 1962. And she sang it for me, very low, there in the restaurant while we waited for David. There I was sitting there in a New York restaurant, with this fabulous, talented, beautiful woman singing 'The Sweetest Sounds' to me. Imagine: my very own lullaby of Broadway. Those were great days."[267]

And crucially, Carroll was also embraced by the Frost family – for example, visiting Whitby on two occasions to stay with Margaret and her family. "She sat on the end of my bed, and showed me how to do my makeup," remembers Frost's niece Sally Wardell. "She was so glamorous but very warm and friendly." During such visits

– indeed, during all such visits by Frost's girlfriends – Margaret's husband Kenneth Bull insisted on separate rooms. "They were always welcome, but the rule of the house was the rule of the house."[268] And for Carroll, such visits and such a relationship were vital, for it was no mere everyday matter for Frost to be conducting thus a relationship with a black woman – a second black woman – in those still tense years following desegregation. "Frost was part of a big change, an important change," says Joanna Lumley. "When he went out very openly with Diahann Carroll, I think everyone was surprised that it was him stepping out with this fabulous, tall, *black* singer. People thought it should have been Dudley Moore or Peter Cook, but no, it was David."[269]

Certainly, Frost's employers at Westinghouse were chilly in the face of the relationship, so much so that Frost was summoned to a meeting, at which he was called upon to sign up to a "corporate code" upholding the morals and ethics of the Westinghouse company. The content of such a code was not explained to Frost – probably because it did not exist – and his smooth response was to request details, and to agree to sign on the understanding that every member of the Westinghouse board do likewise. This strange initiative was duly stopped in its tracks.

It was all the more important, in the face of such unpleasantness, for the wider Frost family to demonstrate visibly its values. And, as Carroll recalls, they did so:

His mother was extraordinary really, and so in favour of the relationship, and that was very important to me. I had lived such a broad life, much more so than the Frosts had, and I wanted to know how comfortable or uncomfortable they were with me, and I wanted to know that they were real, genuine people. And the truth is that I was bowled over by their humanity, and their willingness to bring me into their lives. I had enormous respect for my own mother and father – and when my mother met David's mother, there was an extraordinary, instant connection. We saw them walking arm in arm along a hotel corridor, and they wore the same sort of clothes, and they were the same height, and it even looked as though the same person must have done their hair that morning; and they were so happy to be in each other's presence. It was a lovely time for all of us.[270]

In May, 1971, Frost won his second Emmy – and Carroll wrote the following day to congratulate him: "My Darling, Just a note to say how happy for you – I was so very proud, but darling – you deserve everything – and you'll accomplish everything you want in life. My love (last night was thrilling), Diahann." The two became engaged in November 1972, and Frost presented his partner with an egg-sized diamond ring to seal the arrangement. "I remember David putting his hand in his pocket, and as he was reaching into his pocket, I thought, *Oh, my God, it's going to be an engagement ring*. I could see it in his eyes. And it was a beautiful ring – he had seen me admire it one day at Asprey's, and this was the moment, and I felt incredibly wonderful, and also validated by someone I admired; and I kept looking down at my finger and thinking, *Is this real?*"[271]

Mere weeks before the wedding, however, the engagement was off. Frost's wish to have children was one problem. Carroll had one child from her first marriage, and had had two miscarriages, and had no wish for further children; in addition to which, her doubts about a move to Britain intensified as the wedding day drew near.

Married: for a long time we didn't use the word, probably because he saw the fear in my eyes when I heard it. And there were issues, besides. I was such a busy lady, moving around and around and around, and David was really not keen on a working wife, by the way; he was really quite old-fashioned that way. We had spoken about living in England, which I really did not wish to do. A career is one thing in New York, but it would have been quite another situation in England. The thought of recording in London, for example, was not attractive. And in general it was difficult for him to accept: that marriage might not be the best thing for us, individually. And also he wanted to have children, and I had a wonderful child, but I really had not planned to have more children. He would have been a wonderful father, I knew that. But I don't think he quite realised how much attention children need, and the change in his life that would be required for him to bring that about. And it would have been terrible of me to say, 'Yes, we have to be together, but we can't have children.' I could not have done that.[272]

In the long term, and after a period of painful silence, Carroll and Frost remained friends. Carroll later said that Frost was "the best thing that ever happened to me"; and he would visit her, for example, years later on the set of *Dynasty*. But there was no doubting the pain the broken engagement had caused even one so optimistic and impatient of introspection as Frost. This sense of pain was accentuated by Carroll marrying very rapidly indeed: within weeks to the Las Vegas restaurateur Fred Glusman. That marriage broke down, also within weeks. As for Frost: talking over lunch with Janette Scott in London shortly afterwards, he confessed his feeling of humiliation, before rallying and looking once more on the bright side: "'It would never have worked. England was too cold for her. I walked into my kitchen one night and there [Carroll] was in her mink coat, putting out the dinner.' He roared with laughter, and so did I."[273]

There would be other women. In fact, there would be another broken engagement before too long: early in the following year, the Estée Lauder model Karen Graham left him virtually at the altar. If the Carroll saga was quickly forgotten about, however, the Graham equivalent was a good deal more traumatic – even sensational. Graham too had been brought to meet the Frosts, and had clearly made an impact. At Beccles, Mona Frost pronounced her "just like family", and the engagement seemed set fair. But it was not to be. Several weeks before the wedding, in January 1974, Frost's friend David Niven – who had been due to act as Graham's witness at the wedding in New York; Frost's witness was to be his friend the *New York* magazine publisher Clay Felker – received an extraordinary phone call threatening Frost (and Niven himself) with murder unless he broke off his engagement – and Niven was left in no doubt that those making the threat had the means and ability to carry it through.

Then, four days before the wedding itself, Niven returned home in California to a long string of telephone messages from Frost. "Call me, call me, call me," implored the messages, each once more panicky than the last. Niven did call him, to discover that the wedding had been called off abruptly by Graham. Frost was distraught. Niven's reaction was to fly to New York, collect Frost, and take him off to Paris, for a few days' recuperation in a culture in which press intrusion was frowned upon. "I couldn't suggest we go to London," recalls Niven, "because the media would have ripped him to shreds." From there, Frost would fly on to Australia, where he had filming commitments. "This flight to Paris cost me a fortune, by the way," Niven remembers dryly, "because there was no question of Frostie flying coach or business class."

When Niven arrived at New York and the pair got on the flight to Paris, Frost told him the whole appalling story, as he understood it. Graham had announced that she was leaving him: "He was crying on the plane beside me, spewing out this terrible story, in floods of tears. [Graham] had phoned him, had announced on the phone that she had changed her mind, that the engagement was off. He'd been crazy about her."[274]

Although Frost had the good sense to keep the extraordinary story of threatened murder largely to himself, he did relate it to several close friends years later. Karen Graham repented her broken engagement at leisure: "I respected David a lot and still do. It was a big mistake not marrying him, possibly the biggest of my romantic life."[275] But the last word on this story comes from Whitby. Kenneth Bull, Frost's brother-in-law, was not very pleased by this turn of events. "We had gone out and spent a lot of money on a new coat," remembers Frost's niece Sally Wardell ruefully, "for the wedding and for the New York winter – and then, as we set out for the airport to catch our plane, we heard that the wedding was off. It was too bad – though at least Dad got a new coat out of it all."[276]

*

Unfair as this might have appeared, his sunken relationships with Carroll and Graham marked him as no longer an inevitable winner. Frost, though, was no busted flush. He had established a presence first on British and then American television, and now in these early years of the decade he began cultivating a presence in a third significant Anglophone market. In 1972, he visited Australia for the first time, initially to interview the prime ministerial candidates for the upcoming federal election. John O'Loan, who was then director of programming on Network Ten, made his way to Melbourne Airport for his first meeting with Frost. "One of the perks in those days was to chopper our people from the airport. This was the VIP treatment, and I wanted to meet him and make sure he didn't fall out of the helicopter. And I instantly liked him: a very person-able bloke, a big star, but a very nice bloke."[277] And indeed, Frost could now manifest his chameleon qualities once more. Here, now, he could be "blokey" in a manner exactly calibrated to suit the egalitarian culture of Australia, just as he had earlier evoked a quite different air – metropolitan, patrician, patronising – in his inter-view with Rupert Murdoch, the Australian newcomer to London. He could do what he felt the specific context and viewership required of him, and do it seamlessly. Further visits would follow. His interview series *Frost Over Australia* was broadcast on Kerry Packer's Seven Network from 1972–77, in what would prove to be the beginning of a long broadcasting relationship with Australia and New Zealand. Further series and specials would follow in the course of the decade.

Frost's adventures in Australia won him prime-ministerial friendship: the election at Christmas 1972 of a Labor government under Gough Whitlam brought twenty-three years of conservative rule to an end, and keen winds were soon blowing through the cor-ridors of power in Canberra. Frost had interviewed Whitlam and the incumbent Prime Minister William McMahon in advance of the election and, in 1973, he secured a further interview with Whitlam, and another with his wife Margaret. Frost and Gough Whitlam struck up something of a friendship, and in September 1974, during an official Australian visit to the United Nations, a chance meeting between the two men in the foyer of a New York hotel caused the prime minister to abandon a planned dinner meeting with Rupert Murdoch in favour of time with Frost. It was a snub that Murdoch must have found difficult to forgive, the more so given the fact that he had been an enthusiastic Labor supporter and donor to the party's successful 1972 election campaign. In the aftermath of the election, he had hosted a celebration dinner at Sydney for leading Labor and media figures, and had himself taken pains to establish a personal relationship with Whitlam, albeit a strained one, for the two men were distinctly ill-matched in terms of personality.

Whitlam had form in this regard – this was not the first meeting with Murdoch he had cancelled in peremptory style – and now, here he was, favouring David Frost as a dinner companion. Murdoch thereafter progressively withdrew the support of his Australian newspapers from the Whitlam administration, which collapsed the following year in circumstances that remain deeply controversial to this day. There were, of course, very much larger and more substantial reasons why Murdoch moved away from his support of the Australian Labor Party, reasons that had as much to do with economics, with the tense relationship between Australia and the United States in the Whitlam years, and much to do also with his own evolving political views. But it is impossible not to conclude that Murdoch was at least a little angered and affronted by the (albeit minor) part played by David Frost in the tangled personal and political narratives of these years.

*

Frost's engagements in Australia were played out against a background of financial change at home. In 1972, he had become friendly with the financier Jim Slater, who was best known at that time as the founder and controller of Slater Walker, one of the most prominent of a new wave of merchant banks established during the property boom of the early 1970s. Slater was a self-made man, the son of a London builder who had left school at sixteen, gone on to train as an accountant, and worked for a spell in the sales department of British Leyland, the strike-plagued and notoriously inefficient British car manufacturer, before getting down to the business of mastering what was to him at this point the mysterious universe of stocks and shares. By the late 1960s, the *London Evening News* had named him as one of the nation's most dynamic young people under forty: also on this list was Peter Walker – later a Conservative minister under Margaret Thatcher – and these two thrusting young men established Slater Walker, with the intention of making money on a volatile stock market. Buoyed by the sight of an expanding stock market, and encouraged by Slater to imagine the prospect of building his own production company into a much larger commercial entity, Frost now considered floating Paradine and in so doing, freeing up a good deal of equity for future investments. But Michael Rosenberg – whom Frost had met during the long process of negotiations leading up to the birth of LWT, and had come to trust implicitly – was deeply worried at the prospect of Frost tying his destiny thus to the market. "I said, 'No, no, no.' There was a very great deal of talk, or rather, a good deal of anxious discussion."[278] Rosenberg and Frost now brought in a young lawyer named Victor Blank, in later life also a good friend of Frost, and instrumental in forwarding Frost's charity concerns. The trio mulled over the situation and came to the conclusion that it was not a good idea to float Paradine. The idea, then, was ultimately abandoned, and the effect was to seal the relationship of trust between Frost and Rosenberg. The latter began to play a role in the running of Paradine and a much greater role in general in the smooth running of Frost's finances.

The summer of 1974 also saw a consolidation of what had been a wildly see-sawing personal life. In August, Frost was once more on Cap d'Ail on the French Mediterranean coast outside Monaco, as a guest of Lord and Lady Rothermere. Viscount – Vere – Rothermere was a noted newspaper magnate. As chair of Associated Newspapers, he was publisher of the *Daily Mail*, recently relaunched in tabloid form and now on the ascendant as one of Britain's most influential newspapers. Viscountess – Patricia – Rothermere was known to *Private Eye* as "Bubbles", on her account of her rotundity, love of champagne and generally frothy lifestyle. The Rothermeres holidayed in style on Cap d'Ail. Al fresco dinner parties and luxury were taken for granted, and on this occasion, the hosts and Frost were joined by an Englishwoman named Caroline Cushing, New York-based and employed by the Monegasque tourist authority.

Thirty-five-year-old Cushing had been born Caroline Knott into comfortable circumstances in Berkshire. Like Frost, she had been raised in a household of women (the menfolk in her case gone to war), had gone through a Swiss finishing school and Chelsea Art School and had been a debutante – one of the final waves of well-to-do young British women presented formally to the Queen – before leaving for new adventures in the United States. Now, in the summer of 1974, she had recently emerged from a luxurious but stifling marriage to the American blue-blood Howard Cushing. She had two children from a previous marriage to an Austrian aristocrat. With a prodigious network of her own – now including Prince Rainier and Princess Grace and a web of connections in American publishing – plus ambition and a certain flair, then, Caroline Cushing was more than a match for David Frost.

That evening at Villa Roc was "ridiculously romantic", Cushing says, "with dinner on a balmy starlit evening, a beautiful location on the Riviera. It was unbeatable. And sitting next to David was an eye-opener. I hadn't seen his programmes; rather, it was his humour and his sense of fun that seemed completely unique, at least in comparison to the world in which I'd been living. We had a wonderful night, and afterwards headed back into Monaco where we were both staying." And the pair hit it off. Like all of Frost's women, Cushing was poised and striking, handsome, clever and independent of mind; while Frost himself, "was all quick jokes; he would say ridiculously silly things in a Monty Python way. We got on well because of all that silliness: we both had a silly sense of humour."[279]

Frost and Cushing would be together for five years: the longest and most significant relationship since that with Jenny Logan – and the sheer amount of time she spent with him enabled Cushing to get a good sense of the man with whom she had thrown in her lot. She noted that, in many respects, he was thoroughly spoiled: unwilling – and never required, not once in the whole course of his life – to pick up after himself, to cook a meal, iron a shirt, pack a case. She noted his love of ostentation ("he was a terrible show-off"), and that he was not at all the sort of man who would apologise; other people did that, but not Frost. Nor would he always take instruction. He would follow his own instincts, come what way. She noted the sense he retained of being an outsider, of being somehow beyond the pale, a sense that stemmed from those opening, satirical years of his career. The Establishment, he told her, was out to get him. "Britain was different in those days. I would say, 'What are you talking about?' But I knew he had a right to think as he did."[280] And she noted that Frost was, at heart, a loner. He loved thronged rooms and he loved making connections between different groups of friends, and relishing the energy that might be set free as a result. But in the final analysis, he himself belonged only to his own group, and the inner part of his heart he kept to himself.

There could no doubting the range and complexity of his ambition. Frost wanted to expand Paradine, his own outfit, into a major film production company, but there were various issues that stood in the way of these ambitions, in particular the very large amounts of money required to get a film off the ground. There was another challenge to these ambitions: Frost lacked a degree of knowledge and interest in film as a medium, that instinctive feel for what would and would not work. This lack was part of a larger absence of hinterland. Throughout his life, he was comparatively uninterested in most aspects of popular culture: in film and theatre, in the visual arts, in reading, and even, for the most part, in television itself. Which is not to say that he never engaged in such cultural pursuits. Years later, as his eldest son Miles recalls in vivid detail, he was pressed into attending a Bruce Willis blockbuster, much against his will, and the results were surprising: "On a family trip to see *Armageddon* at the Southampton Odeon, which must have been particularly dreaded by him, I remember looking across at him as Billy Bob Thornton delivers cinema's cheesiest lines ('Permission to shake the hand of the daughter of the greatest man that ever lived') – and noticed he was crying. When we talked about the movie afterwards, it was clear that he had not the faintest idea what the film had been about, but had found it emotional enough nonetheless to shed a few tears." But these were family occasions. Frost would never contemplate a movie night as part of any downtime when he was working or on his travels. It would have been, quite simply, a waste of time. And so, when he was preparing to interview an actor or director, Frost's producers and administrative staff would distil the necessary facts, and these would in due course reappear written in thick felt-tip as notes on his buff manila folders. But he seldom experienced these media for himself, and inevitably this lack of experience told.

Over the course of many years, however, a body of significant film and television work did emerge from Paradine. Some of this was successful popular entertainment, such as Frost's long-running *Guinness Book of World Records* slot. Other work ventured into drama: for example, the series *Clayhanger*, based on the quartet of novels by Arnold Bennett, which became a 26-part series broadcast on ITV; *Jennie: Lady Randolph Churchill*, a period drama focusing on the life of the American mother of Winston Churchill; and later, the popular drama *Riley, Ace of Spies*, overseen by the celebrated producer Verity Lambert and sold to ITV. Later still, in 1995, Frost secured for Paradine an important scoop: he was permitted to enter the German jail where Nick Leeson – the notorious city trader who sensationally brought about the collapse of Barings merchant bank – was incarcerated whilst awaiting extradition to Singapore to stand trial. Frost's interview with Leeson was subsequently broadcast on the BBC (which would itself dearly have loved to secure a Leeson interview) – and Paradine went on to co-produce with Granada Television a feature film version of the Barings saga: *Rogue Trader*, which starred Ewan McGregor.

One cinematic outing, however, caused a frisson of tension between Frost and his old friend John Cleese, who was now enjoying international success as a key component in the Monty Python phenomenon. In 1972, Cleese and Graham Chapman had sold to Frost the rights to a film script called *Rentasleuth*, with a smart cast that included the two Ronnies, Barker and Corbett, together with Marty Feldman, Cleese, Chapman and others. For Cleese, the film was clever and funny – like his later movies *Clockwise* and *A Fish Called Wanda*, it hovered just on the right side of silliness – and the production seemed set fair. But there was trouble raising the finances needed for its production, and instead of holding his nerve, Frost quietly sold the film rights on to Ned Sherrin, who would go on to change the name to *Rentadick*, and produce a poor film, which sank without trace. By this stage, the Pythons had washed their hands of the production: later, Cleese would be scathing of both film ("a stinker") and producer (describing Sherrin as "tasteless, slimy and incompetent" with "a great fondness for smut") – but it was Frost's decision to bundle away the film rights that caused most pain.[281] "It was the one time I was disappointed with David […] I never spoke openly with him about it; but it was a very strange thing to do."[282] The two stayed friends, indeed, Cleese became godfather to Frost's second son Wilfred in 1985, but they would see a little less of each other as time went on.

Frost and Paradine enjoyed one particularly significant cinematic success in these years: *The Slipper and the Rose*, a 1976 musical retelling of the Cinderella story. The script was written by Bryan Forbes, who already had a significant career behind him – he was best known at this point as the director of *The Stepford Wives* (1975) – and who would ultimately become a crucial figure in the British and wider Anglophone film industry; songs were supplied by Richard and Robert Sherman; and Frost himself was executive producer. Funds were supplied by the British-Palestinian businessman and publisher Naim Attallah, who became one of Frost's regular lunching partners in the years that followed, and who was enchanted by his new friend's *joie de vivre* and zest for life: "a man who eats well and enjoys his food: such a man is very sexy. We would go over to the Wolseley for breakfast, and in grouse season, we would go over to the Hyde Park Hotel for lunch and order grouse, and he would eat his grouse with his hands, and it would get all over his face and his tie; and such a man is genuine; there is no hypocrisy; also, he loved women and so do I."[283] And the film that came about as a result of this relationship was charming, if perhaps a little too sugary for some. In the *New York Times*, Vincent Canby noted that the leads, Gemma Craven and Richard Chamberlain, "have impossible roles that are less like characters in a fairy tale than pictures on a jar of peanut butter."[284] Smoothly sugared charm notwithstanding, however, the film did brisk business, and earned the Shermans an Academy Award nomination in the following year.

Frost and Cushing at this time enjoyed an easy, uncomplicated relationship. Neither was looking for a great deal of commitment. For Frost, fresh from his recent emotional travails at the altar, there was no incentive to invest much emotional capital in any romantic relationship. Instead, there was an emphasis upon fun and adventure. As Cushing told *People* magazine, "We are like two English children exploring the world. We both grew up in small villages and we feel we can conquer the world if we set out to do it."[285] Before long, Cushing had relocated from America to join Frost at the house on Egerton Crescent in London. Her children went to boarding school, joining the couple in the school holidays. The silliness continued: "We would get into a car to go off somewhere. He was due to give a talk, and we would pause and he would say, 'Where on earth are we going? I don't know. Do you know?' He loved people, meeting them, greeting them – there was nothing he liked more. He took his life in both hands, and he was terribly inclusive and generous. The effort he put into living was phenomenal."[286]

Cushing placed her own life and career on hold for a period, instead accompanying Frost on his travels, and joining with Luisa Carmo in keeping his domestic life steady and comfortable. And there were further shifts in personnel. Joan Pugh, his personal assistant of long standing, had now left to take up a senior position at LWT, and Frost, rather deftly, poached another LWT staffer to take her place. This was Libby Reeves Purdie, like Pugh, a clever, warm, efficient Englishwoman who had in previous years already worked with Frost on his weekend shows at LWT. Reeves Purdie would go on to witness some of the highest highs and the lowest lows of Frost's life, and as had been the case with Pugh, she criss-crossed the globe with Frost, working now at the house in London, now in the Paradine offices in Manhattan, now in Los Angeles or in Australia on the characteristically wide range of Frost programmes.

It was part of Frost's life and work to directly face the criticism that this range of activity spawned. There was a sense in some quarters that one simply could not work in light entertainment while at the same time interviewing a prime minister – or in an American context, film a segment for this or that popular programme one day, and keep an appointment at the White House the next. Frost's long-standing producer in America, John Florescu, laughs that Frost's abilities in this regard, "deeply rankled the White House press corps [...] The truth is that they were incensed that this interloper from London would repeatedly outfox and outmanoeuvre them for scoops."[287] There were complaints from critics that Frost was making a mistake in breaking down the divisions between silos, but what they really meant, as Libby Reeves Purdie notes, "was that one *ought* not to do so – and yet there was David, showing that both could work without any sense of diminishment. One minute we would be in Australia, filming *The Guinness Book of World Records*, and the next minute we would be in London, interviewing Harold Wilson on the role of the British prime minister."[288] And observing Frost's later career, the television presenter Carol Vorderman adds that, "Not only was he incredibly intelligent, but he was a genius political interviewer, and could charm an answer out of any politician. And at the same time, and uniquely, he was a true entertainer. That versatility was his secret weapon."[289]

Reeves Purdie's essential point, of course, is that Frost was entirely comfortable in the medium of television itself, and that he saw it as the most potent tool for reaching his cherished audiences. Once more, that childhood is glimpsed, spent absorbed in the radio, aware of the power of transmission waves and the human voice to connect with and sway and entertain a vast audience, a throng beyond number.

Reeves Purdie's recollection also points to the connections that David Frost in those days had at his disposal. "I remember that Marcia Falkender [Wilson's all-powerful and much-feared private secretary, famous for her lavender writing paper] really did rule the roost at Number 10, waving her purple paper around all day long – and I also remember that she took the most enormous shine to [Frost]. She schmoozed around him very noticeably. At one stage, Marcia had to go away for a while, and because there was nobody else in Downing Street that Wilson trusted, [Frost] offered to send me over to help him. 'Certainly not,' I said, and David said, 'Oh, but why not?' And I said, 'Because I'm a Conservative. I'm not going to work for a Labour prime minister, and if you make me, I shall make a point of wearing a bright blue dress every day.' Needless to say, he didn't make me go."[290]

In the same vein, David Frost's social life continued unabated in these years. Annabel Goldsmith remembers one evening at Egerton Crescent, in the period when her marriage with Mark Birley was in its final stages of disintegration and she was in a relationship with Frost's friend, the financier James Goldsmith: "[Frost] and [Goldsmith] had become very friendly, hugely enjoying each other's company, though they were complete opposites. David was canny but very gentle, and of course [Goldsmith] wasn't gentle at all, was the opposite of gentle. I went for dinner at Egerton Crescent, and hardly said a word all evening. I was watching Michael and Shakira Caine and Elton John, and taking it all in. And just like Jimmy, David would leap up and down from the table during the course of the meal, unable to contain his boundless energy. The reason I remember it all so well now was because David was moving from being a television man in my eyes to being a friend. And we stayed friends after that."[291] Frost's relationship with Elton John was also turning into friendship in this period. After John bought a substantial shareholding in Watford Football Club in 1976 and became its chairman, Frost came to the club to interview him, and the pair were filmed on the pitch, with Frost in goal and John kicking penalties. "We hit it off immediately," John says. "David seemed interested simply in everything: obviously we had common ground on football, but we had common ground in all sorts of ways. He was intensely loyal, always turned up for things, always turned up for charity events. A good friend is someone you don't have to see all the time, and that was the way it was with David – but he was there for me when I needed him. He was a great conversationalist and so funny. I love people who don't stay within the boundaries of what they do, but instead expand those boundaries, and I loved watching him do this, all the way through his career."[292]

Frost was brought into Cushing's family. He acted as witness at her sister's wedding in London, and inaugurated a tradition – charming, and typical of the man – of sending Cushing's mother a bouquet of tulips each year on her birthday, one for every year of her life. She in turn was shown off to the family at Whitby, and to Mona Frost at Beccles: "She was a very dignified woman, she took on everything as though it was all another sermon – and David was the apple of her eye. She was very easy-going, but tremendously influential, and very strong because she had been through a lot herself. And though he never spoke with any emotion about his family life – he never spoke with emotion about anything – he never strayed from being a member of that family. Some people stray, but he was so completely secure in his background and his identity that it would never have occurred to him to stray or do anything of the kind."[293]

Frost continued his frequent visits to Australia and, during these visits, he tended to stay with Kerry Packer in Melbourne. Packer was another of those larger-than-life characters who tended to populate Frost's life. "He was wild," recalls Cushing, "informal, six-foot seven, very Australian – and he loved goading David. The two of them would spark off each other's cleverness."[294] On one occasion, while staying with Packer in 1977, Frost and his agent Richard Armitage mourned the fact that they had caught only a small part of that year's Melbourne Cup, then as now Australia's principal horse-racing event. "You want to see it again?" exclaimed the flamboyant Packer. "No problem!" He picked up his telephone, dialled through to his television station – with the result that the first showing in Australia of that year's James Bond film, *The Spy Who Loved Me*, was interrupted unceremoniously in order to screen the Melbourne Cup all over again. Such were the fruits – and perils – of travelling with David Frost.

*

During the early months after his resignation Nixon was a soul in torment. Shut away behind the well-guarded walls of his ocean-side home at San Clemente, California, he made a brave show of keeping up appearances while deteriorating both emotionally and physically to the point where he had close calls with a nervous breakdown and with death. The atmosphere at San Clemente […] lurched between surrealism, fatalism and despair. The surrealism came from Nixon's efforts to remain presidential without the presidency. Each morning he arrived promptly at his office at 7am, immaculately dressed in coat and tie despite the 100-degree heat. He was guarded by a detail of eighteen Secret Service men; given medical attention by Navy corps men; provided with transport by the Marines and supplied with secure communications by the Army. […] In private he was crumbling as a human being.[295]

Richard Nixon tendered his resignation as thirty-seventh president of the United States in the East Room of the White House on August 9th, 1974. He had delivered his final address to the nation the previous evening. The resignation itself took the form of a terse note to his Secretary of State, Henry Kissinger ("I hereby resign the Office of President of the United States"); and was followed by a speech to officials in the White House ballroom, which was televised and watched by a global audience. He had then walked, accompanied by his wife Pat, to the waiting helicopter for the short transfer to Andrews air-force base, where he took the Marine signature salute for the final time. Then he boarded the plane waiting to take him to retirement and – it was assumed – painful obscurity in California.

There had been little or nothing in that break-in at the Watergate building two years previously to suggest that it might end thus, with the resignation of the president so ignominiously, so sensationally and in the shadow of the threat of impeachment by Congress. It is highly likely that Nixon himself had no prior knowledge of the violation of the Democratic National Committee premises in that election year, with the intention of placing a bug, and yet it was the response of Nixon himself and his administration to this crime that ultimately swept them from office. A few days after the break-in, Nixon's spokesman Ron Ziegler referred to "a third-rate burglary attempt". A few months later, Nixon himself congratulated his legal counsel on having undertaken a full and thorough investigation, when in fact no investigation had taken place. And, as the scandal drew closer to Republican Party operatives and to the Committee for the Re-Election of the President – a member of which, electronics expert James McCord, was one of those arrested at the Watergate building – Nixon attempted to block further investigations by the FBI, which was in the process of discovering connections between the burglars and the Committee.

In November 1972, these shadows notwithstanding, Nixon won re-election to the White House by a landslide, but in the aftermath of his second inauguration, the scandal gathered pace. Tenacious investigative reporting by journalists led by Carl Bernstein and Bob Woodward on the *Washington Post*, assisted by well-placed moles (notably the so-called Deep Throat operative Mark Felt of the FBI) helped to lay bare the scandal, and to prove beyond any doubt that its roots ran deep into the institutions of the Republican Party and the US government, including the Justice Department and the White House itself. It also gradually became apparent that the White House had fought a clandestine battle against individuals – journalists and government officials – it perceived as the enemy, using the arms of the state itself against them in a serious of measures including phone tapping and vindictive tax audits.

Then, in the summer of 1973, it was revealed that the Nixon's administration had installed a clandestine recording system at the White House. This was not so very remarkable in itself – both Lyndon B Johnson and John F Kennedy had also installed such equipment – but Nixon's system, in a gesture to the difficulty that the president had operating even simple technologies, was designed to be switched off only with the greatest difficulty, meaning that he could not break or damage the system without meaning to do so, and this in turn meant that reams of ostensibly secret conversations had been recorded endlessly, verbatim and as standard. Following bitter court battles, the Supreme Court ordered the release of these tapes, and ironically, the president himself was now caught on record authorising and facilitating further extensions to the ongoing attempted cover-up, while consistently using coarse, ugly language. Support for Nixon now collapsed. The previously supportive *Chicago Tribune* described Nixon as "humourless to the point of being inhumane. He is devious. He is vacillating. He is profane. He is willing to be led. He displays dismaying gaps in knowledge. He is suspicious of his staff. His loyalty is minimal."

All of these factors, combined with a president weakened by this long run of scandals and waves of resignations, led inexorably to that short note written and handed to Kissinger – and to the sensational end of the Nixon administration. He and Pat Nixon retired to La Casa Pacifica, his house and estate overlooking the Pacific at San Clemente, on the Orange County coast south of Los Angeles, and while there were indeed bouts of ill-health and depression to follow, Nixon was back on his feet and back on his game with surprising speed. Swimming, golf and a walking regime improved his fitness, and the occasional party kept his inadequately lubricated social skills from seizing up entirely. More significantly than all of this activity, he began assembling his memoirs. In this, he was assisted by a team of researchers that included the future prominent US news anchor Diane Sawyer, who bore the brunt of Nixon's punishing schedule of dictating, editing and correcting. But the work simply had to pay off. A mere month after Nixon's resignation, the former president secured an advance of $2 million with Warner Books for his as-yet-unwritten memoir.

David Frost had watched the televised resignation speech from a hotel room in Sydney, where he was once more on Australian assignment. He felt a certain proprietorial interest in what was unfolding in Washington. Although Nixon had consistently avoided appearing on *The David Frost Show*, Frost had of course interviewed Nixon himself back in 1968, and had been a keen observer of the American scene in the intervening years. And Frost remembered the often substantial achievements of the Nixon Presidency: the tentative rapport achieved with China which culminated in his visit to the country in February 1972; and an anti-ballistic missile treaty with the Soviet Union that helped to improve Cold War relations. Now, Frost was watching as this episode dragged on to its miserable end, and in characteristic style, he was absorbed by curiosity with the man himself, with his emotions, his secrets and with the paradoxes which ran like electric wires through this most complicated of characters.

He could not but be aware of the high-minded words with which Nixon had opened his spell in office in January 1969: this would be a peace-making presidency, dedicated to civility and reconciliation. But he was mindful too of the aggression of the man, his reputation for dogged vindictiveness, compulsive secretiveness, and bitter anger and hatred of his opponents that darkened his personality, and that seemed to find expression in a saturnine, shadowed visage. And so the germ of this idea, he told Joan Bakewell in a BBC interview recorded thirty-four years after the event, "started with the fact that clearly [Nixon] was the most interesting and mysterious figure in the world to interview at that moment. To unearth that story was simply irresistible."[296]

The question was, whether Nixon would be open to such a television probing: would he simply retreat behind the walls of his property at San Clemente? At first this seemed the most likely scenario. It appeared perfectly possible that the world would hardly hear from this strange, disturbed and disturbing man again. But the announcement of Nixon's upcoming memoir, and the presidential pardon granted to Nixon by his successor, Gerald Ford, altered the landscape. Nixon was signalling that he might be available, and it "seemed to me," Frost wrote, "that Nixon would one day want to talk".[297] It was just the idea to excite Frost: and the ghost of that younger wireless-listening boy that he had once been, imagining a web or network of other listeners strung out across the country, now came to the fore once again. The notion of that disgraced man, walled into his house on the coast of California, fed back into a central well of his own philosophy: that people and their stories were invariably worth listening to, and that it was always worth, in moral as well as other terms, facilitating such a conversation.

At first, there were few opportunities. Frost had no direct connections to the former president. But he continued to meditate on the scheme. He placed a few phone calls to the Nixon estate at San Clemente, which went nowhere, and he discussed his idea with Clay Felker, who had now moved on from *New York* magazine to publish *Esquire*. For Caroline Cushing, who watched the intricacies of the process from within, Felker was a critical and largely unsung figure in the process. "Clay gave David courage," Cushing says. "He was a great creator, a great journalist, very innovative, and he forged new ways to tell stories – and he was able to counsel and talk David through and around any pitfalls. He provided steel and quality."[298] And, in the end, an opportunity presented itself with relative speed. In June 1975, less than a year after Nixon's resignation, Felker ran into the former president's agent at a glossy Hamptons summer party outside New York, and was able to report back to Frost that it was indeed game-on.

Nixon's agent was the gloriously named Irving "Swifty" Lazar. He was, as Frost later remarked, "noted for his legendary ability to enter a revolving door behind you and come out in front".[299] It was Lazar who had negotiated Nixon's $2 million advance, and now he was on the scout for his master once again. He was sixty-eight years old that summer, with a long career and a wealth of experience behind him, and he was a ferociously tough-minded agent, a keeper of secrets and maker of deals, accustomed to fighting his clients' corner and to getting his own way. And now Clay Felker had reported back on the specifics of Lazar's new task: to test the wider media waters, to see if the television networks might be willing to go a few rounds with Nixon, and, again, to see how much they might pay. Lazar was as tough as they came, but Frost was happy enough to see this adversary hove into sight. Both men understood the game. Frost could potentially work with such a man, though in the event the negotiations were fraught in the extreme, with brinks-manship, bluffing and counter-bluffing the order of the day.

Lazar already had a price in mind: his client the former president wanted $750,000 for four one-hour shows – no more, no less. NBC had already come up with an offer a good deal less than this. $300,000 had been pushed up by Lazar to $400,000, and Frost thought he could go higher than that in order to secure the rights. But he had a string of conditions: that he retain full editorial control; that Watergate (reasonably enough) be fully up for discussion; that Nixon sign *exclusively* to Frost; that Frost have access to the former president for sixteen hours, rather than a mere four; and that the resulting interviews be released at least three months prior to the publication of the Nixon memoirs. Lazar said he'd think about it.

A few days later, in early July 1975, he rang Frost in London. Nixon had agreed to relinquish all editorial control of the project to Frost; agreed to the release of the interviews before publication of his memoir; and agreed too, with minor caveats, to the exclusivity principle. ("I took a deep breath," Frost wrote. "I rarely seemed to have the time to look back to my childhood, but for a moment I wanted to pinch myself that a Methodist minister's son from

Beccles, Suffolk, was really laying down conditions like this for the former president of the United States."[300]) And finally, Nixon agreed to discuss Watergate, so long as that discussion did not get in the way of the legal disputes relating to the scandal that were still wending their way through the American courts.

And the money? Frost beat Lazar down – or Lazar cranked Frost up – to an agreed sum of $600,000 payable to Richard Nixon for these interviews, with $200,000 of that payable on signature; plus twenty per cent of any profits that accrued. The second clause in the fateful contract set out the financial details:

> In consideration of the rights granted to me hereunder and for the full and faithful performance of all of your covenants and agreements contained herein, I agree to pay you the sum of $600,000, as follows: (a) $200,000 upon execution of this agreement, in consideration of the performance of your services described in paragraph 1 (b) above and for your services on the first program; (b) $100,000 upon completion of the second ninety-minute program; (c) $150,000 upon completion of the third program; and (d) $150,000 upon completion of the fourth program.

In return, Nixon ceded control of the interviews to Frost, irrevocably:

> I shall be the executive producer of the program with the full right and authority to designate a producer and all members of the crew necessary for the production of the programs. In this connection, you agree that as the owner of all film, tapes and the programs, I shall have all creative, business and production controls and I shall have no obligation to submit questions or other material to you prior to taping or filming any interview.

The notion that Nixon should be paid anything at all was by no means a universally accepted principle: even Jonathan Aitken, a most sympathetic biographer of the disgraced president (and in the future himself a disgraced politician) notes that Nixon himself had formerly been of the opinion that ex-presidents should not receive honoraria for speaking and other engagements.[301] But such notions had now been sloughed off, not least because his lifestyle, his general expenditure and his legal costs could not be met – not by what seemed to Nixon his inadequate presidential pension, and not even when the advance for his memoir was taken into account.

And Frost himself felt obliged to address this moral issue of what was coming to be called "chequebook journalism":

> It seemed to me that if our concept of privacy means anything, then a man's life has to be his own to dispose of in any way that he wishes – after he leaves public life. While in office, the time of a public servant belongs to the people he was chosen or elected to serve. It would obviously be unconscionable, for example, for a president or secretary of state to sell his time exclusively to selected media while in office [...] Beyond that, however, I could not for the life of me see why, after leaving office, it was perfectly proper for a member of the executive or legislative branch to accept a position in a Washington law firm, or on the board of directors of a leading corporation, or a chair at a prominent university or a senior position with one of the many national "think tanks" – all of which trade directly on his knowledge and experience gained while on the public payroll – but improper for him to receive payment for a book of memoirs or an exhaustive series of television interviews.

Frost's words, written in 1978 in the immediate aftermath of the Nixon interviews, are forceful, almost combative: and from this temporal distance – at a time when such migrations from the public to the private payroll have become even more *de rigueur* – they seem prescient. They certainly underscore the hypocrisy and inconsistency of opposing such forms of journalism while not opposing other breaches in the membrane between the public and private sectors. And as Frost himself noted tartly, it was not as though Nixon was setting any remarkable precedent. Lyndon B Johnson had been remunerated amply by CBS in interviews broadcast by that network, and the fact that Nixon had resigned in office in disgrace ought not in this regard to set him wholly beyond the pale.

Frost flew into Los Angeles on Friday, August 8th, 1975, ready to meet Nixon and Lazar the next day and hand over the $200,000 down-payment which would seal the deal. In advance of Frost's arrival in California, however, there had been tense scenes surrounding the raising of the money itself, in particular of that enormous deposit. Frost had been convinced that the financial side of the operation had been secured, that the cash was there, but this proved not to be the case. The costs to Frost of the entire Nixon adventure had been estimated at somewhere in the region of $2 million – between $7 million and $8 million in today's values. This was an extraordinary amount of money for a relatively small entity such as Paradine to raise, and a testament to the gamble that Frost was taking at this time. He was putting everything on the line.

For he had, after all, no commercial partners. NBC, having been foiled in its attempt to engage Nixon, was now not about to assist Frost by buying broadcast rights, and the other big US networks followed suit. "The joys of being an independent are considerable. But I had never felt as much of an independent as I did over the next few weeks. [...] The initial response from all three networks was no."[302] Frost would instead have to sell broadcast rights individually, station by station, by syndication. This was a process to which he was no stranger, of course, given his dealings with Westinghouse and *The David Frost Show*. He knew how it worked; he knew it *could* work; he knew the rewards that could accrue if it worked; and he appreciated, now as always, the sense of independence and control that it brought. This had always been his modus operandi, but equally he knew that there were, quite simply, no guarantees. It might just as well simply not work at all.

And so he had set about raising this frightening loan. The initial $200,000 down-payment had been secured from private backers, but, when Frost arrived in New York en route to California, he discovered – "during the most rancorous meeting I can ever recall" – that this promised money would not now be forthcoming, essentially, that the backer in question had welshed on the deal, leaving Frost with little or no time to find substitute funds.[303] This was a crisis. Paradine had a little over $200,000 in the bank, earmarked for another project; this project would collapse if the cash was swept away by Nixon; yet without a cheque ready for Swifty Lazar, the Nixon deal would fall through too. These were zero-sum games.

It was just as well, therefore, that Frost had such an enviable network on which to fall back. Later that night in New York (Thursday, August 7th, 1975, with two days to go before the date with Nixon), he met the financier and banker James Wolfensohn – later the president of the World Bank, but at that time president merely of the Schroder banking corporation, and an acquaintance of Frost from the interior of Concorde. Wolfensohn was equally scandalised by the collapse of Frost's financial arrangements, and he offered a bridging loan of $200,000, ensuring both Paradine's own short-term financial security, and the security of the Nixon project. It was, Wolfensohn told the *Daily Mail* years later, "totally an offer of friendship that didn't have any commercial or political motivations behind it. [...] In those interviews with Nixon [Frost] did something in television that no one else could have done."[304] The loan offer was in fact made in the teeth of opposition from Wolfensohn's own colleagues. Frost understood within days that his friend's reputation rested on the loan being repaid in full within the stipulated twenty-eight days.

And so, the following morning, with this deal not finally ironed out – and, of course, the remainder of the estimated $2 million budget absolutely nowhere in sight – Frost arrived in Los Angeles. He telephoned Janette Scott, his former girlfriend who was still married to Mel Tormé and living now in California. Frost and Scott continued to enjoy a warm friendship. They were accustomed to meet from time to time for cheery lunches and drinks, but on this occasion Scott understood that she was there to provide a little distraction:

He invited me to the Polo Lounge of the Beverly Hills Hotel. He was already seated at a table against the wall when I walked in, and almost instantly I was aware that he was terribly tense. He kept asking me questions over lunch and it seemed to me that he wanted me to take his mind off whatever it was that was troubling him. From the little information he gave me, it appeared that "funds" were the problem. But since I was no longer part of his life, I felt I could hardly press him for details. So instead I kept answering his questions and chattering on and on. I talked about San Francisco where we had spent a little time back in the Sixties, and Reno and Lake Tahoe where Mel [Tormé] was performing with Sammy Davis Jr. And this may sound comical, but the main reason I knew he was stressed was because he was eating his side salad with his fingers, something I hadn't seen him do for years. So I saw that I was there to provide a distraction. But I don't think I managed to do this very well. We didn't linger over coffee, and I left feeling quite concerned. In hindsight, of course, I needn't have worried ...[305]

The following day – the first anniversary of the presidential resignation, though this was merest coincidence – Frost set out for San Clemente to meet Lazar and Nixon and sign the fateful contract. The visit was wholly consumed by tension which emanated from any number of sources. It would have been a peculiar meeting in any case, the strangest of episodes even without the horrendous few days which Frost had just experienced: a considerable sum of money was to change hands; a potentially significant professional relationship entered into; and the prospect of small-talk with a saturnine Nixon to oil the conversation. But in the event, it all went well enough: "Small talk. Always the most difficult part of any conversation with Richard Nixon. But today there was news in the papers of [Soviet leader] Leonid Brezhnev. Clutching at straws, I mentioned it. 'I would not like to be a Russian leader,' said Nixon, shaking his head. 'They never know when they're being taped.'"[306]

These final negotiations took place over six hours against the backdrop of the blue Pacific, and were finally sealed when David Frost handed Richard Nixon the cheque for $200,000. In the *Frost/Nixon* film, the tension at the moment is switched neatly into something like farce as Lazar demands the cheque be given to him, and not to Nixon for deposit, and in fact, the film at this point was essentially a reflection of what actually took place: "With a firm hand but a slightly trembling mind, I wrote the name 'Richard M. Nixon' and then the words 'Two Hundred Thousand Dollars' and then the numbers '$200,000'. Nixon reached for his billfold, but Swifty cut him short. 'Can I have the cheque, please?' he demanded. 'It's made out to me,' the former president protested. 'I'll deposit it.' 'No, no, give it to me. That is the customary procedure.' 'But what about the bank?' 'I'll take care of it.' 'But – but—' 'Will you give it to me – *please*,' said Swifty, this time enunciating every word separately and distinctly. Nixon handed the cheque to Swifty with the forlorn look of a little boy not allowed to consume the cookie he has swiped from the jar before dinner …"[307]The deal was made public at a Beverly Hills news conference the following day.

The financial side of the Nixon deal now began – fitfully, belatedly – to come together. Frost was able to raise the $200,000 to repay Wolfensohn via a deal with the music group Polygram. AIG, the giant New York-based insurance company headed by Hank Greenberg, provided funds: "[Frost] was dignified," recalls Greenberg, "and intellectually stimulating. When he spoke, it was in a way that made people want to listen; and it seemed to me that he spoke *to* people, rather than above their heads."[308] James Goldsmith promised funding too – though none of this was ultimately forthcoming. The BBC signed on to screen the interviews in Britain, and later, Frost did a deal with Kerry Packer in Australia, the final total agreed on the toss of a coin. This was part of a painstaking construction of a mosaic, a jigsaw of deals and negotiations stretching over months, but that eventually raised the cash necessary to fund the operation. It was a year before Frost finally cracked the syndication deals that would see the Nixon programmes broadcast across America. It took longer still – taping of the interviews, indeed, was actually under way – before the advertising slots were finally filled. Nixon, after all, had a touch of toxicity to his image, and it took all of Frost's powers of persuasion to finally bring major brands on board.

And even then there was a shortfall. Frost was obliged to sell the shares he still owned as a founder of London Weekend Television in order to fill the gap. Michael Rosenberg operated at this time as, in his words, as a:

> back-of-house operation, helping David with the money. The idea to sell the share was his – and it was typically audacious – and a great gamble. After all, nobody knew what the result of the Nixon adventures would actually be. And besides, David loved a gamble; he hardly gave it a second thought. But he did focus a certain amount of bile on a certain Ron Hodges, a grey-faced bank manager at the Midland Bank who had declined to advance any money to fund the Nixon adventure. For some time after that, we used to host a Ron Hodges Memorial Dinner. For my 40th birthday in 1979, for example, we took over the ground floor at Quaglino's, with a menu headed "The Ron Hodges Memorial Dinner". The point being, of course, that we did it anyway, without Ron Hodges, and by selling the LWT shares. It's never a good thing to lose money, as he did on LWT, but it was critical to his career. It was a grand gesture of confidence and commitment to himself and in his career. We didn't even have to talk about it for very long before taking the plunge.[309]

Nevertheless, there was pain involved in the decision – and there would be more pain to come. When LWT was eventually sold to Granada Television in 1994, it became apparent that Frost had lost the fortune – approximately £37 million – he would have made in retaining his company shares. He would actually generate little money on the Nixon phenomenon. And yet, Rosenberg was correct: there is little sense that Frost ever regretted the decision. The

Nixon interviews were too significant, too vital and – as it proved – too central to his career for him to have made any other decision. "Never underestimate," Piers Morgan notes, "Frost's cheery bravado and personal courage in carrying through this deal – few people in the world of television interviewing would have chosen to follow such a risky road."[310] And they signified something else too, for anyone prepared to notice: they demonstrated that there was indeed life and commercial and financial scope beyond the three big networks which ostensibly dominated American broadcasting. Frost had already established that this was the case, with *The David Frost Show*, and now here he was, taking this entrepreneurial spirit a step further. It was not without difficulties, certainly, but it could be done – and this, arguably, was David Frost's greatest gift to the generation to come.

*

In March 1977, Janette Scott and her daughter Daisy once more dropped by to see David Frost at his Beverly Hills hotel. By now, he had moved into a suite at the Hilton.

I arrived at the penthouse suite in the Beverly Hills Hilton around 9am. I had taken Daisy with me to introduce her to "Uncle David" – and we walked into a very pleasant room with a balcony overlooking the south side of Beverly Hills. But it was more or less like walking into a production office at a television station: paperwork, research notes, books lying everywhere – all over the bed, the desk, the dressing table, the chairs; it was just as well we played with Daisy on the floor. She and I had eaten breakfast earlier, but David ordered room service for himself. I think we joined him in a little juice. He ate a vast bowl of cornflakes and milk. He always said the milk that was left in the bowl was the best part, and that if it were up to him he would have all the milk in the world run through cornflakes before being bottled. It was, I remember, quite hard to carry on a conversation; phone calls kept coming through, so after a half-hour or so, I told him we had to get going, and wished him well with the programme. As we went down in the elevator to the hotel lobby I heaved a sigh of relief. I was glad to be out of it and glad to be returning to the calm of our house in Coldwater Canyon.[311]

In the almost two years that had passed since the interview deal had been signed by the ocean at San Clemente, David Frost had not been idle. Part of this period had been spent finalising the details of a series called *Crossroads of Civilisation*, a gargantuan project organised by Paradine in partnership with the government of Iran. The Iranian monarchy had celebrated its notional 2,500th birthday with extravagant celebrations at the former Persian imperial capital at Persepolis in October 1971, attended by a throng of the world's royalty, and the Paradine series was very much of a piece with this story of an ancient civilisation.

Crossroads of Civilisation traced three thousand years of Persian and Iranian history, and the not inconsiderable cost of the series was met by the Iranian state. Indeed, the armed forces of Iran were pressed into service as necessary, required to dress in ancient garb and to take part in elaborate reconstructions of ancient Persian conflicts and battleground victories. Part of the process involved a month spent by David Frost in Iran, observing and tracking the series, and interviewing Mohamed Reza Pahlavi, the shah himself, amid the ruins of Persepolis. As Frost remembers, "the majestic symbol of Iran's monarchical heritage. [...] even today, its ruins have an extraordinary atmosphere, the light changing every hour as the sun shines on the carved stones. [...] No one lives for miles around Persepolis, but there was still extremely heavy security: snipers were stationed in key positions around the site. That morning, just as we were about to begin the interview, Shapur Shahbazi, the director, insisted that I sign a piece of paper saying that I would take responsibility for the life and safety of the shah. [...] I did as I was told: for the next two hours, I was responsible for the shah's security."[312] The idea was that *Crossroads of Civilisation*, like the Nixon interviews, would be syndicated around the world, and indeed there was every reason to believe that the series – ornate, elaborate and lavish – would sell well and be distributed widely.

That it did neither – that *Crossroads of Civilisation* would turn out to be singularly ill-timed and ill-starred – was as the result of geopolitical changes that neither the Iranian state nor Paradine could control. Tensions in Iran had been rising steadily through the course of the 1970s. Civil disobedience and demonstrations against the shah became widespread in the autumn of 1978, and within months the shah had left Iran and gone into exile. Michael Deakin, who was on the fringes of the production, remembers the whole episode as "one of David's more ridiculous constructions: battleground scenes recreated in Iranian fields and so on".[313] *Crossroads of Civilisation* was never broadcast; it remains unaired to this day – and its failure to find an audience remained one of the few abiding frustrations of Frost's professional life. But his dealings with Iran and his personal relationship with the shah himself (the latter had a taste for English treacle tart that Frost was able to indulge by flying to Iran with boxes of tarts freshly made in Berkshire; and flying home back to Britain with tins of Caspian Sea caviar given in exchange) would later provide an interview opportunity that he could hardly have imagined.

And in the meantime, his business with Nixon was ongoing. He had assembled the team necessary to work on such a complicated project – and had set about finding the producer that could pull all aspects of this project together. "The job definition, as I ticked it off, was daunting. My producer would not only have to be a first-rate journalist in his own right, to be able to command the respect of other first-rate journalists on the project, he had to be someone who could deal diplomatically with the Nixon people, who could make wise decisions fast under what might have become incredible pressure, and who would constantly test my own instincts and conclusions. He had to be a conceptual thinker and, at the same time, know television technique and equipment as if it were second nature to him. Did such a paragon exist?"[314]

Happily, "he" did. Frost had turned to John Birt, his former nemesis-turned-producer at LWT. Birt took temporary leave of absence from LWT – and now the remainder of the team began to coalesce around the figure of Bob Zelnick, an experienced, canny, clever New Yorker with a background in National Public Radio. "At first, I was a little bit reticent," says Zelnick:

> because you wouldn't have listed David Frost among the serious practitioners of journalism in Washington – but then I recalled seeing David on *That Was the Week That Was* some years before, and I recalled that the programme was clever and had had a thrust to it, and so that was a balancing factor. And so I met with David and John [Birt] in Georgetown, and I soon saw that David was considerably more clever and informed and knowledgeable and well-read than he was sometimes given credit for. And I saw something else too: that [Frost] understood that his future and his reputation were wrapped up in this project; it would have to show seriousness of purpose. I came away from that meeting with a feeling that this could be terrific, that we would be going into it with the right kind of attitude and sense of purpose; as far as I was concerned, it was something to which I could commit.[315]

For Zelnick and Birt – crucially, given the time they would inevitably be spending together – it was a genuine meeting of minds. The two men formed a close personal connection from the off. The latter describes Zelnick as "the very best kind of American journalist, with a deep moral commitment to high professional standards of accuracy, fairness and integrity". Zelnick returns the compliment, calling Birt, "one of the most intelligent men I had ever met".[316] The two men understood that the project had to become the trial that Nixon had never had, the trial for which the American public was thirsting. "David told me that the answers I had given to the questions that John [Birt] posed were as though I had been present at the very first discussions that had been had on the subject."[317] Frost, Zelnick and Birt also understood another critical aspect of the whole endeavour: that Nixon in fact had as much of a stake as Frost in the success of this project, and in its form as a broad, purposeful enquiry. If Nixon made a fool of Frost, the American public would take it as a sign that their fallen president would never be prepared to tell the truth over Watergate, would never acknowledge any wrongdoing or criminality, would for ever sidestep the substantive issues of the case, would forever be willing to live with and eyeball this taint.

Other team members included a young novelist and lecturer, James Reston, and the investigative reporter Phil Stanford, with Libby Reeves Purdie as an essential administrative link – "a Jill of all trades", as she puts it – that connected all parts of this endeavour.[318] Birt and Reston did not get along especially well. The latter was passionate about his task: he regarded Nixon as a thread of venom in the American body politic, and his job to delve into the man's background, expose the roots of what he regarded as a poison-ous personality type, the better to expel it from the system. Birt's approach, in contrast, was rather more holistic and certainly less passionate: he saw his objective as remaining in the present, follow-ing, that is, the course of Nixon's term as president and tracing his political record, his failings and accomplishments. His mission was to explain Nixon the politician, to set the public figure and politi-cian within as full a context as possible.

Birt began to suspect that he and Reston could not work together, but Frost took the view that Reston brought necessary strengths to the table, in particular a passion and creativity that balanced Birt's cerebral, analytical approach. His early episode of tension and Frost's role in resolving it demonstrated his ability to form connec-tions, certainly – but more than this, it demonstrated that for all his clubbable affability when it suited him, he was a tough-minded impresario at heart. He saw that the correct components had been brought together into one team, a team that worked for him, and he was determined to ensure that it functioned well. Caroline Cushing remarks that "that impresario side came through visibly: it didn't always serve him well because he wouldn't always take instruction, but he knew to surround himself with the best people".[319] In this case, his instincts regarding the composition of his team would soon be shown to be completely correct.

Together, this team set about researching, reading, pulling information together about Nixon and his White House, putting a shape to the programmes that were to come. And indeed, soon it became clear that Frost's decision to override Birt and retain Reston on the team had been simply invaluable, for as he sat in the project's offices in Georgetown and pored slowly, meticulously over the voluminous transcripts of the White House tapes, Reston began assembling the crucial material, the matter that would fell Nixon. In September 1976 – and not the night before Frost's Watergate interview with the fallen president, as was portrayed dramatically in the film – Reston chanced upon a conversation between Nixon and Charles Colson, dated June 20th, 1972, a few days after the break-in; and others dating from the following February. These conversations were incendiary, for they demonstrated that the president was not a bystander in the Watergate cover-up, as he sought to portray himself, but an active participant in and director of the process. "These tapes were new," Frost notes, and goes on for good measure to underscore in generous terms Reston's critical role in the process, "and the dates on which they had been recorded were devastating. It was the best kind of scoop, developed not through a leak or a breach of ethic on anyone's part but through Jim's own sheer shoe-leather diligence."[320]

Gradually now, the focus of operations shifted from Washington to various bedrooms and suites at the Beverly Hills Hilton, filled with lockable safes and as tight security as could be mustered. Zelnick prepared draft after draft of each interview topic: detailing the material under discussion, and anticipating the work that the Nixon team would undertake to present their man in the best possible light, framing Frost's responses to these counterblasts. Rehearsal followed rehearsal and, "It began as a science, and it ended up as an art: all of these endless dress rehearsals ended up with my taking on the guise and language of Nixon – in a way becoming Nixon. 'You're so into this thing,' they would say, that, 'you sound like Nixon. I hope you won't end up in jail.'"[321] Michael Parkinson was sent out by the *Sunday Times* to cover the preparations for a week: "It was fascinating, to see the rehearsals, question after methodical question; to see [Frost's] complete professionalism."[322] Reeves Purdie, meanwhile, now more than ever acted as the kingpin of what was always a complicated, stressful operation. All inward phone calls were channelled to her hotel room, all journalists' queries were filtered through her, and the notes that accumulated every day were typed by her, sometimes well into the early hours, before being distributed to the rest of the team. "'I feel like the hotel tart,' she told Frost, 'running from room to room from midnight until two every morning. My liaisons are many and my satisfactions few.'"[323]

The team also had to find a new location for the interviews. The radio equipment at the San Clemente coastguard station would apparently cause a "rolling glitch" – a thin, waving line – on any television footage recorded at La Casa Pacifica, and this equipment could not be switched off. After scouring the area, Frost settled on a detached house at Monarch Bay, a community on the coast of Orange County ten or so miles north of the Nixon estate. The house was well-maintained – split-level, with fine views of the ocean and furnished in the style of the times, with an abundance of wood veneer, heavy curtains, thick shag-pile carpeting and beige velour loose covers – and Monarch Bay itself was prosperous and comfortable. On the other hand, this was essentially a regular suburban home, surrounded by other regular suburban homes, and as such it was a distinctly odd place to encamp for the weeks it would take to record the Nixon interviews.

The house at Monarch Bay belonged to Martha and Harold Smith, long-time friends of the disgraced president, and the Smiths' lavatory, by all accounts, sealed the deal: it flushed quietly, meaning that if one of the forty-odd people gathered in the house for the duration of the recording sessions was caught short, the noise would not be caught on tape. As the interviews approached, the Secret Service took the house apart searching for hidden menaces to the life of their charge, though they unaccountably missed Harold Smith's gun collection that was stored in the hall closet. It was agreed that the Smiths would absent themselves during the day: they roamed the California landscape, shopping, having lunch, visiting the country club; while their main reception room became a semi-permanent studio; and two spare bedrooms became offices for the opposing Frost-Nixon camps. Helicopters buzzed and aeroplanes droned overhead; neighbours and strangers gathered in front of the house – and these noises, if not that of the Smiths' flushing lavatory, would prove to be clearly audible in the interviews. "We wouldn't ever do it again," Martha Smith said years later.

Caroline Cushing remembers the house at Monarch Bay with no great affection:

It was an hour and more by car from Beverly Hills. The drive, day after day, there and back, became tedious. The atmosphere was tense, and the house itself not big enough for all the people crammed into it. Just being there was unpleasant: driving out there, then hair and makeup; the house claustrophobic, the rooms too small, and all the researchers buzzing around – and all of this relentlessly, day after day. And then David, cool and calm as always in the face of what he knew was the biggest project of his life – but clearly anxious, suffering from stress and aware that many destinies were riding on this. [...] And it always seemed to me that this whole experience in any case wasn't *him*. He had dreamed it up, he had committed to it, he *was* committed to it, but all these crowds of people around simply did not suit him very well. He was better and happier going solo, and in spite of the interview format, the one-on-one, there was really nothing solo about this project. But then, I also saw something else: the steel in his nerves. In the mornings, he would scrabble around looking for matching socks – but his focus was absolutely unrelenting.[324]

The first recording session was scheduled for Wednesday, March 23rd, 1977, and Frost and his team arrived at Monarch Bay to find the media camped on the pavement. Nixon's white Lincoln Continental arrived on schedule thirty minutes later, and after posing for the cameras, the two men went inside. They were clad in the garb they would wear – for the purposes of consistency – for the duration of the interviews: Nixon in his regulation blue suit and bluer tie and looking healthy and well; Frost in a more flashy striped shirt, balanced with a sober jacket; the extravagant sideburns of the early Seventies now mercifully trimmed and tidy; and healthy too, although the fatigued, deeply-pouched eyes of the older Frost are already apparent in this still young man.

The interviews began – and they began badly. David Frost opted to plunge directly into the maelstrom of Watergate. "Mr President, we are going to be covering a lot of subjects in a great deal of detail over the course of the next six hours, but I must begin completely out of context by asking you one question, more than any other, almost every American and people all over the world want me to ask. They all have their questions, but one of them in every case is, 'Why didn't you burn the tapes?' Nixon's surprise is very evident: the order of the interviews had been arranged precisely, with Watergate to be raised in due course – but he rallied quickly enough. "Since you have that as a major concern among your listeners and viewers, there is no reason why I at least can't respond briefly to it now, and you can explore it at greater length later if you like."

In beginning, thus out of context and aware of Nixon's temperament, Frost was attempting to bowl his interviewee a googly – and it was a measure of Nixon's own state of preparedness that he could reply with a degree of grace and mildness to this unexpected opening. And indeed, Nixon had the better of that day's exchanges. In taking up Frost's implicit invitation to explain the intricacies of his recording policies during his tenure at the White House, he led the discussion into a morass of technicalities and extensive detail which caused that day's interview to sag. It was by no means a disaster. Indeed, nuggets of useful information emerged, with Nixon, for example, regretting the colourful, expletive-filled language he had deployed in the course of some of the Watergate recordings. This "disappointed a lot of my friends," he admitted. "Although I must say, it is not the first time that it's occurred."

But it is certainly the case that Nixon led Frost a merry dance in that first session. He soaked up the available time effortlessly by means of long replies, circumlocutions, deviations and descriptions in the matter of just about everyone's sensations and emotions in the face of this event, or that one. The president himself, however, kept his private face essentially private. There were several mawkish side avenues to the conversation that might have been calculated to appeal to public opinion, but hardly anything, Frost judged, that he could actually use. And yet Nixon did give an answer to Frost's initial question. Why *had* he not destroyed the tapes? – because to do so would have seemed an admission of guilt; because he simply never believed until it was too late that the courts would compel the president to release the tapes into the public realm; and because his judgement was that there were other methods by which the presidency might be defended from its enemies. As Frost notes, "[Nixon's] judgement proved faulty …" – and Nixon himself admitted morosely on that first day of recording that, "if the tapes *had* [my italics] been destroyed, I believe that it is likely that I would not have had to go through the agony of resignation … I think it would have been well, looking at it from our standpoint, to destroy them all."[325]

But such insights were the paltry results of two hours of recording: most of that first session was unusable – and this set the scene for many of the opening sessions between the two men. Frost and his team had been meticulous in their preparation, but it was impossible to prepare for Nixon's counterblasts, and difficult to continue to control the agenda in the face of them. "I was fearful," says John Birt, who with Zelnick watched the recordings unfold amid the claustrophobic environment of a spare room in the house at Monarch Bay, "that even edited down, overall the material lacked punch. An early assembly of a possible first programme demoralised us. The team was nervous. We felt the eye of history and of America on us. We feared that David was not taking control and was not driving the interviews hard enough. There was some plain talking between us all. David felt strongly that we were over-reacting and resented our criticism. For a few days relations were tense."[326]

Strong material followed. On April 1st, the two men debated the American relationship with the brutal Pinochet regime in Chile (Frost asked, "If you had to choose a word to describe the Pinochet regime, what adjective would you use ... *brutal*?" Nixon preferred "dictatorial, I would say, *dictatorial*") and with Latin America in general; and the former president's difficult relationship with his National Security Adviser, Henry Kissinger. Frost remarked later of this relationship that, "two more gifted, insightful, jealous, patriotic, secretive, self-promoting, reflective, manipulative, power-grasping public servants had rarely graced the same administration at the same time."[327] On April 6th, 1977 – the day before his thirty-eighth birthday – Frost took Nixon over domestic ground, specifically, the unrest on the streets and campuses that accompanied the American presence in Vietnam. Yet spirits remained low. As Frost says, "the project was experiencing a decline in momentum, a sinking in morale and a shaking of self-confidence."[328] Frost gave the president a difficult time, suggesting that Nixon had betrayed his campaign pledges to be a uniting, conciliatory leader of America, before moving on to the so-called Huston Plan, the report commissioned by Nixon that had proposed much more by way of internal surveillance and espionage upon American citizens and corporations, and that had led directly to the original Watergate burglary. Frost's line of questioning led to one of the interviews' most famous moments:

DF: So in a sense what you're saying is that there are certain situations, and the Huston plan, or that part of it, was one of them, where the president can decide that it's in the best interest of the nation or something and do something illegal?

RN: Well, when the president does it, that means that it is not illegal.

DF: By definition?

RN: Exactly, exactly.

It was a signal moment, but the gloom remained. Bob Zelnick recalls particularly excruciating episodes at this time. On the eve of Frost's thirty-eighth birthday, he invited Clay Felker and others to review the recordings as they stood. The feedback was appalling. "Some of the criticism was pretty harsh. When you have so much riding on a project, and people you respect are telling you that you're going about this the wrong way, or telling you to do it a better way or in the case of Clay Felker falling asleep on the couch ten minutes into the screening, well, that's pretty tough. And it's pretty tough to go out to celebrate your birthday, as David did, and to see [the musician] Sammy Cahn on the stage, and to realise that he's seen you, as David did, and has begun singing about how the project is in a state of crisis. 'I really hate to burst your bubble / But the Nixon interviews are in trouble!' But David took it all as a challenge, and ensured that he improved."[329]

And there was another problem too. Nixon's sheer wordiness and Frost's inability to stem the flow meant that the recording timetable rapidly fell behind schedule. At first, Nixon's team refused to permit more time to be made available, but when Birt threatened to leave out any material on detente with China and the Soviet Union (Nixon's great foreign-policy achievements), Nixon's team hastily gave way. It would never do, after all, to have the whole adventure potentially dominated by Watergate, to the exclusion of so much else.[330] Of course, the Frost/Nixon project *would* inevitably be dominated by Watergate, both in theory and, as it turned out, in practice. And everyone was aware of the fact. Frost's own excellent memory, his ability to master a brief and his rapid grasp of detail would prove a great defence against any form of obfuscation placed in his way, and in this sense he was indeed the perfect candidate to interview Nixon.

And yet, there was anxiety as the Watergate sessions – timed for April 13th and 15th, 1977 – approached. In the early hours of April 13th, Libby Reeves Purdie delivered a note written by John Birt to Frost's hotel bedroom at the Beverly Hills Hilton. Frost and Nixon were to begin the process of discussing Watergate the following morning, and Birt wanted to ensure that his anchor avoided the errors of previous sessions, and was primed fully, completely, without a shadow of a doubt for the task ahead:

It is not a conventional interview: you are exchanging interpretations of the known facts; you should talk almost as much as he does. Most importantly, don't be tempted to put brief and "pointed" questions that elicit long and vague answers: when he paints a picture that you know to be false, respond by painting, at the same length he does, the alternative picture as you understand it. Always keep firmly in mind that Watergate is a difficult subject for a mass audience to follow and at each stage it is your responsibility to point out clearly to the audience the implication of any question, fact, event, statement or admission that you consider relevant. Stay cool and firm, but be polite. Only raise your voice if and when you are pushed to. And, finally, keep up the pressure at all times: you will win only if you can, so to speak, sprint the mile.[331]

Birt's note was impregnated with strain, and with a very real fear that Frost would net little or nothing of enduring or commercial value from his encounter with Nixon. During the ride down to Monarch Bay the following morning, Birt added to his notes – and to the atmosphere of tension – with additional nuggets of advice that were probably less useful at this rushed, claustrophobic moment: Frost must be *physically* present as well as mentally focused. But by this point, Frost was attending to his manila folders, and now Birt's final notes were little heard. Not that this prevented Frost from injecting a note of humour into this otherwise fraught moment. In a short speech to his crew, he asked them to maintain the security of the operation for just a little while longer: "Gentlemen, you've all been superb. Every reporter in the country wants to know what the former president has to say about Watergate. I must ask you not to tell them. Don't even tell your wives or the women you love. In fact, don't tell either of them. Thank you."[332]

But John Birt's overnight note had certainly been heard, and its substance absorbed. Frost's demeanour was indeed respectful in this critical joust with Nixon, but his mastery of the brief was almost palpable, and there was also an edge of steel in his questioning. Nixon's intention was to use legalistic arguments to complicate an already extremely complicated scenario, but Frost's tactic of carrying the war into Nixon's territory and underscoring his *own* opinions regarding Watergate, changed the energy of the encounter. One moment – key, though relatively underplayed – came when Nixon attempted to flourish his legal credentials in the matter of the definition of "obstruction of justice". Frost had pressed his interviewee hard in the approach to this point, seeking to demonstrate beyond doubt that Nixon had indeed been participating actively in a cover-up since June 23rd, 1972, less than a week after the break-in at the Watergate building, and that he had intended to obstruct the course of justice afterwards. "You perhaps have not read the statute with regard to [...] obstruction of justice," says Nixon, with the loftiness of a background in legal matters. Frost replies, *sotto voce*, "I have," and Nixon almost recoils. "Well, oh, I'm sorry, of course, you probably have read it ..." Frost was telling no lies: he *had* indeed read the relevant statue, though in a glance, in the back seat of his car a couple of minutes before arriving at Monarch Bay. But Nixon was not to know this.

At this point, Frost flourished the new material that James Reston had unearthed several months previously in Washington:

DF: But there's one, ah, very clear, self-contained quote, and I read the whole of his conversation of February 14th, which I don't think has ever been published, but ... and there was one very clear quote in it that I thought was ...

RN: It hasn't been published, you say?

DF: No, I think it's ... it's available to anyone who consults the records, but, ah ...

RN: Oh. Yes.

DF: —but, ah, people don't consult all the records.

RN: Just wondered if we'd seen it.

DF: Well, I'm … I'm sure you have, yes, but ah … where the president says this, on February 13th, um, "When I'm speaking about Wa— […] when I'm speaking about Watergate, though, that's the whole point of the election. This tremendous investigation rests unless one of the seven [the aides to Nixon indicted by a grand jury for their suspected role in a Watergate cover-up] begins to talk, that's the problem." Now, in that remark, it seems to me that someone *running* [my italics] the cover-up couldn't have expressed it more clearly than that, could they?

The transcript in its entirely is arresting enough at this point – but the visual record is truly gripping: for it is at this point that the president's body language begins to speak almost audibly. He touches his face, his chin, the knot of his tie; he smiles a sudden, ghastly smile; a tiny tell-tale bead of perspiration – always Nixon's bugbear, as evidenced in his ostensibly sweaty, ostensibly unshaven interview with the telegenic John F Kennedy in 1960 – begins to twinkle on his upper lip; he is on the ropes. Frost, in contrast, has an almost studied nonchalance, with a hand resting on the beige velour chair arm – but one which betrays just the same a tension and awareness of the significance of the moment. And he adds a final jab – for the moment and for good measure.

DF: I still just think, though, that one has to go contrary to the normal usage of language of almost ten thousand gangster movies, ah, to interpret "This tremendous investigation rests unless one of the seven begins to talk, that's the problem" as anything other than some sort of conspiracy to stop him talking about something damaging …

RN: Well, you can – you can state …

DF: … to the press and making the speech.

RN: … you can state your conclusion, and I've stated my views.

In the second session, two days later, Frost again drove his own voice further into the narrative – and again, the result is a visually striking record. Nixon's composure remains – indeed, his legal wordiness remains too; this is no highly coloured soap opera script – but the main sense in the session is of gradual fragmentation and disintegration. While not conceding the specific suggestions – of cover-up, of a trail of lies and corruption beginning and ending in the White House – Nixon's emotions and memories come to the surface as he regrets his own mistakes and lost opportunities, and concedes the general point of a failure of ethics, of idealisation, of an American dream being shattered, of a tainting of the system and of that taint being administered by Nixon himself.

And Frost's own conduct is highly significant: he combines a sense of proactivity with an understanding, once again, of the critical significance of silence. "Would you go further than 'mistakes'? That, you've explained how you got caught up in this thing [...] You've explained your motives. I don't want to quibble about any of this, but just coming back to the sheer substance, would you go further than 'mistakes'? The word seems not enough for people to understand." Nixon responds by putting Frost himself on the spot – "What would you suggest?" – and Frost's response is to toss his clipboard onto the ground, and in the process to change the tenor of the whole exchange. His youngest son, George, recalls his father's memories of the moment:

> He took great pride in the calculated, intentional act of putting the clipboard down. He said that this was a sign that he was going off-script, that he was talking from the heart and that this was in no way planned. I remember him saying to me that without doing this, Nixon would not have said what he did.[333]

And at this point, Frost certainly takes the initiative, directing the conversation into a channel of his own choosing. "My goodness," he says, "that's a … I think that there are three things, since you asked me, I would like to hear you say, I think the American people would like to hear you say. One is, 'There was probably more than mistakes, here was wrongdoing.' Whether it was a crime or not? 'Yes, it may have been a crime too.' Secondly, 'I did ...' and I'm saying this without questioning the motives, right, 'I did abuse the power I had as president, or not fulfil the totality of the oath of office.' That's the second thing. And thirdly, 'I put the American people though two years of needless agony and I apologise for that.' And I say that you've explained your motives. I think those are the categories. And I know how difficult it is for anyone, and most of all you, but I think that people need to hear it, and I think, unless you say it, you're going to be haunted for the rest of your life."

Following this pivotal, proactive moment, Frost steps back, remains essentially quiet, remembers his own rules of silence, of giving the interviewee free rein where appropriate, and enables the interview to flow through to that critical moment, in which Nixon's confession is elicited and electrifies the air.

> I let down my friends. I let down the country. I let down our system of government and the dreams of all those young people that ought to get into government but think it's all too corrupt and the rest. [...] I let the American people down, and I have to carry that burden with me for the rest of my life. My political life is over. [...] Technically I did not commit a crime, an impeachable offense – these are legalisms. As far as the handling of this matter is concerned, it was so botched up. I made so many bad judgements.

In the aftermath of these dramatic days at Monarch Bay, it could almost be forgotten that the project was still ongoing, that there were three more sessions to be filled – a little anticlimactically – before a frantic schedule of editing kicked off in advance of the first press screening. It was an exhausting process for all concerned, though it was now becoming clear that the advertising flow had settled: the project would at least break even. The first press screening of the Watergate interview took place at Washington on the afternoon of

May 4th. Frost stayed away. He and Birt remained in Los Angeles to continue editing, and left it to Zelnick to run the Washington show. Which began badly – the video player wouldn't work, and had to be wrestled with for nineteen excruciating minutes in front of the silent elite of the Washington press corps.

Bob Woodward and Carl Bernstein were in attendance, and afterwards, once the reporters had scattered to file their stories, these two remained behind to congratulate Zelnick on a good job. Frost, meanwhile, had decided to throw a party to mark the end of this particular road, also that same evening, when the first interview was aired in California. This took place at Chasen's restaurant, for many years a noted hang-out of Hollywood's rich and famous. It began with a viewing of the programme, and afterwards, Frost and Birt were invited back to the mansion of the *Playboy* publisher Hugh Hefner, to explore its pink flamingo-filled grounds, and peek at the rooms scattered with sexual paraphernalia. The word had gone out: Frost had hit his target – and at this moment, he and his team were the talk of Los Angeles. The *New York Times* reported that this first programme drew an audience of some forty-five million – the largest ever audience for a news programme; and the *Washington Post* remarked that "the Nixon-Frost, far and away the best piece of journalism to pop before our eyes on the TV screen in a very long time, couldn't get on any of the networks. […] Frost not only asked the right questions the right way at the right time, but, and this is rare among television magpie news performers, knew when to shut up and listen."[334]

This culminating moment in the interviews did what Nixon desperately needed it to do: it lanced the boil that had pulsed angrily around him ever since his resignation. Certainly, his life henceforth would be a process of gradual rehabilitation and an increasing degree of the sort of public sympathy that had been lacking before he sat down in that split-level house at Monarch Bay. When Nixon died in April 1994, his funeral in the grounds of the Nixon Library at Yorba Linda, California, was attended by President Bill Clinton, First Lady Hillary Rodham Clinton and by all four living former

US presidents: Bush, Reagan, Carter, Ford. It was a sign of the completeness of this rehabilitation process, at least in the eyes of the American Establishment.

For those involved in the process, the project became a source of some satisfaction. "The years have been kind to this project," says Zelnick. "You have a little compartment in your mind where you file away the major work you have done, and you sometimes wonder how everything worked and how they could have been improved. But the Nixon interviews, with Frost chairing and Birt overseeing and – I don't want to clap myself on the back, but the tenacity and the lawyerlike intuitions that I brought to the project – I think it worked very well." As for Frost himself, Zelnick remembers, "a very smart, substantial man, well-read and well-informed. And a very considerate man, pleasant to spend time with, and a very sweet man who treated me very well, always, and who was pivotal in kicking off my career with ABC when the Nixon interviews ended. A really good guy."[335] When he and his wife Pam returned to Washington, they built a house on five acres of land in northern Virginia – and named the property Frost Acres.

Before Frost and Nixon went their separate ways, they met at La Casa Pacifica for a formal leave-taking. In the film, this ceremony is shot through with melancholy and a counterintuitive sense of regret: after all, no two men could possibly have been more pleased to see the back of each other. In reality, however, there were undoubtedly mixed feelings. By now, the interviews were making waves, and both Frost and Nixon were aware they had played a part in something that was significant, that would last. Years later, Caroline Cushing remembers her sense of pity for Nixon as she and Frost took their leave:

> I felt sorry for Nixon. David never was one for giving opinions on anything emotional, but, yes, I felt for him. I felt pity for this man who seemed so lonely, and who seemed to want to show off to us, his captive audience, and Pat [Nixon] like a ghost upstairs. He asked, "Do you like good wine?" I said, "What, do

you mean would I prefer bad wine? Yes, I like good wine." He
said, "Well, I have a cellar filled with good wine, and I'll bring
some up for you." As if we were children being offered sweet-
ies. He was like a lion outside his cage, showing us pictures
of himself and Brezhnev. He was a very strange man, and the
whole interviews ordeal, because that's what it was, seemed to
me also very, very strange.[336]

As for David Frost: he had been well aware of the momentous risk
he had just taken. "It was a risk," he told ITV thirty years later,
"in the sense that people predicted it would be impossible to get
Nixon to say anything that wasn't self-serving. It would be impossible to get a *mea culpa* out of him – and we did get a *mea culpa*
out of him and a very dramatic one. But it was a big risk because
there was such hostility to Nixon in the media that, you know, if
I had not laid a finger on him, as it were, I would have been done
for."[337] Now, having laid more than a finger on Nixon, it must
have appeared to observers that David Frost's American career,
moving slowly in second gear as it had been for several years now,
would immediately take off following the Nixon adventure. But this
proved not to be the case: indeed, Nixon did rather better out of
the whole "ordeal". The networks, having disdained Frost and his
plan to take on the fallen president, and as a result having missed
out on this significant story, remained cold on the matter of this
interloping Englishman. In addition to an inevitable sourness at
having dropped the ball in this regard, there were understandable
fears that Frost had reached some sort of high-water mark, that
he would never again be able to scale these heights. And so, Frost
failed to capitalise on his success, failed to carve out new terrain for
himself in America. His career there would remain unresolved for
ten more years to come.

There were, however, two substantial American projects – both
produced in concert with John Birt – still to come in the course
of that decade. One, in October 1979, was a series of interviews
produced for NBC with Henry Kissinger, Nixon's national-security

adviser from 1969; the second, two months later in December 1979, with the deposed and exiled shah of Iran and produced with ABC. Both interviews were deeply uncomfortable, though for rather different reasons. The interview with Kissinger went profoundly badly, and his shadow hung over the meetings with the shah, as Frost recalled in notes written later in his life. The interview was "big news":

> ... and also controversial. The *New York Daily News* said Henry Kissinger had been furious that I had been granted the interview and claimed that he had pushed the shah to speak to his "very close friend" Barbara Walters, or failing that, Walter Cronkite or Mike Wallace – in other words, anyone rather than me. [...] Kissinger was said to be a big influence on the shah, and so when news of my impending interview came out, someone asked [Kissinger] if it had been on his recommendation. Kissinger was livid at the suggestion that he was doing me a favour. "If I was that influential with the shah do you think I would let him be interviewed by David Frost?" he thundered.[338]

This time, the strained relations were between Birt and Frost, to do with the tone of the meeting with the shah, who was suffering from terminal cancer and who did in fact die six months later. The deposed monarch's life in exile was being played out against an atmosphere of extraordinary tension. For the greater part of 1979, the shah and his entourage had travelled from country to country before finally being admitted in October to the United States for medical treatment. A month later, the US Embassy in Tehran was stormed and fifty-two Americans taken hostage as bargaining chips to force the US government to return the shah to Iran to face trial on charges of murder and corruption. In December, the shah left the US for the island of Contadora off the Panamanian coast – and it was on Contadora, and against this extremely fraught geopolitical context, that Frost and Birt recorded their interview for ABC with the deposed monarch. Bob Zelnick was the ABC manager on the ground, Michael Deakin was the producer and Libby Reeves Purdie provided the administrative backup on Contadora – this collection of individuals once more underscoring the sense that Frost preferred always to work with small groups of known and trusted individuals.

For Birt, the interview – recorded over four days – was a disappointment. It "was flat" and Frost was now resistant to the idea that he approach the shah in more combative fashion. It was, Birt admits, "distasteful to put a man with little time to live through a hostile grilling", and yet a grilling was surely necessary for the interview to retain its credibility.[339] Certainly, the shah was asked awkward questions – in the matter of his abundant wealth, for example, and its sources, and the use of torture by members of his regime – but it is almost undeniably the case that the interview is a relatively gentle affair. There is a degree of mellifluity that cannot be explained away by the shah's illness, that can, perhaps, be put down to Frost's previous and highly cordial relationship with the shah in the course of the *Crossroads of Civilisation* series a couple of years previously.

Relatively gentle: there are moments to do with issues of morality – the morality of torture, for example – in which the content of the interview is difficult and awkward:

DF: Do you, as king of kings, who in a sense gets all the credit and therefore all the blame, do you accept in your concept of kingship, a sense of responsibility for those tortures although you did not know about them?

RP: That must be some kind of self-sacrifice or some kind of masochism, because I could not take responsibility if I did not know about it.

DF: You don't have responsibility for everything that goes on in a culture in which you are king of kings?

RP: I was receiving the head of security for twenty minutes twice a week for twenty minutes, twenty-five minutes, and he will have his reports on important things, not just petty details like that [...] that, yesterday we have tortured this fellow or that fellow.

DF: Given the fact [of] the damage to the image of your country and given that I don't know any defence of [torture], I don't think with respect that it turned out to be petty or was petty [...] in all of these areas, one is too many.

But, for the most part, the deposed monarch is given a good deal of space in which to explain himself and rationalise the excesses of his regime, and there is little of the focused questioning that characterises the best of the Nixon tapes.

Birt and Frost, though they maintained – indeed, enhanced – their professional relationship in the years ahead, never worked together in this context again. "David certainly found it challenging," remembers Libby Reeves Purdie, "to deal with a man, to interview a man, who was dying in front of his eyes."[340] And there were further sources of strain: Reeves Purdie describes one electrifying moment when Zelnick, having made his standard evening call to ABC in New York, returned to the hotel dining room to announce that the head of the Panamanian military government, Omar Torrijos, had just done a deal with the new revolutionary government in Iran to despatch the shah back to Iran, and that Frost and his team needed to make plans to leave the country immediately. The deal never materialised, and Frost remained in Panama, but this underlines a sense of the fraught context within which he was working.

His own last words on his experiences of the shah tend to pan back, and look at a larger political and historical canvas:

What the last two years of [the shah's] reign seemed to prove was that an autocracy, as it ages, is a dangerous and sensitive instrument, slow and erratic in its responses, unfeeling in its nerve endings, and – finally – the victim of its own hubris. Whatever your judgement about the rights and wrongs of the Pahlavi dynasty, it was not possible to leave the island of Contadora without a Shakespearean sense of the fall of kings – and of life's ironies. It was, after all, Richard Nixon's visit to Iran in 1972 that had triggered off one of his periodic outbursts about the relatively straitened circumstances of the leader of the western world, when compared with those of a hereditary monarch such as the shah. After my visit to Contadora, I suspected that Nixon – like most of us – would no longer have any desire to change places.[341]

There were other changes too in the wake of Nixon, most particularly on the personal front. In 1979, after five years together, Frost and Caroline Cushing decided to go their separate ways. It had been the most substantial relationship of Frost's life: mutually enriching and fulfilling – and stabilising amid the frenzy of his itinerary. "I can pack in two seconds flat," she had told *People* magazine in May 1977, describing the success of their relationship at the height of the Nixon frenzy; and, "I love him and we are very happy together."[342] At the end of Nixon interviews, however, Cushing had opted to remain in California, where she gathered together once more the threads of her career. She and Frost kept things going – for a while. But ultimately the long-distance connection failed, and Frost was not now, and had never been, willing to relinquish his main British base. And there were other reasons too. "I want to get married," Frost told Joan Bakewell in these years, "and I want to have sons."[343] But Cushing already had sons and wanted no more children, and some circumstances could not be negotiated to the satisfaction of all. "I don't think marriage is the ultimate thing," Cushing had told *People*, and this proved to be the case, at least in terms of this particular relationship. David Frost *would* marry and *would* have sons, but not before the passage of a deeply painful episode in his life.

But Cushing and Frost would remain friends. They continued to meet in London during her frequent visits to Britain, and to pool information as her new career, first at Condé Nast and then in public relations, developed; and Frost continued to send Cushing's mother an ever-larger bouquet of tulips for her birthday each year.

"I could never understand this incessant travel," Cushing says. 'Why don't you stay at home,' I'd say, 'and have people come to you?' And he would look at me. 'What? Oh, no,' he'd say, 'I have to go, I have to.' Could we have settled down? No. I think perhaps we knew too much about each other."

CHAPTER 6

Tabula Rasa

"The truth is that [David Frost] is such a pioneer inhabitant of the shadowlands, the tricky terrain that separates show business and life, appearance and reality, that no slippage or seepage is discernible."

Observer

n January 1981, and after two broken engagements, David Frost married. His bride was Lynne Frederick, a twenty-six-year-old London-born actress with clear, delicate good looks. Frederick had notched up a number of films and television appearances in the course of the 1970s. By decade's end, however, she was best known as having been the fourth and final wife of the *Pink Panther* star Peter Sellers. The two had met in March 1976 and married the following February in Paris. She was "a wild young thing [...] and ambitious," notes Ed Sikov in his biography of Sellers. But other observers are more nuanced in their assessment of this young woman.[344] Sellers was, after all, a profoundly troubled figure, obsessive in his habits, deeply demanding of his friends and lovers, and with – for good measure – a drug habit that exacerbated long-standing health problems. Frederick was perhaps out of her depth in her relationship with him, and as the future of her life would demonstrate all too amply, she was herself troubled and unstable. Within three years, her marriage to Sellers was disintegrating. He died in July 1980, before the divorce was finalised and before he had a chance to alter his will to remove any legacy from his wife. The result was that Frederick inherited his substantial estate by the skin of her teeth.

panding family: Carina, Miles and David Frost with baby Wilfred, 1985, outside the Lindo Wing at St Mary's
spital in London.

the garden at Carlyle Square: David, Miles, Wilfred and Carina Frost, with Norland nannies Ruth Smith (l) and
eanor Dawson (r), 1985.

Special White House talks between Miles Frost and President George H.W. Bush (David Frost as special adviser), 19

'Mr Frost, you must be bonkers!': David Frost questions a tetchy Margaret Thatcher on the sinking of the Belgrano, 1985.

Royal appointment: David Frost and Elton John at a party hosted by The Duke of York at Windsor, c.1988.

avid Frost in the Oval Office with Ronald Reagan – the effects of whose Alzheimer's was clearly visible on the day Frost and crew, 1987.

Family Frost, now complete: Carina, Wilfred, David and Miles Frost with baby George, 1987, outside the Lindo Wing at St Mary's Hospital in London.

Proud godparents: Ronnie Corbett, the Princess of Wales, Jean Pearson and the Duchess of Norfolk at the baptism of George Frost, All Saints, Chelsea, 1987.

godmother and godson: the Princess of Wales and baby George Frost, 1987.

David and George Frost in the nursery at Michelmersh Court, the Frosts' country home, 1988.

David, Wilfred, George and Miles Frost building sandcastles on the beach in Sardinia: the family were guests of Mara and Lorenzo Berni, 1989.

David Frost amid typically chaotic office scenes at TV-AM, c.1985.

Dartith –

Welcome Back to the Oval Office.
With Regards

Gy Bush.

4-16-91

ooting the breeze in the Oval Office: David Frost and President George H.W. Bush, 1992.

What a duo we would have made!
Happy Birthday, Dave × Paul.

'What a duo we would have made!'
David Frost interviewed Paul
McCartney many times between
1964 and 2012.

'Arise, Sir David': the Frost family at Buckingham Palace, 1993.

Allowed to stay up late: the Frost family celebrate David Frost's 55th birthday at Michelmersh, 1994.

At the time of his wedding, David Frost was forty-one years old. In a sign of the interest the media had in this relationship, the newspapers had reported that he and Frederick planned a Christmas wedding in Whitby, where he and Mona Frost had gone as usual to spend a brief holiday with his sister Margaret and her family. "There had been rumours," recalls Margaret Frost, "and the press gathered in some force, and began questioning the stewards at our own church, and focusing cameras on the windows of our house, and a report emerged that he had been seen standing in the kitchen window and drying saucepans. Drying saucepans, of course, was a thing David never did – and besides, they were never going to get married here in the first place."[345]

Michael Rosenberg recalls Frederick in those days as being "fun, jolly, lively, outgoing" and the courtship was pleasant enough, if sometimes not quite plain sailing. Rosenberg recalls a day spent on business outside London, and then an evening dining and drinking a little too much before climbing into Frost's car – Rosenberg and his wife with Frost and Frederick – to return to the city.

We drove down in his big posh car. He was going to open a nursing home I controlled in Surrey; and of course he was the world's worst driver – first fast and then slow and all over the road; and a glass of cheap red, and off we went. Lynne said, "Be careful, be careful, the police patrol this section of the road." Soon enough, we were pulled over by a patrol car. David decided to query whether the police had a right to ask him to take a breathalyser test. Reinforcements arrived. They said, "Come on, sir, just do it." And David said, "I'm not refusing to do this, I'm just asking whether you have a right to ask me." So he took the phone from his car – he was one of the few people at this point who had a car phone – and rang his solicitor, and it ended up with the women driving the car back to London, and us men marched off to Woking police station, where David was indeed arrested for refusing the breathalyser. He kept on repeating that he wasn't refusing to take the breathalyser, he was merely query-

ing whether they had the right to ask him. He kept repeating his
over and over. He was playing for time, of course. In an hour or
so, the wine would have vanished from his system. Finally, the
police car took us to Woking railway station and off we went to
Waterloo, and the following morning it was all over the press.
The police spent a lot of time trying to incriminate us for using
drink and drugs. And sure enough, there was evidence of sleep-
ing tablets in his system. So it went to court, and David was
found guilty of failing to take the test. "I plead guilty of failing to
take the test," he said, "but the levels of alcohol were equivalent
to a wine gum." Which captured the headlines, and captures his
cleverness too. He knew how to control the story.[346]

Rosenberg was Frost's best man when he married Frederick, on
January 21st, 1981 – not at Whitby, but near his Suffolk cottage
at Beccles, not far from Mona Frost's home on Ellough Road.
Frederick was by this time estranged from her family. Her mother
had been appalled by her marriage to Sellers, and the relationship
had never recovered. She was given away instead by Marcus Sieff, at
that time chairman of Marks and Spencer and a close friend of both
Frost and Rosenberg. The latter recalls turning to Sieff just as the
wedding got under way and murmuring, "What are we doing here,
two Jewish boys as good as officiating at a non-Jewish wedding?"
And later, Sieff had a running gag that he was setting up a company
to be called Rosenberg and Sieff, available for non-Jewish weddings.

The courtship between David Frost and Lynne Frederick had
been brief, and had followed rapidly on the back of Sellers' death,
but according to Sikov, there was at least an element of context.
Frost and Frederick had had a brief affair in the mid-1970s, before
Frederick married Sellers. But a distinct air of claustrophobia clung
to the situation and that underscored the relative smallness of the
circles within which Frost moved. This brings to mind the fact
that Sellers had had a discreet relationship with Janette Scott just
before she met Frost in 1963; and now, here was Frost marrying
Sellers' widow, and with what must have seemed like surprising

and incomprehensible haste. Frederick had, however, kept tabs on Frost and his life throughout the course of her marriage to Sellers. She had taken pains to maintain a connection with Lulu Carmo and with Libby Reeves Purdie, both of whom were uncomfortably aware of Frederick's consistent gaze upon Frost and his household. "She was absolutely not my favourite person," Reeves Purdie remarks.[347] And now, as Frederick asserted herself in Frost's life, Reeves Purdie moved to end her employment with Frost. "It wasn't precisely because of Lynne," she says. "It was time I moved on in any case. But Lynne's presence certainly didn't help."[348]

Frost's circle of female friends had always tended to look at Frederick rather narrowly. Joanna Lumley remembers that, "I heard that he was going to marry Lynne, and I thought, *That's not great, that will never work, that's a terrible idea.* Lynne was extremely pretty and she had a way with her, she had what they used in the old days to call *it*. Men would tumble at her feet: clever men, men like David, who knew their way around the world, but who would fall for an extreme woman. I suppose the courtship was fun, but the marriage certainly wasn't."[349]

And for Reeves Purdie, the reasons behind the marriage were perfectly clear: "Because David himself was a real gentleman, I think he responded to the horror stories she told him about her time with Sellers. He saw himself as her knight on a charger, coming to save her from the bullies. She simply bowled him over. The veneer wore off, very rapidly indeed, and when it began to go wrong, it was terrible for David. He was quite old-fashioned, he saw a marriage as being for life, and I think he found it difficult to accept that he had made the most enormous mistake."

And indeed, the marriage did very rapidly go wrong. Caroline Cushing, who in her years with Frost had become friendly with Lulu Carmo, recalls hearing tales of a "monstrous" Frederick stalking a now benighted house at Egerton Crescent. "I remember seeing her at Nice airport when David and I were going out, and David went over to talk to her, and I suppose I was a little jealous, and I said, 'What are you talking to her for?' And I think David married her because now he wanted at that point to settle down and have children, and that was that."[350] The relationship soon ran its ill-starred course. Frost and Frederick divorced in July 1982, after seventeen months of marriage. Following the divorce, Lynne Frederick moved to Los Angeles, married and had a child. She died of alcohol and drug abuse in 1994.

The marriage, then, had been a jarring aberration. Lynne was attractive but she was also manifestly troubled. "I never understood how David got so far into that relationship," recalls Victor Blank, who at this time was moving from being a business contact to being a friend. "Attractive and all as she was, the marriage seemed to show an extraordinary lack of judgement. But he never talked about it to me."[351] Or to many other people. Janette Scott recalls that during phone conversations with Frost at this turbulent time, "he always steered the conversation away from her and their life and on to other things. Of course I thought it odd at the time, but after a while I began to hear that all was not well; and then it seemed a little less odd."[352] Some had simply kept their fingers crossed. "Lynne seemed fine," remembers Michael Rosenberg, "although of course one never knows what lies behind the eyes."[353] In any case, it was at such junctures that Frost's tendency to personal discretion and a form of self-defence came through most clearly. He disliked talking about his personal situations, even if these situations might have benefitted from the ballast and support that frank or healing conversation might bring. His personal issues could, generally speaking, not be dragged out of him, even by his small circle of very close friends.

*

And it was at this critical juncture that another woman moved into Frost's life. He had been stepping out with the television newsreader Selina Scott, as Victor Blank recalls: "He had been out with Selina twice, and was wondering whether he should take her out for the third and crucial time, or should he ask Carina out instead. And in the end, he opted for Carina. A great decision."[354] This was Lady

Carina Fitzalan Howard, the second daughter of the seventeenth Duke of Norfolk, and a member, therefore, of one of Britain's foremost aristocratic families. The Fitzalan Howards were also the most prominent of Britain's recusant Catholic families. They had succeeded in the centuries since the Reformation in maintaining their wealth and their lands in the south of England and Yorkshire. The family seat is at Arundel Castle in Sussex. They, then, held a distinctive place in the social and historic fabric of Britain, and Carina was distinctive too: a tall, slim, athletic figure with striking good looks; strong-willed and with a mind of her own.

This was a turning point – *the* pivotal moment – in the life of David Frost. His friend Peter Chadlington notes, "All those relationships which punctuated his personal life in his middle years, were a search to establish what he really knew he valued: a home with a family which shared the values that his parents had given him and that he held most dear. Finding Carina was the most important thing that happened in his life. It opened the door to what he would regard as his most important achievement – a wife, a home, three marvellous children – all of whom are, like him, ambitious, fun, extrovert and essentially good people."[355] Nor, in these early days, was Carina even much of a stranger. Frost had in fact known her for some years. They met regularly on the social circuit, and they had always got along very nicely. They were both entertaining company and they had both lived a little, for while Frost was tearing from Britain to America and Australia, bouncing from one studio to another, Carina had been following a life of her own.

Lady Carina Fitzalan Howard was born in February 1952. Her childhood had been colourful and profoundly peripatetic: her father had been an army general and the family had from time to time joined his tours of duty abroad. At the age of five, Carina went to live in Berlin and later Munich. At the age of nine, she and her family moved to Kenya where they lived until that colony gained independence from Britain two years later. The family's British base, in the spaces between these tours of duty, was at Carlton, an extravagantly Victorian-Gothic country house outside Selby in North Yorkshire.

Carina went on to attend convent school at Woldingham in Surrey. She then spent time after school studying art and learning Italian in Florence, and then there were additional years spent modelling in New York, with weekends in the Hamptons and with distant relations in Baltimore, as well as much time on the Caribbean island of Barbados, with her lover Noel Charles.

At length, however, Carina's relationship to Charles came to an end, and she returned to Britain, and there she began regularly to meet Frost on the London party circuit. At one south London dinner, for example, she was placed between him and John Cleese: "All I remember is that [Cleese] did not say a word; he was going through a moment and was impossible to talk to. And on the other side, David was hilarious; he was so much fun, we always got on so well. And I confess I was amazed that he didn't call me the next day, because men always called me; and eventually I just got on with my life. 'Ah, but I always had a plan!' David said to me."[356] Eventually, in 1982, the relationship clicked. Frost was in the midst of his separation from Frederick. He had flown into London from Los Angeles, and that evening went along to a drinks party a few doors along from his own house on Egerton Crescent. Carina was at that time living in her own house on Christchurch Street off the King's Road. On this particular evening, she "walked into the room – and it was just different, and I fell in love. And I had never before fallen madly in love with someone who was a friend. It was extraordinary, because we had always really liked one another, so these sensations took a little getting used to."[357]

The couple kept these early months of their relationship discreet, which was not especially straightforward. Newspaper photographers were still in the habit of following Frost, and it took a certain ingenuity to keep them off the scent:

> I told some female friends, I told my brother. Everyone was startled because I had been considered completely, irredeemably on the shelf. Otherwise, we kept the relationship secret for months. Just before Christmas 1982, David suggested we go to

New York. It was to be my first ever trip on Concorde. I knew the slightly wacky, fag-hag New York from my modelling days, but David promised to show me another side to the city – a rich and rare New York. But on the morning of the trip, I woke up in my lovely little house on Christchurch Street, feeling violently sick. I rang my brother, Edward, I said, "What will I do? I keep being sick." And he said, "For God's sake, if David can't handle you being sick, then he isn't the man for you." So I got ready. I was sick on the way to the airport, and sick at the airport, and I was sick on the plane too. But we had a lovely time in New York when we got there.[358]

Very rapidly in this new relationship, both parties began probing the other regarding the future. David Frost had never enjoyed the sensation of wasting time – this was one of the great rules of his life – and now, in this new situation, there was a degree of urgency, and no more time to waste. For Carina, now thirty-one years old, there were no ambiguities. She wanted to marry Frost and she wanted to have children ("I was too selfish before"), and for the forty-three-year-old Frost, surveying the wreckage of his recent first marriage, children and a stable marriage remained his wish too.[359] Frost proposed to Carina in early March 1983, and the couple were married eleven days later, on March 19th, at a ceremony at Chelsea Register Office. "I was able to walk from Christchurch Street," remembers Carina, "along to the register office. I wore a copy of a 'Carina' dress in cream, designed by Ossie Clarke; my sister Tessa had it run up for me in ten days. It was so quick, it was so exciting, it was fabulous; with three nieces and a goddaughter as bridesmaids; a Catholic blessing in Notting Hill; and then a lunch at Les Ambassadeurs on Park Lane."[360]

Michael Parkinson was Frost's best man that day ("Carina's father, the old duke, had it in his head that I was the fellow who cut the hedges on his estate; and he was staring at me when I gave my speech, as if to say: *What's this chap doing here? What the hell's going on?*"[361]). It was Michael Deakin's task, meanwhile, to shepherd Mona Frost through the day. "When we got to Notting Hill and the ceremony – which was a Catholic marriage in all but name, such was the clout of the Fitzalan Howards – was over, I could see that Mrs Frost was clearly not at home in a Catholic church, but she had a £5 note in her hand to place in the poor box, and after the ceremony, we set off around the church looking for the appropriate box into which to pop this fiver. Eventually, we came to a slot in the wall, and a notice: 'For The Little Souls In Torment'. Mrs Frost took in this notice and said, 'But if I put it in there, how do we guarantee that these souls will get the money?' I couldn't very well provide the sort of guarantee she was after – 'I really don't know, Mrs Frost,' – and eventually she shrugged and put her money into the slot; and that was that."[362]

The newly married couple honeymooned in a crisp, clear-skied Venice, staying at the luxurious Cipriani hotel, which faces St Mark's Square across the mouth of the Grand Canal. Never one for walking a single inch more than was necessary, Frost declined to spend any time sightseeing. The honeymoon was spent instead eating and drinking in a succession of gourmet restaurants, and grazing their way through the remainder of the day. It was the beginning of a marriage that would last for the remainder of David Frost's life.

He was, says Annabel Goldsmith, "very lucky to meet Carina. She was his salvation. The moment he got together with Carina, he began to change, and to soften up. That toughness began to slough off in favour of something softer; he kept the wit, but began to become a family man. And Carina played an enormous part in that change in his life."[363] Goldsmith recalls too an episode that for her encapsulated Carina's personality:

Before they married, I invited Carina to [Goldsmith's Richmond home at] Ormeley and she has never forgotten the drama of that Sunday. All my six children were there and Carina, though too well-mannered to comment, was clearly surprised at the speed with which lunch was devoured. My entire family has always eaten much too fast, but none of us were ever a match for Jimmy, whose habit was to retire to the study for coffee when most of his guests were still enjoying their main course. On this particular Sunday, having wolfed down lunch, David and Jimmy retired with the rest of his group to the study and Carina and I went upstairs. Admiring the garden from my bedroom window, she said, suddenly, "Annabel, do you realise there are two horses careering around your lawn?"' And I instantly knew, to my horror, that they must have escaped from the stable. Followed by [Annabel Goldsmith's son] Rupert, Carina flew into the garden, and the next thing I knew she and Rupert had caught the horses and put them back in the stable. My knee was in plaster at the time and I hobbled down to thank her for her skill in handling the two animals; it wasn't the first time they had escaped, and I knew how difficult it was to coax them back. I imagined Carina must have been something of an accomplished horsewoman and was amazed when she admitted that she had never had anything to do with horses in her entire life. I was awed by the dexterity she had shown, and it was then that our deep friendship began.[364]

Certain enduring tropes of this marriage would now be established, and these had much to do with Carina Frost's instinctive sense of how best to handle both her new husband and his lifestyle and work. In some areas, there were few if any challenges to address: her own background and social confidence, for example, ensured that she would certainly not be intimidated or overawed by any of the circles in which Frost moved. And in addition to this, she brought as an invaluable part of her trousseau an insight into the nature of her new husband and of their evolving marriage:

I knew that David had never had been short of girlfriends, of course, and I could not be bothered with any of them – except Diahann Carroll, whom I adored. We really got each other. I knew that she and David had really understood one another, both their lives had been so complicated, both were stars; and so of course I could see how it would never have worked between then – because when *we* married, I had to become second-best, and look after him, which I did willingly. That was part of the deal. [...] I think I was his salvation, but he was my salvation too. We gave each other different things, and it all came together. But we both understood that you can't have two stars in a marriage. I understood the need to stay in the background, to be comfortable in my own skin, to be willing and able to carry an ego. To be the woman behind the man, essentially: this was the role I wanted and understood.[365]

And it was well that Carina willingly occupied such a role in her marriage, for she was marrying a man who, for all his virtues, was not the easiest housemate. Frost remained thoroughly spoilt, for just as Mona Frost had handed her son over to the domestic staff at Caius, and – after the briefest hiatus – onwards to Luisa Carmo, so now Carmo was handing him over to Carina, and it was now she who was charged with organising his wardrobe and seeing to his nutritional and wider domestic needs. Because Frost was essentially institutionalised in these terms, these needs had to continue seamlessly. This was a job Carina was willing to oversee.

But there were aspects to her new husband's life that she was determined to influence and remake. In particular, she began to dispense with many of what she considered the hangers-on who crowded his days. "David could never bear to feel he was being nannied," remarks Carina, "so he had to be *managed*. I boiled it down to a small team. We answered our own front door – which David would very often leave wide open, by the way, so I had to be on red alert at all times – and we worked as a team." And she ran the tightest ship, curbing his excessive expenditure where she could.[366] This process of boiling-down meant that that space was now opened up between Frost and many of his oldest friends and associates. "It was rather painful," notes Michael Deakin, who was one of the friends on this list. "I think that [Carina] thought that this network was fluffy and frivolous and didn't amount to much, that we were in it for the ridiculous Christmas presents that David would despatch each year from Asprey's. But what it in fact meant

was that quite an elaborate social and professional support structure was altered. I continued to see him for lunch every six weeks
or so, but the context was now quite different."[367]

For the remainder of their married life, Carina Frost would
manage her husband with the support of a smaller circle: her own
female friends; Frost's personal assistants and drivers; and such
pivotal figures as Michael Rosenberg, who continued to manage
Frost's business affairs. In many ways, therefore, Carina adapted
her new systems to fit the model that had existed previously. Frost
had never been one for large organisations, preferring to distil his
own systems down to a small number of trusted individuals who
knew his habits and worked the way he needed them to work.

Twenty years after their marriage, the same systems were operating. Reeves Purdie had been replaced by the American Tricia
Pombo, who became Frost's faithful secretary for fourteen years,
and she – and later still an efficient young Englishwoman named
Miranda Gallimore – came rapidly to understand the lie of the land:

> I was employed at first on a trial period. [Frost] worried I was too
> young and so did Lady C, and they both obviously worried that
> I would be off after a couple of months and were also concerned
> that I had never been a secretary before. So, my first job was to
> convince a very protective Lady C. that I wanted a routine, and
> that I wouldn't be going anywhere. I wanted them to see that I
> was a bit of a nerd and not a bit flighty, and I saw at once that I
> had to pass a test with her as well as with him. Which I thought
> was fair: in a job like that, you spend so much time with your
> boss's family as well as with your boss, so it needs to work for
> everyone. And I understood the particular culture of a family
> business, so I knew how critical this element actually was, and I
> was able to convey this to Lady C. It's essentially a *personal* posi-
> tion, and I understood this, and they were a good family to work
> with, and generous and kind to me.[368]

*

Gallimore was now in a position to observe, as Joan Pugh and Libby Reeves Purdie had observed before her, the personality and unchanging habits of her boss: his workaholic personality; his tendency to micromanage, even down to proofreading each and every letter she typed in his name; his burst of energy not in the morning, as in most work environments, but in the afternoons and evenings; his preference for small, trusted teams; his inability to master new technology, and unwillingness to try. She noted too his generally benign view of everyone who crossed his path, although there were occasional exceptions, as when the galley copy of a new biography of Nina Simone arrived at the office with the request that Frost supply a sales blurb. "He kept putting off writing the blurb, putting it off and putting it off, for weeks and weeks. I had to keep badgering him: and finally, he said, 'Oh, very well, bring the pad in.' And I said, 'But why can't you just say something, say anything?' And he said, 'The problem is, I can't think of a single nice thing to say about her. She was a thoroughly foul person to work with.' And I said, 'Well then, say something about her musical talents.' And he said, 'I suppose I shall have to, but everyone else will say the same thing.' I still like her music – but now when I hear it, I think, 'Oh dear, you must have been very bad, Nina, for David Frost to dislike you.'"[369]

Gallimore remembers that "he wanted to spend all his time working" and, similarly, Graeme Wilson, his final chauffeur (Frost nicknamed him Fangio, after the Argentine Formula One racing star), was in a position to observe that the now much older Frost maintained the same habits – of work and of play – as his younger counterpart had done.[370] Work remained "his hobby: he loved his weekends in the country, he loved his times with his family, it was clear to me – to everyone – that he regarded his children as the great achievement of his life. But he needed to work. It was every-thing, and I got used to him sitting in the back of the car writing and writing with his big black felt-tip pen across the back of his piles of manila folders."

Wilson also observed his adoration of Carina, and his willed inability to cook or in any way fend for himself without her. When his wife was out of town, Frost's greatest dilemma was whether to repair to the nearest restaurant, or go to the local Tesco to buy a sandwich. He observed Frost's enduring recognition quotient. On driving him to a Centre Court date at Wimbledon, for example, Wilson realised too late that his employer had left his valuable ticket in the car, now parked in hot sunshine a considerable distance from the tennis complex. But: *Don't worry*, he realised, *they'll allow him through anyway, ticket or no ticket.*[371] He observed Frost's love of performing – even if it was, in this case, inside a car to an audience of one, to Wilson himself: of telling him elaborate jokes that culminated in a nicely delivered punchline. And – in a touching glimpse of the man – he recalls the pleasure Frost took in his splendidly big cars, on one occasion, sitting in the back of the car with the diminutive Ronnie Corbett – whose feet barely touched the floor of the car – and exclaiming delightedly at the plentiful leg room that was available to them.

*

We based ourselves in America for a little while. David had a house in the Hollywood Hills with a pool. But I couldn't wait to get home – after three months, it was time for me to go. Thereafter I stayed at home. When he was working in New York, it was a part of his contract that he would come home every week on Concorde – as it was in those days – because I wanted to bring the boys up in England.[372]

In the weeks that followed their marriage, Carina Frost's first objective was to move house. Frost had lived in his highly desirable property on Egerton Crescent now for close on twenty years, but the property held disagreeable associations for his new wife, not least among them the memory of a host of ex-girlfriends and of an energetically bachelor lifestyle, in addition to which, Lynne Frederick had made the house over from top to toe. It was of paramount importance, therefore, to begin their married life anew and elsewhere, and after a good deal of hunting, offers made and withdrawn and disappointments in the Chelsea area, Carina fixed on her quarry. But it would involve a degree of strategising on her part to bring Frost to the auctioneer's offices. He was profoundly uninterested in the whole process, and it took Carina's hint that they might lose the house to another bidder that brought him there:

> Even though he was the most generous man I have ever met, he was tough on me financially at the beginning of our marriage. I had the sense that Lynne [Frederick] had managed to get through a lot during their relationship. I remember I had lunch with David and [Frost's lawyer] John Stutter at Claridge's just before the auction, and David said he wasn't going to come to the auction, and his lawyer would do the bidding, but I knew and John knew that David *had* to be there, that he hated to lose, and that we would only get the house if he *was* there, if he was determined to win the bid. I thought to myself, I have to get him to buy it, or we'll regret it for the rest of our lives. And so he came, and we bid against a rich divorcee with pots of money behind her, and in the end, we got the house, and we got it because David was there.[373]

Their new home was an imposing and elegant Victorian property at 22, Carlyle Square, on the north side of the King's Road. The elongated rectangle of the large gardens at the centre of the square formed a splendid prospect from the main, south-facing rooms of the house, while the square itself had agreeable connections. Laid out in the 1860s, it had been home to the actress Sybil Thorndike and the Irish writer Edna O'Brien, as well as the scandalous figure of the Cambridge spy Kim Philby. The house was in a sorry state at first. The renewal process was overseen by Carina, Frost himself having scant interest in such matters. The Frosts, having sold Egerton Crescent, rented while the new home was being renovated, and on the day they were to move in, Carina's first pregnancy was confirmed. "It was God's gift: the doctor called at 11am while I was surrounded by boxes and papers, and Lulu [Luisa Carmo] came up and said, 'Lady Carina, Lady Carina!' and after I spoke to the doctor, I telephoned David, and he came rushing back. We both wanted sons, a whole football team worth of them – and we got them."[374]

Their first son was born at the private Lindo Wing of St Mary's Hospital in London on June 2nd, 1984, and was named Miles, for his maternal grandfather. A few days after Miles was born, Diahann Carroll arrived at the hospital, bearing the gift of a khaki baby-sized Burberry mac. Carroll had been asked by Frost to come to London, as she understood at the time, to close the circle of their former relationship:

> I received an invitation from David to fly to London. It felt important for both of us for me to see this child, and to acknowledge that it was a thing that we had missed; and Carina was kind enough, and secure enough in herself, for this to happen. And it was lovely to be there and to see this child, and I was so happy I was there, and of course then I withdrew, because this was Carina's moment.[375]

This was the beginning of a close, touching connection between Diahann Carroll and Lady Carina Frost. And two more sons would follow for the Frosts in the course of the next three years: Wilfred, on August 7th, 1985, and named for Frost's father; and George, on April 22nd, 1987 ("The idea was to name me Gerald, for my mother's brother: but it turned out that nobody much liked the name, so they settled on George instead."[376]). And with the birth of George, Diahann Carroll reappeared, now bearing three new Burberry macs.

David and Carina Frost enjoyed a whirling social life, but for Carina, her life with the children dominated her daily routine: "I loved it. I could never wait to see my boys. I remember that one day, my dear friend Alan Russell stopped me, and he said, 'Oh, do you always drive around listening to Postman Pat, I mean, even when the boys aren't there?'; and there I was, I was driving around London completely batty. But this is what I was born for, to have onttht:

these children and to be David's wife."[377] And Carina also found an ally in Mona Frost, who was a frequent visitor to Carlyle Square, and who quickly formed a bond with her only son's new wife.

With David Frost gregarious and Carina Frost an apt and willing hostess, the house at Carlyle Square soon became a centre of hospitality. The dinner-party book maintained by Carina tells a tale of film stars, politicians, princes and presidents gathering in the house for convivial meals. Joanna Lumley recalls that there were "two tables, one in the dining room and one in the kitchen; a visiting prince or a prime minister would always be placed in the kitchen, with either Carina or David presiding. Each table very grand, there would always be some big beast or other sweeping in, but everyone was equal. I don't remember that we ever talked about serious things; instead, we skipped around. But I do remember David's kindness: he was sensitive to the fact that someone might feel excluded from this or that conversation; he would never dwell on a conversation if he did not have the inside track; instead, we would be moved on sharpish."[378]

Elton John remembers that "David and Carina never ever failed to put a bunch of people together who got on with each other: this potpourri of writers and actors and politicians and princes".[379] And Victor Blank recalls an evening at Carlyle Square, in which "[Prime Minister] John Major arrived: he slipped upstairs to read a bedtime story to the boys before coming down and having dinner. They were very comfortable, companionable evenings", evenings that ran according to "Carlyle Square rules", in which a sense of mutual discretion engendered an atmosphere of trust.[380]

The Duke of York recalls an occasion late in 1985 which sowed the seed of friendship: "David had just interviewed me in connection with a book on photography I had published, and then he asked me to lunch at Carlyle Square just before Christmas, and my then girlfriend, Sarah Ferguson, said, 'But hasn't he asked me too? Well, I'm going to ask Carina myself!' And so, let's just say that that lunch carried on well into the evening, and after that, our Christmas lunches became a tradition we've maintained, in fact, up to the present day. They mean a great deal to us. Then, a few months later, David and Carina invited us to a weekend party at Arundel. Sarah and I were already engaged, but we hadn't made this news public yet. David and Carina were the only ones in the Arundel party to be in on the secret, and the editor of the *Sunday Times*, Andrew Neil, was there too – and not a word was breathed until the engagement was announced. It was a very natural, trusting friendship. A classic friendship: no sides, no requirements."[381]

For the-then Sarah Ferguson, that Christmas lunch was in fact a means of catching up with an old friend. "I said to [Prince] Andrew: 'But I do know them! I've known Frostie for a very long time!' So I rang Carina up, and I said, 'Please may I come too?' And Carina thought it was hilarious. I brought her hyacinths: then, since neither she nor Andrew drank, Frostie and I proceeded to drink the lunch away. Goodness knows why Andrew asked me to marry him after seeing that! And it has been a lovely Christmas tradition to continue in all the years since then; and I always bring Carina hyacinths. She is one of the most enthusiastic, one of the most kind and most loyal people I know. She always tells it exactly as it is, regardless of who you are. And I admire that about her most of all."[382]

Six months after that Christmas lunch, Sarah Ferguson became the Duchess of York; and the friendship with the Frosts was sustained – throughout the course of her marriage to Prince Andrew, and then in the aftermath of the couple's divorce. At this juncture, indeed, the friendship was underlined: "They never left my side, even at rocky moments; they always supported me, rather than move away from me, and I was so grateful for that. If you were their friend, then you stayed their friend: that was the rule. After [the Yorks'] divorce, David and Carina saw that we remained a loving family unit, and that was the most important thing for them; they knew there was simple no need to judge, and they never did."[383]

Frost would in due course support the Duchess in professional terms too, by means of offering advice and support on her nascent television career in the United States. "Frostie was my mentor. He was the man who guided me through every aspect of my television work: how to behave in front of a camera, how best to do everything. I remember sitting with him on Concorde, and getting lessons and tips and good practical advice. I owe so much to him. And I remember most of all, that he had the ability to deliver advice in such a way as give me the confidence to think I *could* do it."[384]

The house at Carlyle Square was in due course fully restored, and Carina turned her attention to the garden, which rapidly became a source of pleasure and creativity amid a busy London life. She caused the space to be landscaped on two levels, and, when George was two years old, she threw a party to show the garden off to close friends. The boys, in matching pyjamas, circulated offering bowls of peanuts, and this was the origin of the annual Frost summer party, held around Wimbledon time at the beginning of July each year, and soon a fixture on the London social calendar. The boys' costumes remained. "When we were young," Wilfred told the *Sunday Times*, "Mum liked dressing us up in horrendous matching outfits, probably until too late an age – twenty-two or something."[385]

Within a few years, the party switched to the central gardens at Carlyle Square to cater to its increasing size, and social desirability: it became a mark of status to secure an invitation to the Frost summer party; and the presence of bouncers and security guards at the event was mute testimony to the status of very many of the guests. "Eventually," recalls Joanna Lumley, "they had to have security men on the roofs, and once you got in through the security cordon, you would know the name of everyone there because they were so famous. Of course there must have been masses of people there who simply hated each other – but it never showed: opera singers and cricketers and prime ministers – and David in the middle of it, the man of the people, and people sensed it. It was in a sense quite frightening. It felt like a children's tea party, except we were the children in the middle being looked at, with the photographers outside doing the looking."[386]

In later years, it was Miranda Gallimore's job to maintain the guest list – Carina Frost would strike names off the list, David Frost would follow behind and add them again – and to stand guard over the list on the day of the party itself. "The way the guests conducted themselves at the gate was the judge of them," Gallimore recalls. "Certain people who shall remain nameless would sail past and never even look at me, much less pause to let me tick their name off the list, but others would show their class. Michael Palin would come over to me and say, 'Hello, it's Palin, with a Pah.' Billy Connolly would always thank me on the way out. Margaret Thatcher would say, 'Perhaps my name is on the list? It's Lady Thatcher.' Frank Langella came one year, before *Frost/Nixon* was released. I didn't recognise him, but thought he might be someone big at the BBC and so I decided I should suck up to him, hoping Paradine might get something commissioned. And so I practically linked arms with him and said, 'I think your host is over there; let's go and find him,' and I ushered him into the crowd – and later, [Frost] said, 'Oh, Frank Langella said you were so awfully friendly!' – and I was mortified because I got it so wrong."[387] And while it was not quite the done thing, given the circumstances, for guests to ask other guests for autographs, there was certainly a good deal of ill-disguised gawking going on for the duration of the party.

The summer parties at Carlyle Square would continue for the duration of the quarter-century that the Frosts lived in the house, the guest list changing with the years, as the political complexion of the country changed and changed again. By the mid-1990s, with a Labour government now in sight after sixteen years of Conservative rule, Tony Blair's press spokesman Alastair Campbell could record: "Wednesday 5 July, 1995. David Frost's summer party. Huge mix of political figures, media, business, lots of Frost interviewees. I asked David English [editor of the traditionally Conservative *Daily Mail*] if the *Mail* had ever considered backing Labour. Loud enough for lots of people to hear, he said, 'There's always a first time.' Peter [Mandelson, then the Labour spin doctor] working his way around. Imran Khan and Jemima Goldsmith, Conrad Black, Alan Yentob, of course. He was quite an operator, old Frostie."[388] It is significant, however, that the following summer – with Labour enjoying an even greater lead in the opinion polls and the incumbent Conservative administration exhausted and fractured from incessant infighting – Campbell sniffs, "Tuesday 2 July. We went to David Frost's party at Carlyle Square. There were very few Labour people there […] Loads of Tories."[389]

Campbell's observation highlights a significant element in what by any account continued to be a frenetic Frost life. His interest and absorption in the lives of the famous was sometimes used as a stick with which to beat him, but it is worth noting that he did not particularly distinguish between those who were on the way up, and those plummeting downwards. If anything, indeed, his friends noted an essential native sympathy for the latter category, and a willingness – rare in the deeply cynical media and political circles in which he moved – to be seen fraternising with the unfortunate. Margaret Thatcher, for example, was a visitor to the Frosts for Sunday lunch the week after her sensational ejection from Downing Street in November 1990; and David Owen – a Labour Foreign Secretary in the 1970s and a founder of the Social Democratic Party in the early 1980s – notes that his close friendship with Frost only took off in earnest, "after I stopped being particularly in the public eye." Frost, notes Owen, was the very opposite of a fair-weather friend: he was more likely, indeed, to hove into view when times were tough or personally challenging. "He never forgot people when they were riding low […] he would always be there on the phone, saying, 'Let's have lunch.' He was a true friend."[390]

In particular, the story of David Frost's dealings with the Tory Cabinet minister David Mellor is a useful example of an essential kindness and lack of calculation in his character, and a willingness to befriend when there was little or nothing to be gained from the association. The two met in 1983, at which point the politician was a junior minister and regarded as one to watch on the political front. "I first met him at an event at the Royal Opera House in Covent Garden, at which Princess Diana signed a pledge against drugs, and at which a good many people gathered in support, David among them. The two of us retreated into a corner, decided we'd have lunch, did have lunch, and ended by racking up nine or ten of these lunches a year, every year. There was a reason at that point why David might have wanted to get to know me – I was in politics and then in the Cabinet, but that reason came to an end soon enough."

The reason it came to an end soon enough was because Mellor's mistress, Antonia de Sancha, sold the story of their extra-marital affair to a tabloid newspaper, trimmed luridly by this newspaper with additional – and, as emerged subsequently, entirely false – details of Mellor's various sexual peccadillos. The result was the end of his political career, and a hefty accompanying dose of public humiliation – and in such a context, it might have been in order for Frost to keep his distance. "But he didn't. When I slipped off the greasy poll, David was as much present then as he was before; and I remember that when the Variety Club presented him a with life-time award later that year [1992] at the Dorchester, he asked me to introduce him – and I could see well enough that he was asking me in order to underscore the fact that we remained friends regardless of my private humiliations. He never changed, in other words: and it was really extremely kind of him."[391]

After Frost died, Mellor received a letter of condolence from Miranda Gallimore. The letter was framed and hung in Mellor's downstairs lavatory:

I have been meaning to email to say that my thoughts have been with David since Sir David Frost died. I don't know whether I ever mentioned this before: but I used to love seeing that it was one of the regular Bibendum lunches in the diary with the two Davids, because Sir D would always come back so happy and so full of playful joy, even more than his usual default setting! Once he came out of the lift which was opposite my desk doing his usual two-step shuffle across the floor and singing a show tune. I distinctly remember giggling and saying that if I hadn't known it was a Bibendum lunch with the two Davids that day, I would have guessed – because he just loved them, as I know I won't have been the first person to say.[392]

And the television impressionist Rory Bremner recalls a vignette which adds to this sense of an essential kindness of nature: "I was doing the commentary at one of David's charity cricket matches, and I saw David arrive with David Mellor, and I rubbed my hands and thought: *Oh, I'll have a little fun with this.* And next thing, there was a knock on the door of the commentary box and in comes David and David Mellor's son, and David says, 'Oh, here's little Freddie Mellor, he's a great fan of yours.' He knew of course that I wouldn't take the mick out of Mellor with his son sitting right there beside me. So very kind and generous – a touch of grace which I think was part of his religious side."[393]

*

Early in their marriage, David and Carina Frost had augmented their London home with a second property in the country. The couple had discussed the possibility of acquiring a weekend retreat, and Carina disliked Frost's existing country cottage at Beccles. Lynne Frederick had married from there, it was too far from London, and it was, "so small and so poky, I nearly killed myself half a dozen times on corners and low ceilings, and I also nearly killed a baby or two."[394] At first, the idea had been to take over a ramshackle property on family land at Arundel, but in the autumn of 1986, Carina, now pregnant with George, went down to Hampshire to look at a house in the valley of the river Test.

This was Michelmersh Court, an extraordinarily beautiful late-eighteenth-century property, perfectly symmetrical and with the look of an exquisite doll's house, set in a wide sweep of gardens, meadows and woodland outside Winchester. The house was originally built as the startlingly fine rectory attached to the relatively modest and much older nearby church, and on the chilly morning when Carina arrived to view the house for the first time, she found a fire burning on the hearth in the morning room. The house was, in truth, a good deal larger than the country home Carina had set out to find and certainly it was larger than requirements – but its beauty was bewitching. Several days later, she picked Frost up at the airport, at the conclusion of another foreign trip, and brought him down to look at the house. They bought it shortly afterwards, and Carina began the process of restoration with her own individual style. Both homes would later be featured in *Country Life*, a fact which gave both Carina and David Frost a good deal of pleasure.

Between them, the houses at Michelmersh and Carlyle Square provided the focus of Frost family life for the next quarter-century. Weekends and school holidays were spent in the country, the grounds providing Frost with space to kick a football with his sons as they grew up. The dining-room, meanwhile, and the former schoolroom-turned-kitchen that opened off it provided ample space for entertaining.[395] Commuters at Winchester railway station soon became accustomed to the sight of David Frost early on a Monday morning, pacing the platform restlessly and shrouded in a cloud of cigar smoke as he waited for the train to Waterloo.[396] Michelmersh would become a familiar spot to many. Although it was a good eighty miles from London and therefore not quite conveniently located, it began to host a weekending cross-section of Britain's political, cultural and sporting elite, invited down for a casual Sunday lunch and a game of football afterwards.

Not that David Frost was a countryman at heart – far from it. Michelmersh was surrounded by beautiful grounds and by the splendours of the Hampshire landscape, but Frost had no more feeling for or interest in nature now than he had ever had. "Look at that wisteria!" Victor Blank exclaimed on his first visit to Michelmersh, the mature wisteria a tremendous sheet of blue across the walls of the house. "Where?" replied Frost. And Miles Frost recalls an episode which encapsulates his father's spectacular absence of interest in the natural world:

My Uncle Eddie [Edward, Duke of Norfolk] was giving a talk at Sotheby's on the English partridge, specifically the importance and method of its conservation. Most people there were deeply interested shooting types, avidly taking notes on how best to mirror the remarkable achievements at Arundel on their own estates. The same could not be said of Dad, who had absolutely no interest in country pursuits. He was there purely to support Eddie, who was passionate on this topic. Despite his best efforts, Dad frequently nodded off, and was somewhat relieved when it ended. We had a drinks party to go to next, where we met Charles Delevingne, an old family friend. Talk soon turned to catching up. "So, Frostie, all well?" Dad said, "Fantastic, Charles, though I've just come from a VERY long talk about squirrels." Charles said, "Squirrels? What on earth was that about?" And Dad said, "Well, people conserve them to then shoot them, all these shooting types, and the whole talk was about that: hedges, predators and other details." Charles: "Shoot them?" Dad: "I know! Odd, isn't it, that people do this?" At this point, I was in uncontrollable fits of laughter, incapable of speaking, and not wanting to stop this fabulous misunderstanding quite yet. After I eventually resolved it, Charles laughed, Dad nonchalantly shrugged with a sort of "tomayto-tomahto" look, and we giggled on through the party.

Michelmersh, then, certainly did not sate some hidden, passionate desire in Frost for countryside pursuits: its role in his life was very different. Rory Bremner, a friend of Frost from the late 1980s onward, recalls in vivid detail the disparate crowds who gathered for these Hampshire Sunday lunches: the "football match with [Conservative politician] Michael Howard in midfield, David Seaman in one goal and [Canadian newspaper proprietor] Conrad Black in the other: nobody on earth could put together such a group of people. I used to tease him by imitating his fulsome welcome to all and sundry: 'Oh, and have you met the Pinochets?'"

Equally, Barney Jones, Frost's later producer, remembers that, "[Frost] never said who'd be there; you would just turn up, not knowing whether you'd be having lunch with Benazir Bhutto or the chancellor of the exchequer and playing football afterwards with Archbishop of Canterbury on the wing."[397]

But for the Frost boys, Michelmersh was a place of delights. "It was a very grounding place," says George Frost, "and it meant we had a country childhood. And it was a sign of how much we enjoyed each other's company. The cool kids were hanging out at weekends in London, but not us." And Miles Frost adds that, "Saturday morning breakfasts at Michelmersh always went on for hours, fuelled in part by Dad's subscription to every single newspaper available. He'd begin with a review of the serious ones 'for work', but it was never long before duty gave way to passion: he was happiest hosting a debate with the three of us on whether it was the *Mirror*, *Sun* or *Daily Mail* whose football transfer speculation was most credible that weekend. And then, of course, the boiled eggs: a weekly ritual of him acting out excitement at attacking his eggs – only to crack them open and find they were duds, turned upside-down. Once, twice, thrice we'd make him do it [with five-, four-, and three-year-old Miles, Wilfred and George] laughing hysterically as he delivered another performance."[398]

These London evenings, these Hampshire weekends: they operated on a number of levels. In one sense, they provided the milieu that Frost himself needed in order to thrive, to express himself. This was once more the context of the impresario, the driving force, the enabler, the promoter, the producer – operating now not over breakfast at the Connaught, but on home ground. Here he was producing energy, creating stages for himself and those around him. It pleased him to live and work like this, to keep many plates spinning, to keep a mass of conversations energised. They were networking events, pure and simple, with Frost himself – as he had begun to do at Cambridge and continued to do thereafter – inserting himself into these networks; and as host, placing himself at the centre of each. And indeed, it was all the more necessary for him to do this, because his career in the course of the 1980s had placed him squarely at the centre of British political and cultural life.

And yet, for all this wall-to-wall socialising, Frost was at heart a very private man and very discreet – about his own life as about the lives of others. This meant that, "one would tell him things that would never be told to anyone else," says David Mellor. And, while it was an easy matter to see into certain aspects of his life – his enjoyment of his marriage and his family life and his pride in his children – "this need for privacy also meant that one saw the substance of his life only through a glass, darkly. He was a private man, and extremely well-defended." And this in turn meant that his close friendships were few – and all the more prized for it. "I became quite close to him," says Mellor, "and I was amazed and impressed by his durability: I had watched him on TV when I was in my teens, and forty years later there he still was, still enjoying his career – and having lunch with me. Yes, I was made happy by his friendship; it was a matter of pride for me."[399]

All of these friends sensed nevertheless an aspect of David Frost's character that was not easily glimpsed: that fence of impenetrability that, to a casual observer, appears as one of his most surprising characteristics. He was a private man, or rather, there was an element of privacy that sat oddly set against his ostensibly gregarious, open and sunny nature. His openness to the lives of others, the questing curiosity that defined his character and that made him a keen, skilled interviewer, was also a shield: asking questions and delving into the stuff of other people's lives left less space and time available for any delving into his own. Brenda Yewdell, his make-up assistant, noted this trait: "He was very private. He had his life that he wanted to keep private. The family was his domain and he didn't want to talk about it. He was so proud of his boys, and he doted on Carina; but all this was *his*."[400] And the Countess of Wessex, a friend in his later years, sensed the strategies he deployed to maintain this privacy: "I always had a feeling I really ought to prepare myself, do a little bit of homework, for a lunch with [Frost], simply because he was fully engaged with everything one said, he was full of questions, he had the knack of making one feel the most interesting and absorbing person in the world. I felt as though I had been through the wringer: a lunch with him was a little like the Spanish Inquisition. And I would take my leave afterwards, and realise I had hardly had the chance to ask him a single question about himself."[401] This was simply an aspect of his *modus operandi*, a means of holding the world at bay, and to prevent too much by way of prying into his own life.

*

> One can always sense when one individual is being catered to more than others, and that became gradually apparent to us: other parents, teachers and so on – they were aware of him, and we were aware of that. This sense diminished as he aged, certainly – but certainly it was there when we were children; and there was a sense that he was the centre of the world for a period of time when we were children.[402]

Miles, Wilfred and George Frost enjoyed a comfortable, loving childhood, amid an environment in which they wanted for nothing, and within a social milieu that in turn moulded and shaped their own sense of identity and of social confidence. Their own personalities soon emerged: Miles, the eldest, was clever, generous, with an analytical cast of mind; Wilfred, the middle boy, was focused and strong-willed, with a touch of Stoic stubbornness; George was light-hearted, a comic, in many ways most like his father.

Their lives were, at first glance, hardly conventional: dining with political leaders, kicking a football with sports stars, yarning with actors and spin-doctors. All this was part of the normal weft of their routine, and so was having a father who was in himself a personality, appearing at least weekly on their television screens and enjoying the friendship of a host of household names. As for their own version of this, "That the house at weekends was filled with famous people," remarks Miles Frost, "was neither here nor there."[403] The Frosts, however, kept their children away from the cameras. Photos exist of the family lined up before the summer party at Carlyle Square or in the forecourt of Buckingham Palace for David Frost's 1992 knighthood – the boys in (matching) suits and ties, with gaps in their teeth and thatches of hair – but for the most part they were shielded from any limelight and taught the value of normality.

The Frost children were also conscious, however, that they had an unusually empathetic father, and a demonstratively loving one. Miles Frost remembers that, "Dad would drive home how wonderful he thought each one of us was, that we were as capable and talented as we simply wanted to be. I always grew up buoyed by this: that, if I tried, I was able to achieve anything. I can remember him saying, 'You can do anything you put your mind to,' and he'd emphasise this point, again and again. This sounds achievement-based, but in fact it extended far beyond into deep fatherly love. While always keen to achieve things he would be proud of, I never felt at all worried of sharing concerns, personal shortcomings or mistakes with him. And he would often call me at weekends as I grew up and left the house, asking how Wilf and George were getting on, and if this or that was a problem. He was constantly inquisitive about how we were getting on."[404]

All three children, as they grew up, were fully aware of Frost's work ethic – what Rory Bremner called "the Methodism in his madness" – and his unwillingness to waste a single minute. Miles Frost recalls that his father was perfectly capable of cracking the whip if the occasion demanded it, and that he was particularly irked by idleness. "I have a lazy side: and there were times in my life where I was really scared of him, and those times were when I had been lazy, or idle. *Bone idle* was a phrase he used a lot. Work was not simply work: it was a gift, something wonderful." Wilfred Frost adds that, "Dad was busy, and because of that, he wasn't always very good at disciplining us, and so we knew how to play him. In that sense, Mum had the hardest job, as tends to be the case with mothers. She had to take up the slack, though we were not so very aware of this. He would go through our report cards, very much in a pupil–headmaster sort of way, and this was one of the few occasions when we would approach him with apprehension. On the occasions when he did lose his temper, when we did something wrong, he was terrifying. It was really quite scary." And George Frost notes that his father, "was always the academic pusher, while our mother was more relaxed. I think he looked on our time at school as a means of maximising every opportunity we had. I had lots of bad reports. I wanted to be the centre of attention, which never puts you in a good position at school, and which obviously I inherited from Dad. And so, he was a little more likely to empathise: glass houses and all that."[405]

The school in question was Eton, which all three Frost boys attended, and the choice of which helps to underscore the sense that David Frost had indeed joined the very Establishment that as a young man he had helped to pillory. The Frosts had made the decision to bring their children up, not as Methodists or – as might have been expected – as Catholics, but in the Church of England. Carina had been surprised, as she got to know Frost, to find that he had a daily habit of prayer. "He prayed every night, without fail. I used to say, 'For God's sake, come to bed, it's freezing, what are you praying for? – I'm the Catholic, I'm the one who should be praying.'"[406] But he made only periodic efforts to inculcate religion in his sons: marching them across the lawn to the little adjoining church at Michelmersh, for example, to sit in the pews while he read a prayer or lesson, until fits of laughter put paid to this exercise in piety. "He wanted us to go to church," says Wilfred Frost, "and was disappointed and upset when we didn't. At Michelmersh, since he was always busy on Sunday mornings with the show, he tried to get the parish to put on a later service, a small prayer service, or a reading before lunch – but we would get the giggles, and then Mum got the giggles; and then it just didn't work at all. And later, we would avoid discussing these sorts of issues rather than upset him by admitting to a lack of interest or belief in God."[407]

The boys' Eton housemaster was Bob Stephenson, who recalls being struck by Frost's own obvious backbone of morality and his clear opinions and views, all delivered during regular Friday-afternoon phone calls, "in the course of which the world would, between us, be set to rights".[408] And Wilfred Frost notes that, "when [Frost] was younger, I think he would never have imagined the possibility of Eton for his children. But he saw, I think, that this in itself was hardly a reason not to send us there. We had quite a cocooned childhood, spending more time with our parents' friends than with children our own age, and we were a little green around the gills when we went off to school. And Eton had a good effect on us, giving us the resources to grow into rounded adults. I remember that Dad cried on the phone when I told him I'd just been made house captain at Eton: a geeky achievement, of course, but something I was proud of – and something he was too."[409]

The decision to send their sons to Eton was, in part, a reflection of his long-standing sense of duty, refracted now through a more focused prism, and in the direction of his sons and their prospective futures. Certainly, his friend Peter Chadlington recalls that Frost became an enthusiastic Eton standard-bearer, urging him in his turn to send his own son to the school. "He completely changed the education of my son James, who wanted to go to Radley. David shook his head; 'No,' he said, 'don't send him to Radley, send him to Eton: elitist, separatist and all as it is, it's a wonderful place.' And so I dragged James off to Eton, and took him around and we walked out of the house and he said, 'I'm going there, Dad.' What was so persuasive about him? He was a friend, and he had my interests at heart, and he was a good man."[410]

And the Eton decision was also an acknowledgement of the essential facts and texture of David Frost's life. He occupied, through the trajectory of his work and through his marriage into the British aristocracy, a certain place on the country's social ladder, and he moved in certain circles. A friendship, for example, developed in the course of the 1980s between the Frost family and the family of the Prince and Princess of Wales, the connection nourished by the presence on the scene of five boisterous children who were much of an age. This relationship had its apotheosis in April, 1987, when Carina and David Frost asked Diana to become godmother to the infant George Frost. Diana was delighted. "I am just so thrilled to be asked to be godmother to George," she wrote to Carina. "It was such a touching thought, and I hope I will be a good one." Diana, indeed, took pleasure in the company of all three Frost boys, to whom she referred as "Carina's little men".

Diana's private letters to Carina, redolent as they are of a warm, trusting relationship between the two families, illustrate clearly the reasons why the Princess was asked to become godmother to the youngest Frost boy. "A big hurrah!" writes Diana to Carina in September, 1986, "to know that there is a small Frost on the way! [...] Huge applause!" The letters also give an indication of the texture of the Frosts' social life in the period and the sense of fun and energy that prevailed at Carlyle Square. In one letter, following a dinner in March 1986 with both couples, Diana pronounces herself star-struck – to such an extent, she writes, that, "For once I was speechless, and that takes quite something." She describes how she had been particularly excited to be seated next to John Cleese – although touchingly, her favourite part of the evening consisted of a visit to the nursery floor to kiss the little men goodnight. It was the splendid Frost country home in Hampshire that Diana loved best. Michelmersh was "heavenly" and "beautifully decorated with a cosy atmosphere".

As the boys grew up, the two families came to see a good deal less of one another. Nonetheless, the Frosts were saddened by Diana's death in 1997 – and George Frost, then aged eleven, was particularly distressed: "She was such an enormous character, and everyone wanted a piece of her, and there wasn't enough to go round – she didn't have time for everyone. But what this relationship meant for me was that I could be aware of energy and warmth and a desire to do good."[411]

The three Frost children would eventually leave Eton and emerge into the adult world: Miles studying Politics and George Economics at Newcastle University, before returning to live and work in London; Wilfred studying Politics, Philosophy and Economics at St Edmund Hall, Oxford. And the family remained close, the specific rhythms and patterns of Frost life continuing as the children grew up. They continued regular holidays *en famille* – to the Caribbean, to France and Ireland – and, in what became an annual tradition, to Spain to holiday with Annabel Goldsmith and her family at their estate at Tramores in the dry, tawny foothills of the Sierra Nevada. A close friendship developed between the Frost boys and Ben, the youngest of the three Goldsmith children and David Frost's godson. Indeed, a close general bond grew between the Frosts and Goldsmiths, especially following the death in 1997 of James Goldsmith – so much so, indeed, that Carina Frost took to referring to "our twin families".

Annabel Goldsmith has described the easy, comfortable tenor of these Spanish holidays. Jimmy Goldsmith was an enthusiastic gambler and "unlike their reluctant father – Jimmy could never persuade David to gamble – the boys, taught by Ben, enjoy the odd flutter and the noise of the dice rattling on the backgammon board and the dashing up and down the stairs to catch the racing on Channel Four, accompanied by the odd crash as David knocks over another vase, are the defining sounds of our holidays. [...] David is one of the kindest people I have ever met. His loyalty and empathetic intuition are second to none, and it is an absolute pleasure and privilege to be his friend. I don't think there is anyone else I know who is quite so riveting to talk to. [...] Years ago, when he was staying at Tramores, on the way back from a day trip to the old town of Ronda, we decided to take a short cut home over the land owned by the businessman Adnan Khashoggi, who at that time was in some kind of business trouble. When I asked David what the problem was, he replied, 'Well, to cut a long story short, I think it's a case of plenty of Shoggi, and no Khash.'"[412]

*

After six months of marriage, I called my brother Eddie and I was sobbing, and he said, "Oh, Carina, for God's sake, we finally have you married, what's wrong now?" And I said, "I'm exhausted, being married to David Frost is the most exhausting job I've ever had." And Eddie said, "That's because you've never had a job!"

Every day in the course of their Venetian honeymoon in 1983, David and Carina Frost took the boat from the hotel dock at the Cipriani across the mouth of the Grand Canal to St Mark's Square.

David Frost disliked most forms of physical exercise, but there was no avoiding this particular trip. The vicinity of St Mark's was the best place to pick up the latest British newspapers, and there was a particular reason why the happy couple had to get their hands on the latest news. At home, all hell was breaking loose, and the British media were feeding like sharks on the story.

This chapter in the life of David Frost began well before his marriage to Lady Carina Fitzalan Howard: in January 1980, when Michael Rosenberg – flying from Britain on a business trip to California – came across a small story in his newspaper. The latest ITV franchise round was looming, and this was in itself of some interest to Rosenberg: he had, after all, been part of the operations that resulted in Frost's consortium winning the London ITV franchise for LWT more than a decade previously. But this time, the Independent Broadcasting Authority (IBA) – the regulative successor to the ITA which had awarded LWT its licence – was minded to introduce a novelty to British broadcasting. Breakfast television had been part of the pattern of daily life in the United States since the 1950s, but, as the television historian Ian Jones has written, there were all kinds of reasons why it had not been contemplated in Britain:

> Since television was first launched in Britain in 1936, few within the media establishment had ever serious countenanced the idea of breakfast programmes. For a start, it was too costly – only a fool would throw money away transmitting at such an anti-social hour. It was considered too problematic: a host of awkward union negotiation and staffing issues were bound to be involved, which would invariably take forever to settle. [...] Above all, it was a genre with roots in the United States, which meant – to those reared on fiercely home-grown and patriotic sentiments, of which there were many – it was simply out of the question.

And Jones puts a finger on a fourth factor: a pervading cultural snobbery in a television industry which was still laced with a degree of patrician values, and that saw the very notion of breakfast TV as "simply too down-market for the discerning viewer".[413]

None of these factors daunted Rosenberg. "I spent the flight putting numbers and a business plan on an airline sick-bag – I had no paper with me – and when we landed at LAX, I got off the plane, rang David who was in LA at the time, told him I had a great idea. David hadn't, in fact, even heard of the breakfast idea, but he went off he went to think about it and – being David – do something about it."[414] There was little time to waste – and besides, Frost soon got wind that other prospective bids were possible. He now set about wooing Peter Jay, former British Ambassador to Washington, son-in-law of the former Labour Prime Minister James Callaghan and one-time television presenter on John Birt's *Weekend World* programme for LWT. Jay and Birt had become known in the years since for their idea that television suffered from a "bias against understanding", which was a somewhat weighty way of suggesting that the medium needed to become more generally highbrow, and feature rather more explanation and rather less by way of visuals which had the potential to explain little and leave the viewer unenlightened. Ian Jones notes the converse opinion of some critics, that such notions were "cerebral nonsense and a recipe for driving viewers away from news programmes, and TV companies out of business".[415]

Critics or no critics, however, Jay had cachet and contacts – as many contacts and as much cachet even as Frost himself. He joined the infant Frost consortium for a number of reasons: he liked Frost personally; he saw the fact that Frost's ideas were as yet unformed as a good thing, meaning that the bid could be moulded to take a shape that pleased Jay himself; and he liked the team that Frost was forming, which included his friends Rosenberg and Michael Deakin, who had an established reputation as a creative and talented writer and programme-maker. Deakin remembers these beginnings as decidedly haphazard: "David rang me up and said, 'Breakfast television is going for grabs; shall we make a bid for it?' I saw it as something that would amuse David, so I said, 'Yes.' I was fond of him and it sounded like fun. And he said, 'OK, well, we have two days to put in a bid; you must come down to Egerton Crescent and we'll do it.' And even though it was a bank holiday, I did it. He had a computer, which was very new-fangled in those days, so I used that: it was miraculous."[416] Jay himself would take a plum position in the new station, were it to win the franchise, and so, over a cheery lunch at La Caravelle in New York, he said yes, and formally joined forces with Frost.

The ITV franchise round, as had been the case a decade and more ago, remained "a beauty parade: it did not hinge completely on money – but of course the figures had to add up".[417] It was left to Rosenberg to achieve this, and, "One day the phone rang: Barclays Bank, asking questions about backing ITV franchises. And I said, 'Well, but have you thought about investing in the breakfast franchise?' And they said, 'Oh! Well, no, we actually haven't,' and ultimately they provided the cornerstone backing of the £10 million fund we needed to launch the station." Other funds were supplied by the Conservative MP Jonathan Aitken and his businessman cousin Timothy, who with Frost were part of the management board; and the consortium now adopted the title TV-AM. And meanwhile, Frost and Deakin focused on attracting the talent. "I do think, sometimes, that the problems that TV-AM suffered subsequently, that they were all my fault," says Deakin wryly. "It was my idea to sign up a roster of talent, without thinking too much about how such a collection of large personalities and large egos would manage to work together."[418]

This eventual talent list was by any standards impressive. Frost made a shortlist of names, took out his address book and began ringing around his intricate web of connections. The names on his list were offered extremely lucrative salaries, six months off every year, and a say in how TV-AM was run, and soon he was joined by television newsreaders Angela Rippon and Anna Ford; the august journalist and writer Robert Kee; Michael Parkinson, his old friend from LWT who had now carved out an impressive broadcasting career in Britain and Australia; and Esther Rantzen, who like Frost was a client of the Noel Gay Agency and whose Sunday night *That's Life!* programme regularly racked up the BBC's highest weekly viewing figures. Rantzen eventually dropped out, choosing instead to recommit to her career at the BBC – and the remaining star names were christened the Famous Five.

Alex Armitage had now joined his father Richard at the agency, and he recalls that, "We cleared the decks for these negotiations. We were aware of how huge it potentially was. These five massive contracts were finally, finally drawn up, with last-minute adjustments and lawyers creeping all over them. They were ultra-confidential, and then some of the contracts were placed in the wrong envelopes and sent out. And so the five discovered what the others were being paid – and so of course a new round of negotiations was sparked off."[419]

In December 1980, the franchise bid was won – the result partly of what Deakin calls celebrity "starfire", partly as a result of what Michael Parkinson calls the "marvellous ideas pulled together" by Jay, and partly due to a speech given by Frost at the interview, at which he spoke of the "chemical reaction" that would exist between members of the Famous Five on screen.[420] (This was the source of the "sexual chemistry" reference often ascribed to Frost – one assumes that he had Rippon and Ford in mind, rather than Kee and Parkinson.) In advance of the decision, Frost had been at pains to keep the IBA on-side, "to play down the idea that we were presenting an image too rich and too posh, and so he issued a decree that in future everyone travelling to one of the numerous outposts in Britain to present our case to the public should not travel first-class on the railway. To his disappointment and anger we all disobeyed him on a long trip to Darlington; after all, we were paying for ourselves! Having been scolded by David, who requested that we walk down the corridor when the train arrived at Darlington station so as to be seen to disembark from the second-class carriages, we were amused to see on the platform David's Rolls-Royce complete with chauffeur in peaked cap. The driver had arrived at the station on his own initiative rather than at David's order – and David was not pleased to see him. In fact, he ignored the driver and began to walk along the platform to the exit. He was pursued by the driver in the Rolls-Royce, like a rather expensive lapdog trotting after his master. In the end, David had to tell him to bugger off, much to the interest of the journalists awaiting our arrival. I think it was the only time I saw David discomfited and at a loss for words."[421]

In the aftermath of the bid victory, Frost threw a lunch party at Egerton Crescent to seal the fact that what had begun as an intrepid adventure had become – to the surprise of many – reality.[422] The pleasure was dulled a little when the IBA decreed that the new station would not launch for two more years, meaning two years without advertising revenue; and dulled a little more when the BBC announced twenty-four hours later that it too would be launching a breakfast television programme. Indeed, all the pleasure on evidence in the Egerton Crescent dining room that day would soon be swept away entirely, as the new TV-AM ran into the sand of managerial, financial and personality problems. Tension developed in particular between the Aitkens and Jay. The former felt increasingly that Jay was simply not the right person for the job, and morale at that station – which had of course not even begun to broadcast yet – was already sinking.

And the BBC launched its programme first: *Breakfast Time* went on air in January 1983, fronted by the fatherly Frank Bough (reassuring in a cardigan) and Frost's one-time girlfriend Selina Scott (to supply a balancing youthful appeal). It was launched smoothly, professionally, with a cosy set consisting of soft lighting and comfortable sofas, and with the BBC's broadcasting muscle at hand to supply news, weather and well-resourced programming. When TV-AM launched a fortnight later, the station was still struggling with all sorts of problems: conflicts with unions had slowed the flow of advertising revenue to the station; and there was an obvious conflict, as yet unresolved, between Peter Jay's high-minded-but-chilly "mission to explain" and an evident need to build audiences and establish rapport.

And while hindsight is a treacherous thing, a viewing of that first morning's edition of the programme seems burdened with discomfort and awkwardness. TV-AM's synthesised music in the opening credits is shrill and unbecoming to a morning show; and while Rippon and Parkinson seem comfortable in their skin, their three fellow stars clustered there on the cream L-shaped TV-AM sofa certainly do not: Ford seems nervous, Kee hopelessly out-of-place, and, most curious of all, David Frost, that most experienced of broadcasters, radiates a tense energy that sets one's nerves on edge. "Hello, good morning and welcome," he carols as the programme opens, and as the closing credits roll, he twice grasps the beskirted knees of Ford and Rippon in a gesture that could not possibly have been welcome even in 1983.

And it got no better. Frost and Ford were rostered to appear together for the first month, and they made an awkward, uncomfortable pair seated together on the sofa. Ford seemed to lack spontaneity, Frost looked exhausted and the pair sparred rather than purred together. There was certainly no sexual chemistry. "We just never gelled, the five of us," says Parkinson.[423] This might in theory have made for television that was riveting, albeit in a horrifying way – but the public would not be riveted. Ratings were dire, registering after a few weeks at essentially zero, while *Breakfast Time*, well settled in and running smoothly, was sailing ahead. Jay resigned on March 17th, as the result of a boardroom coup led by the Aitkens. The minutes of the meeting reveal that Frost objected to the move. Later that evening, David Frost and Carina – with the clock ticking on their upcoming wedding, now two days hence – dined with Jay and a friend in a Greek restaurant in Soho. Instead of the dinner for two which had been planned to finalise the wedding arrangements, the meal became an emotional ordeal for all concerned, as Frost begged Jay to withdraw his resignation, and Jay refused. And so it was against the backdrop of this coup, and the bitter conflicts in the days that followed, that David and Carina Frost married in west London and set off on their Venetian honeymoon. And the reason why they made the daily trip across the water from their hotel to St Mark's to stock up on British newspapers was to check whether Frost, in the midst of this blood-letting, still had his job to go back to at TV-AM.

Frost kept his place – he was still a board member and could not be so easily dislodged – but by the end of March 1983, he had been booted off his prime-time week-day perch in order to concentrate on an as-yet-undefined big interview slot. It was clear to all that his early-morning television appearances, laced as they were with evident fatigue and lack of spark, were seen as a weak element in the TV-AM line-up. But his move from the week-day schedule was a mortifying development. "He never quite showed his emotions about this," remembers Rosenberg. "He was quite reserved in that sense, but it was clear enough that he was upset. This was his baby and he had given birth to it, and all the flak fell on his shoulders; and of course people loved a glimpse of failure. They fell upon it with abandon."[424] And Michael Parkinson remembers his sense that Frost had been, "treated shabbily at best by an organisation that, remember, he had helped to found. Happily, David was the most forgiving of men. He was under enormous pressure – we all were – but he never lost his cool. We had adjoining offices at TV-AM overlooking the Regent's Canal. You could stand in the frame of the windows and look down on the water, and one day, when we were knee-deep in the crap, I was standing there, and I glanced across and there was David, standing and looking down, and he says, 'So, come on then, who gets to jump first?'"[425]

But at least he still had a job – for others were not so lucky. Within three months of TV-AM going on air, Ford and Rippon had been sacked; Parkinson had threatened to leave with them, but relented when offered a position on the board, and went on broadcasting at weekends; Kee became an occasional special correspondent. The problem – the essential problem amid a throng of breakfast problems – was that TV-AM had been founded upon a flawed premise: that the "starfire" of the Famous Five would in itself ensure success. The old United Artists model had resulted in Hollywood stars calling the shots – but TV-AM was not Hollywood, and such a model was doomed to fail. Many relationships unravelled in those several hellish months. Although David Frost certainly did pride himself on speaking no ill of anyone at any time, there were several exceptions that proved this rule. "He hated the Aitkens," remembers Carina Frost, who still recalls vividly the torrid atmosphere that prevailed in advance of her wedding. "They had stitched him up. They were despicable, totally and utterly despicable. All I could remember was that I was trying to get married, and there were these crisis meetings every ten minutes." And Michael Parkinson recalls that while Jonathan Aitken would be, "smoothly, emolliently buttering you up in this or that meeting, Timothy would be simultaneously digging a tunnel under your feet like the Viet Cong."[426] In 1999, Jonathan Aitken would be sent to prison for perjury and perverting the course of justice. "We knew two people," recalls Carina, "who went to prison: Jeffrey Archer and Jonathan Aitken. We were happy to see Archer again, but Aitken? No, never."[427]

In the aftermath of the purges, a bearded young television producer named Greg Dyke was drafted to set the station back on an even keel, and to address its disastrous ratings. Dyke had – as was the case with so many people in Frost's life – had a career with LWT. Michael Deakin had attempted to poach him for TV-AM when the station first began, but Dyke had sensibly declined to have anything to do with the new enterprise at that point, and now he stepped into "a total shambles: I like a challenge, I was up for a challenge, but this was a much tougher task than I had imagined. It was hysterical – I was shocked when I looked at the books – but we turned it around in the course of the year that I was there, and turned it from a champagne place to a pint of bitter place."

Timothy Aitken had sacked Anna [Ford] and Angela [Rippon] on the day I arrived. There they were, sacked, and Parkinson threatening to walk out in sympathy. I was sitting there with Dick Marsh, the deputy chair, and he had had a vasectomy that day; and Marsh was saying to Parkinson, 'We really need you,' and then he screamed in agony and grabbed his crotch. Parkinson did stay, but Marsh's crotch only added to the insanity of those days.[428]

It would indeed soon become evident that Dyke, a tough-minded, pragmatic populist, was the right person to address TV-AM's woes. But he was not unaware of the challenges involved, and was certainly aware that for Frost, this was a challenging time. "David was a mega figure, and this was the first time I had ever met him. The Nixon interviews hadn't been so very long ago, and he might have been very hostile to me. But he wasn't. He helped, he made it easy. And I decided we would locate David's show on a Sunday morning, and of course that continued for thirty years. We built his career, or rebuilt it, and it was at that point that I got to know him. The thing about David was that he was always on to the next thing, always running. And he had amazing connections. I remember the Harrods bomb [the bombing by the IRA of Harrods department store in central London on December 17th, 1983], and in its aftermath we all rushed into the office to get the programme up and running. We thought, *Let's get Enoch Powell* [then an MP in Northern Ireland], and he had him on the phone. He could pick up the phone and get anyone. We were having a discussion about English fast bowling – and he said, 'Oh, let's ring up John Snow,' and picked up the phone and phoned him. He had access to everybody; he could get anyone."[429] Dyke and Frost remained friends after the former departed TV-AM a year later, in the face of Bruce Gyngell's appointment as managing director. Dyke and his family bought property in Hampshire, and became regular weekend guests at the Frost house at Michelmersh. Frost's relationship with Dyke, then, had begun in the most inauspicious possible context, but the relationship of substance that developed would pay dividends for Frost well into the future.

And even against the immediate TV-AM background, good fortune was smiling on Frost. He had been bumped to the weekend, but this seeming demotion ensured that he would settle by chance on a format that suited him. The Sunday-morning slot, which kicked off in September 1983, was unfashionable, but it was also a *tabula rasa*: empty television territory to be colonised by the first comer. For Marie Jessel, a young producer from Northern

Ireland who became Frost's first editor on the Sunday show, the opportunities were clear: to use this programme to take possession of the news agenda for the coming days, "with Frost the person to do the big interviews". The first shows addressed the issue of the leadership of the Labour Party, which was in disarray following an overwhelming Conservative general-election victory; leadership candidates Neil Kinnock and Roy Hattersley appeared on the programme in consecutive weeks, and, "now we had the ball rolling; and David came into his own. And we got into the habit of having breakfast with the guests afterwards – and he was in his element. I watched him charm his guests, and there was no pretence; this was simply the way he was. One day, [Conservative politician] Edwina Currie complained to me as though I was a scullery maid because her breakfast hadn't arrived quickly enough for her liking, and afterwards David apologised for her. 'I didn't like the way she spoke to you.' He had observed how rude she was, and I was young, and I appreciated it."[430]

Jessel also noted Frost's relationship with the royal family: in those days, with Princess Anne, and Prince Andrew and his new wife Sarah. In one revealing memory, Jessel recalls Frost showing Andrew around the TV-AM building, what were then brand-new headquarters with state-of-the-art recording and broadcasting equipment. "He took his time, and gave Andrew the full tour. A little while later, we received a letter from a viewer in Barrow-in-Furness, telling us he had watched TV-AM every single day since its launch. So we invited him down to take a tour of the studio too, and I noticed that David gave him exactly the same tour, and spent exactly the same amount of the time with this man from Barrow-in-Furness as he had spent with Prince Andrew. And I thought that said something about the man: he was very, deeply egalitarian."[431]

Soon, he was sculpting the Sunday show in his own image, complete with long-form political interviews that did indeed have the effect of controlling the news agenda for the coming days. It became standard practice for news bulletins later on Sunday to lead on the news broken by Frost, and for the following day's newspapers to take their cue from the programme too. Frost's interview with Kinnock in May 1987 – in the days leading up to the general election of that year – is a case in point. Kinnock was now four years into his tenure as a modernising leader of the Labour Party. He remained the focus of much bile on the part of many Fleet Street newspapers, which were eager to fasten on anything that might be perceived to be weak or excessively left-wing. One such was Labour's policy of unilateral nuclear disarmament. And so, when David Frost invited Kinnock to speculate as to what a non-nuclear Britain might do in the face of a threatened Soviet nuclear strike and invasion, there were many observers ready to pounce. "In those circumstances," Kinnock replies, "the choice is again posed [...] of either exterminating everything that you stand for [...] or using resources that you've got to make any invasion totally untenable. And of course any effort to occupy Western Europe or certainly to occupy the United Kingdom would be utterly untenable, and every potential force knows that very well and are not going to be ready to engage in attempting to dominate conditions that they couldn't dominate."

Kinnock's reply might, under certain circumstances, have been spun as Churchillian: that Britons would fight any invaders on the beaches and on the landing grounds. As it turned out, however, Kinnock's unwise reply to Frost's question brought a wave of criticism: the Conservative press claimed that Kinnock was advocating a policy of retreat, of taking to the hills; and two days later, the television news bulletins took up the story, which dominated the second week of the general-election campaign, and badly damaged the still-weakened Labour brand. And all this, ignited by one open question posed by David Frost days earlier.

In establishing his own strong credentials, Frost also managed to create a firebreak between his show and the rest of the TV-AM operation which continued to resemble an especially lurid soap opera. Bruce Gyngell was Australian, and his profile was relatively low when he arrived on the British television scene. His various sackings and axings did not endear him to TV-AM employees. He banned black from the TV-AM building on the grounds that "black is not a colour," while his fondness for shocking colours – bright pink shirts, canary-yellow office walls – and such habits as exercising on a trampoline installed in a corner of his office as a means of relieving stress, made him a gift to the tabloid press.

It is only fair, of course, to add that Gyngell's efforts were duly rewarded: cost-cutting, efficiencies and a roster of popular presenters including Nick Owen, Anne Diamond and a stuffed puppet named Roland Rat ensured that TV-AM at length changed from being a broadcasting basket case to one of the world's most profitable television stations. But Gyngell's dedication to balancing the station's budget topped every other concern. When in October 1984, for example, the IRA bombed the Grand Hotel at Brighton in which Prime Minister Margaret Thatcher was staying – narrowing missing assassinating her and most of her Cabinet – outside broadcast budget cuts ensured that TV-AM could not provide adequate news reports from Brighton itself; the BBC, in sharp contrast, threw its extensive resources at what was clearly a seismic story. There was simply nothing even-keeled about TV-AM, which underscores the achievement of Frost's enduring and indeed profitable presence at the station. Though even he was obliged to adapt himself to Gyngell's various strictures. In the first years of the show, such strict budget curbs meant that the Frost Sunday show was recorded as live, usually a day in advance. It was only later that the shows were actually broadcast live on Sunday mornings. The programme ran until TV-AM lost its franchise in 1992, at which point it sported the title *Frost on Sunday*.

Andrew Lloyd Webber offers a tantalising glimpse of a private David Frost at this point in his career, just as his Sunday slot was bedding in, but before it was fully established. Lloyd Webber and Frost had known each other slightly much earlier in their lives, but "we became closer after his marriage to Carina, and when I was married to Sarah Brightman; we would often go out for a meal together. I remember how nice he always was to Sarah, and I also remember how depressed he was at the poor beginning of TV-AM. We used to have to jolly him along." Lloyd Webber notes how much

Frost was "a child of, and an addict of television. He loved popular television, and he loved the deeply serious side too. Sometimes people simply did not or would not understand this, would not understand how someone could simply love the medium."

But there were limits, and Lloyd Webber can be credited with warning Frost off from committing to host the ultra-brassy ITV game show *The Price Is Right*, which began broadcasting in 1984:

He called me up one day and went out for lunch to a fish restaurant in Kensington – he hated fish, so I'm not quite sure why we went there – and he said, very enthusiastically, "Lunch is on me, I have good news; let's have a bottle of wine, and I'll tell you. I'm going to present *The Price Is Right*. I've decided. Nobody wants to watch this political stuff any more." And I was appalled. I knew about this show, and I knew that it was too much, that it would destroy his credibility. And so I said, "No, you're absolutely not! If you do that, your political interviewing will be over, blown to bits." And he stared at me and he said, "Oh, do you really think so?" And I said, very firmly, "Believe me." Imagine: there we were, convened for a celebratory lunch, and I had to say, "No, I really, really don't think so." And later that day, Carina rang to thank me. I can remember the table we sat at, I can remember the whole thing, it was so horrifying. And the interesting thing is that he had completely underestimated the impact that his Sunday slot was beginning to have, that the ratings might have been low, but it was a question of *who* was watching, not how many people were watching.

Frost and Lloyd Webber sustained their friendship in the following years. The Frosts would often visit Lloyd Webber at his homes in Ireland and the south of France, and their friendship became closer still following Lloyd Webber's third and final marriage to Madeleine Gurdon. Lloyd Webber too saw and came to value Frost's loyalty and empathy as a friend: "He was the opposite of a fair-weather friend; and as far as was possible, he tried to see the best in everyone."[432]

There were other advantages to the eventual success of TV-AM and to Frost's enduring relationship with the station. Not least among these were the beginnings of two trusted and enduring connections. One was with Brenda Yewdell, who for the next thirty years would act as his make-up artist. "He was a great man, with his lovely red socks: we used to sing hymns while I was making him up. And, 'God bless you,' he would say, and put a little cross on my forehead. I think he was very aware of God; it was just in him."[433] The other was with Trevor Poots, a television producer from Northern Ireland who in 1988 took over from Marie Jessel as producer of the Sunday show, and who became indispensable to Frost's work at Paradine.

Another benefit was the fact that a short slot called *Through the Keyhole*, a format devised and owned by Frost and shown on the original form of TV-AM, survived the initial station purges; and went on to have a life – and a highly profitable life – of its own on ITV, BBC and other channels. It first launched as a programme in its own right in 1987, and was recorded at the studios of Yorkshire Television in Leeds. And it was a programme that was distinctive, as well as indicative of a profound cultural shift. *Hello!* magazine launched the following year, ushering in the era of celebrity in Britain, with the homes of stars opened up to a voyeuristic public view. But *Through the Keyhole* had pioneered precisely this sort of cultural change. Frost had been ahead of his time. Yet in spite of this – and much to his surprise and irritation – Frost was never able to sell the format to the United States, a market that one would have assumed would be enthusiastically open to such a form of programming.

The format of *Through the Keyhole,* though resolutely populist, showcased a different and more low-key populism than that exhibited on *The Price Is Right*. A roving reporter – for many years the American Loyd Grossman – allowed the viewer a peep inside the home of a celebrity, with a panel of other celebrities in the studio tasked with guessing the identity of the homeowner. It was a simple, attractive format, though not everyone agreed. "One well-known broadcaster on the TV-AM team," says Grossman delicately, "was absolutely appalled by the idea, thought it was very downmarket and disgraceful and refused to have anything to do with it, but the interesting and revealing point is that David himself had no hierarchical approach to these things. There was no television Everest versus Death Valley in his mind: there was only television, and he was never imprisoned by genre; and he knew that *Through the Keyhole* would be a success, and that he could interview the prime minister one moment and present a light entertainment the next, and make a success of both."[434]

Carina Frost and her children would occasionally travel north to Leeds for the recordings. Margaret Frost and her family would also come – sometimes in a bus, having collected a group of friends and neighbours – over the moors from Whitby to Leeds too, and the extended family would convene afterwards for fish and chips in a local café. Andrew Neil – then the editor of the *Sunday Times*, and an influential media figure in his own right – recalls a touching episode from this period:

We had spent the day and evening together recording several episodes of *Through the Keyhole*. Normally, we would have dinner together: but I explained to David that I had an early morning meeting and the show had laid on a car to drive me back from Leeds to London through the night. He looked at me and said, "I'll come with you! – and we'll go in my car." So we headed off from Leeds around 11pm, sitting in the back of his Rolls – but not before David had loaded up with quiche from Marks and Spencer, together with several bottles of Chardonnay and a box of Montecristos. We sped down the M1, munching the quiche straight from the box, sipping the wine (glasses provided), then lighting up a couple of stogies, solving the problems of the world and sharing war stories as we went. About two and a half hours into our journey, when we were both in full flow (along with the wine), David suddenly gripped my arm, looked me in the eyes and said "Isn't this marvellous?" And that summed up David for me: the most famous TV interviewer in the world, who spent much of his time with the most famous and powerful people in the world, thought driving through the night down the M1 with a mate was the sort of small thing that really made life "marvellous".[435]

And Grossman recalls Frost's essential democratic take on life, and the ways in which it manifested itself. "The world of television is full of real monster egos," notes Grossman, "with outsize egos at the very least, and so one of the most interesting things about David is that I never saw him pull rank. People are very aware of their status in that world, but David dealt very fairly with everyone around them, regardless of who they were. He was very refreshing and collegial. He had been on the scene for so long and had seen people rise and people fall, but he was immensely loyal to the people with whom he worked, and that was very evident at the summer parties. Which was pretty nice. And because he gave loyalty, he got it back. And he was boyishly curious about people, and that curiosity never seemed to dim. That was his greatest asset, I think."[436]

*

It is rare to get the chance to relive a treasured experience, but late in 1986 just such an opportunity presented itself. A bright young man by the name of John Florescu, who had produced *Great Confrontations at the Oxford Union* for PBS [Public Broadcasting Service], came to me with a suggestion: "Wouldn't it be a great idea to interview all the 1988 presidential candidates for a series to be called *The Next President?*" I told him I found it very easy to agree that it was a good idea ... because I'd done the same thing myself, under the same title, back in 1968![437]

Not least among the many virtues of Frost's Sunday slot on TV-AM was this: it absorbed only six months of his year, leaving him free to pursue other projects. This in turn meant that when, one day in 1987, his secretary put through a call to Frost from an American, he was at liberty both to take the call and to take the proposition it contained seriously.

John Florescu was the Bostonian son of the Romanian-American academic Radu Florescu, who in 1972 had appeared on *The David Frost Show* to promote his book *In Search of Dracula*. (In another loose connection with Frost, Radu Florescu had studied at Oxford with Michael Deakin's father, the historian Sir William Deakin.) This book explored the connections between Bram Stoker's famous literary creation and Vlad the Impaler, the actual blood-soaked figure from Romanian history. It had been received enthusiastically, had sparked many more Dracula-themed books, and it was this memorable connection which enabled his son to get past the Paradine switchboard in the first place, and to be connected directly to Frost. John Florescu himself was thirty-three years old that year, and he was rather more than a bright young man: he was a polyglot cosmopolitan young man educated at Boston College and Oxford who, furthermore, having served for some years as communications director of the Democratic National Committee in Washington, was already a highly networked insider on the American political scene.

Florescu admits freely that he had had no idea that Frost had already devised another *Next President* in the approach to the 1968 presidential election, but Frost had certainly not forgotten, and now he suggested that Florescu take a flight to London and that they meet for breakfast to chew the fat. "I imagine that by making such a suggestion, he was checking me out: was I prepared to stump up the not inconsiderable fare for a last-minute airline ticket to London? Well, I was."[438] The pair did indeed meet for breakfast – at the Four Seasons in Mayfair – and the project began to take wing. John Florescu's trump card was his connections: he knew personally most of the six men – once again, all of the candidates were men and there were in fact seven Democratic candidates before Joe Biden of Delaware dropped out of the race – planning to run on the Democratic ticket. He could secure interviews with each of them with a phone call. And once the Democrats were secured, the six Republican candidates would inevitably join them at the party.

And there was another idea to add: instead of the rather formal and certainly static one-on-one format of Frost versus candidate, as had been the case in 1968, the new series would take the viewer into the candidates' homes, and would meet their spouses into the bargain. This was an opportunity to perhaps see a more human candidate, in a more nuanced setting; certainly it would increase the attractions of the series to the candidates themselves. This was a recognition by Frost that the landscape of politics and of television had altered significantly in the course of twenty years. Fewer American viewers would be prepared to watch a studio interview, and fewer advertisers would be prepared to stump up the cash for a slot on such a programme. Nowadays, the people wanted programmes that were rather more down home, and filmed against a backdrop of kitchens, porch swings, fixtures and fittings, yachts and dogs.

These logistics, then, were simple. It remained only to build a team, and to secure the funding for the programme. The first was soon done: the money, however, was less simple, because once more, the three major US networks declined to touch Frost and his idea. Florescu remarks that that the networks simply found it too challenging to deal with a figure such as Frost who "went from silo to silo, from hard news to entertainment and back. This wasn't the thing to do in America, and it simply made people jealous and defensive to see him crossing boundaries so easily. Many American television executives were, frankly, very glad he was gone."[439] This remark echoes the sense of Frost's American career in the aftermath of Nixon, which promised – but failed – to remain highly visible, also as a result of industry conservatism. It seemed that little had changed in the course of the intervening ten years. But nobody knew better than Frost himself that Florescu's phone call and suggestion had provided him with a perfect opportunity to resurrect his American career, and he threw himself into the project with gusto.

If there were challenges in America, there were also opportunities. Thatcher's Britain was deregulating the television industry as it was deregulating every other industry, but the American model of a free and flexible market had been definitively in place for a vastly longer period of time, and it was a marketplace that Frost knew well: both its challenges and its opportunities. "You could sell to anyone," as Florescu notes, "and you could raise money from anyone, from private sources and corporations, and so of course this was great for David, because it played to his strengths of getting to know people, socialising with them and getting them to invest. He could make it work nicely for him. And these tough American business guys, they weren't used to people like David, with an approachable, garrulous, entertaining manner, and an ability to make people laugh."[440] And it was on these tough American business guys that Frost now focused his charm, schmoozing and fund-raising energies, helped by the essential soundness of the idea he was marketing, and by the already existing relationships in America that he had continued to foster over the years.

One of these tough guys was not in fact American at all. Mortimer – Mort – Zuckerman, forty-nine years old at the beginning of 1987, was a Canadian-born Anglophile who had founded the Boston Properties real-estate firm in 1970. Ten years later, he had acquired the upmarket Boston-published *Atlantic* magazine, and four years after that, the venerable news magazine *US News and World Report*. For Frost, Zuckerman was the perfect quarry: "[Zuckerman] liked the idea of a good-quality television connection with his magazine, and in addition he was a liberal and he liked Frost for having slain Nixon."[441] Zuckerman himself recalls his personal and professional relationship with Frost with a good deal of warmth:

We had delightful chemistry: he was a hell of a lot of fun, but I saw too that he was a serious thinker. He took the time to read and research, he had a wonderful perspective on life, he knew how to leaven his conversation with humour, and it was extremely refreshing to be in his company. I had been in the world of journalism for some time, and focused on American politics and American leadership and American national security, and we both found this topic absolutely riveting. It was a magical dialogue, whenever we met, and I found myself after every conversation coming away feeling much more intelligent than I actually was. I've always been grateful for his friendship.[442]

Zuckerman adds that there was another connection: both men had been born abroad, and both were absorbed by and appreciative of American openness, flexibility and ways of doing business. Together with Fred Drasner, a smart lawyer from Brooklyn who was the co-publisher of the New York *Daily News* and who would go on to co-publish *US News and World Report*, Zuckerman put together an investment package that would fund the production of *The Next President*, and that would add a number of gleaming enhancements in the form of radio, a dedicated book and, in partnership with the *New York Times*, print syndication too. The project had now become a "multi-media extravaganza", and surely the advertisers would bite.[443] The tense atmosphere of that L-shaped cream sofa at the TV-AM studios in early-morning north London now seemed very far away indeed.

It was a triumph for Frost, who now saw the possibility of resurrecting his American television career at a stroke. In this greater scheme of things, it mattered comparatively little – though it did matter – that Drasner and Zuckerman, for all of their personal connection with Frost and their enthusiasm for the project, displayed their business prowess by paying their partners $1.6 million to conclude the deal – before adding the marketing bells and whistles that brought in almost $4 million – a clear profit that went to them, and not to Frost. ("I think we got the better end of that deal," notes Drasner wryly.[444]) In particular, Drasner ensured that the project was underwritten by a significant investment by the insurance corporation AIG, at that point still headed by Hank Greenberg, who had invested in and assisted in facilitating the Nixon interviews and who remained well disposed to Frost. Paradine had been stung – considerably stung – but Frost was able (not that he had much choice) to take a longer view. "In the end, we knew that David got what he wanted too," said Drasner, who like Zuckerman went on to forge a warm relationship with Frost.[445]

And besides, Frost had unrevealed secrets. Once the deal with AIG was signed and sealed, and marked with a lavish party in mid-town Manhattan, Frost and Florescu walked back for a final celebratory drink at Essex House, the famous Art Deco hotel on Central Park South in which Frost maintained a suite on the nineteenth floor. There they opened a bottle of Californian red, and drank, and reflected on the deal that had just been signed. None of their partners had apparently realised that the money might now be in place, and the advertising assured, but Florescu and Frost had not a single presidential candidate signed yet. Even more importantly, they had no television stations – not one – signed up either. The all-important web of syndication (that Frost remembered so well from his Nixon days) simply did not exist.

Ultimately, then, the two men had had the last laugh: at this point in the process, they had spun dollars from straw. And in due course, the contacts would be made. Florescu's political connections did indeed ensure that the Democratic candidates for president came on board, and were inevitably followed by their Republican rivals, and the project was further enhanced by interviews with the incumbent president, Ronald Reagan (whom Frost had already interviewed, of course, back in 1968) and his immediate predecessors, Jimmy Carter and Gerald Ford. The syndication network was built – eventually over one hundred stations took the series. *The Next President* would take the final form of fourteen forty-minute episodes which aired from November 1987, just as America's unending election cycle was moving up several gears in advance of the looming Iowa caucuses.

The series kicked off with Frost's interviews with Reagan, Carter and Ford. *People* magazine reported – using revealing language – that, "Frost has scored his biggest journalistic coups not with confrontation and accusation but by being a chummy, sympathetic peer to his subjects [...] now the British interloper is on deck with *The Next President*."[446] And after that first broadcast, the *New York Times*, which did after all have the chance to look at the series in advance, was a little sniffy in its reporting: "We get an anecdotal Mr Reagan, a solemn Mr Ford and a slightly peeved Mr Carter. We also get a circumspect Mr Frost [...] The program [...] opens and concludes with Mr Reagan in the Oval Office. Mr Frost nods agreeably with the President and chuckles at his mildest jokes. The mood is rather as if the two are having after-dinner drinks, and the older man is holding forth. Mr Frost shows a certain deference to Mr Reagan, which considering his office, is not out of place."[447]

And it is certainly the case that these sessions with Reagan, Ford and Carter were indeed no more than a curtain-raiser to the main business of the series. Frost offered Reagan – now seventy-six years old and with a year remaining in office – the gentlest of questions and received the Reagan standard-issue folksy replies, and the best remembered part of the interview was Reagan's remark that his marriage to Nancy Reagan "is kind of like coming into a warm, fire-lit room when you've been out in the cold". There was, however, significance in the meeting between Reagan and Frost that day, even if that significance would pass unnoticed by any viewer.

The critical moment came during a break, when Frost – prepping the president for the next recording session – floated a few questions to do with his Hollywood years, and then asked him what he would remember most about his years in the White House. "Expecting a good-guy bad-guy cowboy tale of triumph over the Evil Empire," remembers Florescu, "we were shocked. 'One of my Virginia buddies,' the president started rambling bizarrely, 'had to have his home-phone rewiring done just to prepare for his buddy's [i.e., the president] visit ...' This tangential tale went on for several more twists, and David glanced across at me. It was alarming – and none of us knew what to think."[448] It was only some years later, when the now-retired president's Alzheimer's was confirmed, that White House staffers confirmed that the disease had begun its assault on Reagan when he was still in office. Frost and Florescu had witnessed its depredations, there in the Oval Office itself.

In the book of *The Next President*, Frost also provides a rare first-hand glimpse of his own method in preparing for such interviews. In the course of filming, Florescu had already had a steeping in this method, in particular the rigorous rehearsals, role-playing and compiling of dossiers of facts and figures related to the interviewee. Frost himself, however, goes a little further than was generally his habit:

On the actual day of the interview, while the rest of the taping team – producers, crew, and any additional personnel – would be on the set quite early, I made it a practice not to show up until just before the interview was scheduled to begin. I did this partly because I have found through the years that the interview works better that way. If the interviewer and the interviewee have been standing around talking for a while before the tape starts to roll, the initial spontaneity that I so value is often lost. There was one even more practical reason. I like to spend the last few hours before any major interview transposing the team's questions, the "skull sessions" questions and my own questions onto buff-coloured folders. This not only fixes the thoughts in one's head, it reveals any last-minute gaps. I would then try and fill those in. (Though of course in any interview, it is often the totally ad lib, entirely unpredictable moment that is the most memorable.)[449]

This mirrors squarely the comments of others, in particular on this matter of his timing. Trevor Poots, however, was also in a position to reflect on the impact these last-minute arrivals had on Frost's colleagues. "He loved live shows," remembers Poots. "He much preferred them to recorded shows. He had the adrenalin rush in the run-up to the live broadcast and he could be very tetchy. Of course it *is* scary: like rolling a ball downhill, it's impossible to fully control – so his response was to go at the very last minute into the studio. He would stay in his dressing room until the very last minute, even if all hell was breaking loose around him: *Where is David? Where is David? One minute to air!* Then he would appear, the sound guy would rush to mike him up; and sometimes there was no time for the sound man to vanish again, so he had to hide behind the sofa or whatever furniture was about."[450]

Florescu was also in the position of being able to observe his colleague's own personal responses to his programmes, or rather, his reaction to how these programmes were perceived, and his thoughts once more reveal a Frost less confident, less grounded than one might assume. He was consistently focused on the matter of reviews. Nothing pleased him more than a positive review, and he would work his way, station to syndicated station, across the network, sitting up late in a hotel suite, for example, trawling the coverage for positive notices. "Good reviews were like Christmas presents, and worst of all was not getting a review at all. He gathered ratings city by city, like a giant chocolate cake being eaten slice by painstaking slice."[451] And Frost was delighted when the chairman of the Democratic Party, Paul Kirk, dropped a note declaring that *The Next President* was the best thing on television in the course of the whole presidential campaign.

*

In the aftermath of *The Next President*, Paradine had been given a fresh infusion of life in America, and Frost was now determined to capitalise on his higher profile. He asked John Florescu to run his operations in America, in typical style. On the short shuttle flight from New York to Washington, he proposed the idea, and suggested that he and Florescu both write down a prospective salary on a piece of paper. Florescu suggested $80,000, Frost $100,000. "Too bad," Frost said. "I'm the boss: $100,000 it is." Florescu already had a new idea up his sleeve: a series showcasing the virtues of what had always been David Frost's speciality – the long-form interview, which was distinctly unfashionable in the America of the day. In the absence of anything other than chilly looks from the major networks, Florescu proposed that the concept be pitched at PBS: upmarket, highly regarded and the closest channel that the United States had to a public-service broadcaster – but always short of funds. A deal between PBS and Frost would be a good fit – this would in a sense be natural terrain for Frost's interview format – and in addition, PBS lacked an anchor or heavyweight presence. Again, money was raised. In this case the principal funder was Sanford "Sandy" Weill, a wealthy American banker, philanthropist and financier who among other companies controlled the Travellers insurance corporation. In 1991, the new show aired for the first time.

Weill had been aware of Frost's body of work in advance of the approach made to him, and it was this Frost imprimatur, rather than the PBS scheduling or any other factor, that swung the deal. "David was why we chose to invest: frankly, without him we would not have supported the programme. I saw that he was at the top of his game, and only a few other people could rival his ability to attract and interview some of the most best and most interesting people in the world, and then get them to relax and feel comfortable, and end up with an interview that rewarded the time you spent watching. You simply learned a lot, and that was part of his art."[452] Weill and his wife became very good friends with Frost and Carina (a "great sport") and spent a good deal of time with them, staying with the Frosts at Michelmersh and at Carlyle Square, where the then Prime Minister John Major and the last British governor of Hong Kong Chris Patten turned up one evening for dinner.

Talking with David Frost would run on PBS for seven years – a total of sixty-seven monthly one-hour shows – and a glance at the roster of interviewees who volunteered to be questioned by Frost makes for impressive reading. In January 1991, George and Barbara Bush were the first guests. The former was now president of the United States, making this first booking a coup indeed. In that first year, they were followed by the likes of John Major, his predecessor as prime minister, Margaret Thatcher, the actor Robin Williams, media mogul Ted Turner and Iraq War commander General Norman Schwarzkopf. In the years that followed, Frost met the former Soviet President Mikhail Gorbachev; South African leaders FW de Klerk and Nelson Mandela, against the background of a South Africa in the midst of breathless change; writer Maya Angelou; the Palestinian leader Yasser Arafat and Israeli Prime Minister Yitzhak Rabin in a joint interview; the actor and director Clint Eastwood; Benazir Bhutto, the first female prime minister of Pakistan – and an extraordinary host of others, dozens of them from the political, cultural and entertainment spheres. "Very few people have made that cross-over from Britain to America," reflects Piers Morgan. "David was a star of American TV, and he was very proud of that. When years later I used to interview celebrities and presidents for American television, they would always say – 'Hey, do you know David Frost?' He had a grace and a style about him, and he loved people and was fascinated by them."[453] Such clout and such names indicated Frost's renewed reach in America, and his stature in attracting such figures. It also demonstrates that there was indeed an appetite for the long-form interview, if only a television station had the nerve to invest in a format that had the potential to provide absorbing, arresting television. Frost's interview in advance of the 1992 presidential election with the young governor of Arkansas, Bill Clinton and his wife Hillary Rodham Clinton is a showcase of this ability. The programme was broadcast in May 1992, towards the end of a gruelling Democratic primary season, after the Clinton team had weathered various scandals and with the nomination now in sight. Some of the attractions of this interview, of course, come with the benefit of hindsight: the Clintons were still relatively new to the national stage; Bill Clinton had not of course even begun his fascinating presidency; the American obsession with the Clintons and their marriage had only just begun; and both Bill and Hillary, seated before Frost, were young, fresh-faced and with the world and all its adventures before them. And Frost's manila folder, almost a fourth star in this tableau, was prominent in the foreground: scrawled-upon, intricate, utterly illegible.

And Frost's questioning of the Clintons – first Bill Clinton, then his wife, then the two together – foreshadows many of the characteristics of the Clinton presidency and how it was covered in public discourse. Even at this point, it is impossible to separate the Clintons' public life from their private relationship. Frost probes delicately the scandals and challenges their marriage has already weathered, and asks what continues to provide the glue that keeps the relationship together. Bill Clinton answers very much as a politician, albeit an engaging and charming one. Hillary Clinton is an altogether more fascinating interviewee, being both more enigmatic *and* more obviously passionate and motivated. She wants "to be a voice for children in the White House. What my husband and I would like to be able to say at the end of his first year, his first term, is that we really finally had a children's and families' agenda in America and that we were able to implement it."

Has Hillary Clinton been muzzled in the course of the campaign, Frost wonders, as part of a deliberate effort to disentangle the potential president from the dangerous notion of a strong-willed spouse? She laughs, or grimaces. "I say *we* a lot," she replies, "because what has happened in Arkansas is that we, meaning … literally hundreds and thousands of people, have tried very hard to change conditions and I have this feeling that there's that number of Americans, millions of them. This, she says, "is a very inclusive *we*." A minute or two later, she calls media portrayals of her by remarking mildly that there "is still some stereotyping that goes on … so that a man is called *assertive* and a woman called *aggressive* and a man is called *strong-minded* and a woman called *opinionated*". She is reaching beyond the confines of the studio in seeking to chime with every woman in America, and Frost is enabling her to do so while at the same time underscoring the reasons why, even at this early point in the Clintons' extraordinary national adventure, elements in American society fear and hate her. It is a delicate balancing act – but executed marvellously. And it shows precisely Frost's knack of providing coils and coils of rope to his guest, and then sitting back and allowing her or him to do with these coils what they will. In this case, Hillary Clinton uses this rope not as a noose, but as a lasso – reaching out to and drawing in the women of America. Frost and Bill Clinton would meet subsequently on a number of occasions, and an interview with Clinton and Tony Blair at the G8 summit at Birmingham in May 1998 – an appearance designed to energise the faltering Northern Ireland peace process – was the only time that Frost would interview a president and prime minister together. When Frost died, Clinton wrote in a letter of condolence to Carina Frost that, "David was an extraordinary man and truly one of the greatest journalists of our time. His legacy is already deeply ingrained in British and American history and I know he will be long remembered for his honest, insightful, and entertaining commentary on our modern world. I always enjoyed our talks, on and off camera."[454]

This was only one of many editions of the show to underscore the range and reach of David Frost in this period of his professional life. Another– the third to air, in late March 1991 – was with General Norman Schwarzkopf, the leader of the Allied forces ranged against Saddam Hussein's Iraq in the first Gulf War. This war had begun in August 1990, when Iraqi troops had invaded and occupied Kuwait, and had exploded in earnest in January 1991, with the onset of Operation Desert Storm, the American-led military campaign against the Iraqi occupation. This had swiftly succeeded in achieving its objectives: by the end of the following month, the Iraqi occupation of Kuwait had ended. President George Bush had given the order that the pursuit of the retreating Iraqi forces should cease: this, following extensive media coverage of the scene on the so-called Highway of Death, portraying scenes of bombed and burning Iraqi military equipment on the highway from Kuwait back into Iraqi territory, and of bodies strewn across the road and sands. The Allies also permitted Saddam the use of helicopters in his own territory, although it was later shown that he had used this permitted air transport to drop chemical weapons on rebels in Iraq itself.

With the war obviously winding down, David Frost focused on securing an interview with Schwarzkopf for PBS, and, his invitation taken up, flew with Florescu and their crew into the Saudi capital Riyadh, en route to Allied military headquarters in a bunker below the desert outside the city. On the flight, Frost had tried his very best to persuade the Saudi cabin crew to serve him a glass of Merlot, and when that failed, a glass of rosé, on the grounds that the latter in its lightness was as good (or bad) as a soft drink. (This, while his Saudi fellow travellers were in the midst of prayer, using an intermittently functioning GPS device sunk into the cabin ceiling to find the direction of Mecca.) At the bunker itself, they descended in an elevator three storeys into the ground – "like a James Bond movie", remembers Florescu – and emerged into the nerve centre of the

Allied military headquarters, itself surprisingly spartan, tatty and by no means hi-tech, with paper maps pinned to the walls in the manner of a World War II military briefing room. Frost was clad in a light tan suit, as close to battle fatigues as his wardrobe could come; and there was Schwarzkopf, surrounded by men who clearly adored this hero of the war.

Schwarzkopf was a considerable figure: not only physically but intellectually and diplomatically too. He was extremely experienced, courageous – and he possessed a fondness for theatrical flourishes, all of which made him an interesting figure to the press in this media age. Moreover, he had a good grasp of a non-American world view, having lived abroad (including in Iran and Switzerland) before enrolling in the US Military Academy at West Point – this in advance of a strikingly successful and much-decorated military career, of which Desert Storm marked the zenith. And he was no gung-ho military apologist. "War is a profanity," he said on his return from a tour of duty in Vietnam, in remarks that might have been directed at many civilian politicians. "It really is. It's terrifying. Nobody is more anti-war than an intelligent person who's been to war."[455] But at the time of this interview with Frost, Schwarzkopf was unhappy and frustrated at being obliged to implement policies from on high with which he fundamentally disagreed: in particular, the decision to leave Saddam's regime in power in Baghdad.

This was simply a policy with which Schwarzkopf fundamentally disagreed – that, and the decision to allow Saddam to use air transport – and now he told Frost that he had advised his superiors to permit Allied forces to invade Iraq and had been overruled. ("I think they suckered me," were his words. "I think I was suckered because I think they intended […] to use those helicopters against the insurrections that were going on.") And this statement was of enormous importance: it was reported in Washington, created a firestorm, and brought attention to the contradictory advice being issued there at the top of the Allied command. After the interview was aired, his military superior Colin Powell issued a statement that contradicted Schwarzkopf, who was told to keep silent.

"The interview definitely caused tension with the Bush White House," remembers Florescu. "It was front page news, and it had brought record-breaking ratings for PBS. It was a real Frost coup but it must have irked the White House, which seemed out of step with its top military commander. But Bush was ultimately a pragmatist: he had never ignored Frost's status as a news man, and he understood the importance of the bottom line: in this case, that Frost himself felt the obligation to push and press Schwarzkopf, this major figure who was staring him in the eye and signalling clearly that he had something significant that he wanted to say."[456] And indeed, it was a sign of the enduring relationship between Bush and Frost that the pair, together with the president's key aides, convened later in 1991 at Camp David to record an interview on the inside story of the Gulf War.

The war had just ended and, "the idea was to get the story down when the story was fresh in his mind. Bush had been exhausted by the experience of overseeing a war – he was tired, ashen, exhausted. The White House idea was to hold the recordings for history, and so David and Carina flew into Camp David, along with [White House Press Secretary] Marlin Fitzwater and [National Security Adviser] Brent Scowcroft – and with the president they recorded this very moving hour of footage; and he became emotional as he recollected sending young men off to war. The footage was actually recorded by the White House Signal Corps, and it was agreed that the tapes, which covered the president's most intimate and candid thoughts on the war and his fellow coalition leaders, would be embargoed."[457] Sections were released five years later, following a Frost visit to Kennebunkport where he made the case for such a move. "We'd play tennis in the morning, and edit *Lessons of the Gulf War* in the afternoon, saying, 'We'll leave this in, we'll leave this out.' David could play tennis well enough except for the fact that he didn't have a backhand, so he'd switch hands to avoid the backhand, and he'd hit moonballs all the time, and Bush was totally flipping out about it: 'That's some tennis, David!' It was an intimate relationship built on trust."[458] Other sections have never been broadcast, and to date they remain sealed in the hands of Wilfred Frost at Paradine.

A second episode in these American years dramatically illustrates the reach and remit of the programme. In July 1995, *Talking with David Frost* aired an interview with Radovan Karadžić, the leader of the Serb entity within a Bosnia-Herzegovina now consumed by civil war. The Bosnian war was in now in its third year – it would continue for a further year, until the Dayton Accords brought an imperfect peace settlement to the country – and the gruesome playing-out of the siege of the Bosnian capital Sarajevo was dramatised night after night on western television. Nobody could doubt that now, in the summer of 1995, it took nerve and a degree of personal courage to report from or travel within Bosnia. David Frost flew into the Serbian capital Belgrade, therefore, under no illusions as to the difficulties that awaited him. "We were told that it was difficult," Florescu remembers, "but David needed to get to the centre of the action."[459]

Their access to Karadžić, a poet and psychologist who had studied at Columbia University in New York and who spoke fluent English, had been guaranteed as a result of a connection between Karadžić's daughter Sonia and a colleague of Florescu inside the DNC. But the trip had been arranged with caveats: the Bosnian Serb administration would guarantee their visitors' safety during the passage to and from their headquarters at Pale, in the hills above Sarajevo, only in the hours of daylight. It was critical that Frost, Florescu and their team reach Pale before nightfall. And they did not: held up by delays on the frontier post between Serbia and Bosnia, the convoy's members found themselves crawling towards Pale on narrow mountain roads, having absorbed the New Zealand-born CNN war correspondent Peter Arnett at the border, and bundled him into their team. After several hours, Florescu took the decision to remove Frost from the most comfortable and modern vehicle in the convoy and place him in an older, more clapped-out transport – this on the understanding that now a sniper would be much less likely to target him. Florescu had already had the disagreeable duty of organising insurance from Lloyd's of London against the death of Frost and the rest of the team, and to digest the knowledge that his anchor's finger was apparently worth more than a Serb team member's whole body. And now, as the convoy set off again into the summer twilight, Frost settled back into the dusty, uncomfortable interior of the vehicle, and retreated once more into his buff folders, felt-tip pens and preparation.

Once at Pale, close to midnight, the group changed cars once, twice, three times – before eventually reaching Karadžić's bunker in the early hours and being obliged to undergo the Ruritanian protocol ("he was hooked on protocol") that the Serb leader thought reflected his rank, before the interview at last began. Once he was seated with Frost, however, Karadžić used the interview to set out a series of demands that might lead to the cessation of violence: that the Serb population inside Bosnia be granted fifty-six per cent of the country's territory; and that Goražde, the remaining Bosnian government enclave in eastern Bosnia, be handed over to his forces in return for several suburbs of Sarajevo itself.

But the interview is best remembered not for Karadžić's posturing, but for Frost's line of questioning, which focused on the human toll of life taken by the Bosnian war, including the mounting casualties in nearby besieged Sarajevo. The interview itself, indeed, would be broadcast shortly after a massacre of Bosnian men and boys by Karadžić's forces had taken place in Srebrenica.

David asked him questions to do with ethnic strife, with Karadžić's role in fomenting this – and he really began to bear down on the dead, on the numbers, on the statistics – and Karadžić got angry; and it was now three in the morning, with an angry boss and this dusty bunker full of intimidating soldiers all beginning to stir and cock their rifles. But just the same, David kept pushing and pushing, we were more and more uneasy, and I was relieved when finally the interview ended and we asked for a military escort to get us the hell out of there. I felt that it wasn't beyond the Serbs to take a shot at us before we managed to leave Bosnia. Finally, an escort did arrive. We scattered the Serb guys and our people around the three or four cars. I frankly admit I was terrified, and

I felt I couldn't shut my eyes until we were over the border. I felt the responsibility to my team and to the work we had done.[460]

Naturally, episodes such as these – driving through a civil war at nightfall; entombed in a military bunker beneath the Arabian desert – were far from Frost's standard-issue experiences in these years. He was rather more likely to be found shooting his interview in the controlled environment of a PBS studio; and his guest list was generally less tempestuous too. But it is worth noting Frost's appetite for a story remained sharp, and his energy to find the stories and ability to net them remained strong too. He was fifty-six years old on that Bosnian summer evening, not a young man any longer, and with a wife and three young children at home to think about, and it says a good deal about the professional hunger of this now mature Frost that he was prepared to undergo such adventures. And taken together, Frost's output in this second impressive career wave in America was prodigious. For US viewers and critics, he had made his mark once again – and as often as not, he was considerably more famous than the guests who beat a path to his door.

He remained the showman, the performer. It may have been unspoken and underplayed, but there was something of a fanfare about such interviews that appealed to him enormously. "The performer in him, the theatrical person: it was a very strong vein running through his system and his career," remarks Trevor Poots, "and he liked scenes that were set up to be dramatic."[461] And combined with this was that congenital restlessness and urge to travel that was never far below the surface. By maintaining an onward momentum, Frost would never have the leisure for introspection, for the sort of self-examination that did not attract him. And finally, there was that third, never-absent urge, that strong moral impulse that in such contexts found full expression: to hold to account, to educate and inform, to broadcast to a web of listeners and viewers. Such a combination of powerful instincts would continue to find full expression during the remaining years of his life.

CHAPTER 7

The Cashmere Doug Hayward

"I sewed a Miles Frost school nametag into his coat, which he left behind all over the world. It was always a cashmere Doug Hayward, and he left it behind in so many restaurants and on so many flights – but the nametag meant it always came home to us."

Carina Frost

1991 was a difficult year for David Frost. On April 23rd, Mona Frost died at Whitby, at the age of eighty-eight. The previous Christmas had been spent in Yorkshire as usual with Margaret Frost and her family – but while she was there, Mona had fallen ill, and her final months were spent in a nursing home on the edge of the town. Her funeral, which was well covered by the regional and national press, took place at Beccles on April 30th, a large congregation gathering to hear the Rev. Alfred Loades note that Mona Frost was "a person who lived life to the full and had an easy rapport with people from all walks of life whether they were heads of state or country folk".462 A few days before it took place, Jean, Margaret and David Frost received a letter from a Beccles neighbour:

Dear Children of Mrs Frost,

There are few people who would be greatly missed in Beccles for it is too large a town, but your Mother will be very greatly missed. She had the happy knack of bringing out only the best in people, and expecting them to live up to her own high natural expectations. [...] I thought it might comfort you to know how much we all admired her, and how proud we were to know her. I am not a Methodist, but a friend told me that when the Methodists and the URC [United Reformed Church] combined, it was Mona Frost who really made them feel welcome. Beccles is a very pleasant place, but it is rather insular, and your Mother brought a touch of the greater world outside which was most refreshing. It will be some time before we stop saying, "I must remember to tell Mrs Frost that, it will make her chuckle," or, "She will understand."[463]

In that same year too, and in spite of his prospering American career, there was looming professional distress: for TV-AM lost its franchise. It had been on air at that point for eight years, and had developed from being a television disaster area to one of the most profitable stations in the world – albeit one which still retained its highly developed taste for behind-the-scenes drama. The ITV franchise round had now changed from being a so-called beauty pageant to a revenue-generating round for the government of the day – and in the end, TV-AM's attempt to retain the breakfast franchise was outbid by a consortium led, ironically, by TV-AM's earlier saviour, Greg Dyke. The news was released in October 1991 – and David Frost's reaction was blunt. "When I was at school," he told the media outside the station's building in north London, "I was always told that the important thing is not the winning, but the taking part. I didn't believe it then, and I don't believe it now." Behind the scenes, however – back inside the building – he was distraught.

There was further disagreeable news to come. Frost had formed the CPV-TV consortium with Richard Branson and others including the Charterhouse merchant bank to bid for three separate ITV franchises in the same auction round – but all bids failed at the first, or programming "quality threshold" round. And Frost also had a stake in raising money in the bid for the proposed new British terrestrial station Channel Five, as David Keighley – at that point the head of corporate affairs at TV-AM – recalls: "I remember he brought out his address book and was going through the names of these financiers and influential people – 'We could try him, and we could try him; no, not him and not him' – but although we did put together a very well-resourced bid, by the following summer the numbers could not be made to add up. We had planned a press conference at the Grosvenor House Hotel to announce this: [TV-AM boss] Bruce Gyngell was speaking at one end of the function room telling the press that the Channel Five bid would not now go ahead; and David was at the other end, telling the media desperately that the bid *was* going to go ahead; and I was shuttling back and forth from camp to camp. And at one point, a *Sunday Times* journalist tugged my sleeve and said, 'Gosh, isn't it time to think about moving on?'"[464] And it was indeed time to move on – for all concerned. David Frost also now cut his losses. In June 1992, as TV-AM was entering the last six faltering months of its dramatic broadcasting life, he left the station. (Margaret Thatcher had been the final guest on his Sunday show before it wrapped: "Margaret, thank you very much indeed for a memorable morning.") His activity in Britain over the next few months was instructive in several ways, for it illustrated his own pragmatism, the professional respect in which he was held, and, perhaps most interestingly, the sense in which a reservoir of good will existed for David Frost, to be tapped as needed.

Frost had already, by the time he left TV-AM, made a new mark. In that year's general election, held on April 9th, he with Selina Scott anchored coverage for Sky News. The quality of its broadcasting mattered especially to Sky, because this was the first time since its launch three years previously that the channel had had the opportunity to cover a national election. Sky's political editor Adam Boulton had originally been pencilled in to anchor the night's broadcast, but there was a lingering sense that a more established figure was needed, and in an indication of the stature of Frost's programme on TV-AM, the owner of Sky, Rupert Murdoch, weighed in to give the chair to Frost instead. This was a significant moment: it marked the entry of Sky News as a substantial player on the British media scene; it laid to rest once and for all the sense that Frost and Murdoch could not have a meeting of minds, even when their interests were in alignment; and it consolidated Frost's own position as a political heavyweight on the British scene.

There was additional good news. John Birt was appointed director general of the BBC in this same year of 1992, and now an opportunity opened for Frost to take his successful TV-AM format and transplant it to Sunday mornings on the BBC. Birt – like his successor as director general, Greg Dyke – saw it as his role to foster Frost's career, and to offer protection from the eddies of the world. Birt mentioned his idea to Tony Hall, director of news at the Corporation: and Hall met with Frost to discuss the idea: "I knew I wanted to sweep up the show and bring it to the BBC. David had just come off an overnight plane from New York, he had obviously had a jolly time on the flight, and he was wonderful, energetic, enthusiastic, and we just took it from there. I knew already that his pulling power was quite extraordinary and his enthusiasm for joining the BBC was very gratifying."[465]

The BBC made its offer, and Frost jumped at it. And of course the move was in the interests of both parties: Frost saw the chance to take an existing brand and to use the BBC's resources and imprimatur to make it even stronger; Birt and Hall understood that here was an opportunity for the Corporation to exert considerable control over the news cycle, in the manner in which Frost had done on TV-AM. There was a sense that, with the BBC behind it, Frost's programme early on a Sunday morning could be even more successful in attracting every news-maker and -influencer who mattered, and could control the headlines well into the following week.

Barney Jones, who would become Frost's long-time editor at the BBC, illuminates the means by which these arrangements were made to work:

John Birt contacted Frost and said, "Come to the Beeb, you're an enormous talent, and we'll find you the slot for your skills." I wasn't privy to discussions, but it was decided to give him to the editor of BBC Breakfast News, and see what happened: factor in an hour-long Sunday show to add to the week-day roster, and

watch the results. It was imagined as loosely part of our breakfast family of programmes, though we didn't know how it would
work. David being David, he of course wanted to bring all his
old friends from TV-AM with him, and he also wanted it to be
a Paradine production. But the Beeb drew the line at this. "No,
no," they said, "we need you under a BBC contract, adhering to
our editorial world," and after much huffing and puffing, that's
what happened.

This was a significant moment in British politics. Many people
had expected and many polls had forecast that the 1992 election
would see Labour returned to power under Neil Kinnock. Instead,
John Major was back in Downing Street, and Labour was soul-
searching, gripped once more with introspection, and wondering if
the party could ever form a government again. The Conservatives,
meanwhile, were in many ways no better off. They had won the
election, but were riven internally by the issue of Europe. It was,
in other words, an extremely fluid and volatile political phase, and
one pregnant with opportunity. Frost and the BBC were anxious
to perfect their formula, including, as Jones recalls, agonising over
a title for "ages before we settled on the *Breakfast With Frost* tag.
It had to have Frost in there somewhere. And at least we managed
to have some fun with the title sequence: that was always the most
fun you can have, with titles and set. And so we sat around, the
production team and Tony Hall and I and we cooked the whole
thing up."

From the beginning, the BBC was aiming at a comfortable, populist programme. So early on a Sunday morning, it could realistically
aim at nothing else. If it scheduled a programme on, for example,
the trade deficit, a Sunday-morning audience would have switched
off in droves. "So, we settled on a big interview, surrounded by lots
of other stuff: newspaper reviews, and a clutter of newspapers on
the coffee table as people would have it at home. We wanted something – not cold, not analytical, but warm and cosy, an extension
of our viewers' own Sunday, and an extension of their homes. And

David in the middle of it, rattling papers, flicking, pointing out material, deliberately discursive."[466]

Breakfast with Frost began early in January, 1993 – kicking off with an interview with the prime minister, John Major, who later remarked that, "As an interviewer, he was deadly, but he was always a fair interviewer. He didn't play cheap tricks, he didn't look for a cheap headline, his determination was to get out of the interviewee what they had to give."[467] The second show featured the new Labour leader, John Smith; the third featured Paddy Ashdown of the Liberal Democrats; and the fourth – in something of a flourish – Frost's friend George Bush, who had only weeks before relinquished the Oval Office to Bill Clinton. At this time too, Frost flew to South Africa to interview Nelson Mandela against the backdrop of a country preparing for its first democratic elections for more than fifty years. This interview was teamed with a session with Frost for PBS, and was instrumental in establishing Mandela's post-incarceration credentials as a man of peace, with a vision for a new, post-apartheid South Africa. "There is no time to be bitter," Mandela told Frost, underscoring this message. "There is work to be done." It was the first of three meetings with Mandela – including a question-and-answer session on a Cunard liner sailing between Cape Town and Durban.

By this stage, ITV's lunchtime politics programme was indeed eclipsed: it had been blown out of the water, and Frost was off and away. And Barney Jones was getting accustomed to working with a new and sometimes idiosyncratic colleague. Frost had underlined the importance of his family weekends with Carina and their children – Miles was nine that year, Wilfred eight and George six – in the Hampshire countryside, and had also observed that he liked to arrive in the studio with only minutes to spare before broadcast. Neither of these factors was especially welcome. Hampshire was a long way away, and the technical staff in any studio prefers its quarry to be dressed, made-up, seated and lit well in advance. But as Jones soon discovered, there was little room for negotiation on either point. These arrangements suited his new colleague. Indeed, life suited his colleague now more than it had ever done. "Although I'm very grateful obviously for the contribution that my girlfriends have made to my life, and Lynne too, the present is very much Carina and the boys. In that sense, it feels like I've never been married before, though I know full well I have. [...] Even allowing for the fact that I'm a Pollyanna, I think it's the happiest time of my life so far."[468]

And indeed, family life was at this time a source of great happiness. The boys, now growing up, shared their father's love of sport, and Michelmersh provided the perfect context. As Wilfred Frost recalls:

All Miles, George and I wanted to do was to play sport. This was football all year round, with tennis and cricket added in the summer. Dad was now in his fifties, but he was still quite the sportsman, and certainly better than us until we were well into our teens. But Dad of course had to work on Saturdays ahead of *Breakfast with Frost* on Sundays. So it would be a battle to tear him away from his desk (not that hard) – no doubt to Barney Jones's frustration! We used to like to hide in his huge study and jump out at him – he would of course pretend that he didn't know we were in there. But at times, if there was a very important call to take, then we were not to disturb him. Mum developed a traffic-light system at the study door: red meant we mustn't disturb him, green meant joking was fair game. Of course, sometimes this didn't work. I remember a few occasions when we were already hidden, and then a phone call would come in, and Dad would answer: "Prime Minister, how good to hear from you," or, "Mr President!" We would then have to sit tight for what felt like the longest and most boring conversation in the world to finish ...

The BBC, then, devised a new regime to fit around the Frost family timetable. Frost would be collected from Michelmersh early on Sunday morning, to arrive at a reasonable time in studio – in the first years of *Breakfast with Frost*, the programme was shot in Studio One at Television Centre, where *That Was the Week That Was* had been filmed thirty years before – in time to be made-up and seated. The process worked: that is, Frost was never actually late for a programme; but it set nerves on edge weekly. As Joan Bakewell – frequently on the guest roster as a newspaper reviewer – notes: "He always left it to the last minute to arrive, which drove us all mad. It was terribly stressful. The producers liked people there ages before – 7.30am for a 9am show – and David would come blowing in with ten minutes to spare. But having said that, he had filleted the newspapers in the meantime, there in the back of his limo: so it all tended to work."[469]

Jones noted other Frost characteristics: while the production crew agonised about budgets and deadlines, Frost breezed through on a wave of positivity. And he was extremely difficult to pin down: this or that production meeting was paused, postponed, delayed because Frost had a meeting at Paradine, or a trip to the United States (where *Talking with David Frost* was now at full tilt) or a dinner with the Prince of Wales or the Archbishop of Canterbury. And so, "nailing him down was – it was a problem. It was always a problem. He had so many business interests he was looking after too; always a million schemes under way."[470]

And Frost was – BBC contract notwithstanding – certainly taking care of Paradine at this time. His deal with the BBC provided for domestic rights only – a clause the Corporation discounted or failed to note during the drawing up of contracts. As a result, Frost was free to sell the show internationally, and he did so, agreeing with Sky News that *Breakfast with Frost* could be shown following its broadcast on BBC1. The deal showed Frost's business acumen, not to say his opportunism, and it was not without its comical side, although the BBC was, perhaps, less than amused when it realised the situation.

We ran the show a half-hour after it was broadcast on the BBC. And we scratched our heads and said, "But the BBC will never agree to this!" and he said, "Oh! No, no, we own international rights; the Beeb only has domestic rights! Now, you're an

international broadcaster, so do you want the show or not?"
And I said, "Yes, please!" and so all we had to do was to revise
it. In fact, it was a delicate editing process to take out the BBC
News logos, slot in commercial breaks; and I did this myself, a
very quick editing process, always very touch and go. And so the
BBC now realised it had missed the loophole in David's contract.
I had cut around BBC logos and so on – but the following week,
the BBC *filled* the screen, the set, the studios, the books on the
shelves with the BBC logo. It was then impossible of course to edit
around – so we just had to go ahead and show the programme as
it was – the point being that it became a plus point for us, to be
thought worthy of screening heavyweight BBC shows – and this
was worth a great deal in those early Sky days.[471]

The programme was now fully established – and it would continue
to attract a line of political and cultural worthies. John Smith's
death in May 1994 brought the young and fresh-faced Tony Blair
to the fore as the next Labour leader, and soon he was nurturing a
relationship. In the leadership contest that followed Smith's death,
Blair was anxious to appear on the show as a means of cultivating
the image of a leader in waiting. Later, the leadership secured, he
and his advisers continued to use the clout that the programme
now possessed:

Sunday 12 June, 1994: TB did well on *Frost*. Looked the part,
spoke well, nothing untoward came out of it. TB called later and
said that he didn't think he had done that well. Frost was tougher
than he expected him to be, and he didn't think he had handled
the tougher questions that well.

Saturday 7 October, 1995: I called Barney Jones of the *Frost*
programme and asked him not to discuss [the impending defec-
tion of Conservative MP Alan Howarth to Labour] this with
anybody but Frost himself. I did not give a name, but said that
a Conservative MP would be defecting to us during the course

of the day and we would like his first interview to be on Frost. He was gobsmacked. [Next day] Alan Clark had been on *Frost* reviewing the papers and of course he slagged off Howarth in the tribal way you would expect.[472]

David Frost and his programme continued to pepper Campbell's diaries: now, Campbell is lunching with Frost at the Carlton Tower hotel in Belgravia: "[Frost] was convinced we were on course for a big win. He was desperate for us to agree to a TV debate when the election came, and to back him as anchor. [...] I always find David Frost funny, interesting and charming. With most people, I would have found it unacceptable to have them lighting up a cigar and billowing out smoke all over the place while I was eating; but with him it was somehow acceptable"; now, he and Blair are role-playing (as Frost himself did in advance of his big interviews) in the back of Blair's car en route to the BBC, early on a Sunday morning in March 1996; now, Campbell and Frost are lunching at Bibendum in October 1996, with Campbell parrying Frost's requests both for a TV debate, and for an interview with Blair's wife Cherie Booth.[473] Campbell noted other idiosyncrasies, in particular his messy eating habits, which were part of the general miasma of chaos – mislaid bags, mislaid coats, leaking pens and dishevelled suits – that tended to surround Frost. He recalls one particular breakfast amid the august surroundings of Claridge's: "David had ordered smoked salmon and scrambled eggs, and David topped his forkful of scrambled eggs with a quail's egg and bit into it – and out popped the yolk, sailed through the air and landed on his tie in a lurid streak – and of course David simply carried on talking regardless."[474] And to quails' eggs may be added ink stains: Sarah, Duchess of York, recalls, "David always used Tempo pens, I remember, and he would have the ink from them all over his hands and his face, rather than on the page."[475]

The connection between Blair and Frost in many ways mirrors the relationship the interviewer had had with George and Barbara Bush. The Frost boys remember games of football at Michelmersh and at the prime-ministerial country retreat at Chequers, following the landslide Labour victory in the General Election of 1997. It was a mutually beneficial relationship, and was nurtured on both sides. Blair recalls his conversations with Frost on the nature of faith and religion: a joint interest, but a topic which Frost tended in general to be wary of discussing in public. There were few chances to broadcast on this topic. Trevor Poots remembers one such opportunity, *An Easter Enigma*, broadcast on the BBC in 1996, which led to unease. "We collected an excellent panel: Karen Armstrong, AN Wilson, Robin Lane Fox, Paul Johnson. At a certain stage in the discussion, the panellists began pointing out how little actual evidence exists for the Resurrection, and David was desperately ill at ease. He did not want to hear this, or have to chair a discussion on such a topic. I could see him wriggling, obviously very disturbed. This belief in God affected much of what he did."[476] In spite of this personal discomfort, however, the programme – much to Frost's pleasure – was a critical success.

For Tony Blair, Sunday-morning interviews with Frost soon became part of the political furniture. "I wouldn't go so far as to say that we arranged the political year around the Frost programme," Blair says, "but it is the case that we did plan to make certain policy statements on his show, the better to get the news out in the media, to kick-start the policy as well as we could." He trusted Frost to keep the personal side of things personal, the professional side of things professional – and never to rupture the invisible but critical membrane between the two. "He was professional, is the bottom line: he was a professional at what he did. He understood the need for trust, for discretion, not that I would have gone through the Cabinet papers with him in any case, of course, but I knew I could speak with him in the knowledge that any information wouldn't be used against me the next time I was sitting on his sofa in the studio."[477]

As Frost paid attention to his relationship with Blair, so he paid attention to the programme itself. It assumed many of the characteristics that he liked to attach to himself – and in particular it began to build the reputation as a safe and hospitable place for its guests. As had been the case at TV-AM, a cheery breakfast was laid on for guests. Barney Jones had feared that a parsimonious BBC would never run to such luxuries as a cooked breakfast, but he undertook a little sleuthing which brought good news. "'Let's have a celebratory breakfast,' said David on that first morning, 'let's have some drinks.' But I knew that the Beeb would never sanction drinks, we drew the line at drinks – so David brought his own bottles of champagne. And then I discovered that there actually were always BBC chefs on duty on a Sunday morning, who never had anything to do – so we had a nice breakfast afterwards, and David said, 'Well, the guests enjoyed that, didn't they, so let's do it every week. Let's really bind the guests in, let's make them see that there is more to this programme than work. let's cultivate a loyalty that way!' And we did, and it worked, and we still do it today. So that you'd have a situation where the conversation would go something like this: 'Oh, Prime Minister, and have you met David Seaman?' Very jolly occasions."[478] Jolly – but not without a certain tough-minded intent. Frost himself was never off-duty – indeed, this was one of his defining characteristics – and while his guests were tucking into hot breakfasts, letting their guard down and enjoying the champagne, he was listening, and logging everything as knowledge for future use.

Frost's name became a talisman of sorts – it served to open many doors, and succeeded in getting his colleagues past the doorkeeper. And from time to time, he delivered the guests personally – and in particular, his flourishing American career opened a world of opportunity to his British producers. As Jones notes, it was easier to get a secretary of state because Frost's stock, in the aftermath of *The Next President* and with *Talking with David Frost* still running, was again so high in the States. This was a crucial point: Frost's British peers in the media simply did not have his clout and his international reach. And this relationship flowed in both directions. US guests were pleased and reassured by Frost's new BBC credentials too, and reassured by his connection with a trusted global brand.

This symbiosis underscores once more the sense that Frost's activities on both sides of the Atlantic nourished one another, and underpinned his broadcasting career as a whole.

And of course, Frost himself was at this point in his life also a trusted brand. He was sufficiently known and sufficiently trusted and understood that guests were already likely to gravitate towards him. Late in his life, he acknowledged this essential point himself:

> I think after a time if people have seen you on television, they can make their own decision. And if they like what they see in terms of you being fair or whatever, they can make their own decision. So I think that is the visiting card really, that they have seen you on television. And one of the other things about it is people you've never met before, because they've seen you on television, it's like a reunion rather than getting to know you. So, when I was interviewing Al Gore for the first time in 1988 in the States, he said, "Oh, I used to love *That Was the Week That Was*," and so on and so forth in the States. And you know, it was like we'd known each other for years. We hadn't, of course! – but it enabled the interview to get going much quicker.[479]

Tony Hall notes that, "People would come to the show because of David. They knew they'd be treated correctly, that a certain style came along with David. [...] It was successful above and beyond even what I had expected."[480] And Barney Jones observes, "We liked to get big names. It built up an aura around the programme that was very necessary, and made the future easier to build and structure. And we liked to get them in certain contexts – the Élysée Palace, the White House – it built prestige, and David helped with all this."[481] Some of this professional success Joanna Lumley puts down to Frost's "empathetic quality, which was uncommon in a man of a certain age, and especially uncommon in powerful men. His name opened doors, in a way that was extraordinary and rare; it carried an authority, and doors would swing open. But he was never grand or swanky about it."[482] But not everyone was pleased: it continued to madden functionaries and intermediaries when Frost simply bypassed them and went straight to the top.

It was one thing to make connections that would ease the production process, but quite another thing to mingle indiscriminately the various networks of his life. And in particular, David Frost preferred to keep his British and American circles separate. This was part of his tendency to micro-manage and maintain small and trusted teams – all as a means of retaining control over the various arms of Paradine, and of his business in general. This had its uses, to be sure, but it also created weaknesses in Frost's business structures, and atomised his vision. "His advisers were few," remembers John Florescu, and his business acumen:

> had its limits. He had no long-term strategic vision of where he wanted to take his company. Planning memos were summarily ignored. During one late-night call from LA, I asked him, "What do you want me to do with this company [Paradine]?"; and he cut to his corporate philosophy succinctly: "Make money while I sleep." And, unless cross-selling of shows was involved, the American staff and the London staff were mostly unaware of what the other was up to. Even though his one-man conglomerate often swelled to dozens, depending on shows in production, Frost had a Metternich-like divide-and-rule approach to his organisation. I always felt that he liked to control the show.[483]

Michael Rosenberg, who had guided his business affairs for three decades, agrees that Frost had little in terms of a strategic vision. "Many, many times we would try to get him to talk business and get Paradine to evolve into a major production house, but he was unwilling to divorce the personality from the company. *Through the Keyhole* exemplified this. He identified very closely with the brand, and when the rights were sold, as they were, for example, to Fremantle, he resisted very much the idea that the format might travel without him. Which of course it did and very successfully: and the fees came rolling in without him having to lift a finger. He ought to have enjoyed this, but he didn't. He was very possessive, and a bad delegator, and found it difficult to let go. Eventually his advisers would have to bang the gavel to get him to see sense."[484]

Only from time to time would David Frost permit his various worlds come together. This might take the simple form of an American partner joining Frost and British friends for dinner in London; or the regular summer jaunts to London undertaken by his old friend Herb Siegel and his family, filled with pleasant, companionable visits to Michelmersh and to Wimbledon; or a favour done for a friend, as in the case of Howard Stringer, who in 1996 had just completed a spell as president of CBS. "I never knew his entire circle because of course I was in America and outside his London operations. But in 1996, I was awarded the Medal of Honour at the St George's Society of New York, which is presented to a person who furthers British interests in America. I called David and asked him to be the one who would present the medal to me, and he flew over – I didn't pay for it – and he dazzled with his speech, he had the place in stitches; and so I threw away my speech, because I couldn't come close to him! The organisers said, 'I don't suppose he'd come over every year?' It was the sort of thing he would do for you, that had nothing to do with self-interest."[485]

And it also from time to time involved Frost's ongoing charity work – as was the case in 1987, when Princess Diana, who was royal patron of the charity Wellbeing of Women (then known as Birthright), asked Frost to engage in a fundraising drive for the charity in America. Wellbeing of Women had been founded in the 1960s: its original aim had been to raise awareness of the number of women and babies who died in childbirth and during pregnancy more generally; and to raise funds for research into the reasons for such deaths and how they might be prevented. It was as a result of research funded by Birthright, for example, that folic acid was discovered to bolster a healthy pregnancy – and soon this became a standard pregnancy supplement across the western world. Research sponsored by the charity led to advances on many other fronts. Diana connected with the charity in 1984, and Frost several years later – an interest whetted by his sense of gratitude that he and Carina Frost had had three healthy children.

In 1988, Diana – now godmother to the small George Frost – had agreed to attend a lunch in support of the charity at the Savoy in London. Fundraising in general, however, was not going especially well, and it was for this reason that she intervened with Frost and made the request that he undertake the task. In America, as John Florescu remembers, this led to a meeting at the Melrose Hotel in Washington:

"Let's have a little fun with this," he says; and he whisks out his big black address book – and he calls the King brothers from New Jersey, syndicated-access television kings of North America; [Frost's British friend] Howard Stringer, who was president at CBS; Richard Gelb who was CEO of [pharmaceutical corporation] Bristol Myers; Clay Felker. And he calls them one by one and tells them to stump up for Wellbeing of Women, and I was to be the secretary of this society, and in about two hours he had raised $400,000. And more: he had convinced those paying that they were lucky to be called. Time flicks forward to February 1989. David had told these funders that there would be a chance to meet Diana when she came to New York, and in due course she arrived, and he asked could he arrange to have a little reception at her hotel, the Plaza Athénée on 64th Street. She liked everything just so – certain flowers, certain colour schemes, apricot juice in her suite – and we were all invited for a quick hello; and the British ambassador to the United Nations at the time was there, high with nerves and worried whether all these corporate people that Frost was bringing along could muster the delicacy necessary to meet a British princess. And it was true, these tough CEOs were standing there cowering like children – or lined up like bowling pins, is much more like it – to be introduced. And I noticed that Diana did have a wonderful way of looking directly at you and making you feel like you were the only person in the room; this was a knack she shared with

David. And so there she was, splendidly beautiful and dressed all in white; and there all these men were, behaving as though they were on their first date; and the British ambassador watching this scene with a raised eyebrow. And one by one, David effected the introductions – and we got to the King brothers. Now these guys were hugely successful but were essentially working-class boys-done-good from New Jersey. And one of them pipes up: "You may be the princess, but we're the Kings," and the ambassador's face imploded, just like that – and then, in for a penny, in for a pound, the other King brother invites Diana to go on *Wheel of Fortune*, and she very skilfully smiles and moves away; and the ambassador just about has a cardiac arrest.[486]

Frost had run his fundraising activities in America past his friend Victor Blank, tabling them as an example to follow in Britain. But the sums of money involved could not readily be duplicated in London society, and it was unlikely that the format would go down especially well either – and Blank knew it. Instead, Frost's activities for Wellbeing of Women took on a distinctly English form: his long-running charity cricket match, held each summer in the English countryside. "The phenomenal levels of cash that [Frost] was raising at a stroke in the United States was simply not in our league," remembers Blank, "and so when he mentioned Wellbeing of Women to me, I told him this – and then I said, 'Look. I've just bought a house and some land in Oxfordshire, with a flat meadow that I was thinking of having as a cricket pitch.' And I said, 'I'm thinking of putting on a cricket pro-am for charity and what do you think of that?' And time went by, Christmas ... and then it was February 1988, and suddenly David phoned and said, 'OK, I have the following people ready to play: Imran Khan, Phil Edmonds, Dennis Lillee, Clive Lloyd and John Edrich.'"[487] Blank rounded up a number of wealthy friends in the City of London who were willing to pay £10,000 for the privilege of sharing a ground with such players. That first charity match for Wellbeing of Women, in the summer of 1988, raised £150,000 – and in the course of the next twenty-five years, David Frost, Victor Blank and the England cricketer Mark Nicholas would help to raise an extraordinary £6 million for charity.

Miranda Gallimore, Frost's personal assistant from 2003, remembers "telling my dad, 'Oh, yes, today, I watched Shane Warne bowl to Sunil Gavaskar being caught out by Allan Lamb, while being umpired by Ian Botham, and I was sitting on the boundary at a table with Mike Brearley,' and my father was speechless, as well he might have been".[488] And Warne himself recalls that Frost "had such energy and such a sense of fun. He was tremendous to be around".[489] But not everyone was pleased. Carina Frost fretted, especially in later years, that the effort was too much for her husband, and that it was absorbing energy he no longer had to spare as the shadows of age grew longer: "I was always having to stop people from taking too much of him."[490]

And Carina was right to be concerned. Shane Warne recalls Frost at the wicket as "a tough bugger" – but tough or not, a near-miss at the charity cricket match in the summer of 2005 caused him to call it a day.[491] "His enthusiasm knew no bounds," recalls Nicholas, "but the fact is that he wasn't any good. On this particular day, he was keeping wicket as usual, with Wasim Akram coming in on a short bowl, and we said, 'Frostie, come back a pace or two, come back a pace or two, come *back* a pace or two.' So, eventually, he said, 'I shall defer to your better judgement,' and he came back a pace. And the bowler bowled – and without the batsman even having a chance to pick up his bat, the ball thumped into David's chest – and he fell forward on his face, out cold, his glasses smashed. We all held our breath. We went to him, we gathered him, he was breathing, the ambulance came, he was whisked off. And, thank God, he came back around 6.30pm, bruised and battered – never to play again. 'I think I probably learned my lesson,' he said. He still came to every match, he was still committed fully – but he never played again."[492]

*

Breakfast with Frost ran for twelve years – and Barney Jones recalls programmes that in hindsight seem exceptional. In July 1993, John Major and his Cabinet critic and leadership rival John Redwood – named in a leaked conversation as a Eurosceptic "bastard" by the embattled prime minister – were coaxed to appear on the same edition of the programme. In a sign of the dysfunctional nature of the government of the day, these two party colleagues were interviewed at separate times, Major being ushered out of one BBC door as Redwood entered by a second. And Alastair Campbell recalls Frost's distinctive reaction when the prospect of a dual Blair–Clinton interview was in sight: "How would you like an interview with Tony [Blair] at the G8?" Alastair Campbell asked Frost. "Great," replied Frost. Campbell said, "And how about we throw in Clinton?" Frost replied, "Orgasmic!"[493]

In 2000, Tony Blair used an appearance on the Frost show to declare that the government intended to raise British health spending to the European average in the course of the next few years. This was a pledge that would cost billions, and that had not been disclosed in advance to Blair's colleagues. It was reported that Chancellor Gordon Brown was apoplectic at the news – but Blair himself recalls that the decision had not been spun out of him by Frost. "No, no. We intended to do it; it was part of the plan of the interview."[494] And Alastair Campbell adds that, "David loved being in on this kind of news. He loved exactly this sort of professional buzz."[495] The episode made waves, and demonstrates that the programme remained a political forum of choice.

In December 2002, footballer David Beckham and his England manager Sven-Göran Eriksson were interviewed together – not at the BBC studio, but in a small room in the basement of Buckingham Palace, on the fringes of a Palace reception being attended by both men. "We snuck a few cameras in and put together a mock-Frost studio set down there, and David was completely thrilled with this because he was so completely football-mad." The set was manifestly too small: Frost, Beckham and Eriksson were squeezed together, and Frost's red socks were set off nicely by a theatrical backdrop of a pair of sweeping crimson Buckingham Palace curtains, but nobody complained and the interview passed off smoothly. And in March 2004, his old friend Annabel Goldsmith appeared on the programme to publicise her memoirs. "He was very kind. He said, 'Divine one, you are definitely coming on my programme, aren't you?' And of course once I got there, I made a fool of myself. I mentioned my two husbands and I said to David, 'I sometimes wish I'd been a sort of, could have been a one, a sort of one-woman man,' and then I did a David, and knocked a lamp over on my way out of the studio, which is exactly the sort of thing he would do himself. It was sweet of him to have me on. Needless to say, I only went the once."[496]

Frost's *divine one* was, in fact, of a piece with his usual form of expression with family and close friends. Naim Attallah wrote in the *Daily Telegraph* how he and Frost "often bumped into each other at airports when he would cheerfully greet me at the top of his voice, unfazed by the multitude of passengers around, calling out, 'Hello, sweet prince!' – an affectionate expression I'm unlikely to ever forget, despite my embarrassment whenever it happened at the time."[497] Meanwhile, George Frost recalls visiting his father's office and hearing "Dad ending a phone call with, 'OK, wonderful – I cannot wait to see you, gorgeous, gorgeous person.' I asked how Mum was, was she back? And Dad replied that it hadn't been Mum on the phone; it had been Peter Chadlington."[498] Carina Frost, meanwhile, was the "child bride" to Goldsmith's "divine one", and the latter has provided a glimpse of a private Frost life that was content and jolly:

David still calls me the "divine one", which dates back to something that happened years ago on Sandy Lane beach in Barbados. While David was busy making sandcastles for the boys, Carina and I were having a dip in the sea to cool off. As we emerged, David looked up, opened his arms wide and shouted at the top of his voice everyone on the beach to hear: "Ah, here comes the child bride and the divine one!" Heads turned in bewilderment, as Carina may have looked every inch the beautiful child bride, but they could see no sign of the divine one.[499]

*

In the years they worked together successfully on *Breakfast with Frost*, Barney Jones was able to get to know his colleague reasonably well, and several characteristics stood out. He continued to have a weakness for good-looking women, sometimes at the expense of his professional judgement. "We clashed, I remember, about [the model] Elle McPherson. David had met her at a party, and he said to me, 'I think she should come on the show.' I asked him why exactly Elle McPherson should come on the show. 'Well, because she's very beautiful, and famous and successful.' Yes, but what was her handle? What would she have to actually say? 'No, I mean, I don't know – but she's very beautiful.' He was quite personality-led."[500] Jones also realised – as others had realised throughout Frost's life – that the man continued to lack interests outside of work, that he lacked the hinterland that one might have taken for granted, given his career and its longevity. He remained uninterested in culture in general: in the visual arts, in radio, cinema and theatre. He even lacked an interest in television itself as a visual experience – he understood how it worked, and was passionate about programme-making – but he hardly ever actually watched the box. And in addition, his resistance to new technologies had now hardened: they were set in stone, even as the world of television – and the BBC itself – began to probe new frontiers unthinkable even a few years previously. And there was little else that would stimulate him. As Miles Frost notes, "He had no hobbies as such: he loved cricket, loved Arsenal and Norwich City; but there was little apart from that that he did for pure joy."[501]

John Birt stepped down as director general in 2000, to be replaced by Greg Dyke. This was another instance of good fortune smiling on Frost: Dyke, like Birt, continued to respect David Frost's talent, and Dyke, like Birt, continued to defend Frost from detractors inside the Corporation. For there certainly were critics: voices murmuring that Frost had lost his edge, had lost his bite, had gone soft with his interviewees.

And so, when Dyke left the BBC prematurely in January 2004 – having resigned in the aftermath of the Hutton Report into the Corporation's coverage of aspects of the Iraq War – Frost was, perhaps more than he realised, left exposed. He had applied for the position of BBC chairman, which had also fallen vacant in the aftermath of Hutton. But it was evident to friends that his application was made ambivalently. The job paid £80,000 per annum for essentially a two-day week, but he understood the constraint it would nevertheless apply to his other business interests; and there was no heartbreak when he failed to land the post. Meanwhile, *Breakfast with Frost* ran in its existing format for another year. But in 2005, it was announced that Frost would be leaving the show in May, to be replaced by the journalist Andrew Marr. When the decision was made to let Frost go, the BBC had nobody lined up to replace him – there was, at that point, no actual Plan B – but "the bosses had decided that David had less fire in his belly, and that he needed to go. There was a sense that the big beasts were finding it all too easy, too cosy – and that if a prime minister was due an interview, then they needed to be hauled through a *Newsnight* or a *Today* studio instead. And there was a sense too that David had had a good run, and that it was now time to let someone else have a go. And my own sense was that he was now losing his physical vigour physically; that age was catching up with him."[502]

It was, by common consent, a profound shock for David Frost. His week was structured around a Sunday slot that suited him precisely. Carina Frost remarks that "the breakfast slots had been perfect for him; it was good for his family; and there was a continuity in it, which he adored. And the programme inherited an address book that it would never have had without David – it was a window on the world that the programme could never have opened on its own."[503] For Miranda Gallimore, "I never heard him say a bad word about anyone at the BBC: he was annoyed, and frustrated because he had been able to bring a huge amount to that slot, but he didn't go on about it. Lady C was much more distressed, as is usually the way with these things."[504] George Frost agrees that his father "loved

Breakfast With Frost: he loved the structure, the slot, the space it gave him."[505] John Florescu says that "the BBC let him go too soon – and it was a terrible shock, because it was the centrepiece of his life. When it went, the central pivot of his life was removed too."[506] And Greg Dyke is scathing of the BBC's decision: "Some people at BBC News were embarrassed by Frost, they didn't think he was right for the show. It didn't seem to matter to them that he got all the names, that he could get anyone he wanted; all of that seemed irrelevant, which I just didn't understand."[507]

It is certainly the case that Frost's departure from his show created a flurry in media circles. In his autobiography, the journalist and former politician Gyles Brandreth made much of Carina Frost's distress at the circumstances in which her husband found himself. Wilfred Frost remarks in response that Brandreth "was a close friend of my parents – he even spoke at Miles, George and my shared twenty-first birthday party – and yet he reported a private conversation of his recently widowed friend to help his book. That's pretty damned cheap. The point is, I think, that my mother has been a wonderfully loyal wife and mother; and her disappointment at Dad's pain was hardly surprising."[508]

Andrew Marr himself speaks with grace and warmth of his predecessor:

I thought of [Frost's interview style] as "caress, caress, nod, smile – kidney punch – smile, smile". It could be devastatingly effective. [Politicians] come on expecting an easy ride, and they leave behind headlines they hadn't expected. I think my style is different. I interrupt more, I smile slightly less; but I have learned a great deal from the master. I keep an entire interview in my head before I start, I know where I'm going, and I have learned the power of a short, direct and preferably unexpected question, when the interviewee is starting to feel relaxed. What I haven't learned is how to deal with a robotically-prepared politician who isn't really listening to the questions and doesn't want to: how rude can you be in jolting them. I'm sure [Frost] was bitterly upset to lose the programme. All I would say is that none of us holds any of these things as of right, and my time will come too. I know something of the hurt of losing a big job […] I also know that it is entirely human to resent whoever takes over. I say this because David himself was always entirely charming, pleasant, courteous to me. He didn't help me, as such – why would he? – but I never got the impression that he wanted the programme to fail without him. It has developed very differently over the past decade, but we still get well over two million viewers many weeks, make front-page headlines again and again, and I hope have retained a relatively warm atmosphere: in all these ways, David's spirit still stalks our studio.[509]

With the end of *Breakfast with Frost*, David Frost was thrown back very much on his own resources. For a period, the atmosphere at the Paradine offices was frenetic, with Frost hustling for work, for new commissions, for new material to keep the momentum of his career. "When it ended," remembers Miranda Gallimore, "he just began taking on more stuff; and getting busier and busier. When it went, it was glorious chaos – I worried it was going the wrong way – but he put in longer and longer hours, and later and later finishes. He also began drinking less: he had the habit of bringing me a glass of wine at my desk between five and six – a good management technique because it kept me working late – but it seemed to me that his consumption of alcohol began to diminish." Although certain habits remained much as the same as usual: much time, for example, was spent pursuing his cashmere Doug Hayward coat from restaurant to restaurant across London, and from plane to plane across the world. "I used to suggest that he just get a cheaper coat, but that wasn't seen as a very practical solution. He would never forget his briefcase, but as the seasons changed, he would forget his coat every single day."[510]

This frenetic period also included a second appearance on the BBC's *Desert Island Discs*. Whereas his previous luxury had been an endless supply of potato crisps, now he chose a supply of the

Sunday newspapers; and swapped the complete works of Chaucer for the London *A–Z*. His choice of music was instructive: tracks by Elton John and The Beatles nodded to long-standing personal friendships; Ray Charles's rendition of "America The Beautiful" glanced at Frost's love of that country; while a track by Coldplay acknowledged the central role in his life now taken by his sons. This period would culminate a year later – in a highly audacious move that surprised media observers and David Frost's friends alike. And at much the same time, David Frost's long-ago encounter with Richard Nixon re-emerged, most surprisingly, into his life.

*

At certain points in *Frost/Nixon*, my role called for me to stand on the stage of the Donmar and look out into the audience as part of the play. I knew that on the evening of the very first preview, the audience had been filled with Frost's lawyers; and now, on *this* preview, I caught sight of a profile that I thought looked familiar. And afterwards, Michael Grandage popped his head around the door of my dressing room and said, "Frostie's in; he's waiting for you in the bar." So up I go, and there Frost is, standing with a drink and his hands shaking slightly, and I said, "So, what did you think?" And he said, "In the words of Yogi Berra: it's like déjà vu, all over again." And he was very supportive after that. The lawyers peeled away, and he came to the play again with his family, and everything was good after that point.[511]

The Donmar is a small London theatre, seating a bare 250; and since its foundation in the years after the Second World War, it has established a reputation in British theatre for innovative writing and excellent productions. Michael Grandage had been artistic director at the Donmar since 2002 – and now the theatre was producing a play by a writer new to the stage. Peter Morgan, forty-three years old that summer, had established his reputation with a piece written for television. *The Deal*, set in 1993, dramatised the agreement between Tony Blair and Gordon Brown – reputedly struck over a tense meal at the Granita restaurant in north London – concerning the leadership of a British Labour Party on the verge of achieving power. Morgan's focus in that superb piece had been the fraught connections between fact – the actual verifiable stuff of documentary and of history – and its relationship with fiction, with extrapolation, with how the weave of history might be dramatised and represented on television. Now, Morgan was again parsing the relationship between fact and fiction in a game similarly played for high stakes. The title of the play was *Frost/Nixon*.

In some respects, Morgan's focus on David Frost's relationship with Richard Nixon was an odd choice. The mid-1970s was for many a distant era, and the subject matter lacked the immediacy and electricity of *The Deal*, the principal figures from which were still on the political scene. David Frost himself was now sixty-six years old. His weekend programme had established him at the centre of British political journalism, but the obverse side of this status was a lack of immediate relevance to a younger generation, to those not yet born when he was fronting *That Was the Week That Was* in the early 1960s. In addition, his dealings with Nixon were remembered as a foggy episode from the past – if they were remembered at all.

On the face of it, then, Morgan, Grandage and the Donmar were taking something of a chance in developing this production. "Peter Morgan had become fascinated by Frost and Nixon," remembers Matthew Byam Shaw, the show's producer. "I remember him speaking about Frost, about Nixon, about Nixon's fall, but also about the trajectory of Frost's career, which he found intriguing. He fixed on this idea that Frost had had an amazing run on television and had enjoyed genuine television achievement – and he was also interested in the idea that a generation was beginning not to know who Frost was."[512]

But this prospective show had certain intrinsic factors in its favour. It had a strong cast: Nixon was played by Frank Langella, seasoned American actor of stage and screen, who had lately been seen with George Clooney in *Goodnight and Good Luck*, but whose career stretched back to the 1960s, and encompassed a pair of Tony awards. Frost was played by Michael Sheen, who had with uncanny likeness portrayed a broadly smiling Tony Blair in *The Deal*. And Morgan's work was now attracting wide attention. It had, for example, been widely reported that a new film scripted by him would be worth a look: *The Queen*, starring Helen Mirren and dramatising the startling and dramatic days that followed the death in Paris in 1997 of Diana, Princess of Wales, was opening at the Venice Film Festival the following month. In a striking further blurring of the distinction between fact and fiction, Sheen was to reprise the role of Blair in the film. "I returned from a trip to France for the opening," recalls Byam Shaw. "London in summer – very warm, very sultry – and I became aware of a lot of important people who would normally have been in the country or in Tuscany at that time of year, and I saw that, yes, *Frost/Nixon* was onto something."

David Frost did not attend the opening performance at the Donmar. He and Carina had gone along instead to a preview – and their presence there in the small theatre had been noted and had caused a further heightening of this sense of unreality, with the audience responding tentatively and with embarrassment to what was unfolding on stage. It was challenging for the actors too, to have such a figure lurking in the stalls. The show, as was usually the case at preview stage, remained jagged, bumpy; the principals had a good deal of work still to do to iron out the production. For Sheen, as for Morgan himself, Frost had become a figure of some fascination:

> He intrigued me: the trajectory of his career from Cambridge to *TW3*, the tremendous success that had come so early; and what this meant to him. I was interested too by the impact that people's reactions had on him: the fact that certain people had reacted very badly to him, the fact that that he had, in certain quarters, been so divisive. He had never been allowed into a certain club – into the *Beyond the Fringe* club – and so I thought that there must be always have been a separateness there in his head, and an armour, a defence. I found myself wondering

about the impact all that had on him, and I speculated about the interior steel he must have had to handle all that. And I was also interested in his work on what Kenneth Tynan had called "low art" and "high art". Frost had always worked in different formats and he simply *expected* his serious work to be taken seriously, which was another aspect of his personality that ruffled feathers. A week into rehearsals, I had gone along to a party organised by Channel Four, and as I was about to go into this party, I saw David Frost coming out – and instead of going to the party, I decided to follow Frost instead. We hadn't yet met, and so I followed him along the street at a safe distance and watched him move, seeing him as an animal in the landscape.[513]

And now, here was the silhouette himself, glimpsed disconcertingly in the stalls. Frost had been ambivalent about the production – for there were aspects to *Frost/Nixon* that he was hard pressed to like very much. Morgan had – as he had every right to do, for this was a fictionalised dramatisation, not a telling of history – rearranged the evidence at his disposal, had collapsed one character into another, had concertina-ed the timelines. And the "Frost" character was portrayed as thoroughly lightweight, an opportunist, a television personality with an Australian-based career teetering on the verge of failure. And so Frost, sitting there in the stalls that night, watched as the material of his life was pushed and raked around, like so many counters on a card table. It was a disconcerting experience, and he was for a while duly disconcerted. It took the quality of the script and the production, Sheen's marvellous portrayal, Carina's pleasure, and the absorption of the audience to remind him that something extraordinary was taking place in his life: a West End show *about* his life and career, about to take wing.

Morgan and Byam Shaw had first met him several years previously, at a breakfast appointment in London, at which he blew cigar smoke across the table at his guests, and insisted on ordering kidneys for the entire party. The two younger men were enthusiastic about their idea, and that meeting and many others to follow were pleasurable and engaging – but ultimately Byam Shaw and Morgan required Frost's cooperation and consent in order to bring their idea to life. Both were essential: with his customary acumen in the matter of rights and permissions, Frost had ensured in that long-ago contract with Nixon that he held ownership of the recordings of his interviews with Nixon.

The Nixon interviews had been critical to the course of David Frost's career, but in truth, he and his colleagues had in the intervening years paid scant attention to the original material. The five original tapes had lain mouldering in the Paradine files for ten years after the interviews had taken place: they had all but disintegrated before they were rescued and brought in the nick of time to the only studio in Los Angeles capable of converting two-inch tapes to digital. And now, twenty years later, they were being given new life once more. Nothing, however, could happen without Frost's express permission. After much conversation, he gave this permission in principle; he also gave Morgan and Byam Shaw the rights, *gratis*, for the run at the Donmar, and for any West End transfer that might result – though not for any further iteration of the project.

Several months later, Frost also consented to a third request: that he relinquish any form of editorial control over the project, the better to strengthen it creatively and editorially. He understood that it could flourish only if it was independent of his own input and that of Paradine. But this third request nevertheless went against the grain, for it had always been a key Frost characteristic to retain control of his material, in all its forms: this aspect had been a mainstay of his career; and an example of his clear-minded business acumen. Now, here he was signing over certain rights, relinquishing any financial reward – at least for the time being – and stepping back from any creative involvement whatsoever. "I don't know how we managed it," remembers Morgan drily, "but we did."[514]

At that initial cigar-clouded breakfast, Frost had been "highly avuncular," remembers Byam Shaw, "and at that point very enthusiastic: he knew [Morgan] from *The Deal*, and he seemed to feel the whole idea was a total hoot. It was a happy, happy, easy meeting. Then [Morgan] went off and began to develop the play – and after a while, the experience stopped being so very happy, happy, easy." At the heart of Frost's developing unhappiness was the germ of the story that Morgan wanted to tell.

It was *Rocky* with words, we told David: at its heart was a figure called David Frost, and he was on the ropes. He needed Nixon as much as Nixon needed him – and then he needed to beat Nixon. Peter saw the arc of the story, the arc of the character; and he wrote it that way – and there were parts of the story that [Frost] simply could not stand. "But I won, I won," he would say – but we said, "Look, if you won every round with Nixon, if you simply won and won, then we won't have a play."[515]

David Frost was nothing if not pragmatic. He was fully aware of the time that had slipped past since these momentous interviews had been recorded; he was pleased that thirty years later they were being hauled out once more into the light; and he was mindful that, given a little luck and the right form of husbandry, the possibilities for the *Frost/Nixon* project were endless. And so: "I decided that the advantages just about outweighed the advantages," Frost later wrote rather delicately, "though when I saw the first draft, I was not so sure."[516]

The truth, in fact, was even less mellifluous. As the production process took shape slowly and the drafts emerged, Frost was appalled – and he said so, loudly and in the course of a good deal of vexed correspondence. In a letter to Morgan and Byam Shaw of October 6th, 2005, Frost wrote:

I look forward to seeing the next draft but in closing a word to you, Peter. I appreciate completely that you may never have shown your first drafts to anybody and that it makes you uncomfortable. However, please do realise that this process is uncomfortable for me too. I have never allowed anyone to semi-fictionalise any part of my life, least of all one of its highlights. I wish I had not done so, just as you probably wish you had never given me the right to see every single draft. That is why, as I said, I would prefer you to tear up the script [...] That would be a great relief for me, and perhaps for you. However, if you think that good can still come out of all this for us both, then let's give it a go at least until the next draft.[517]

For Morgan, his script went "to the heart of what a dramatist – or a portrait painter or a biographer – must do: they must strive to bring a person fully to life. David wanted the David Frost of his dreams and imagination to appear there on the stage. He wanted a portrait his mother would have created, a portrait without flaws, which pointed to his achievements only. The irony is, of course, that my portrayal of him was entirely sympathetic. I always intended to make him the underdog who won. But he was resistant to the satire that he himself as a satirist had applied to others earlier in his career. Having satirised others, he proved remarkably thin-skinned when it came to himself."[518]

Ultimately, issues were handed over to lawyers, but facts remained facts. Frost had stepped back from the production, and he could not now step forward into it, regardless of his bruised ego and regardless of the pressure he placed on the *Frost/Nixon* producers. The anxiety and concerns he felt concerning his portrayal in the earliest versions of the script were understandable. To be sure, later versions rounded out the characters, tightened the action – but Morgan's essential vision survived. In the mid-1970s, according to this production, Frost had been down on his luck – chronically so. The Nixon tapes, then, saved his bacon. "David wrote me a letter," recalls Byam Shaw, "saying that he thought he'd given away the shop. But there was no way around that. The ironic thing was that he really, really wanted the story of the greatest success of his professional life to be recounted – and of course it was! He got what he wanted and needed. It was resolved eventually – through lawyers and agents, but it was resolved. Our relationship was a little tense after that. I would see him from time to time, and he would be very

the Kremlin with Vladimir Putin: David Frost interviews the Russian leader for *Breakfast With Frost*, ahead of a te visit to the UK, 2003.

ecting pace into the Northern Ireland peace process: Frost with Bill Clinton and Tony Blair, G8 Summit Birmingham, 1998.

Hitting it off: Frost with Nelson Mandela on *Breakfast With Frost*, 2001. Frost interviewed the South African statesman on a number of occasions.

At Highgrove: Carina and David Frost with The Prince of Wales, c.2002.

Frost's guest on the first edition of *Breakfast With Frost* was the incumbent Prime Minister, John Major. The two men were close friends.

own time: with George H.W. Bush at Kennebunkport, Maine, 1991. Frost – still – couldn't swim.

nd professional time: for David Frost, work was seldom far away.

Another President: Frost with President George Bush, 2003.

Frost with Barney Jones, his *Breakfast With Frost* producer. The pair enjoyed a television partnership lasting twelve years.

t on the town: David and Carina Frost arrive at a party for David Mellor, 2004.

lfred, David, Carina, George and Miles Frost at the Frost summer garden party at Carlyle Square, 2006.

Television statesman: Frost on Al Jazeera with the Prime Minister, David Cameron, 2012.

Facing the cameras: Carina and David Frost, 2012.

The contemporary Frosts: Miles, Wilfred and George celebrate Miles's thirtieth birthday in Ibiza, 2014.

The wisteria blooms at Michelmersh, the Frosts' country home for thirty years, 2013. © *Country Life*

The Sunday Times reflects on the life of David Frost in advance of his Memorial Service, February 2014.

Courtesy of *The Sunday Times Magazine*

The Prince of Wales lays flowers at the memorial stone to David Frost at Poets' Corner, Westminster Abbey, 2014. From left, The Dean of Westminster, The Prince of Wales, Miles, Carina, George and Wilfred Frost.

careful, very watchful around me, as though he were afraid I was going to pinch something from him. The situation was never really *personally* resolved, is the bottom line, and that was a shame."[519]

But there was delight too. Frost responded to the critical praise of the production, and naturally there was electricity in seeing himself on stage. At the Broadway opening, remembers Byam Shaw, "there was the usual grandstanding as to who would sit down last in the stalls – and of course David won: he was the last man standing. He sat at the Broadway opening as though he were the producer – all a very far cry from the Donmar preview. He really loved it in the end."[520] Others noted his ambivalence. Joan Bakewell, for example, saw that, "the project appealed to his vanity. He didn't much like aspects of it, but he was able to balance this against the fact that it existed at all; and so he absorbed it, assimilated it, and put it out publicly that he was delighted."[521] And in fact, there would be much to delight Frost, for the play was a tremendous success. It did indeed transfer to the West End, and to Broadway the following spring.

Critical opinion for the play was reasonably positive. "The real fascination of Morgan's play," the *Guardian* wrote, "lies in its suggestion that there was a symbiotic link between Frost and Nixon. Frost, having lost his American and Australian shows, desperately needed the interviews to restore his dwindling fortunes; Nixon, for his part, craved public redemption."[522] The *New York Times*, meanwhile, was more ambivalent: "Structured as a prize fight between two starkly ambitious men in professional crisis, *Frost/Nixon* makes it clear that the competitor who controls the camera reaps the spoils. Mr Morgan, a specialist in fact-based fiction for screen and television, has spoken of 'the difference between accuracy and truth' in eliciting private drama from public records. But here, he sometimes seems to be forsaking accuracy less in the pursuit of truth than of conventional entertainment value." Frost, the newspaper added, "is presented as a bit of a celebrity bimbo, a vain man who lives for the perfect tale in the best restaurant amid A-list companions. What makes him worthy of concentrated attention here is the raw hunger of his ambition and the insecurity that feeds it."[523]

By then, a film was in the works. The Oscar-winning director Ron Howard had made a point of coming to London to see the play at the Donmar, and was immediately taken with the idea of producing it as a movie. He had already considerable experience of portraying still living subjects – in, for example, *Apollo 13* and *A Beautiful Mind* – and now he felt that here was another life worth dramatising on screen:

> I had met Peter Morgan previously, and had actually seen a manuscript of the play and been riveted by it. And I also knew that people like Martin Scorsese and George Clooney and Mike Nichols and other significant names had already expressed an interest in producing and directing a feature – plus I was already hearing about the strong reviews for the play itself. So I flew to London to see it for myself – and by intermission I knew I wanted to make it. I loved the way it had been staged and it captured my imagination. So during the intermission I made a commitment to myself to make the film, and to make it with these actors. And after the show, I went out on the sidewalk, called my agent and asked her to begin the ball rolling to get the rights. And it all happened very quickly – really, the movie came together more quickly than any movie I have ever made.

For Howard, there was a personal element at play too: he related to his subject's drive and ambition. He had watched Frost's broadcasting career develop over the years, and had been aware that here was a kindred spirit, someone who, like Howard himself, had declined to remain within defined career boundaries. As Howard had moved from acting into movie direction and production, so Frost had moved from one career silo to another and another, demonstrating considerable entrepreneurial and commercial nous on the way – and for Howard, the film would provide the scope to portray Frost's genius and nerve, as showcased in the Nixon project, "in bypassing the American networks, going for syndication, proving to media entrepreneurs that there was life beyond the existing model. He dared to prove that there were other ways available out there; and I wanted to celebrate the risks he had taken." For Howard, Frost seemed, "the quintessential extrovert, very quick, very witty, a very impressive man – and a great host. And I saw something else too: he retained the entertainer's wish to earn a laugh. He was like Jimmy Durante: 'Always leave 'em laughing.'"[524]

Shooting on the movie of *Frost/Nixon* began in the summer of 2007 ("We finished the Broadway run on the Sunday afternoon," says Michael Sheen, "and the following Thursday morning, I was shooting my first scene in the film over in California; that's how quick the turn-around was.") and the film opened in the United States in December 2008.[525] And by now, the rights had once more reverted to Frost. The *Frost/Nixon* project, then, was a success – and for Frost, a lucrative financial success too, leading to joint appearances with Michael Sheen at the BAFTAs and Academy Awards – but the fact remained that he had been presented in a certain light in both play and film; and Frost knew better than anyone the importance and durability of the image, of a certain presentation of history. It was unusual, looking at the context of a long career, to see himself presented in such a light – normally, it was Frost himself who managed the presenting side of things. But it was certainly true that his customary pragmatism had won the day – in the face of doubts that were personally extremely challenging.

In essence, then, the experience proved to be a long-running episode of pleasure for Frost and his family. "It gave Dad the most enormous boost," remembers Wilfred Frost, "just as *Breakfast with Frost* had ended. Mum, Miles, George and I adored it too: the opening nights, red carpets, the excitement of it all. For my brothers and me, we could hardly believe how cool Dad was – and he was aware of that. For us as a family, it was a wonderful moment. And it introduced Dad to a younger generation: and it highlighted to people under the age of thirty how important a political interview could really be."[526]

The *Frost/Nixon* phenomenon, then, was ultimately a deeply satisfying event in the life of David Frost – all the more so, perhaps, for having emerged from the deep past in a way that was unexpected, and profoundly and delightfully affirming. But there remained the question of Frost's contemporary career, which ostensibly had been holed below the waterline by the demise of *Breakfast With Frost*. Here too, however, events were to turn in Frost's favour.

The Al Jazeera network had launched in 1996 as an Arabic-based television system, its explicit intention to provide a counterbalance to the Western television channels beamed into the Middle East. The first Gulf War of five years previously had emphasised the power of television to influence minds and policy – and Al Jazeera was founded and funded by the government of Qatar, which maintained an arm's-length policy towards the fledgling station. The result was broadcasting the tone of which occasionally disturbed and shocked conservative television viewers in the Middle East: boisterous and not beyond providing a stage for all manner of dissenting political opinions which had previously been seldom aired in the region.

Its actual independence from the Qatari government remained a moot point: regardless of this, however, the Al Jazeera audience expanded rapidly – and three years after its launch as a spindly outfit broadcasting six hours a day, the station became a twenty-four-hour operation. Its roots in the Arab world meant that it could provide an intimate knowledge of the region. It was, for example, the only international broadcaster to have a bureau in Kabul for the beginning of the American-led war there in the aftermath of the 9/11 attacks (though this bureau was destroyed in the course of the war). And it was able to flourish what was increasingly seen as a trump card: it could provide news uninfluenced by an Anglo-American mind-set, and claim the loyalty of vast audiences wholly unaccustomed to trusting the output of any news channel. It was for this reason that, for example, Tony Blair was willing to appear on Al Jazeera – to address directly the network's vast audiences and to engage in a battle for hearts and minds.

By 2006, Al Jazeera was contemplating a further addition to its family of channels: Al Jazeera English, a twenty-four-hour news and current affairs channel with headquarters in the Qatari capital Doha and in London. The intention of the channel could not have been more explicit: Al Jazeera English was established "to reverse the North to South flow of information" – to bring an alternative news source to households all over the world. This was an intention to be welcomed or disdained, depending on one's political point of view. Certainly, the looming birth of this station was a disconcerting event, with the potential to upend traditional ways of generating and consuming news. But for Al Jazeera, there was at this point one over-riding challenge: to establish the station's credibility, fast – and it was with this need in mind that a connection was formed with David Frost. Late in 2005, several months after the BBC had dispensed with Frost, Alex Armitage met with his client:

> We had breakfast at Claridge's: always an ordeal for me, really, because in those days before the smoking ban, David would insist on smoking these awful cigars with breakfast; and in addition to this, I was dreading to see how he was coping with the BBC rejection. "Well, Al," he said, "what next?" *Big question: what next?* And the truth is that at that point I felt sorry for him. I could see him slowing down, and I had no answer to give him. And then, a few weeks later, I was having lunch with one of the team at Al Jazeera, and he mentioned that they were short of presenters. I said that the channel's essential problem at that point was that it had no figure-head, no focus, no face – and then I said I had the solution: "Sir David Frost!" I also said that this solution would be hugely expensive – but that we could do a deal there and then. And I wrote on a napkin: "David Frost, forty-two programmes, one million pounds a year." And we ended up pretty close to that.[527]

The deal may have been done rapidly, but Armitage then went off and did a good deal of research on the new station. Was it for real? What did people make of it? Was it a propaganda station, the terrorists' friend? For Frost, "The reason that Al Jazeera was such an irresistible opportunity was that I felt that it might be the last time that a brand-new network covering the world would actually emerge. It made Al Jazeera English's trailblazing plans very much irresistible."[528] Others required a degree of reassurance, and a long telephone conversation ensued between Carina Frost, David Frost and trusted confidantes, designed to tease out the facts and principles behind Al Jazeera. Certainly, it is the case that these questions emphasised the actual, fundamental difficulties that many people in Europe and North America had with the very notion of an Arab-based news network broadcasting in English.

Armitage, Frost and Al Jazeera itself also approached Barney Jones – now directing Frost's successor, Andrew Marr, on BBC Sunday mornings – for advice. Frost was concerned that his stock, accumulated painstakingly over years, would plunge, that his vast network of friends would be afraid of appearing on a channel seen as being in some way unreliable. Armitage was worried that the channel would follow through with this huge offer, only to find that Frost would be unable to deliver the guests. And Al Jazeera fretted that audiences in America would not be at all keen about the idea of watching the station, and that American guests in particular would make their excuses. "'Think about the end result,' I told David. 'You'll make a big splash, but it won't last. Blair and Bush will be advised to stay far away; they'll feel tainted.' And I said to Al Jazeera, 'Can he pull in the names? I would be wary.' And I'm very happy to say," Jones says, laughing, "that both sides completely ignored my advice."[529]

By the following summer, plans had progressed smoothly, and Frost and his new editor, former *Independent* journalist Charlie Courtauld, were invited to visit the newsgathering "hubs" in Qatar, Malaysia and the United States. For Frost, this was the busiest of moments, for of course the lights were just about to go up on *Frost/Nixon* at the Donmar, and he had much on his mind:

The hubs were a shambles of dangling wires and cardboard boxes. DF loved it. But that's not our subject for today. It's the flight. As is his way, DF was in First Class, seat A1. As is mine,

I was in Stowaway Class with caterwauling babies and excess luggage in shitville at the back. DF toddled down the aisle to me with a copy of a new play by Peter Morgan, and asked me to read it and pass on comments. He then toddled back, and I settled down to read. A few minutes later, a stewardess rushed out of first class. "Is there a medical doctor on the plane?" she pleaded. My immediate thought was, *Oh, crap. My presenter's copped it.* But I carried on reading and didn't go up to First till I'd finished. It turned out that the alarm was nothing to do with DF. He was sitting in one of those cubicle-type seats, sipping a glass of his usual white. I handed back the play.

"What did you think?"

"Do you want my honest opinion?"

"Go on."

"You don't come out of it very well. You look like a twit, frankly. A total lightweight. It looks like your only interest is in getting the interview, and it's only the determination of your team which forces you to ask the right question."

"Oh, I thought that when I first read it. But John Birt said it was OK."

"That's hardly surprising. John Birt comes out of it all right."

Then it was back to economy for the remainder of the flight …[530]

For Miranda Gallimore, the incipient deal with Al Jazeera meant something else entirely: an opportunity to practise her diplomatic skills as Qatari representatives and lawyers came and went from the office. "On signing day, I learned an Arabic greeting: and when they all came out of the lift, I stood up and said my greeting – and they stood looking at me, in a row, silently. And DF said, 'Bravo!' and gave me an enormous wink, and off they trooped into his office."[531] Once in the office, meanwhile, there was a little misunderstanding: "The lawyers mistook Frost's salary for the show's annual production budget – and the Qataris were looking confused and asking, 'Is there a problem, is it too little?'"[532]

For Alex Armitage, the Al Jazeera deal was, "a rabbit out of a hat. When David died, I remember thinking, *If the BBC hadn't cancelled him, Al Jazeera would never have happened, and really, would David have been happier ploughing on for years to come at the BBC?* I'm not certain. He was probably happier joining a start-up – but of course David being David, ideally he would like to have done both." George Frost remembers that, "I thought it seemed to make sense, in that the focus of the world was changing, and that region was becoming more and more important. Besides which, it gave him a platform!"[533] Joanna Lumley, however, says that Al Jazeera was, "such a weird thing for him to get involved in. Very daring; and I wonder if it lost him kudos."[534] Such a range of opinions demonstrates the impact that the deal had on Frost's circle of friends, as well as on media society as a whole. It was a disconcerting deal and challenging to the preconceptions of a great many people – and many people were duly disconcerted. In the final analysis, however, it introduced David Frost to a vast swathe of the population in whose media lives he had barely before figured.

And Al Jazeera English went on to launch successfully. In the aftermath of the launch, Frost received correspondence – especially from the United States, American citizens sending emails that suggested that it was Frost's presence on the channel that provided the symbol of respectability they were seeking; they would have avoided the channel had it not been for this. As John Florescu notes, this indicated that the station had known exactly it was doing when it hired Frost: "If a family from Massachusetts writes and says, 'Oh, if you work for these guys, then they must be OK,' well, frankly, this spoke volumes; and it meant a good deal to him, reputationally. It buzzed him up at the time." That said, not everyone in America was pleased. "The fact is that many of his friends in America were very disappointed and almost scandalised – *Why is he doing this, why is he with the enemy?* – and many people stayed annoyed about it and were critical of him. But the thing is that it allowed him to stay in television and it opened him up to a potentially vast new audience, much better than, say,

CNN – and besides, the fact is that these guys don't want to leave the screen."535

Frost Over the World was first broadcast in November 2006, from the Al Jazeera broadcast headquarters in Knightsbridge. Frost was now sixty-seven years old, and he was working with a new editor – but much of the method, honed over the decades, remained identical. "We did not work in the same building as David: questions etc. were emailed to [the Paradine offices in] Kensington. David read it all and rewrote questions, long-hand, with a blue fibre-tip pen onto a buff cardboard folder; a different folder for each interview …"536 And the first Frost programme launched with a flourish – and in a manner that recalls the original edition of *Breakfast with Frost*: the show landed the current prime minister, Tony Blair, and it landed a scalp. The war in Iraq was over, and Blair, in the final months of his premiership, was invited to look back on a scene of carnage:

DF: In terms of Iraq […] in the light of the latest figures from the Iraqi health ministry, that the number of Iraqis who have died is between 100,000 and 150,000 and so on, with those scale of figures, if you had known that that was the scale of bloodshed, would you still have gone to war?

TB: Well, the alternative was leaving Saddam in charge of Iraq, where hundreds of thousands of people died, there were a million casualties in the Iran/Iraq war […] So the idea that Iraqis should be faced with the situation where they either have a brutal dictator in Saddam or alternatively a sectarian religious conflict, why can't they have in Iraq what their people want? Which is a non-sectarian government, a government that is elected by the people and the same opportunities and the same rights that we enjoy in countries such as this.

DF: But, but so far it's been, you know, pretty much of a disaster.

TB: It has, but you see what I say to people is …

The transcript does not do justice to the drama of this tingling moment: the first moment at which Blair acknowledges the ruin of Iraq which flowed from the war. Blair's delivery speeds noticeably in the aftermath of his admission, as though to blank or overwhelm it with words – and of great interest too is Frost's own demeanour and body language as the pouncing moment arrives, as he stoops a little and slips in the question: "David fidgets and looks at his fingernails – and this was his technique, a lowering of his voice, a shrug and – 'It was a disaster, wasn't it?' And, 'Yeah, it was, but ...'" But he had said it. And we had taped him saying it. We whisked the tape away, but within minutes we had Blair's people calling us in the car as we made our way back to the studio, demanding to see a transcript. The calls continued all the way through the edit."[537] Blair himself is blunter: "He got me. And it was a mark of his skill; you can't take it away from him."[538] It was a coup for Frost, Poots and Courtauld – and *Frost Over the World* was set fair.

Several years later, as Wilfred Frost was taking his first steps into his own career as a television interviewer, he studied this moment, and others like it:

> For me, it was a masterful moment. The way that Dad essentially made the statement to Blair, but did so in his very warm and charming manner in order to elicit an "affirmative" from Blair, such that he got the impossible out of him – he got the admission that "the Iraq war had been a disaster" – but just not in so many words. It's a tactic I have observed in some of Dad's other interviews too. I've tried to use it myself in my own career – but thus far it hasn't worked at all! But I'm still learning ...[539]

For Al Anstey, who directed operations at Al Jazeera English, Frost "was much loved by the people who worked with him at the channel. He was a fantastic operator, and a true professional, and so completely engaged with the stories and with his interviewees. He relished the opportunity that this new station afforded him, and it became perfectly evident to me that he supported the vision of the channel: to cover the world on a level playing field. He badly wanted this infant channel to succeed, and frankly he was one of our best advocates." Anstey recalls a meeting in Doha, the first hour of which was taken up with a long discussion about the Afghan driver who had ferried Frost from the hotel to the studios, about his life and background. "David was captivated by this gentleman, the family he was obviously missing, his life experience. It underlined for me that he was still just as interested in the story of an Afghan taxi driver as he was in the story of a president of the United States, and he had the same passion for the human stories that he had ever had."[540]

*

Over the last fifty or sixty years, from the very bland interviews that people did with politicians back in the fifties, interviewing in politics has got sterner and tougher, which is all for the good. At the same time, in terms of film stars and celebrities, interviews have got softer, because more and more spin doctors are involved. […] The basic point is that it's no good going into an interview in a really combative way unless you've got the goods. […] In other words, yes, of course you can be confrontational, as long as it's a real confrontation. Doing it in order to sound tough, but without the good, it won't work.[541]

In October 2014, in a lecture delivered in the Chapel of St Peter's College, Oxford, the BBC's David Dimbleby explored what he considered the decline over time of the political interview in Britain. Dimbleby's remarks explored the evolution – or, as he saw it, diminution – of the interview form in the television age, its arc from an accepted long-form structure to the short, rapid slots of today's sound-bite age, and a consequent loss of a sense of theatre and, essentially of prestige and meaning. Dimbleby counselled against the creeping sterility of the political interview in an age when, more than ever, politicians needed both to be held to account, and to explain to an increasingly sceptical public the critical role they had to play in a mature democracy. The interview, in other words, had an absolutely essential role to play – if only it was allowed to play it.

One of Dimbleby's points, delivered in the course of this thoughtful and detailed lecture, was that the decline in the utility and function of the political interview could be traced back, not only to the advent of the ubiquitous spin doctor, to the sort of media training that every politician now must undergo as part of their trade and to the long withdrawal of ideology from party politics, but also to the advent of the sofa on our television screens. Or rather, to the advent of that which the sofa represents: a loss of rigour, of critical intelligence, and its replacement by an anodyne "lifestyle" interview that was of little use in getting to the heart of the politician or of the policies being espoused. The intelligence of the form was being eaten away by such factors, as termites eat at the foundations of a house, leaving a void in their wake.

In the course of *Frost Over the World* – and its successor programme, *The Frost Interview*, which involved a punishing travelling schedule – David Frost interviewed nearly thirty heads of state (including Lula da Silva of Brazil; Evo Morales of Bolivia; Michelle Bachelet of Chile; Ilham Aliyev of Azerbaijan; and Viktor Yushchenko of Ukraine), nearly thirty heads of government (includ-ing Tony Blair, Gordon Brown and David Cameron of the United Kingdom; Recep Tayyip Erdoğan of Turkey; Helen Clark and John Key of New Zealand; and Julia Gillard of Australia), former world leaders (including Benazir Bhutto of Pakistan and FW de Klerk of South Africa) and dozens of other policymakers, political leaders, directors and others (including Margaret Chan, director of the World Health Organization; the environmentalist James Lovelock; chef Heston Blumenthal; writers Amos Oz, Terry Pratchett, Mario Vargas Llosa and Gore Vidal; sports stars Martina Navratilova, Oscar Pistorius, Novak Djokovic and Roger Federer; and actors Patrick Stewart, Emma Thompson, Robin Williams, Catherine Deneuve, Michael Sheen, George Clooney and Vanessa Redgrave) from around the world. This is by no means an exhaustive list – and it indicates the reach and clout that the mature Frost still enjoyed.

There were particular highlights. Frost's meeting with Mikhail Gorbachev, in Berlin in November 2009 to mark the twentieth anniversary of the fall of the Berlin Wall, is a case in point. Frost and Gorbachev had long had a friendly relationship and, as was the case with the first President Bush, this intimacy was evident on the screen. In this final interview between the two, Gorbachev looks back on those heady days with a combination of satisfaction and regret, satisfaction that the unification of Germany had been completed in a manner which showcased international cooperation, even as tensions pulsed below the surface, but regret that the Soviet Union had then dissolved with such startling speed.

Gorbachev reflected that French President François Mitterand had commented, "We love the Germans so much that we let them have two Germanies. And then Mrs Thatcher rejected the idea of German unification; she thought it would be bad for all. It was a difficult process." As for the subsequent break-up of the USSR: "The reasons for the break-up of the union were all internal. There was a severe political battle and some people wanted to take advantage of it." And any idea that the union might be preserved was of course scuppered by the coup of 1991. Frost remarks that Gorbachev's place in history is secure – he is, after all, the man who changed the world. "I have always thought that history was a fickle thing," Gorbachev replies. "Any time you feel the need to talk, let me assure you that I will make time, I will always find the minutes."

Frost Over the World and its successor were a success, in terms both of critical response and of ratings. They had the sort of global outlook and reach that Al Jazeera required, and Frost had proven that he still had what it took to run a successful career as an interviewer. "You only get the quote," as he put it, "if you get the guest."[542] And he still knew the rules of the game, in particular the critical importance of openness and flexibility of approach. The Wimbledon champion Andy Murray recalls asking Frost what made a great interviewer: "I haven't forgotten his answer, which was simple and incisive. He told me that it's someone who asks a question and then *listens* to the answer and then adapts his or her next questions. He said he was amazed at how many interviewers stuck with pre-planned questions, regardless of the answers – sometimes, he said, you simply needed to let interviews flow and see where they carried you. He didn't do too badly, I guess!"[543] Others agreed: the former prime minister, Sir John Major, recalls Frost's "insatiable curiosity", remarking that he, "asked the questions that need to be asked and listened to the answer, and then followed up the answer not with a pre-prepared question but from something that *arose* from the answer".[544]

Formula One champion Lewis Hamilton recalls the sense of respect he felt for "anyone who manages to remain at the top of their game for so long. He achieved a lot and he was still out there working incredibly hard [...] still wanting to get to the deep roots of any conversation he had."[545] "He did his homework," adds Elton John, "and he tried to find the human being inside the interviewee."[546] The actor Liam Neeson, who first met Frost on a New Year holiday on Anguilla, and who became friends with the family, recalled, "David would come in with this lovely, beautifully executed question, and open up the whole interview – assuming that the guest wanted to open it up! And though a Brit, he was an internationalist too, and he didn't have any kind of island mentality. And he was a very, very smart man and a very ambitious man, without ever being ruthless. And crucially, he had a natural affinity for human beings, he knew how to pitch questions, depending on who he was speaking with. And it was never him and you – it was us. He was good at making the links, and he was instinctive, and he understood empathy. He was the same with everybody, whether you were Richard Nixon or Richard Harris or Richard Anybody; he had a real sense of class in that respect."[547] And for the Duke of York: "He understood that an interview was a collaborative venture. Of course he had his editorial imperatives, and if you opened a window or a door, he was very adept at getting in there; but otherwise, he understood that both interviewer and interviewee had a message to get out."

Many observers, of course, were by no means appeased by this ever-growing body of work. Frost had for years taken criticism for being soft, remarks which can be traced as far back as his interview with the shah in 1979 which so irked John Birt. And certainly, it is the case that the now-ageing Frost, sitting – or rather hunched in a chair and wearing a suit that seemed a little too large for him – bore little relation to the youthful Frost who had hauled Emil Savundra over the coals forty years before. Certain policies remained the same: interviewees were never permitted to see questions in advance; the final shape of the interview – as Tony Blair's advisers discovered in November 2006 – was never up for discussion with any interviewee or their advisers. Charlie Courtauld brings to vivid life the context in which Frost and his team frequently had to work. In a description of the team's visit to President Aliyev of Azerbaijan, he recalls the president's flunkies shadowing the team's every move: at the Presidential Palace, "the flunkey was there and had a new level of intimidation: every time I spoke, everything I said, was written down, longhand in the notebook. The interview was good: DF asked all the right questions and Aliyev looked an arse."[548] The interview was good, however, only because Frost and his team had faced down a demand that they avoid difficult questions, a list of which had already been drawn up and presented to them.

Courtauld had already investigated Frost and his career in some depth. The year before being signed up by Al Jazeera, he had written a long profile piece on Frost which delved back into the career of his soon-to-be-colleague. The piece was salty and opinionated, noting Frost's later reputation for "unctuous" questioning and "sycophancy", and noting that his stock had for some years been rather higher in the United States than in a native country that had become accustomed to aggressive questions delivered by blunt journalists. But Courtauld also noted the class-based origins of some of this criticism, the disparaging and frankly ugly comments on the questions of Frost's vowel sounds and his heavily underlined ambition; and Courtauld also noted Frost's curious – given this ambition – lack of joined-up, strategic thinking. At the heart of the piece, however, are comments on some of Frost's particular strengths: his ability to draw people out, to put them at their ease and enable them to speak comfortably and openly. "One of his skills as a broadcaster is encouraging people to talk and being at ease himself whether the camera is running or not. Just last week we had a schoolboy on the show – the star of *Billy Elliot* [Jamie Bell] – and David was as comfortable talking to him as he was talking some months ago to George Bush."[549]

For Joanna Lumley, Frost, "had a strange way of appearing not to be on top of things. I was interviewed by him a couple of times, the last one for Al Jazeera about the Gurkhas [Lumley's ultimately successful campaign to force the British government to grant Gurkha soldiers who had fought in the British army, and their families, residency rights in the United Kingdom]. Sometimes during interviews, it was as if he was thinking about something else, and I would think, *Oh dear, he's not listening, I'm not being interesting* – and then he was snap back into a question. He seemed to be able to sweep in facts like a street-sweeper, he just netted and dragged everything in. He could assimilate facts photographically, osmotically, just taking everything in when for when he needed it."[550]

And there was another strength, one which applied in particular to his later political interviews. It stemmed from the professional ability he had always possessed to be silent, and to use that silence as necessary. "He gave people rope," recalls Alex Armitage, "and allowed them to hang themselves if they wanted to do it. The secret of a great interviewer is not to be afraid of silence, so when people reach the end of their script and the end of what they want to say, he would leave a silence, and they would jump into the silence with the next day's headlines. He knew to shut up, and so they frequently did hang themselves. They didn't mind very much: or at all. Nobody thought: *Oh, that bastard Frost stitched me up.* Because he didn't – they stitched themselves up."[551]

And he was aware too of how to press a button, for maximum media impact in the days to follow. In an edition of *Breakfast with Frost* from September 2002, he questioned Tony Blair on the fringes of the Labour Party conference against the backdrop of the looming conflict in Iraq. The exchange is instructive in that it went to the heart of the sense of unease felt at the relationship between a Blair thought by many to be on an unsettling moral crusade, and a President George W. Bush who was a born-again Christian and gearing up for a war against "evildoers":

DF: But both you and he [Bush] are great, greatly men of faith and so on ... I mean, do you pray together?

TB: Pray together?

DF: Mm.

TB: How do you mean?

DF: Do you say prayers together for peace, you and the president?

TB: Well, we don't say prayers together, no, but I'm sure he in his way hopes for peace and I hope for peace too.

The question was perfectly calibrated: once again, the transcript cannot capture the degree to which this exchange unsettled, not to say mortified the prime minister, a politician to his fingertips as well as a man of faith, and perfectly aware of how such a topic would most likely go down in a largely secular Britain. "People forget my reply," Blair recalls now, "they only ever remember Frost's question."[552] In his memoirs, meanwhile, Blair recalls his sense that:

Frost was still far and away the best interviewer around on TV, far better than those who sneered at him for not being sneering enough. He wasn't rude or hectoring but had an extraordinary talent for beguiling the interviewee, leading them on, charming them into discretion, tripping them, almost conversationally, into the headlines. I lost count of the number of times Alastair [Campbell] would say to me, *What the hell did you say that for?* – after a Frost encounter; and he would explain and I would go, *Oh*. Also David had a revolutionary notion in his head that the audience wanted to hear what the person answering the questions had to say, rather than the person asking them. By this device, he got people to say much more than they intended and on a much broader range of topics. He would always end up with four or five news stories out of the interview. And of course by being insistent but not aggressive, he made it much harder, psychologically, for the interviewee not to answer directly.[553]

For Wilfred Frost, his father's interviewees "understood that his motives stemmed from a genuine interest; and also that he had done his homework. And my father understood something else too, and he never forgot it – and that was a sense of gratitude. An interviewer owes his whole career to the interviewees, and certain styles of interviewers miss this crucial point – but he never did, and it found expression in a certain way: he got them to talk."[554] And for the Prince of Wales, "one of David's most remarkable gifts was his ability to listen – or appear to listen! – with rapt attention to his interviewee, thus lulling his 'victim' into a false sense of security that invariably exposed more of the person's soul than might otherwise have been wise …"[555]

Certainly, there was a method – tried, tested, refined – in Frost's long career as an interviewer. The research and preparation, so often noted and remarked upon, were of course the crux of the matter, the key to perfecting the experience – but the critical point was, as Wilfred Frost notes, "that preparation not simply to be ready and revved up. Instead, it was about communicating this readiness to the interviewee. The person sitting across from [Frost] saw this readiness, saw that he had done his homework fairly and squarely – saw, in other words, that he respected them enough to do this; and I often saw that it made all the difference."[556]

Frost's manila envelopes and thick felt-tip pens also pointed to another element in this process. They indicated something unstructured – or rather, free-flowing – that was rooted in Frost's ability to listen, and if necessary forget everything and respond instead to what was actually being said. His comic timing and background also assisted, as a means of keeping the conversation oiled. And finally, as Wilfred Frost notes, "You have to be liked and you have to be genuine – otherwise you don't have a career at all. There has to be some substance behind the smile."[557]

And what of the criticism of Dimbleby – and indeed, of a line of others over the years – that the introduction of sofa-style journalism signified the beginning of the end of forensic television journalism? Dimbleby's clear implication is that Frost was part of this drift towards laxity: more than this, he implies that Frost must take some of the responsibility for this syndrome, in the sense that he was offering politicians an easy ride, an easy way out of difficult predicaments. The answer is, perhaps, that Frost was certainly forensic, that his understanding of television as a medium and of the expectations and desires of his audience more generally was profound, and that he used this very great understanding and a lifetime of experience to get the best guests and to extract material from them. It was, perhaps, this deep-seated understanding of the potential relationship between viewer and host that was consistently his trump card.

He was not – at least in his later life – in the business of being argumentative, or aggressive, or deadly, of seeking above all else to trip up a politician, of entangling a politician – or anyone – in the bonds of their own careful argument. The Savundra interview was a one-off; any repeat performance would inevitably be subject to the law of diminishing returns. Instead, he was in the business of *amplification* – and again the scene returns to a youthful David Frost caught up in the idea of broadcast as a fine-spun web connecting person to person, viewer to viewer, listener to listener, the better to create a greater community. "As far as I am concerned," he told the *Observer* in 1992, "I am not in any way stylised. I am natural. Natural for *me*. The more I can be myself on television, the more effective I think I am at what I do. I talk the same way I talk to you now."[558]

Taken all in all, he did, to be sure, watch enough interviewees trip themselves up in their own words over the years – often to profoundly theatrical effect. He also conducted enough "soft" interviews that can be remembered merely for the substance of their words. Because he was not, after all, explicitly in the business of the *political* – his career was instead in the business of studying the *human*, that rather broader avenue of exploration stemming from his upbringing, that motivated him throughout his life. "He wasn't ideological," says Tony Blair, "and that was the key to it. Because he wasn't ideological, I knew he wasn't going to sink his teeth in." And in 1995, Frost himself observed that, "You can only judge a question by the answer it provokes. Pointlessly confrontational questions can be self-defeating. The idea is to open people up, not shut them up. You can ask the most testing of questions in a civilised way."[559]

And later, he reflected on the importance of a certain flexibility of mind: "It's very important that anyone in the interview business not only listens to the answers and all those things but does vary their approach in the sense that obviously you would interview Julie Andrews in a different way to Saddam Hussein! And it's always important to link the appropriate techniques to the occasion. And the Nixon interviews were one case where I had to be several different people at different times: prosecutor and defence as we were implying over Watergate – but then Boswell to his Johnson when he was talking about the breakthrough with China. […] And then as he was starting to give and starting to come forward, then one became in a sense his sort of, not his psychiatrist, but his psychologist …"[560]

The last word on this subject belongs to Trevor Poots, his producer and collaborator of many years. And here too, the idea of theatre is evoked. "He was very theatrical. 'Hello! Wonderful to meet you!' It was as though he had trained at RADA – and in this sense he was very unlike those others who were journalists by inclination and training. And this point influenced many people's attitudes towards him. Whereas, for example, Jeremy Paxman was trying to get an *answer*, David Frost was trying to create an *event*. He disliked the very word 'interview'; in fact, he preferred 'conversation'. He disliked the idea of an interrogation; he wanted a chat. So, although he had strong journalistic instincts, he was not a journalist per se. I would say he was a politically extremely well-informed host. He loved the idea of a show more than anything: putting people at their ease, and then getting them to talk about areas they had never talked about before."[561]

He was an impresario, in other words: in the very broad business of getting the very best possible result. He had been an impresario at Cambridge; he was still an impresario as he criss-crossed the Atlantic over the course of decades; or was seated with an uncomfortable Richard Nixon at Monarch Bay; or drinking champagne following a breakfast show, his ears flapping and eyes peeled all the while. It was a mode that did not suit every viewer, every observer or critic; and sometimes distaste eventually cost him his job, as at the BBC. But it was the heart of the man: and to see him as anything else is to mistake the matter.

*

David Frost's *modus operandi* did not always work, of course, and this became increasingly the case as he aged. One example came in the spring of 2013, when the BBC scheduled a special programme on BBC4 between Frost and Joan Bakewell to mark the latter's eightieth birthday. The interview was an agreeable, relaxed affair – but Frost lacked something of his usual acuity. "An odd mix," recalls Bakewell, "though I was with a friend, and it was a pleasant event. I was quite happy about it."[562] David Frost had just turned seventy-four years old that April, but he had the bearing and demeanour of an older man. His stoop was more pronounced, his hair thinner, and certainly the bounding vitality of the young man was at this point no longer in evidence. "He didn't look after himself, certainly: he never did; and later in his life he didn't look well," recalls Michael Parkinson."[563] And many of those around him were frailer too – and there was, perhaps inevitably, a valedictory air to these years. His sister Jean died in May 2010, having suffered from Alzheimer's in the final period of her life; and his brother-in-law Kenneth Bull – Margaret's husband in Whitby – died in November 2012. And Frost had already seen other old friends for what would prove to be the final time: in September 2003, he had attended a memorial service for Thora Hird, the mother of his former girlfriend Janette Scott. "I saw him standing on his own at the reception following the service. I introduced my family to him and I wanted to say more – but there had been two thousand people in the Abbey, and they all seemed to be pushing into the reception, and I had no time to say more. And I regret that."[564]

And the world was changing too: the context in which he was operating was shifting beneath his feet. His admirers saw him as an elder statesman of the television age, there at its beginnings, and still there years later. His critics saw him as a figure who had stayed too long, and whose voice – less clear, less sharp, the voice of an older man that he in fact was – was beginning to fail him. And there are shreds of evidence that he was thinking along the same lines. "I would regularly do a Frost impersonation," says Rory Bremner, "and he would laugh along with everyone else. But one day, out of the blue, he asked me quite vulnerably, 'Do people's voices change as they get older?' What he meant was, *Does my voice as you have begun to impersonate it – a little more slurred and hesitant – does my voice sound like this now?*"[565]

In these later years, indeed, Frost himself was rather more frail than was generally realised. And in March 2011, he had an accident inside the house at Carlyle Square. Carina Frost was in the country, his sons elsewhere – and Frost, on his way to his study in the basement of the house, fell down the staircase and suffered concussion. He remained concussed for a period of time – just long enough for his family not to be able to reach him on the telephone, and to raise the alarm. Miles Frost reached the house first, to be met by his father, who had by now revived and become able to climb the stairs and to open the front door himself. Knowledge of the incident was kept from all but his closest friends. He took time away from Al Jazeera to recuperate, and when he returned to the interviewer's chair, it seemed that he had lost some of the intense focus that had previously distinguished him in his professional life.

The after-effects, including a degree of disorientation and memory loss, could be perceived for a few months, and as Miles

Frost recalls, were distressing both to Frost himself and to his family:

> Even after we had returned from hospital with the diagnosis of severe concussion, it was a very scary time. He was disorientated to the point of not knowing where he was, for weeks after the fall. I remember wondering if he would ever recover, or whether some permanent damage had been done. Mercifully, it was temporary. Over the following weeks and months he slowly got better, with occasional lapses, as the swelling in his brain subsided. But I think it took several months to get back to ninety per cent, and I wonder whether he ever regained that final ten per cent.[566]

John Florescu recalls a lunch date with Frost at a Kensington hotel. His friend was escorted into the restaurant by Carina Frost, who returned to see her husband safely home an hour or so later. In the interim, it was understood that Florescu was responsible for his care. "I had the *Herald Tribune* open on the table, and he glanced at it, and I could see that something was wrong. The headline he was looking at referred to Serbia, but he began referring to Japan, and I realised that he was not seeing what I saw."[567]

But this period passed. He began once again to hold court at his favourite restaurant, the Wolseley on Piccadilly, and his sons and friends recall Frost at a function at the London Hilton in early July 2013 to mark the twenty-fifth anniversary of the charity cricket match he organised with Victor Blank. It was an occasion, indeed, on which Frost was at his witty and sparkling best. He insisted on arranging the event with Mark Nicholas, and then being interviewed on stage by Nicholas too, and, "he was sharper and more sparkling than I had seen him for a long time," remembers Wilfred Frost. "He was back to his very best."[568]

At this time too, there were profound changes taking place in the family's circumstances. David and Carina Frost had decided it was high time to look anew at their domestic arrangements, and in particularly at the properties in which they lived. For Carina, to whom inevitably fell the task of running of two large houses, the job had become tiring – and in reassessing the circumstances in their lives, they decided to sell both Carlyle Square and Michelmersh, and to acquire new and rather more manageable homes in London and elsewhere in the countryside. The decision made sense: their sons had now flown the nest – and the house at Carlyle Square felt now suddenly much too large and much too empty. And this was doubly the case for the splendid house at Michelmersh, which was a property older and considerably more time-consuming to maintain. Still, in each case the decisions involved an emotional wrench: the houses were filled with family history and family associations that the Frosts would now be obliged to leave behind. But naturally the decision was liberating too. In London, Carina and David Frost bought a house south of the King's Road: smaller but handsome, its Georgian façade concealing a dramatically reconfigured interior. And in leaving behind Michelmersh, the Frosts bought a property outside Henley in Oxfordshire: considerably closer and more convenient to London, and with scope and space for the whole family. The sale of Michelmersh and the emotional and practical shift to Henley took place over the course of several years, and was completed by the summer of 2013.

In the meantime, there were a good many other activities to take Frost's mind off the difficulties and inconveniences of moving house. In 2011, he had formed a relationship with the Cunard cruise line, which involved his occasional presence as a guest speaker on the company's ships. In that first year, he sailed on the *Queen Mary 2* and *Queen Elizabeth*, and, in the second year, he sailed with the company three times – on an Atlantic crossing on the *Queen Mary 2* in that year, his task was to deliver a speech on "Interviews I Shall Never Forget", to take part in a question-and-answer session and to introduce a special screening of *Frost/Nixon*. In general terms, Frost's role on these cruises was to provide a focus for evening events on board ship, to describe his interviews and choice interviewees – to present a précis of a life and long career in the public eye. It was a role he took pleasure in fulfilling, for it enabled him to indulge his love of showmanship, of comedy and timing and anecdote in front of a live audience. Sometimes Carina accompanied him, sometimes she did not.

His next Cunard engagement, on board the *Queen Elizabeth*, was scheduled for the end of August 2013. In advance of this trip – from Southampton to Lisbon, the first leg of the ship's Mediterranean cruise – he and his family visited, as they always did in August, the Goldsmith estate in southern Spain. It was by all accounts the happiest of holidays. Frost was in sparkling form. To his godson, Ben Goldsmith, for whom Frost had consistently made time since James Goldsmith had died in 1997, he was mellow, relaxed, with cricket played every evening under the pines. "He would always keep wicket: the form was no pads, no gloves, barefoot, with a softish ball; and I would bowl to him as I would to a man of my own age, and he would lunge and catch the ball as though he was a man of my own age too. We took time to discuss his whole career: Nixon, everything. And at the end of the holiday – and yes, of course this is perhaps the sort of knowledge that comes with hindsight – there seemed to be a sort of finality. There was an extra kind of affection. His interactions with each of us felt like a final parting."[569]

David and Carina Frost flew back to London late in August, and in the final days of the month, they set off for a night at Henley, before Frost embarked on the *Queen Elizabeth* the following day at Southampton. They were joined at Henley by Miles and by George, accompanied by a friend – Wilfred was absent – and the five dined together that Friday night in Henley. "Dad was on cracking form," remembers George Frost.

The following morning was Saturday, August 31st, 2013. George Frost remembers that, "Dad – and this was most unlike him – had forgotten the name of the driver who was to take him down to Southampton. So he sent me out to the car to find out the driver's name. And I did – and then he set off."[570]

This was the last time Carina and their sons would see David Frost.

CONCLUSION

The Star of His Life

David was the star of his own life. He didn't self-dramatise, he just placed himself on this trajectory and went with it, and dispensed with any concept of introspection.

Joan Bakewell[571]

At noon on Thursday, March 13th, 2014, a congregation of some two thousand had gathered at Westminster Abbey. The occasion was a Memorial Service for David Frost, the organisation of which had been undertaken painstakingly by his family, the BBC and the Abbey authorities in the course of the previous months. The Prince of Wales and Duchess of Cornwall were in attendance at the Abbey that day, together with other members of the Royal Family, the Lord Mayor of Westminster and many other dignitaries – and a throng of friends, associates and colleagues. The prime minister, David Cameron, had been due to attend, but was obliged to cancel at the last moment. In a statement issued after Frost's death, he had described "an extraordinary man – with charm, wit, talent, intelligence and warmth in equal measure. He made a huge impact on television and politics".

George Frost had taken a cab by himself to the Abbey that morning. As the car approached Westminster, "the cabbie said to me, 'So, what's going on here this morning?' And I replied, 'It's Sir David Frost's memorial service.' As soon as I said this, the cabbie turned around and said, 'Sweetest man I've ever driven in this cab. I've driven him three times and he was just a complete legend.' And, as if the circumstances weren't emotional enough, I said, 'Well, he's my dad.' It summed up a lot of things for me."[572]

Some of the most significant figures in the life of David Frost spoke in the course of the service: these included his three sons, as well as Ronnie Corbett, Peter Chadlington, Herb Siegel and David Owen – with the eulogy delivered by Greg Dyke. "We sat down in a kind of family committee," George Frost told Mark Edmonds of the *Sunday Times*, "and we decided that of all the people we knew, we should ask Greg. [...] We loved the way he took the piss out of Dad."[573] Dyke's speech was emotional and powerfully delivered, but, fittingly, it was not without its moments of humour, as when he drew attention to Frost's curious and absolute unwillingness to countenance modern technologies: "We live in a world in which some people never come to terms with new technology. David was unusual in that he never came to terms with old technology either. I was with him once when we walked past the cash machine. I said, 'Hang on a moment, I need to get some money.' He looked at me in awe: 'Do you really know how to use that?' He had never used a cash machine in his life."[574]

In possibly the most dramatic and eloquent part of the ceremony, meanwhile, Carina Frost and the Prince of Wales unveiled a memorial stone to David Frost at Poets' Corner. The gravity and solemnity of the occasion, however, were leavened delightfully in the form of a poem written by Joanna Lumley and Richard Stilgoe, and delivered by Lumley from the steps by the High Altar:

Shall I compare thee to Sir Robin Day?
Thou wert more lovely and more temperate.
Earth has not anything to show more fair,
Hello, good evening, welcome, Frostie's there.
When you considered how our weeks were spent –
Those were the weeks that were; they came, and went.
The quips, the japes, the hasty hymn to Kennedy
And now your turn, as we compose your threnody.
For many a glorious morning I have seen
David, bright-eyed, be-sofa'd on the screen,
Or *Through the Keyhole*, or on Concorde's wing,
Bob Hope, a Pope, a President – and Bing.

You've known them all, nor lost the common touch,
Clerics and Thatchers, Screaming like Lord Sutch.
Prince of all broadcasters and the friend of princes,
Loved by the young, adored by the Blue Rinses.
The world's your stage, from Norfolk Broad to tundra,
You skewered Doctor Petro and Savundra.
Colossus in your field, ahead of trends,
Most generous of hosts and best of friends.
I met a traveller from an antique land
Said Richard Nixon: then, as David planned,
Disarmed and charmed by his insistent guest
Nixon let his guard down and confessed.
No more TV-AM, no more Al Jazeera –
We end not a career, but end an era;
For now he's gone, ascended into orbit,
And *I look up to him* (quoth Ronnie Corbett)
In Heaven, and awaiting David's call,
Is the greatest interviewee of them all:
With Frost tonight, on Paradise TV:
'Hello, God – Evening! Welcome!' We shall see.
Much have you travelled with your Rose of Gold,
And left too soon, thus never growing old,
For you were young and sweet in heart and mind,
When Frost has gone, can spring be far behind?

George Frost read his own poem in tribute to his father:

I've had my life and enjoyed every second
But as it is, another life beckoned.
It's important to know that I have not gone,
And I hope that, on you all, my light has shone.
Stay in the sunshine, rest never in the shade,
Don't curse my absence, as this light you evade.
I love in the smiles, the moon, stars and sky,
And I feel eternal pride as I watch you all fly.

And for my darling children who wonder what to do.

Just have a wonderful time, as I will, living through you.

The occasion was "beautiful," says Diahann Carroll, "and handled exactly the way it should have been."[575]

The role of the BBC in the service was significant and highly visible. The Corporation did more than assist in its production and planning: it contributed a touching montage of Frost's broadcasting career, and its new director general, Tony Hall, delivered one of the readings. A month after David Frost's death, at the conclusion of a speech at the Radio Theatre at Broadcasting House that was designed to set out his vision for the BBC of the future, Hall was at pains explicitly to connect the Corporation to Frost's legacy, which, he implied, exemplified the best of public-service broadcasting:

> Last month, we all lost a broadcasting legend: Sir David Frost was everything the BBC aspires to be. He had wit, and he used it to devastating effect. He was bold, fronting programmes that no-one had even thought of before he did them. He had the popular touch, and was never too grand to appeal to his audiences. He was courteous and polite, never thinking himself greater than his guests. He was a journalist and broadcaster known throughout the world for his truth-telling, his imagination, his ability to entertain. That was the BBC that was, that is the BBC that will be.[576]

*

It is tempting to ascribe a certain degree of significance to the timing and circumstances of David Frost's death: aboard a Cunard vessel, and surrounded by the livery and insignia of that historic and august line. Frost had travelled in his youth aboard Cunard liners, crossing the Atlantic on the *Queen Mary*: and now he had passed away amid similar surroundings. Yet, this very setting and the circumstances of his death also ran utterly counter to the currents of his life: it seems counterintuitive for a public figure such as David Frost to die alone, unobserved and in what can pass for silence. A tendency, as natural as it is inevitable, urges us to look for meaning in death: but the only meaning to be found here lies in a sense that Frost died a death that was deeply human.

It was human in that it was surrounded by mundane, trivial details. The ship's log records painstakingly those details of his final known actions of his life and the recording of his death as recalled by Wilfred Frost in the prologue. It was human in that it was disorderly and uncontrollable and the result of chance. Or almost the result of chance. Frost had died young: he was only seventy-four; but there was a sense among those who had known and loved him that, as Joanna Lumley remarked, "he wouldn't have made old bones".[577] Charlie Courtauld notes that Frost's passing was "certainly to me, who'd worked with him for over seven years, totally shocking and entirely unsurprising".[578] He had crammed his life full of incident, after all, had lived so very much on the hoof, year after year and decade after decade, that his early passing could not be a complete surprise to anyone.

But for Margaret Frost, now the last of the three children of Wilfred and Mona Frost, David Frost's death was certainly a shock: she was fourteen years older, and although she had noted that her brother had slowed down, had aged markedly, she had not expected to outlive him. "I took it very badly. A fortnight before he died, he rang up and said, 'I want you to be our first visitor in our new house. My chauffeur will come up for you early on the Saturday and bring you back on Monday.' But of course it never happened."[579] Instead, Margaret's daughter Sally had received a call from Carina early on that Sunday morning, September 1st, 2013: the news of David Frost's death would be released within the hour, there was no way to delay this news any longer – and so Sally was obliged to rush to break the news before her mother saw it on the television. It was an unpleasant but inevitable side-effect of a life lived in the public eye. "At least he went quickly," Margaret adds. "He would have hated being incapacitated."[580]

And this knowledge was shared by others. Lady Carina Frost says, "If I'm really generous, I think he was lucky he died like that

– because for him, it was the best, though for us, it was the worst, because we never got to say goodbye. But I know that he would have been the world's worst invalid. So, yes, for him, it was the best way to go." And on the question of his early death, she adds, "I'm convinced that travel played a big part in it. Those miles in the air – and also those cigars, which I could never get him to give up."[581]

Other friends took the period after the death of David Frost to reflect on the man himself and, in particular, on the man they knew – or thought they knew. "I sometimes think he was rather a lonely man," says Greg Dyke. "At those summer parties, I would look back and think, *How many of these people were his real friends?*; and by extension, was I a good friend? Sure, we went to lunches, and parties, and I saw him all the time – but I find now that I wonder about his emotional hinterland, and the part that friends played in that; and whether they really played any significant part. I used to ask myself: if you have been David Frost for so long, do you really *have* that many friends? Put it this way: I know I wasn't his lifeline; and I don't think anyone was. He didn't like talking about himself; he would always prefer instead asking people about themselves. Which is why, of course, Carina and his children saved him."[582]

For those who knew him longest, however, there was an understanding that David Frost wanted and needed few friends. He was living his life in a manner that pleased him and that made him content; there was no need for further examination. And in the end, this fundamental sense of himself came from the profound grounding of love and confidence and sturdy stability given to him once and for all in the course of his otherwise restless and peripatetic childhood: that gift handled by his parents and his sisters and passed on to him. For a younger generation, he provided inspiration and example. "I loved him," says Mark Nicholas. "There was an element of a father figure there. He became a touchstone, a reference for me. Other than my own family, he and Michael Parkinson and Richie Benaud were the three people in the business I most admired, and whose guidance and friendship came to mean so very much to me. David was simply the most engaging person I have ever met."[583]

For Michael Parkinson, who had watched the course of Frost's career since the 1960s, there was the sense of an impressive man, who made up in values and roots what he lacked in a larger hinterland:

> I admired him enormously. He had an ability to turn any crisis into a joke, even when he was under great pressure. He was extraordinary at gathering friends: and he had the ability to make anyone feel at ease; he lived in an abnormal world, but he himself remained normal. He never lost the sense of who he was, which had everything to do with his religious upbringing. There was something deep in him, from his childhood, his father, which guided him through life. He had a saintly patience for people, a wonderful way to handle pressure – by going back to his basics.[584]

"He was so proud of his boys," Elton John remarks, "and that's what I loved about him."[585] And in words that are close as he would come to a personal reflection, in an interview some eight years before his death, David Frost remarked that, "I think back to my father and I think that if I could be said to be half as good a father to our three boys as he was to me, then I'd be very content."[586] For Sarah, Duchess of York, Frost's marriage was key to the man. "David and Carina were such an extraordinary couple, and they gave such pleasure to so many; and they had such humility."

And for Carina Frost herself, there is satisfaction as well as sadness in reflecting on a life lived well:

> David worked extraordinarily hard, but most importantly, he loved what he did. The warmth with which he treated people – from all walks of life – was both genuine and infectious, Everyone adored him, and he deserved to be the huge star that he clearly was.[587]

Portraits

Margaret Thatcher

David Frost interviewed Margaret Thatcher many times over the years: like Prime Ministers Major and Blair after her, she was frequently to be found occupying a place on the Frost sofa and using his programme as the best available platform to reveal policy, opinions and news.

Perhaps Frost's most famous interview with Thatcher came on TV-AM in June 1985 – and it involved the controversial matter of the sinking of the Argentine warship *General Belgrano* in May 1982, during the Falklands conflict. Thatcher was now at the height of her powers: her landslide general-election victory of 1983 had given her an impregnable majority in the House of Commons, an Opposition which was still in the process of rebuilding itself; and a party which hung on her every word. There was, therefore, no reason to believe that this interview with Frost would not pass smoothly.

The very fact that this interview was scheduled in the first place was seen as a coup, even before it began. It was one of the first times that the Sunday Frost programme on TV-AM featured a political heavy-hitter; and was understood as a sign that after its traumatic beginnings, the station – and this Sunday slot – was now definitively a success. There was a decidedly jolly atmosphere, therefore, in the run-up to the interview: staffers were delighted, and Frost, assiduous in his preparation and surrounded by his manila folders and his felt-tip pens, was focused on the task in hand.

The interview was not confrontational as such – at least not on the part of Frost – but is instead remembered for a degree of tenacity on the part of the interviewer and, as a result, barely concealed anger on

375

the part of Thatcher. The prime minister, resplendent in blue and hoarse with a cold ("They are most difficult to get rid of, but they do not really bother one.") sits upright. Gradually, her lips tighten and she begins to radiate fury in the face of Frost's questioning.

Thatcher uses the patriotism argument: "Everyone accepts that the *Belgrano* had to be sunk. […] I think people recognise that in fact you have to look after your own people on the high seas. […] Do you really think that is worth making such a fuss about?" Frost invokes the figure of Diana Gould: she was the composed teacher and Antarctic expert from Cirencester, who – live on television – had challenged and rattled Thatcher on the question of the *Belgrano* in the course of the 1983 general-election campaign; and as the interview proceeds, he continually brings the argument back to the facts, actual and disputed:

> DF: I was going to talk about the cover-up … but the reason I—
>
> MT: Cover-up of what?
>
> DF: Well, the cover-up of the facts. I mean, you know … […] I mean the fact that […] the fact that it was going in a completely different direction … it was not as he said closing in.
>
> MT: Do you know, ships do zig-zag.
>
> DF: Yeah, but it didn't zig-zag.
>
> MT: But ships do change direction.
>
> DF: Yeah, but it didn't, it didn't though.
>
> MT: That ship did change direction.
>
> DF: On that day, when the government said it had changed direction many times, it only changed direction once to go back home and a ten-degree difference to get closer to Argentina.

In the end, Thatcher's fury is worn on her sleeve: she sits forward and asks Frost in angry tones, "Do you think, Mr Frost, that I spend my days prowling around the pigeon holes of the Ministry of Defence to look at the chart of each and every ship? If you do, you must be bonkers!"

David Keighley, at that point the director of corporate affairs at TV-AM, recalls the episode in vivid detail. It had been decided that, since Thatcher had a weakness for malt whisky, a selection of whiskies be brought to the green room, to entertain her following the programme. Downing Street refused to disclose the prime minister's favourite brand of whisky – and so, to be on the safe side, the selection soon became fifty bottles. "We weren't sure how [Frost] was going to approach the *Belgrano*, but soon we saw the steam coming from [Thatcher's press secretary] Bernard Ingham's ears, and when Maggie emerged from the studio, she headed for Bernard and the two stalked out of the building looking like thunder. She didn't say anything, but it was plain that she hadn't enjoyed it. And there in the green room were fifty bottles of malt, and Thatcher gone so fast that you couldn't see her for dust …"[588]

Frost would interview Thatcher many times over the years, and the two seemed friendly, but to the advertising executive Tim Bell – connected to the Conservative Party, and a close friend to Thatcher in particular, as well as to David Frost – it was evident that, "David was quite unforgiving of Thatcher for the *Belgrano*, for having done something and then, as far as he was concerned, for lying about it. It remained as a scar. He had a clear idea about what was virtuous and what was not. 'I don't believe her about the *Belgrano*,' he'd say. And I'd say, 'Nor do I.'"[589]

A second remarkable Thatcher interview took place on BBC *Breakfast with Frost* in October 1993. The now dethroned Thatcher was appearing to publicise her post-prime-ministerial memoirs – and Frost was keen to hear her views on her successor, John Major. Only eight years have passed, but both parties have aged visibly, and this interview was notable – indeed, it makes for truly riveting viewing – for the sense of complicity between interviewer and interviewee.

Frost is anxious to take the opportunity to ask Thatcher a question or two on the subject of her successor, and on the state of the government and country in general; and Thatcher – following a feint or two for the sake of politeness – is happy to oblige. Frost, in other words, is only too delighted to offer Thatcher coil after coil of rope with which to hang herself, and the Iron Lady, equally delight-edly, ties the knot herself.

Frost focuses on the dramatic final days of the Thatcher leader-ship, with the prime minister at a summit in Paris, her political assassins busily sharpening their knives at home, and her rule unravelling as the results of a disastrous Conservative leadership ballot begin to filter through to her:

DF: If you had your time over again, would you still go to Paris?

MT: I had to go to Paris! We were there signing the big inter-national treaties on reductions in conventional armaments. We were also there signing a great big Magna Charter [sic] of human rights which I had in fact proposed at Aspen. I could not, in fact, having been a main player in the East–West game, have pulled out from going to Paris – look at what headlines there would have been! And also, I was representing my country.

DF: But do you think it cost you votes?

MT: It may have done, it may have done. But there's no point living an *if only* life.

Thatcher then goes on to speak of her Downing Street years as a time of "dynamism, purpose and achievement", but it is evident that she is indeed living an *if only* life. If only her colleagues had backed her; and if only her successor, John Major, had what it took. Frost probes delicately the matter of Major's loyalty to her in those last, fraught days. When she phoned him in his Cambridgeshire constituency to secure his support, how did he react?

MT: A little kind of pause.

DF: How long was the pause?

MT: Well, a pause is not very long, but it's a pause. You are very sensitive at this time. But [pause] he did, he did [offer his support].

And later, Thatcher offers lukewarm support: Major will make a great leader. "I think he has done it in his own way, in his own time … give him a little more time, a little more time." She handbags her predecessor, Edward Heath, noting that he had lost three elections out of four, while, "I never lost an election, and I never had a majority lower than forty-five ... Britain meant something in the world when I left office. And she ends by offering an opinion on the role and utility of elder statesmen – by which she clearly means "stateswomen":

DF: There's nothing wrong with being a back-seat driver?

MT: Not a back-seat driver, but I don't think you should be expected to conceal your views on any particular matter.

DF: So Granny will always be there with her advice?

MT: Granny will always be there with her views.

The result of the interview was to dramatise – at the beginning of the new parliamentary year – the matricidal strife that was threatening to tear the Conservative Party apart at this point; and to underline too the extent to which Thatcher herself had by no means reconciled herself to her loss of power.

George H W Bush

I spent many happy times with David, both for interviews and for just a quiet social get-together. It was always a pleasure to be with him, and, of course, with Carina. He was one of the very, very best, and I had the highest regard for his professional standing and accomplishments. On a personal note, David was my esteemed and treasured friend. He brought great joy and friendship to some significant times in my life and I will always remember him with affection and respect.

President George H W Bush[590]

It was a crowded field surveyed by David Frost for *The Next President* – but the various candidates fell away in the course of that 1988 presidential year, until only two were left standing: and the sitting Republican Vice President George Bush would go on to defeat his Democratic opponent, Michael Dukakis, in a campaign best remembered for its deployment of negative campaigning.

At the end of the summer of 1987, Frost and John Florescu travelled to the Bush summer home at Kennebunkport on the rocky coast of southern Maine to interview the vice president and his wife Barbara. The big networks had now stepped up their complaints: Barbara Walters' producers passed along to George Bush's camp that *The Next President* would be a syndicated series, while Walters was on network television. "When we arrived at Kennebunkport," John Florescu recalls, "I overheard Barbara Bush say to her husband, 'Honey, what exactly is syndication?' George Bush replied, 'I don't know, Barb; who cares?'"[591]

This meeting at Kennebunkport was significant for David Frost. It was the first of seven interviews that Frost would conduct with Bush – and it signalled the beginning of a personal friendship between the Bush and Frost families; and private visits to Michelmersh by the Bushes and to Kennebunkport by the Frosts. In this first instance, it helped that the objectives of both the Bush and Frost teams were identical: to conduct an interview that would reveal an aspect or aspects of the vice president that had never been seen, or seen fully, by the American public.

Naturally, this was always Frost's objective, but for Bush it was an absolutely pressing need: he had been hitherto regarded as a loyal vice president to Ronald Reagan, as a highly successful diplomat and Washington insider, and as a decorated war veteran – but also, as a buttoned-up north-eastern WASP without an emotional life to speak of; and this last image was at this point impacting on his presidential aspirations. Frost set out to forge a personal connection with Bush: and he succeeded, creating a direct line to Bush that paid rich dividends, even if it vexed beyond measure certain Bush staffers, who resented Frost's ability to go over their heads, to place a call in the certain knowledge that that call would be taken. On one occasion, Bush's chief of staff, James Baker, crumpled one of Frost's letters of invitation to his boss and threw it across the room in frustration. And Frost's producer Marie Jessel recalls her colleague picking up the telephone at TV-AM headquarters in north London, and being patched straight through to Bush at Kennebunkport: "And it was: 'Oh, hello, Barbara, is George there?'"[592]

In the book of *The Next President*, David Frost speaks warmly of the Bush that he knew. "I had not realised how funny he can he. From early on in the interview he often made me laugh, which said two things to me about Bush. First of all, this is a man with a sense of humor [sic] and, second, that sense of humor, being unforced, would add to the chances of our having a real conversation. And so it transpired. Nothing the vice president said seemed to be by rote; I don't believe he slipped into automatic pilot – or if he did, he did it so skilfully that I didn't notice." Frost also commented on the personality and presence of Barbara Bush, who was regarded then and later as her husband's greatest electoral asset. There is nothing especially penetrating about Frost's words, but it was certainly the case that his interview revealed a human side to the candidate.

However, it was another aspect of the interview that accomplished what any number of jokes could not have done. In 1953, Robin Bush, the three-year-old second child of George and Barbara Bush, had died of leukaemia – and it was the mention of their daughter that proved to be electrifying:

It was a clear Indian-summer day with a powerful, rolling Atlantic ocean as our set backdrop. Frost and the vice president were outdoors on the back deck, I was seated a few feet away inside the house. I was pitched in front of a bank of TV monitors, with my team to my right and Bush media adviser Roger Ailes and his team to the left. We began to roll tape. After the obligatory jokes, David started to question his guest along biographical and philosophical lines. Before too long, Frost said, "Have you been aware of the presence of God?" It was a Frost-like question, loaded with political implications that made the candidate for the Presidency wince. "I can't point to one example," Bush said. "For me, born again – and this gets awful personal – is knowing that in my case Jesus Christ is my personal savior [sic]. I know that." At that, Frost quickly turned to the subject of Robin Bush. "It was inexplicable to me," Bush said, and suddenly the vice president was struggling to control himself. Inside the house, I could feel Ailes start to tense up, and then to seethe. He could ill-afford to see his man look weak, near tears. Ailes turned to me. "We have to stop this, John," as if it was his production. I said, "I won't and I can't." Ailes said, "Stop it or I will walk into the shot." I said, "You walk into the shot, and I'll air it." And at that moment Bush collected himself, and Ailes retreated. What Ailes – puzzlingly for a man so skilled in television; he would later become president of Fox News – missed was one of the most powerful moments of Bush's television career. Frost was able to achieve in two minutes what had eluded the Bush advisers for months: making their Brahmin, blue-blood candidate look more human, likeable and *real*.[593]

Years later, Frost himself remarked that this first encounter with Bush was his favourite interview. "It's when you get something from a person who everybody told you would not give at all," he said. "A man I greatly respect, the first President Bush – well, everybody had said that he never relaxed on television and when we did the first interview with him up at Kennebunkport [...] Although we'd never met before, within ten to fifteen minutes, he was talking just so frankly about his family and the daughter he'd lost to leukaemia. He was direct and everything that he is in real life, but he'd never been seen that way on television."[594]

Bush went on to carry the 1988 US presidential election, defeating Massachusetts Governor Michael Dukakis by a landslide. The glimpse of a more human candidate certainly did his campaign no harm, as is evidenced by the fact that a few months after that meeting with Frost on the Maine coast, his campaign contacted Florescu to request the footage in question for a campaign advertisement. Florescu refused.

There are memorable episodes in later Frost–Bush encounters too. It will be for posterity to judge the full impact and value of the Camp David interviews recorded in the immediate aftermath of the first Gulf War: these were kept embargoed, and only sections of them have been released. Frost, however, recalls an emotional Bush perfectly aware – as many leaders who never themselves experience combat, and cannot or will not imagine the horror of its impact on individual lives – of the moral dimension of his decision as president to send American citizens to war; and aware too of his reasoning, political, logistical and moral, for halting the Allied advance into Iraq itself and opting not to overthrow Saddam Hussein once Kuwait had been secured. For this, Bush was criticised by many; but it seems likely, especially given the course of recent events, that history will judge this decision as being wise and prudent.

In June 1998, David Frost interviewed George Bush for the A&E network in the United States – and it is here that we see the sense of mutual respect between the two men, and the sense in which Frost has the trust of the former president, and the ability to amplify the older man's emotions in an interview setting. Bush is now seventy-four years old: and while the interview by no means has a valedictory note, there is an understanding that Bush is reviewing his life, his decisions, his relationships.

This interview explores the decision of the young Bush to enlist in the Navy in 1942 – as he puts it, "to get in there and do something [...] the experience [in December 1941] of Pearl Harbor was so monumental that everybody wanted to be in it, everybody wanted a piece of the action." It also, however, provides an insight into a family dynamic, for this situation is established at once as both dramatic and personally tense: Bush's father is anxious for his son to waive his decision and to take up his place at Yale instead, and has said as much – but, "I think he knew then that I had made up my mind and that I was going to go ahead and go into the Navy."

At this point, and very unexpectedly, Bush weeps, and Frost's response is both professionally skilful and personally empathetic: he fills his interviewee's emotional silences by continuing his own narration, while at the same time taking care to widen the space that Bush himself has made available. Bush becomes emotional once more as he describes his leave-taking at Penn Station for training in North Carolina, and Frost continues this delicate process of filling and widening. Much of the remainder of the interview describes Bush's experiences as a pilot, but even here there is a harrowing edge to the interview – Bush confesses to feelings of terror; and to fear – after being shot down over the Pacific – of what the Japanese would do to him if he was captured. "I tried to turn the plane to the right so the crew could bail out [...] and I bailed out myself, and I did it badly [...] you're supposed to dive out on the wing [...] but I pulled the ripcord too soon and next thing I knew I had hit the tail of the airplane with my head [...] it was a harrowing experience. [...] I was scared, I was throwing up."

The result of this interview was to expose Bush's human experience, which was always Frost's objective. Whether it is possible to separate a politician's objectives from their human histories is of course a moot question. An interview with an ageing and retired politician, however, can be another matter, with a renewed scope for insights, reflections and a sense of personal wisdom. This interview is characterised by a sense of spaciousness, and it shows too that David Frost's cultivation of relationships with such figures as Bush had the potential to produce insightful and memorable television.

Bush and Frost met again in November 2009. The channel now was Al Jazeera, the scene was Berlin, and the occasion was the twentieth anniversary of the fall of the Berlin Wall. Early in the interview, Frost divulges a startling and revealing piece of information: that he had been present in the White House that night – November 9th, 1989 – as a guest at a State dinner honouring the then Philippine president, Corazon Aquino. As was now essentially standard in meetings between the two men, the climate was easy, relaxed, almost intimate. Bush, recalling his emotion at the tearing-down of the Iron Curtain in those momentous weeks, jests drily that, "I weep at anything these days, David, I get very emotional. It's a little embarrassing, frankly."

Bush's reflections in this interview take in the flow and skill of statecraft and, in particular, his sense that his good personal relationship with Mikhail Gorbachev governed much of his behaviour in this electric period in history. His initial response to the fall of the Wall, and his response in the days and weeks that followed, had been low-key, eschewing the triumphalism that might have been expected as history played out so dramatically. It was a response that earned the president a good deal of criticism in America itself – but it was necessary, as Bush reflects, to be prudent and "not to be out there grandstanding" for fear of enraging the Soviet military and hastening the fall of Gorbachev himself. "History will say I was right." And history, he goes on, "marches with personal relationships – personal relationships can build trust. Sometimes that trust can be misplaced, sometimes trust can be overwhelmed by events […] but if you know the heartbeat of the other guy, you're less likely to have two dark ships passing in the night." Margaret Thatcher and French President François Mitterand feared the consequences of German unification, Bush goes on mildly, "and I could understand their reluctance – they had seen their own sons and daughters die in two wars in Europe – and they hadn't quite come along as far as I had. But they didn't try to block it."

The interview is, in hindsight, valedictory in tone. Bush remarks that he no longer does interviews; and that at the age of eight-five, prefers to live his life, rather than look back upon it. Frost will still be around in twenty years, he says – but he, Bush, certainly won't.

It was the final television meeting between the two.

Muhammad Ali

David Frost's interviews with Muhammad Ali spanned a period of nearly forty years on both British and American television, from their initial meeting in 1967 to a final retrospective in 2003. The particular strength of this long relationship was that it took place against – and more importantly, it paid rapt attention to – the radically shifting contexts within which the drama of Ali's life has played out.

Ali was born Cassius Clay in 1942, in Louisville, Kentucky – one of five children, and into financially modest circumstances. But his destiny began to be fulfilled at the 1960 Summer Olympics in Rome, when the eighteen-year-old won the light heavyweight gold medal – only to return home to a segregated America in which his triumph, as he told David Frost in 2003, seemed to have little or no meaning. Was it actually the case, Frost prompted, that he had thrown his gold medal into the Ohio River when the staff at a Louisville five-and-dime refused to serve him?

The restaurant said, "No, no black people, no Negroes allowed." And I said, "I'm from Louisville, it's a good time to put them on the spot. I'm the world champion, I've got the gold medal, the Olympic champion of the whole world, from a little town named Louisville, Kentucky, now I'm going to go in there with my medal, see if I can eat, put them on the spot." So I went in, sat down, said, "I want two hamburgers." They said, "We don't serve Negroes." I said, "I don't eat them either. I want two hamburgers," and the manager said, "Boy, get out," and he forced me out. So I went to the Ohio River and I took the medal out and I said, "This thing ain't worth nothing. I'm a gold-medal winner, I'm the champ of the whole world, I'm wearing a gold medal in a little old town, and the medal can't get me a hamburger." So I got mad and threw it in the river. [...] My home town in the country of America, in the little town of Louisville, and I couldn't eat, the medal on, and I couldn't eat.

Ali was presented with a new gold medal at the 1996 Atlanta Olympic Games: and the veracity of this story, as related to Frost, has been challenged consistently. Its strength, however, lies in its symbolic value, because it highlights the existing political awareness of the young Cassius Clay even before he went to Rome. This awareness was made publicly manifest shortly afterwards, when following a visit to a Miami mosque, Clay joined Nation of Islam and shed his original – what he called his "slave" – name and became Muhammad Ali. In 1967, he was banned for fighting for three years for refusing the Vietnam draft: and by this point, Ali had become the charismatic, articulate and poetic black leader of popular consciousness.

In advance of Frost's first interview with Muhammad Ali in New York, Neil Shand set off for La Guardia to meet his guest's plane and escort him into Manhattan – and his memory of the time captures an Ali who was as much a poet as a boxer and political leader: "Ali emerges from his flight. Remember, he was not a popular mainstream figure at that time, having become a Muslim and changed his name, and we get into the limo and begin our drive through the city – and he leans on my shoulder and says, 'I write songs, you know, as well.' And I say, 'Wonderful!' – or something like that. 'Would you like me to sing you one?' he says, and he sings me a ballad with his head on my shoulder. And so I sat back and floated like a butterfly, while hoping he didn't sing like a bee."[595]

The fully-fledged Ali was interviewed by Frost for LWT a year later, and by sparring with the boxer on the question of the Bible, Frost was able to give as good as he got. "I really believe all white people are devils," says Ali. "I'm not gonna be no phoney," and he backs up his claim with reference to St Paul's Letter to the Romans. In a short but absorbing scene, Frost denies categorically that Romans 3: 9 says any such thing. Ali quietly leaves the stage to fetch his Bible from his dressing room, returns, reads the passage in question, and it is clear that here, Frost is on secure ground, and in the right.

Years later, in the 2002 interview, Frost revisited this episode, recalling his suggestion that Ali was well on his way to becoming a mirror image of the notorious George Wallace, the dedicated segregationist and Alabama politician. Why not, instead, Frost had suggested at the time, take Robert Kennedy as a role model? And now Ali agrees, conceding that, "the Devil can be in any man, any colour, black devils, red devils, yellow devils, anybody can be a devil, anybody can be evil," and conceding too that this political journey had indeed been more Kennedyesque than otherwise.

The most famous encounter between Frost and Ali, of course, took place in Kinshasa, Zaire, in October 1974 – as part of the so-called "Rumble in the Jungle", the boxing match between Ali, the challenger, and George Foreman, the incumbent, for the title of undisputed heavyweight champion of the world – and it was a sensational event, one of the great sporting duels of the decade, and a cultural milestone. Foreman, immensely focused and powerful, had been the favourite to win. In the event, however, the charismatic, compelling figure of Ali knocked him out in the eighth round ("That all you got, George?" he murmured in Foreman's ear, just before the final knock-out), in a fight watched by thousands in the stadium at Kinshasa, and by millions around the world.

The entire episode was deeply, intensely political: both contestants were black; the event organiser, Don King, was black; and the profoundly symbolic location of the duel was the former Belgian Congo, a territory stripped and exploited by the worst and most notorious excesses of European colonialism – but now attempting to rebuild itself as a new, modern, resource-rich African nation. The Zairean president, Mobutu Sese Seko, personally stepped in to host the event in a demonstration of national pride. The following year, Ali recalled the fight and its context:

I saw they'd built a new stadium with lights and that everything would be ready and I started getting used to the idea and liking it. And the more I thought about it, the more it grew on me how great it would be to win back my title in Africa. Being in Zaire opened my eyes. I saw black people running their own country. I saw a black president of a humble black people who have a modern country. When I was in training there before the fight, I'd sit on the riverbank and watch the boats going by and see the 747 jumbo jets flying overhead and I'd know there were black pilots and black stewardesses in 'em, and it just seemed so nice.[596]

As it turned out, this optimism and display of national virility were both short-lived. Mobutu was later shown to have presided over a kleptocratic regime characterised by extraordinary corruption and violence; and Zaire itself became a sort of anti-poster child for the woes of postcolonial Africa. But on that hot tropical night, these horrors were yet to be fully realised.

David Frost had already interviewed Ali at his training camp at Deer Lake, Pennsylvania, an encounter best remembered for Ali's all-too-evident mastery of the psychology as well as the science of boxing. The interview – conducted there in the ring itself – was a clarion call to arms, and a mocking challenge to Foreman, who was popularly regarded as the overwhelming favourite, but who was dismissed by his challenger as a stiff-gaited, slow-moving Egyptian mummy. "No problem, no problem," says Ali, "[...] Listen, David: when I meet this man, if you thought the world was surprised when Nixon resigned, wait till I whip Foreman's behind. I'm telling you, David [...] I've wrestled with an alligator, I've tussled with a whale. I'm so mean I make medicine sick! [Foreman] is a bully, he's slow, he has no skill, he has no footwork, he is awkward [...] he shall be known officially as the mummy. And how's a mummy gonna catch me? I shall be the mummy's curse that night. Have you heard of the mummy's curse? It's gonna be some fight, the greatest fight, the greatest event of all times when I get to Kinshasa ..."

In Kinshasa itself, Frost's role was as anchor and presenter of this dazzling show, and he kicked it off in the style of a showman. "From the heartland of Africa, live and direct from ringside in Kinshasa, Zaire, this is David Frost welcoming you ..."; and after the bout, he interviewed the new champion, enabling Ali to speak with fluency and passion.

MA: Will everybody stop talking now? I told you all, all of my critics, that I was the greatest of all times. When I beat Sonny Liston [in 1964], I told you; today, I'm still the greatest of all times; never again defeat me, never again say I'm gonna be defeated, never again make the underdog until I'm about fifty years old, then you might get me. [...] I stayed on the ropes [...] staying on the ropes is a beautiful thing with a heavyweight when you make him shoot his best shots and you know he's not hitting you. [...] I don't know if I'm going to fight again or not, or if I'm gonna retire.

DF: Why was it when you were on the ropes, that he could not hurt you? MA: I have a radar built inside me, I know how to judge his punches. [...] I told you, I'm gonna float like a butterfly and sting like a bee, his hands can't hit what his eyes can't see.

DF: Are you really going to retire?

MA: I'm seriously thinking about retiring [...] I'm gonna hold this title for a few months. They took my title unjustly. I told you, I'm the real champion, I told you, I'm the champion of the world! [...] The stage was set, you made [Foreman] great, you made him a hard puncher – but I want everyone from this moment on to recognise me [...] if you want to know any damn thing about boxing, then don't go to no Jimmy the Greek, come to Muhammad Ali, I am the *man*.

It was typical of Frost, however, that he devoted just as much time and attention to the vanquished Foreman. "We went up to his hotel room," recalls Caroline Cushing, who had accompanied Frost to Zaire, "and I remember so clearly the sad figure sitting on the floor holding his Alsatian dog."[597]

The 2003 interview is inevitably remembered best for the onslaught of Parkinson's disease on Ali's formerly youthful and handsome frame. But he was still more than capable of wit: at one stage in the interview, he begins to snore. Frost glances around, says, "Shall we take a break?" – at which point Ali opens his eyes: "I was teasing: you are as dumb as you look."

Billy Graham

Although the teenage David Frost could not have known it, his visits to witness the London evangelism of the American preacher Billy Graham – at Harringay greyhound track and later at Wembley, one face in a sea of faces in the spring of 1954 – was the beginning of a significant professional relationship. As with Muhammad Ali, the relationship spanned decades. Frost would return again and again for further conversations with the ever more influential Graham; and the connection would be maintained for a lifetime. It was, perhaps, the professional connection that mattered the most.

The first season of *That Was the Week That Was* wrapped in the spring of 1963, and in the course of a typically restless and peripatetic summer, Frost was commissioned to travel to Paris in order to interview Graham for the *Daily Mail*. This was his first experience of Graham since his teenage years and, of course, it was his first close encounter with the preacher. Graham had now brought his evangelical crusade to Montmartre, and Frost was struck once more by the power and hypnotic effect of the preacher's language, which was by no means diminished by language barriers and the need for an interpreter.

Frost stayed at the Hôtel Lancaster – an elegant, timeless place which would in time become a favourite haunt – and conducted the interview in its lobby the following day. Graham explained why he had left England in May 1954, when the masses of people filling Harringay Arena and Wembley suggested that he might have sustained the crusade for weeks and months to come: "I was frightened. That's why I left England in 1954. I don't want people pointing at me. I just want them to point to Jesus. […] I began to feel it was Billy Graham people were interested in, not Jesus Christ. […] Perhaps I was wrong. Perhaps if I'd gone all over England, there could've been a great revival …" In his piece for the *Mail*, Frost wondered what might have happened had Graham remained, whether the country might have morphed into a society "as vibrantly alive and flagrantly Christian as Dr Graham himself? I wish he'd stayed."[598]

Another year passed, and now the relationship between Frost and Graham was folded into the expansion of the BBC itself. In the spring of 1964, the Corporation launched its second national television channel, beginning with a service of dedication to the infant BBC2 at Westminster Abbey on April 19th. There were possibilities here for David Frost and his new Paradine production company – beginning with a long-form interview between Frost and Graham, now back in Europe once more for another round of crusading soul-saving. Frost and Janette Scott were invited to spend a day with the preacher in advance of the interview. Scott, not having met him before and distinctly apprehensive, instead noticed in Graham "that same peaceful spirituality that I had seen only once before – and that was in David's father".[599] And the interview itself proved to be precisely the sort of television that Frost would trademark in the years and decades to come: taking time to dwell a little on issues, to question, to enquire into beliefs and probe why they were held; and to show the human curiosity that drove him forward.

After all, this was – whatever his audiences might at the time have imagined – such familiar territory. Frost's childhood and upbringing in a Methodist household had possibly never before stood him in such good stead as it did now: he was able to roam what might have been daunting landscape in the knowledge that this was familiar turf. He could address issues of morality, of worldliness, of evangelisation and sexuality, with Graham as – and this is crucial – his equal. Some of Graham's thoughts, in an age when sex was an issue more public than it had ever been, challenged the new orthodoxies of the time. Sex before marriage, for example, was always wrong:

BG: It hinders. I've talked to many psychologists on this point. It hinders real love within marriage.

DF: But not always does it destroy a real love, does it? Not always?

BG: I don't know that it always destroys, but it always hurts and blunts real love. Yes, always.

DF: Always?

BG: Always.[600]

Such television has never been common. On BBC2 in that spring, however, this was altogether new, and it is to Frost's credit that he brought the interview off successfully, and in the process opened up a new facet of his television personality to the public and to commissioning editors.

In the course of the 1960s, Billy Graham established his reputation in America as a man of considerable moral stature. And one with political clout too: it became an objective for presidents to be seen to foster a relationship with this Southern preacher, and to receive his seal of ... perhaps not approval *per se*, but of public friendship. Frost had already sealed his own relationship with Graham: in 1969, he was one of Frost's first guests on *The David Frost Show*, by which point, the teenage church-going son of a Methodist preacher from Gillingham had been replaced by a thirty-year-old celebrity who was dedicated to the good life, who seldom darkened the door of a church, and who was certainly not given to moral discussion with friends and lovers.

Yet the effects of his upbringing would linger, and find form in his own social and political creed: "My belief in the intelligence and integrity of members of the public, and their ability to make up their own minds when their democracy supplied them with the necessary raw materials, sprang directly from the attitude of the religious figure I knew best, my father. His appreciation of the value of each individual life and its propensity for good, and his total lack of condescension or pretension, made a subliminal impression and set an indelible example that was every bit as valuable in the studio as it would have been in the pulpit."[601]

Frost's relationship with Graham stemmed, at least in part, from the interest the two men shared in power: its nature, its workings, how it might best be wielded. Of all the conversations over the course of years and decades, then, it is their discussions on the nature of political power that perhaps resonate most clearly. "If He hadn't chosen you to be an evangelist," Frost asked Graham on *The David Frost Show*, "what might you have chosen to be?" Graham's reply is not very surprising: "I probably would have gone into politics. Politics fascinates me."

And almost twenty years later, he told Frost that he had indeed considered entering party politics – by running for president in 1964:

BG: Briefly, until my father-in-law called, and my wife called and said, "If you announce that you're going to run for president [...] I'll divorce you, and America will not [pre-Reagan] elect a divorced man."

DF: But it was there for a moment?

BG: It was there for a moment, and telegrams were coming in from people who said that they would pledge their delegates to me, and so forth and so on. And interestingly, it was the Republicans, and I'm a Democrat![602]

Interestingly, Graham and the Nixon family had enjoyed a friendship which dated back to the late 1940s, and on *The David Frost Show* in 1970, several years before Watergate, Frost engaged Graham on the subject of the now-sitting president.

DF: President Nixon, in fact, publicly gave you part of the credit for persuading him to run again [in 1968], didn't he?

BG: Yes. I don't know whether he did or whether somebody quoted him or not. I've never really discussed it with him. But when he was trying to make up his mind as to whether or not to run, he invited me to come down to Florida and spend a few days with hum, because I had been in bed with pneumonia. And he said, "Come down and breathe some of this good air and get some sunshine and we'll have some talks." So I went down and stayed with him, and we discussed many things and watched a football game and so forth. I gave him the reasons why I thought any prominent American in whom many people had confidence ought to offer himself at a critical period of history – not specifically him, but any American. That was more or less the way we left it. Whether that had any influence in his decision or not, I don't really know … because he's never told me.

Years later, Frost asked him about the nature and potential dangers of such a close relationship with the wells of political power:

DF: People say that Jesus was at odds with the political leaders of his time, he was condemning them. It was an adversarial relationship and yours is not; Jesus's [relationship] would have been different.

BG: It has been adversarial in private. A number of things I have completely disagreed, and argued a point of view that they didn't particularly accept. But I haven't done it in public, because if you do it in public, you never get an opportunity to do it again. I have been asked advice by politicians from time to time, and I've given them exactly what I think I should give them, if that's my conviction. Some of them, they ask questions I don't know the answer to, and I just tell them I don't have an opinion on that.

In that same interview, Frost asked about the sense that politicians and others used their relationship with Graham to further their own objectives. Did Graham ever feel used by politicians?

BG: Yes. By several of them. By the aides. I never felt used by the politician himself so much, never really, because I saw them privately. And I never had been to the Oval Office in all these years more than two or three times. I always see them in their private quarters and become family friends.

DF: Where you have felt used, how were you used?

BG: I couldn't answer that. I … just don't believe that the president, presidential candidate or the president himself, has ever attempted to use me.

These transcripts and others, provide glimpses of the ways in which Graham – and by implication, Frost himself – managed their relationship with power, while still maintaining a sense of their own integrity. Ultimately, perhaps, this process of management was anchored in confidence, in their understanding that personal integrity – their *own* integrity, as they understood it – was not a commodity to be bought and sold. Certainly, Frost's relationship with Graham had much to do with a meeting of minds, and was for the younger man one of the most important relationships of his life. Reflecting on the death of his father, Frost wrote that, "he gave his children all the raw materials for living a decent, honourable life, but left the implementation to us. Like Billy Graham, he believed that faith in God was the path to a fuller life, not a more narrow-minded one. And he believed that all of us had a duty to use to the full whatever time and talents we had been given. Nowadays, when I talk about not liking to waste money but hating to waste time, I know the origins of that emotion. Money did not matter to my father. Time did."[603]

Henry Kissinger

In the autumn of 1979, David Frost agreed with the NBC network to interview Henry Kissinger, the former US secretary of state and national security adviser to Richard Nixon. The interviews would be recorded at NBC studios at Rockefeller Center, and were timed to coincide with the publication of Kissinger's enormous biography.

There was a particular context to this situation. NBC also had a separate, parallel contract with Kissinger himself, having recruited the politician as a consultant – on a five-year contract, worth $200,000 a year – after he had left office in 1977. The station had taken a good deal of criticism for this decision. Kissinger was, after all, not uncontroversial, and now the network needed an interviewer such as Frost, who was seen to be neutral and who might in the process restore the tainted reputation of NBC. "What we didn't realise," remembers Frost's assistant Libby Reeves Purdie, "was that NBC, whilst having made an agreement to air [Frost's] interview, was nevertheless not quite impartial."[604]

Kissinger and Frost had been on friendly terms for years. Kissinger had first encountered Frost on the west coast: the former had spent much time at Nixon's "Western White House" in California: "He was with Diahann Carroll at the time. I thought he was a very interesting, intelligent person, and we had a very friendly relationship. I thought too that he was an unusually good interviewer; and I always enjoyed his company." In subsequent years, they became accustomed to meeting at an assortment of upmarket Park Avenue dinner parties. Kissinger was "wildly charming", Reeves Purdie recalls, "when it was to his advantage to be so", though in the run-up to the interview, Frost was naturally obliged to curb his New York socialising, and to take a step back from any public sense of fraternising with his interviewee.[605] To a man like Frost, hooked as he was on the social circuit, this was a painful task indeed, though one he accepted manfully.

And, in October 1979, Frost, Kissinger and their teams met in the studios at Rockefeller Center. A good deal of preparation had been put into the project, and Frost, who was working once more with his Nixon collaborator John Birt, had in addition recruited William Shawcross, whose recently published book *Sideshow* had exposed in riveting detail the substance of American operations in Cambodia, the bombing of which by American forces from 1970 had killed tens of thousands of Cambodian citizens. But from the off, there were tensions with NBC, which insisted on the format of a single one-hour interview – meaning two forty-minute recording sessions – and which had also privately agreed (in a contract described by Birt as "extraordinary and unprecedented") that Kissinger had the right to review the entire editing process, though not the right to veto any aspect of it. Frost and Birt, unsurprisingly, decided that the best way to untangle what Birt called a "straitjacket" was to embark from the off on rapid, systematic questioning, the better to squeeze as much time and information as possible out of the limited format with which they found themselves.[606]

In an interview with *Radio Times* thirty-three years later, Frost recalled his preparation for the interview, and, revealingly, his engagement with Kissinger as part of this preparation. "I think that you've got to stick to your principles, even if it's with a friend – but the important thing, really, is to make it clear, with someone that you know really well, that this is something different. Something where we are both on duty, on show. We are both putting our points of view as strongly as possible and that, even if it is tough, it will always be fair. [...] I went to see Henry the day before the interview, to say, 'You must remember that this is a professional gig tomorrow, and everything we say is on the record. It is a professional assignment and therefore it will be different in tone to a conversation over dinner.' [...] I don't know how clearly he heard it because his performance the next day was extraordinarily *obtuse*, in many ways."[607]

Frost plunged directly into a series of penetrating questions on the issue of Cambodia. Kissinger of course had played a key role in the formation and direction of American policy and military operations in Indochina. As Birt notes, however, this was the first time that the former secretary of state had ever been questioned in any substantial way on the horrors visited on Cambodian citizens, and he was utterly wrong-footed by the direction of the interview. Frost had, after all, the long experience of Nixon under his belt: the hours of practice, of role-playing, of hypothesising. Gruelling though this undoubtedly was, it now stood him in good stead. Also, he had Shawcross's vast trove of research on which to draw.

I think it was a lot to do with persistence. And I remember saying, "Why did President Nixon say in his key speech [of April 30th, 1970, announcing that there were to be incursions into Cambodia] that, 'We have never moved against Cambodia in any way,' when you had been secretly bombing it for about fifteen months! Why did he say that when it wasn't true?" And Kissinger said, "President Nixon was given to hyperbole." And I said, "In that case, why did you say *exactly* the same thing in your press briefing thirty minutes later?" And he said, "That was a mistake."[608]

Unable to control the flow of the interview and unaccustomed to anything other than gentle handling by American broadcast journalists, Kissinger was, "furious: he accused David of being ungentlemanly, there was an almighty row – and Kissinger walked out of the studios, leaving us sitting there; none of us knew what to do".[609] And this was only the close of the first of two sessions.

"My take on this situation," recalls Kissinger, "was that David and I had been friendly and never confrontational – and so, when he was chosen as interviewer, I thought that he would ask big questions that absolutely needed to be asked. Instead, he made the whole interview about the bombing of Cambodia, without telling me that this was to be the subject; and he had all these details at his disposal as a result of his researchers' work; and I was not at all prepared for this level of detail. I was stunned by the tone of our interview. Naturally, I assumed he would ask challenging questions but, instead, his thrust was to do with criminalising American foreign policy. Had I had the chance to look up the detail of his questions, I would have been in a position easily to answer them."

Something of a deal was tabled hastily by NBC. Kissinger, who had threatened to pull the plug entirely on the production, reconvened with Frost for a rather less testy second session – but afterwards, it dawned on Frost and his team that a third session would be scheduled, during which he would ask his Cambodian questions again, in an order and a manner acceptable to Kissinger. "And David said, 'No, I don't work like that; that isn't the way it works.' And there was another impasse. David wouldn't step back, neither would Kissinger, so we went back to the Paradine offices across the way and just sat there, scratching our heads. Meanwhile, all hell broke loose. I must say that David was enormously professional, in the face of huge pressure and threats [that he would never work for the network again] from NBC."

Frost now resigned from the project, telling the *New York Times* that his position had become untenable, and NBC itself that the network had soiled its hands in its dealings with Kissinger. This was a charge refuted angrily by the station's vice president of special programs, Nigel Ryan (a "debonair, straight-backed, upper-class Briton"), who wrote to Frost that:

> As you know, I thought in certain respects your interview [...] gripping and impassioned though it was, went over the top in places into advocacy. I do not sympathise with Kissinger's claim that he was not expecting your line of inquiry. If, as he says, you tricked him, then his gullibility warrants Freudian interpretation. But I was concerned we did not give him a fuller opportunity to reply. I think we interrupted him too much and I do not find that easy to defend professionally. (That is <u>not</u> to say that I think secretaries of state should never be interrupted at all.) I think that had we run the Wednesday material alone, our critics would have concluded that we were more interested in winning an argument than in drawing out information. At best it was electrifying television. At worst, it degenerated into a squabble which used up too much of our precious ration of time. All this added to the case for recording more material. It also prevented us exploring more deeply the interesting dilemma, in which Kissinger played a historic role, of a powerful, though for the first time no longer all-powerful, America. Some of all this came out in the interview. More might have. A pity. Clearly, people who cannot take casualties shouldn't start wars. Perhaps the same applies to television projects.[610]

The interview was aired, albeit in a form over which Frost had no control. The Frost team watched the final film in a room at the top of one of the towers of the World Trade Center – and in viewing, they observed that NBC had realised that its professional integrity mattered ultimately more than its relationship with Kissinger: the programme was tough and essentially sound. "We had quibbles," writes Birt, "but it was a powerful, revealing programme, and it remained *our* programme. We had just about survived the entrapments of NBC's ill-judged arrangements with Henry Kissinger. As for Kissinger himself, as Nigel Ryan ruefully remarked at the end of the saga: 'Henry showed about as much respect for the independence of NBC as he did for the neutrality of Cambodia.'"[611] And after this episode, it was alleged Kissinger made sure that Frost's name was dirt in New York, a charge Kissinger denies: "It was socially uncomfortable for David for a long time afterwards; but of course the critical point was that he had preserved his professional reputation."[612]

The relationship between Kissinger and Frost was chilly for twenty years after this episode. "I was not pursuing a vendetta against him," says Kissinger. "I was not saying things against him, I simply did not seek his company. After quite a few years, we talked again; and after that, we met from time to time quite civilly. He called me then to go on his Al Jazeera show, and eventually, I did, and that was a normal, high-quality David Frost interview. I normally don't go on Al Jazeera, and I went on this one occasion as a sign of goodwill towards David."[613]

John Lennon

At the beginning of John Lennon's appearance on *The David Frost Show* in June 1969, the long-haired, bearded Beatle reaches his hand into a bag he has brought with him on stage, brings out a fistful of acorns and begins throwing them into the audience, in the manner of a pantomime hero dispensing chocolates to watching children. Yoko Ono, Lennon's brand-new wife, watches quietly. David Frost, though not exactly nonplussed, does hold back for a moment to watch this spectacle unfold, before offering his assistance with the acorns. Later in the recording, Ono gives Frost a "box of smile", a small receptacle with a mirrored base, designed to reflect his own smile.

John Lennon was a regular Frost guest, and his appearances on the show track his evolution from mere Beatle to sixties peace activist and general sage of the age. Lennon and Ono's celebrated 'bed-in' – the seven televised days following their marriage in March 1969 spent in a bed at the Amsterdam Hilton in the cause of world peace – had been followed by a press conference in Vienna which expanded on the subject of peace, and why it should be given a chance. This session with Frost, then, provided an opportunity both for the host to explore these topics with his famous guests, and for Lennon and Ono to disseminate their message to a mass American audience.

John Lennon was twenty-nine years old that summer. He had already demonstrated not only his musical genius, but also his mastery of media control by means of a stream of *bon mots* and controversial pot shots at such Establishment targets as the Queen Mother. At the Royal Variety Performance of 1963 – a moment when *That Was the Week That Was* was at its zenith – he had poked fun at the royal spectators in his audience: "For our next song, I'd like to ask for your help. For the people in the cheaper seats, clap your hands … and the rest of you, if you'll just rattle your jewellery." He was also, of course, a spectacular live performer, and appearances on Frost's stage were bread and meat to him. Frost himself had moved on from being simply an Establishment scourge, but there was nevertheless common ground and a basic, unspoken creative understanding with Lennon, that served both men well.

And Lennon was already an old hand when it came to interviews with Frost. In the autumn of 1967, he and George Harrison had taken part in an hour-long session on *The Frost Programme* on the subject of transcendental meditation, a practice both men had embraced enthusiastically following a meeting with its guru, Maharishi Mahesh Yogi. Of the practice of meditation, Lennon remarked, "Maharishi said that one of the analogies, you know, is that meditation is like dipping a cloth into gold. So you dip it in and you bring it out. If you leave it in, then it gets soggy. If you sit in a cave for the whole of your life, then you'll get a bit soggy.

So meditation is like going in and coming out, in and out – for however many years." Naturally, this interview hooked its audience by means of celebrity – in this case, the starry presence of two Beatles. Nevertheless, it was a serious affair: considered, leisurely, lengthy – an interview and a format for its time.

Two years on, and Lennon and the Beatles were in a very different place. The former's ranging imagination, along with the arrival on the scene of Ono and the couple's increasing political activism, had begun to put distance between Lennon and the band – and Frost's task now was to showcase his palpably restless guest; to illuminate this restlessness; and to see, if possible, where it might be leading. Not that Lennon seemed at all keen – at least at first – to play ball. "Do you really need all these explanations?" he asks his host, before turning to the audience. "I thought he was clever!"

"No, no, no," Frost tells him, and he too appeals to the audience. "The message I had from John and Yoko the other day, when we were planning the programme, was a message with a nice picture that said 'Love + Peace = Bagism'. I need to know more, John." And Lennon obliges:

> What's Bagism? It's like a tag for what we all do, we're all in a bag, you know, and we realised that we came from two bags – I was in this pop bag going round and round in my little clique and [Ono] was in her little avant-garde clique going round and round and you're in your little telly clique and [...] And we all sort of come out and look at each other every now and then, but we don't communicate. We all intellectualise about how there is no barrier between art, music, poetry – but we're still all: "I'm a rock-and-roller"; "He's a poet." So we just came up with the word, so you would ask us what bagism is – And we'd say: "We're all in a bag, baby!"

"You've got in a sack," Frost replies; and Ono tells him, "You know, this life is speeded up so much and the whole world is getting tenser and tenser because things are just going so fast, you know, so it's so nice to slow down the rhythm of the whole world, just to make it peaceful. So, like the bag, when you get in, you see that it's very peaceful and your movements are sort of limited. You can walk around on the street in a bag."

Frost is stagily unconvinced, and Lennon tells him:

JL: If people did interviews for jobs in a bag, they wouldn't get turned away because they were black or green or long hair, you know, it's total communication.

DF: They'd get turned away because they were in a bag.

JL: Well, no, if that was specified that when you interviewed the people that you wanted to employ – and you had this prejudice – and the people had to wear a bag, then you'd only judge them on what they communicated to you and you wouldn't have to think *Oh, he's wearing black suede, is he? Don't like it.* […] It's like, we did a press conference in Vienna and they're pretty square over there […] We were in the bag that time and all the press came in, sort of expecting Beatle John and his famous wife, and we were in the bag singing and humming and all they were asking was, "What are you wearing?" And they're all sort of holding mics to this bag and asking it how it felt, and was it glad to be here and were you really John Lennon and Yoko?

Frost at this point has had enough of bags – and he focuses more explicitly on his guests' peace activism:

DF: And tell me, how has this thing gone with the sleep-ins you've been having. Those are what? To draw attention …

JL: We're trying to sell peace, like a product, you know, and sell it like people sell soap or soft drinks, you know, the only way to get people aware that peace is possible and … it isn't just inevitable to have violence, not just war, all forms of violence. People just accept it and think, *Oh, they did it,* or, *Harold Wilson did it,* or, *Nixon did it,* they're always scapegoating people. It isn't Nixon's fault, we're all responsible for everything that goes on, you know, we're all responsible for Biafra and Hitler and everything. So we're just saying *Sell Peace*. Anybody interested in peace: just stick it in the window, it's simple but it lets somebody else know that you want peace too, because you feel alone if you're the only one thinking, *Wouldn't it be nice if there was peace and nobody was getting killed?* So advertise yourself that you're for peace if you believe in it.

"Make peace, and sell it," Lennon says a little later. "Is it too simple a truth?" asks Frost, with a touch of characteristic doggedness – but Lennon is having none of it. He says, "What is too simple about me not killing you now?" and Frost keeps his cool. "Well," he replies, "I think that's a good idea, on the whole." From the bag of acorns, the interview has accumulated a little heat and become something substantial – and in the process, it has shown a little of Lennon's heart. A few months later, the Beatles formally split, and Lennon and Ono went their own way.

Frost and Lennon would meet subsequently on television. In January 1972, a further Lennon–Ono appearance on *The David Frost Show* degenerated into a slanging match between the duo and members of the audience. It was full of sound and fury, signifying comparatively little; and later on in the same show, Frost scolded his guests for referring to the questions in terms of trickery. But David Frost's screen meetings with the plain-spoken Liverpudlian have deposited something substantial in the archives: a rounded portrait of a Beatle who was energetic, passionate, wilful, complex and driven – a man and icon for his times.

Lady Carina Frost

I n the cold, blue light of day, my heart will always go back to the fireside in the morning room at Michelmersh, the home in the country that David and I created for our three beloved boys, Miles, Wilfred and George. It became the centre for Family Frost and all that it represented, and the haven for thirty years of marriage.

Michelmersh Court was a breathtakingly beautiful Queen Anne rectory, nestling in its own acres at the edge of a hamlet and protected by yew hedges, the winter walk and the conservation area in which it so gracefully lay. The nearby church dated back to 985: it stood in its own graveyard in which sheep grazed quietly; and I can still hear the toll of its pealing bell through the arch in the hedge and the branches of the tall swamp cypress tree.

I had been searching for a country home for two years, while permanently pregnant. But this was love at first sight for me, and the next step was to somehow seduce David, who, needless to say, was on his way back from New York and hoping to view a simple weekend cottage. We drove through the thickest fog I had ever experienced – and there the house stood on the top of its hill, enticing and beckoning patiently, as though it had all the time in the world. I watched his face light up with surprise and expectation as the Court silently emerged through the fog and began to work its anticipated magic on him.

Michelmersh was not a grand house, but instead was proud and welcoming with huge charm; and it became our refuge and strength for the next thirty years. The boys ran wild in the woods, go-karted around the winter walk and later learned to drive in a battered old car in the fields. Meanwhile, David was stationed at his huge desk doing what he loved doing most: preparing for his breakfast programme and, later, his Al Jazeera shows; and watching his beloved boys play football in the garden. On Sundays, he would leave for London at 6am and return caked in makeup – just in time to kick off his legendary Sunday lunches by skipping into the dining room and welcoming his guests. He did so love to make an entrance.

I first glimpsed David on *The Frost Report* via a very small black-and-white TV, in the days when I was a student in the sixth form at the Sacred Heart convent at Woldingham. Bizarrely, the only two programmes we were allowed to watch were his chat show and *The Forsyte Saga*, which shocked the country with the famous Soames rape scene. From the moment I saw David on the screen, I was smitten: I was a tall, lanky, gawky sixteen-year-old, and unbearably shy. I watched from the back of the room – and I developed a serious, schoolgirl crush on him. Little did I know what would develop in the years ahead, in our rollercoaster of a marriage together. It was Mother Wilson who years later I went to see, saying, "Mother, I really do know now the name of the man I am going to marry." She said, "Dear God, Carina, who is it this time?" When I told her it was David Frost and she enquired if he was religious, I told her a little smugly, "Oh, yes, Mother, he thinks he's God."

I first met David at a dinner party in Clapham, where I was placed between him and an extremely silent John Cleese. David and I got on famously that night and shared much laughter. It was impossible not to be tornadoed into his extraordinary cheeky confidence and his huge enthusiasm for life. He was insanely bright, hugely ambitious, extremely self-assured – but in his humble way, never arrogant. The secret of his success was his genuine love for and interest in people; and to this day, I have never heard a bad word said of him. If I remember correctly, I was amazed (such was my ego) that he did not call me the next day; then again, I was already heavily involved with someone, and he was yet to marry the actress Lynne Frederick. Timing was everything with David; and it was around five years later that the mutual attraction happened and our friendship developed into something different.

Days went by, years went by during which we led our different lives – but he would always put a smile on my face when I bumped into him, usually in extraordinary places. I lived in New York for two years when I was modelling, and I remember a huge white limo pulling up as I was striding along Fifth Avenue, late for a down-town fashion show. The blacked-out windows opened – and there was a beaming David, asking if I'd like a lift. I replied, "I wouldn't be seen dead in a white limo." But we did have a yummy breakfast the following day before he left for Australia to interview the Bee Gees. We had little in common in those years in New York. I spent my days on the catwalk – the runway, as it was called in America – and my nights at the Factory with Andy Warhol, or dancing the night away at Studio 54 with Richard Bernstein, who had the only studio at the Chelsea Hotel, where he did all the covers for Andy's magazine, *Interview*; later, he painted a picture of David and me for our wedding present. David, on the other hand, was interviewing presidents, prime ministers, rock stars – and he was way out of my zany league.

I met him in 1979, at the Oscars. I was with the *Deer Hunter* crowd and gobsmacked to be there. He invited me to his fortieth birthday party, which he shared with Rod Stewart, who had just married Alana Hamilton. It was a wild night: Dudley Moore was at the piano, I was seated at a table with Peter Sellers and his then wife Lynne Frederick – and I still have a photograph of David bending down to kiss me hello. Lynne glared at me weirdly all evening, I remember.

One summer evening when I was back living in London, friends rang me to say that they had David Frost coming for a drink, and would I like to join them? To this day, I still don't know what made me cancel what I was doing – but I did, and spent hours washing my hair and deliberating about what to wear. I turned up feeling intriguingly nervous – and that was it: *that was the evening that was*. We fell insanely in love, and the rest is history. There was something rare and special about falling in love with someone I already knew as a friend, someone I admired and always felt safe with – and from that day on, I knew he was the man I would marry.

For six months, we secretly courted each other in an old-fashioned secret romance. We avoided the paparazzi: meeting in airport lounges, quiet, hidden restaurants, at weekends in his cottage in Suffolk, and on trips to New York, staying in his apartment at Essex House on Central Park South. I nearly blew it once at Heathrow by approaching David chatting animatedly to some guy just outside the Concorde lounge – one look from David, and I took myself off to the bookshop. Needless to say, his companion was a reporter and when he said, "David, you seemed to know that leggy blonde," his reply was, "Sadly, no, but I sure as hell wish I did!"

For my birthday in February 1983, he flew me to Paris: and I remember being a touch upset when I spied the wrong-shaped box from Asprey's sticking out of his coat pocket. In fact, it was the most stunning delicate ruby-and-diamond bracelet that I wear to this day – and the first of many such pieces of jewellery he was to give me.

And I didn't have to wait long. On March 10th, he rang the doorbell of my Chelsea house on Christchurch Street, tripped over the doorstep, fell to his knees and at last proposed to me. My reply was, "Yes, yes, yes, I thought you'd never f------ ask." We married nine days later, on March 19th, 1983, in the Chelsea Register Office, with a Catholic blessing in Notting Hill that was arranged by my father – and then a sumptuous wedding lunch at Les Ambassadeurs, surrounded only by our bestest friends. Parky was the best man, my dad gave the most hilarious speech, and my batty Texan grandmother was found in the Gents' loo, saying, "That was such a beautiful funeral – but do tell me: when is dear Carina getting married?" It was a truly joyous and festive occasion – those were David's words.

Afterwards, we jetted off to Venice to honeymoon at the Cipriani. It was the first of many visits to come. I had first been captivated by Venice when I was staying at Florence and being "finished off" and taught to draw by Signora Simi, who had years earlier trained

Annigoni. I fell in love at that time with the light, beauty and magic of Venice – and I vowed then that I would never go back until my honeymoon. The only person who had persuaded me to return in the interim was Ossie Clarke, my modelling mentor, who picked me up two years later on the King's Road.

After a glorious honeymoon, we returned to London, where amid the maelstrom of TV-AM, I found 22 Carlyle Square and began its renovations within days. Six months later, on the very day I moved David (he a touch morosely) out of Egerton Crescent, I had the joyful news that I was pregnant. Inside the next two years and ten months, Miles, Wilfred and George were born at the Lindo Wing of St Mary's Hospital – where Diahann Carroll later visited, carrying three huge boxes containing a Burberry mac for each of them. My dad, who was there at the time, completely fell for her; when she left, he escorted her to the lifts.

We were blessed with Carlyle Square. The house was surrounded by gardens, and the enchanting nursery floor was crammed with an assortment of nannies, friends and cousins. It hosted endless happy little tea parties, with David coming up each evening, glass of white wine in hand, to read a bedtime story. It was the cosiest home for little people; later, it became known as Bunnykin china flat, as nannies moved out and girlfriends moved in.

I fell in love with our secret garden too. It still had a vegetable patch; and here I planted a magnolia tree to give shade to the boys' pram – a reconstructed Sol Whitby, of course! This was the beginning of my obsession with gardening. Our garden was on two levels; and it became my pride and joy. I loved working in it – it provided me with sanity and peace and I delighted in watching it grow.

One beautiful summer's evening, an idea came to me. Although I knew you could never have two stars in a marriage, I thought there would be no harm in showing off the garden to a chosen few. David – who loved a party – was thrilled; and so began the famous Frost drinks parties. The first guests to arrive at that first party were Elton John and his wife Renate, who turned up at six on the dot. They were instantly accosted by the three boys (aged four, three and two, and dressed in their matching striped pyjamas) and offered bowls of peanuts.

The garden grew, the guest list grew, the boys grew – and five years later, we moved it across to the gardens of the square itself. The rest is history: it became the most legendary of drinks parties and the most sought-after media invitation. I never stopped moaning and groaning and taking people off the list – but David loved it, and I shall never forget his animated face as he greeted each and every guest with his "Hello, Good Evening and Welcome". To watch him was sheer joy, and worth all the behind-the-scenes work that went into it.

When the boys were a little older and settled at school, I had the freedom to travel with David on his work strips: to Moscow to interview Gorbachev, to Libya for Gaddafi, to Qatar with Al Jazeera, to Pakistan for Benazir Bhutto – and endless trips to New York and the White House. I remember taking Miles and his nanny Ruth Smith in her Norland uniform to have tea with George and Barbara Bush; and I remember kneeling at George Clooney's feet at the Carlyle Hotel and telling him he *had* to marry again.

The highlight of these trips has to be the visit to Camp David, where David was recording his secret sessions – on the first Gulf War, for posterity – with George Bush Senior. I shall never forget when the Chinook arrived to take us from Washington: it was filled with armed Secret Service men; and one of them had to disembark to accommodate my Louis Vuitton case. How honoured I feel now to have witnessed such fascinating interviews – and how intrigued I was at the time by the security, by the two huge fences surrounding Camp David, with sand spread between them to detect any footprints. George and Barbara were amazingly kind and hospitable. Later, they gave us a truly fun weekend at Kennebunkport, where George took us out on a boat at terrifying speed, to try to lose the Secret Service – never knowing that David couldn't swim!

It's difficult to judge – but I think the ultimate interview for David was when he met Mandela. His gentle humility and huge dignity had a great effect on me; and our visit to his empty cell at Robben Island still haunts me to this day. I still remember the shock of looking down from the helicopter, and seeing the prisoners exercising in the yard – naively, I did not realise that it remained a functioning jail; and I still hear the clang of the double doors as they closed behind us on our departure for Cape Town.

Over the years, I pathetically tried to stop David using the words "pardon" and "lounge". To no avail – and instead, the boys and I began to call the British Airways Concorde lounge the "BA drawing room". To get his own back, however, he later admitted at his investiture at Buckingham Palace, saying, "Pardon, your Majesty," when he realised he had not heard a word the Queen had said!

I always promised my beloved David that one day I would write a chapter. Little did I know it would end up being about him and how difficult it would be to put pen to paper. Forgive me: but the shock of his death was catastrophic and he leaves behind the most ghastly gaping hole that we still struggle to come to terms with. Worst of all was not being able to say goodbye to him, to prepare us for the pain, huge loss and sheer emptiness his death leaves us with.

Quite simply, the boys adored him. He was the centre of our universe and the very reason for Family Frost as we knew it. Yes, he was a legend, a genius, larger than life, with a generosity of spirit that knew no bounds, famous worldwide, stubborn beyond belief – and the bestest dad in the business, giving unconditional love, always equally shared. The life and the morals he gave us were extraordinary, and the people we met both rare and humbling. But at the end of the day, he was a family man – and not a night went by without him kneeling to say his prayers.

Over the years, a lot of people have remarked that it was hard to get to know the real David and that deep down he was a lonely man. I beg to differ. Everyone wanted a part of David and quite simply there was not enough of his precious time to go around; and as always with great success there would follow sometimes great envy. He would never understand this, but I did, and I protected him like a lioness. We let each other into our very souls, and at the core we shared a love, loyalty, trust and sense of humour that is indeed truly rare. How lucky we were and it is this oneness, this depth of life that I now so sorely miss. Ours was a huge love affair and together with our three boys we created a very private family. At the end of the day, through our ups and downs and through thick and thin, we prayed together, we loved together, and dear God how we laughed together.

David's death has reignited my faith – and I thank God that he is buried near to our new property in the country, where I can visit him often. I also go to Westminster Abbey and kneel on his stone placed at Poets' Corner, inwardly smiling at how much he would have loved every moment of his memorial service organised by the Dean, the BBC and Wilfred. And high in the hills of southern Spain, Annabel Goldsmith and our twin families have planted a tree in his memory at her beloved Tramores, in the place where we holidayed together every August. It stands alongside the tree planted for her brother Alastair, David's good friend.

Miles, Wilfred and George have been my salvation – and I know he looks down on them proudly as they soldier on with their successful business achievements: Miles building his venture-capital enterprise Frost Brooks; Wilf anchoring *Worldwide Exchange* for CNBC; and George launching his Duppy Share rum. We feel him everywhere, safe, at peace and now surrounded by his angels. No doubt he is puffing on his cigar with his large glass of Burgundy and preparing his new project, *Prayers with the Popes*.

My darling David, I send you a cross on your forehead, I raise a glass of Becks Blue in your honour – and rest assured that I am with you always, for ever and a day.

All my love,

Your Child Bride

Acknowledgements

No biographer is an island. This book could not have been written without the full cooperation of the family of David Frost, who assisted me generously, spoke with me frankly and provided the insights and access necessary to illuminate a life. With these facts in mind, I should like to thank Lady Carina Frost, George Frost and the late Miles Frost for their patience and grace. I am especially grateful to Wilfred Frost, whose insights and practical support have, from the inception of this book, been simply invaluable.

I should like also to thank David Frost's sister, Margaret Paradine Bull, and his niece, Sally Wardell, of Whitby.

I am indebted to a wide circle of friends, observers and associates of David Frost, for taking the time to share with me their memories and insights. My thanks to Al Anstey; Alex Armitage, Melissa Fontaine; Naim Attallah; Joan Pugh Baff; Baroness Bakewell (Joan Bakewell); Miranda Gallimore Ballard; Lord Bell (Tim Bell), Teresa Woodley; John Bird; Lord Birt (John Birt); Tony Blair, Samantha O'Callaghan, Julie Crowley; Sir Victor Blank, Tracy Lenden; Rory Bremner; Sir Michael Caine; Alastair Campbell; Diahann Carroll, Jeffrey Lane; Lord Chadlington (Peter Chadlington), Spencer McCarthy; John Cleese; Ronnie Corbett; Charlie Courtauld; Michael Deakin; Fred Drasner; Greg Dyke, Christina Magill; Sir Elton John, Elsbeth Watmough; Lady Annabel Goldsmith, Judith Naish; Ben Goldsmith, Georgina Hilliard; Caroline Cushing Graham; Hank Greenberg, Mona Benedetto; Jim Griffin, Ryan Theobalt; Loyd Grossman, Camilla Eadie; Richard Green; Lord Hall (Tony Hall), Amanda Churchill, Rachel McQuinn; Lord Gerald Fitzalan Howard; Ron Howard, Louisa Velis; Mark Itkin, Andrew Kenward; Sir Antony Jay; Marie Jessel; Barney Jones; David Keighley; Imran Khan; Henry

Kissinger, Jessica Leporin; Jenny Logan; Joanna Lumley; Andrew Marr; Millicent Martin; David Mellor, Jacqueline-Ann Fernandez; Fred Metcalf; Peter Morgan; Piers Morgan, Heike Garbelmann; Andy Murray; Sir Paul McCartney, Lisa Power, Marie Weston; Sir Ian McKellen, Louise Hardy; Neil McKendrick; Liam Neeson, Joana Cannon; Andrew Neil; Alma Ní Choigligh; Mark Nicholas; David Niven; Lord Owen (David Owen), Maggie Smart; John O'Loan; Dáithí O'Ceallaigh; Sir Michael Parkinson, Teresa Rudge; Bryan Pearson; Michael Pearson; Libby Reeves Purdie; Lord Renfrew (Colin Renfrew); Janette Scott Rademaekers, Daisy Tormé; Ray Richmond; Mark Robinson; Neil Shand; Matthew Byam Shaw, Annie Pritchard-Gordon; Michael Sheen, Alana Adye; Herb Siegel, Patricia Sibley; Bob Stephenson; Sir Howard Stringer; Joanna Symons; Carol Vorderman; HRH The Prince of Wales; Shane Warne, Elise Biesbroek; Lord Lloyd Webber (Andrew Lloyd Webber), Jan Eade; HRH The Countess of Wessex, Janet Emmerson; Sandy Weill; Graeme Wilson; Brenda Yewdell; Sarah, Duchess of York, Martin Huberty; HRH The Duke of York, Amanda Thirsk; Bob Zelnick; Mort Zuckerman, Clare Probert.

My particular thanks to John Florescu, Trevor Poots and Michael Rosenberg for advice and assistance throughout; to Simon Fuller, Julian Henry and Helen Barnard of XIX Entertainment; to Shona Abhyankar, Caroline Butler, Albert DePetrillo, Ed Faulkner, Dionne Harrison and Yvonne Jacob at Penguin Random House; and to Veronique Baxter at David Higham Associates.

I am grateful to friends who have offered encouragement and practical support: in particular Stephen Faloon, Marie Gethins, Anne Mary Luttrell, John Murphy, Ruth McDonnell, Eina McHugh, Caitríona O'Reilly and Catherine Toal; Lucy Collins of University College Dublin; and John McManus of Trinity College Library, Dublin. Finally, my thanks to my family: especially to my sister Claire Hegarty and the Butler family of North London; to Maureen and Charles Hegarty of Derry; and above all to my partner John Lovett.

Neil Hegarty
Dublin, 2015.

Notes

1   AC to NH, May 18th, 2015
2   DC to NH, April 16th, 2015.
3   David Frost, interviewed on BBC *Desert Island Discs*, April 15th, 1963.
4   JL to NH, February 4th, 2015.
5   MPB to NH, November 11th, 2014.
6   David Frost, *An Autobiography* (HarperCollins, 1994), 4.
7   Frost, *An Authobiography*, 4
8   MPB to NH, November 11th, 2014
9   MPB to NH, November 11th, 2014
10   MPB to NH, November 11th, 2014
11   Richard Green, unpublished MS.
12   David Frost, *Billy Graham: Candid Conversations with a Public Man* (Cook, 2014), 9–10.
13   Alan Bennett, 'Diary', in *London Review of Books*, January 22nd, 2015.
14   Frost, *An Autobiography*, 9.
15   Cited in Rushden and District History Society Research Group website: rushdenheritage.co.uk
16   Frost, *Autobiography*, 14.
17   Frost, interviewed on BBC's *Desert Island Discs*, April 15th, 1963.
18   Frost, *An Autobiography*, 15.
19   IMcK to NH, April 6th, 2015.
20   Frost, *An Autobiography*, 16.
21   DM to NH, March 23rd, 2015.
22   JL to NH, February 4th, 2015.
23   Frost, *An Autobiography*, 19.
24   Neil McKendrick, *That Was Another Life That Was* (unpublished memoir of David Frost)
25   JC to NH, March 13th, 2015.
26   John Cleese, *So Anyway* (Random House, 2014), 134.
27   PG to NH, December 15th, 2014
28   Carpenter, *That Was Satire That Was*, 83.
29   IMK to NH, April 6th, 2015.
30   IMK to NH, April 6th, 2015.
31   IMK to NH, April 6th, 2015.
32   Thompson, *Peter Cook*, 64.
33   JC to NH, March 13th, 2015.
34   IMcK to NH, April 6th, 2015.
35   McKendrick, *That Was Another Life That Was*.
36   MPB to NH, November 11th, 2014.
37   McKendrick, *That Was Another Life That Was*.
38   Frost, *An Autobiography*, 22.
39   *TV's 50 Greatest Stars* (ITV, 2006)
40   *TV's 50 Greatest Stars* (ITV, 2006).
41   McKendrick, *That Was Another Life That Was*.
42   Greg Dyke, Memorial Service for Sir David Frost, Westminster Abbey, March 13th, 2014.

43 McKendrick, *That Was Another Life That Was.*
44 Frost, *An Autobiography*, 7.
45 Ned Sherrin, *The Autobiography* (Sphere, 2005), 48.
46 MC to NH, March 23rd, 2015.
47 David Frost, interviewed on BBC's *Desert Island Discs*, April 15th, 1963.
48 Frost, *An Autobiography*, 37.
49 AA to NH, February 3rd, 2015.
50 Quoted in "TV's Intercontinental Man", in *Look* magazine, March 24th, 1970.
51 PMC to NH, January 23rd, 2015.
52 PMC to NH, January 23rd, 2015.
53 Ronnie Corbett, *My Autobiography* (Ebury, 2000), 87.
54 Humphrey Carpenter, *That Was Satire That Was* (Phoenix, 2000), 208–9.
55 JBD to NH, March 5th, 2015.
56 AA to NH, February 3rd, 2015.
57 Frost, *An Autobiography*, 35.
58 Elisabeth Luard, *My Life as a Wife: Love, Liquor and What to Do About Other Women* (Bloomsbury, 2013), 5.
59 *Observer*, 1962; quoted in Carpenter, *That Was Satire That Was*, 178.
60 *Daily Mail*, August 2nd, 2014
61 JB to NH, February 3rd, 2015.
62 JB to NH, February 3rd, 2015; JBD to NH, March 5th, 2015.
63 AJ to NH, November 24th, 2014.
64 NS to NH, April 21st, 2015.
65 Quoted in Jonathan Coe, "Sinking Giggling into the Sea", *London Review of Books*, July 18th, 2013; quoted in Thompson, *Peter Cook*, 299.
66 PC to NH, December 15th, 2014.
67 Luard, *My Life as a Wife*, xi.
68 Hermione Lee, *Penelope Fitzgerald: A Life* (Vintage, 2014), 13.
69 Sherrin, *The Autobiography*, 66.
70 Carpenter, *That Was Satire That Was*, 205.
71 Carpenter, *That Was Satire That Was*, 199.
72 Sherrin, *The Autobiography*, 106.
73 AJ to NH, November 24th, 2014
74 David Frost, *An Autobiography*, 43.
75 Corbett, *My Autobiography*, 93.
76 Thompson, *Peter Cook*, 139.
77 Sherrin, *The Autobiography*, 109.
78 *TV's 50 Greatest Stars* (ITV, 2006)
79 Frost, *An Autobiography*, 46.
80 Jay, "Here is the News", *Daily Telegraph*, July 14th, 2007
81 MM to NH, January 11th, 2015
82 MM to NH, January 11th, 2015.
83 Carpenter, *That Was Satire That Was*, 222.
84 MPB to NH, November 11th, 2013.

85   Cleese, *So Anyway*, 164.
86   Sherrin, *The Autobiography*, 113.
87   Frost, *An Autobiography*, 54.
88   *Sunday Telegraph*, November 25th, 1962; quoted in Frost, *An Autobiography*, 54.
89   AG to NH, February 2nd, 2015.
90   Luard, *My Life as a Wife*, 53.
91   Frost, *An Autobiography*, 61.
92   Carpenter, *That Was Satire That Was*, 236
93   Carpenter, *That Was Satire That Was*, 236–7.
94   Carpenter, *That Was Satire That Was*, 226.
95   NS to NH, November 15th, 2014
96   Frost, interviewed on BBC's *Desert Island Discs*, April 15th, 1963.
97   Frost, interviewed on BBC's *Desert Island Discs*, April 15th, 1963.
98   AJ to NH, November 24th, 2014
99   Jay, "Here is the News", *Daily Telegraph*, July 14th, 2007
100 Frost, *An Autobiography*, 80.
101 JB to NH, February 2nd, 2015.
102 Frost, *An Autobiography*, 81.
103 JS to NH, January 8th, 2015.
104 JS to NH, January 8th, 2015.
105 JS to NH, January 8th, 2015.
106 JS to NH, January 10th, 2015.
107 JS to NH, January 11th, 2015.
108 JS to NH, January 11th, 2015.
109 MPB to NH, November 11th, 2013.
110 Thompson, *Peter Cook*, 148.
111 JB to NH, February 2nd, 2015.
112 JBD to NH, March 5th, 2015.
113 Thompson, *Peter Cook*, 149.
114 JS to NH, January 14th, 2015.
115 Frost, *An Autobiography*, 92.
116 Booker, *The Neophiliacs*, 211.
117 AJ to NH, November 24th, 2014
118 Frost, *An Autobiography*, 102.
119 JS to NH, January 11th, 2015.
120 Sherrin, *The Autobiography*, 146–7.
121 Sherrin, *The Autobiography*, 147.
122 AM to WF, May 21st, 2015.
123 HS to NH, February 12th, 2015.
124 Frost, *An Autobiography*, 117.
125 Frost, *An Autobiography*, 118.
126 WF to NH, May 21st, 2015.
127 PMC to NH, January 23rd, 2015.
128 Frost, *An Autobiography*, 122.
129 PMC to NH, January 23rd, 2015.

130 JS to NH, January 12th, 2015.
131 JS to NH, January 14th, 2015.
132 Frost, *An Autobiography*, 126
133 "Frost: Still hungry after all these years", in *Observer*, December 20th, 1992.
134 PC to WF, May 19th, 2015.
135 Frost, *An Autobiography*, 128.
136 Frost, *An Autobiography*, 136.
137 Carpenter, *That Was Satire That Was*, 290.
138 Sherrin, *The Autobiography*, 150.
139 Frost, *An Autobiography*, 137.
140 JBD to NH, March 5th, 2015.
141 *Daily Express*, December 14th, 1964; quoted in Frost, *An Autobiography*, 155
142 AJ to NH, November 24th, 2014
143 Thompson, *Peter Cook*, 160.
144 Corbett, *My Autobiography*, 131.
145 Sherrin, *The Autobiography*, 166.
146 Frost, *An Autobiography*, 159.
147 JS to NH, January 15th, 2015.
148 JS to NH, January 15th, 2015.
149 JS to NH, January 15th, 2015.
150 Frost, *An Autobiography*, 161
151 Frost, *An Autobiography*, 161
152 JL to NH, April 10th, 2015.
153 JL to NH, April 10th, 2015.
154 Frost, *An Autobiography*, 166.
155 MPB to NH, November 11th, 2014.
156 Corbett, *My Autobiography*, 133.
157 Quoted in *Sunday Times* magazine, February 23rd, 2014.
158 RC to NH, December 16th, 2014
159 Cleese, *So Anyway*, 245.
160 Cleese, *So Anyway*, 256.
161 HS to NH, December 15th, 2014.
162 JC to NH, March 13th, 2015.
163 Booker, *Neophiliacs*, 286.
164 Frost, *An Autobiography*, 170.
165 AJ to NH, November 24th, 2014.
166 AJ to NH, November 24th, 2014.
167 PMC to NH, January 23rd, 2015.
168 Booker, *Neophiliacs*, 286.
169 Frost, *An Autobiography*, 176.
170 "My Life as King of Comedy", in *Daily Express*, March 4th, 2008
171 Corbett, *My Autobiography*, 141.
172 Cleese, *So Anyway*, 262-3.
173 Cleese, *So Anyway*, 366.

174 RC to NH, December 16th, 2014.
175 Frost, *An Autobiography*, 183-4.
176 Frost, *An Autobiography*, 187.
177 JC to NH, March 13th, 2015.
178 MPB to NH, November 11th, 2014.
179 Frost, *An Autobiography*, 193.
180 Frost, *An Autobiography*, 195.
181 Frost, *An Autobiography*, 195.
182 Frost, *An Autobiography*, 197.
183 Cleese, *So Anyway*, 296.
184 PMC to NH, January 23rd, 2015.
185 Corbett, *My Autobiography*, 146.
186 Frost, *An Autobiography*, 246
187 Frost, *An Autobiography*, 249.
188 Frost, *An Autobiography*, 249.
189 MR to NH, December 12th, 2014.
190 JPB to NH, March 30th, 2015.
191 JPB to NH, March 30th, 2015.
192 JPB to NH, March 30th, 2015.
193 AA to NH, February 3rd, 2015.
194 WF to NH, May 22nd, 2015.
195 JL to NH, February 4th, 2015.
196 Frost, *An Autobiography*, 254.
197 AJ to NH, November 24th, 2014.
198 MR to NH, December 12th, 2014.
199 Frost, *An Autobiography*, 254.
200 Frost, *An Autobiography*, 277.
201 Frost, *An Autobiography*, 281.
202 Frost, *An Autobiography*, 281.
203 Frost, *An Autobiography*, 282.
204 Frost, *An Autobiography*, 282
205 MP to NH, April 16th, 2015.
206 RC to NH, December 16th, 2014
207 John Birt, *The Harder Path: The Autobiography* (2002), 107.
208 JPB to NH, March 30th, 2015.
209 Frost, *An Autobiography*, 327.
210 MPB to NH, November 11th, 2014.
211 JL to NH, February 4th, 2015.
212 Frost, *An Autobiography*, 329.
213 Frost, *An Autobiography*, 329.
214 David Frost, *The Presidential Debate, 1968* (Stein and Day), 40–41.
215 Frost, *An Autobiography*, 343.
216 Frost, *An Autobiography*, 343–6.
217 Frost, *The Presidential Debate*, 121–2.
218 Frost, *The Presidential Debate*, 122.
219 *Guardian*, March 11th, 2012.

220 Quoted in Sir David Frost Memorial Service: Order of Service.
221 Frost, *An Autobiography*, 371-2.
222 Frost, *An Autobiography*, 381.
223 Frost, *An Autobiography*, 382.
224 Frost, *An Autobiography*, 437.
225 JL to NH, February 4th, 2015.
226 JL to NH, April 10th, 2015.
227 JPB to NH, March 30th, 2015.
228 NS to NH, April 21st, 2015.
229 Letter from Prince of Wales to Wilfred Frost, April 2015.
230 David Frost, *The Americans* (Heinemann, 1971), 241–2.
231 Frost, *An Autobiography*, 467.
232 NS to NH, April 21st, 2015.
233 NS to NH, April 21st, 2015.
234 RR to NH, May 23rd, 2015.
235 PIM to NH, June 9th, 2015.
236 "He's no singer, no comedian, no sex symbol: What Makes David Frost Talk?" in *New York Times* magazine, November 3rd, 1969.
237 JO'L to NH, January 27th, 2015.
238 "King of the Q&A", in *Cigar Aficionado*, March–April, 1997.
239 MGB to NH, February 3rd, 2015.
240 *Cigar Aficionado*, March-April, 1997.
241 AA to NH, February 3rd, 2015.
242 *Daily Mail*, September 5th, 2013.
243 BW to WF, May 22nd, 2015.
244 JL to NH, February 4th , 2015.
245 Frost, *An Autobiography*, 467.
246 NS to NH, April 28th, 2015.
247 Coretta Scott King to David Frost, October 16th, 1969.
248 MC to NH, March 23rd, 2015.
249 Barbara Walters to David Frost, June 17th, 1970.
250 Joan Crawford to David Frost, January 15th, 1970 / February 18th, 1970 / June 17th, 1970.
251 "TV's Intercontinental Man", in *Look* magazine, March 24th, 1970.
252 Quoted in "Frost: Still hungry after all these years", *Observer*, December 20th, 1992.
253 RR to NH, May 23rd, 2015.
254 NS to NH, April 21st, 2015.
255 PC to NH, December 15th, 2014.
256 John Birt, *The Harder Path: An Autobiography* (TimeWarner, 2002), 127.
257 Birt, *The Harder Path*, 128.
258 Birt, *Harder Path*, 127; TP to NH, December 12th, 2014.
259 JO'L to NH, February 2nd, 2015.
260 DY to NH, May 27th, 2015
261 DC to NH, April 16th, 2015.
262 David Frost, unpublished notes.

263 DC to NH, April 16th, 2015.

264 DC to NH, April 16th, 2015.

265 DC to NH, April 16th, 2015.

266 JPB, March 30th, 2015.

267 NS to NH, April 21st, 2015.

268 SW to NH, November 11th, 2014.

269 JL to NH, February 4th, 2015.

270 DC to NH, April 16th, 2015.

271 DC to NH, April 16th, 2015.

272 DC to NH, 1April 16th, 2015.

273 JS to NH, January 17th, 2015.

274 DN to NH, January 21st, 2015.

275 "They all fell for Frost", in *Daily Mail*, September 5th, 2013.

276 SW to NH, November 11th, 2014.

277 JO'L to NH, February 3rd, 2015.

278 MR to DF, December 15th, 2014.

279 CCG to NH, February 5th, 2015.

280 CCG to NH, February 5th, 2015.

281 John Cleese, *So Anyway*.

282 JC to NH, March 13th, 2015.

283 NA to NH, March 26th, 2015.

284 Vincent Canby, "Glass Slipper into Sow's Ear", in *New York Times*, November 5th, 1976.

285 "Frost's Frontiers", *People* magazine, May 23rd, 1977.

286 CCG to NH, February 5th, 2015.

287 JF to NH, May 23rd, 2015.

288 LRP to NH, March 25th, 2015.

289 *TV's 50 Greatest Stars* (ITV, 2006).

290 LRP to NH, March 25th, 2015.

291 AG to NH, February 4th, 2015.

292 EJ to NH, May 27th, 2015.

293 CCG to NH, February 5th, 2015.

294 CCG to NH, March 11th, 2015.

295 Jonathan Aitken, *Nixon, A Life* (Weidenfeld and Nicholson, 1993), 529.

296 Quoted in "How Frost Beat Nixon", November 13th, BBC2, 2011.

297 David Frost, *I Gave Them a Sword: Behind the Scenes of the Nixon Interviews* (William Morrow, 1978), 13.

298 CCG to NH, March 11th, 2015.

299 David Frost, *Frost/Nixon: Behind the Scenes of the Nixon interviews* (Harper Perennial, 2007), 7.

300 Frost, *Frost/Nixon*, 9.

301 Aitken, *Nixon*, 540.

302 Frost, *I Gave Them a Sword*, 34.

303 Frost, *I Gave Them a Sword*, 25.

304 "Revealed: The Australian banker who stepped in with $200,000 to save the legendary Frost-Nixon interviews", in *Daily Mail*, September 8th, 2013.

305 JS to NH, January 19th, 2015.
306 Frost, *Frost/Nixon*, 10.
307 Frost, *Frost/Nixon*, 11.
308 HG to NH, April 28th, 2015.
309 MR to NH, December 15th, 2014.
310 PIM to NH, June 9th, 2015.
311 JS to NH, January 20th, 2015.
312 David Frost, unpublished MS.
313 MD to NH, April 1st, 2015.
314 Frost, *I Gave Them a Sword*, 37.
315 BZ to NH, March 18th, 2015.
316 John Birt, *The Harder Path*, 190; BZ to NH, March 18th, 2015.
317 BZ to NH, March 18th, 2015.
318 LRP to NH, March 25th, 2015.
319 CCG to NH, March 11th, 2015.
320 Frost, *Frost/Nixon*, 18.
321 BZ to NH, March 18th, 2015.
322 MP to NH, April 16th, 2015.
323 Frost, *I Gave Them a Sword*, 178.
324 CCG to NH, March 11th, 2015.
325 Frost, *Frost/Nixon*, 33.
326 BZ to NH, March 18th, 2015.
327 Frost, *Frost/Nixon*, 71.
328 Frost, *Frost/Nixon*, 84.
329 BZ to NH, March 18th, 2015.
330 Birt, *Harder Path*, 196.
331 Birt, *Harder Path*, 198.
332 Frost, *Frost/Nixon*, 103.
333 GF to NH, May 24th, 2015.
334 Quoted in Frost, *Frost/Nixon*, 136.
335 BZ to NH, March 18th, 2015.
336 CCG to NH, February 5th, 2015.
337 *TV's 50 Greatest Stars* (ITV, 2006)
338 David Frost, unpublished MS.
339 Birt, *The Harder Path*, 214.
340 LRB to DF, March 25th, 2015.
341 David Frost, unpublished MS.
342 "Frost's Frontiers", *People* magazine, May 23rd, 1977.
343 JB to NH, February 3rd, 2015.
344 Ed Sikov, *Dr Strangelove: A Biography of Peter Sellers* (Pan, 2002), 345.
345 MFB to NH, November 11th, 2014
346 MR to NH, December 15th, 2015.
347 LRB to NH, March 25th, 2015.
348 LRB to NH, March 25th, 2015.
349 JL to NH, February 3rd, 2015.
350 CCG to NH, February 3rd, 2015.

351 VB to NH, February 24th, 2015.
352 JS to NH, March 14th, 2015.
353 MR to NH, March 27th, 2015.
354 VB to NH, February 24th, 2015.
355 PC to NH, May 24th, 2015.
356 CF to NH, December 11th, 2014.
357 CF to NH, December 11th, 2014.
358 CF to NH, December 11th, 2014.
359 CF to NH, December 11th, 2014.
360 CF to NH, December 11th, 2014.
361 MP to NH, April 16th, 2015.
362 MD to NH, April 1st, 2015.
363 AG to NH, February 4th, 2015.
364 Annabel Goldsmith, *No Invitation Required: The Pelham Cottage Years* (Phoenix, 2005), 150–1.
365 CF to NH, December 11th, 2014.
366 CF to NH, December 11th, 2014.
367 MD to NH, April 1st, 2015.
368 MGB to NH, February 3rd, 2015.
369 MGB to NH, February 3rd, 2015.
370 MGB to NH, February 3rd, 2015.
371 GW to NH, March 30th, 2015.
372 CF to NH, December 11th, 2014.
373 CF to NH, December 11th, 2014.
374 CF to NH, December 11th, 2014.
375 DC to NH, April 16th, 2015.
376 GF to NH, December 11th, 2014.
377 CF to NH, December 11th, 2014.
378 JL to NH, February 3rd, 2015.
379 EJ to NH, May 27th, 2015.
380 VB to NH, February 242th, 2015.
381 DY to NH, May 27th, 2015.
382 SDY to NH, 3 July, 2015.
383 SDY to NH, 3 July, 2015.
384 SDY to NH, 3 July, 2015.
385 Quoted in *Sunday Times* magazine, February 23rd, 2014.
386 JL to NH, February 3rd, 2015.
387 MGB to NH, February 3rd, 2015.
388 Alastair Campbell, *The Alastair Campbell Diaries, Volume 1: Prelude to Power*, ed. Alastair Campbell and Bill Haggerty (Hutchinson, 2010), 239–40.
389 Campbell, *Diaries*, 386.
390 DO to NH, March 26th, 2015.
391 DM to NH, March 17th, 2015.
392 Miranda Gallimore to David Mellor: quoted in DM to NH, March 17th, 2015.

393 RB to NH, February 25th, 2015.
394 CF to NH, December 11th, 2014.
395 VB to NH, February 24th, 2015.
396 JSY to NH, January 16th, 2015.
397 BJ to NH, January 26th, 2015.
398 MF/GF to NH, December 11th, 2014.
399 DM to NH, March 17th, 2015.
400 BY to NH, May 28th, 2015.
401 CW to NH, March 31st, 2015.
402 WF to NH, December 11th, 2015
403 MF to NH, December 11th, 2014.
404 MF to NH, May 25th, 2015.
405 MF, WF, GF to NH, December 11th, 2014.
406 CF to NH, December 11th, 2015.
407 WF to NH, December 11th, 2015.
408 BS to NH, February 26th, 2015.
409 WF to NH, December 11th, 2014.
410 PC to NH, December 15th, 2015.
411 GF to NH, February 27th, 2015.
412 Goldsmith, *Pelham Cottage Years*, 151–2, 154.
413 Ian Jones, *Morning Glory, A History of British Breakfast Television* (Kelly, 2004), 11.
414 MR to NH, December 15th, 2015.
415 Jones, *Morning Glory*, 14.
416 MD to NH, April 1st, 2015.
417 MR to NH, December 15th, 2015.
418 MD to NH, April 1st, 2015.
419 AA to NH, February 4th, 2015.
420 MP to NH, April 16th, 2015.
421 MP to NH, May 5th, 2015.
422 MD to NH, April 1st, 2015.
423 MP to NH, April 16th, 2015.
424 MR to NH, December 15th, 2015.
425 MP to NH, April 16th, 2015.
426 MP to NH, April 16th, 2015.
427 CF to NH, February 26th, 2015.
428 GD to NH, January 29th, 2015.
429 GD to NH, January 29th, 2015.
430 MJ to NH, April 9th, 2015.
431 MJ to NH, April 9th, 2015.
432 ALW to NH, March 26th, 2015.
433 BY to NH, May 28th, 2015.
434 LG to NH, April 1st, 2015.
435 AN to NH, June 15th, 2015.
436 LG to NH, April 1st, 2015.
437 David Frost, *The Next President* (US News and World Report, 1988), 12.

438 JF to NH, January 27th, 2015.

439 JF to NH, January 27th, 2015.

440 JF to NH, January 27th, 2015.

441 JF to NH, January 27th, 2015.

442 MZ to NH, April 3rd, 2015.

443 John Florescu, MS.

444 FD to NH, April 10th, 2015.

445 FD to NH, April 10th, 2015.

446 *People*, December 7th, 1987.

447 *New York Times*, November 28th, 1987

448 John Florescu, MS.

449 Frost, *Next President*, 151.

450 TP to NH, December 11th, 2014.

451 JF to NH, March 13th, 2015.

452 SW to NH, April 6th, 2015.

453 PIM to NH, June 9th, 2015.

454 Bill Clinton to Carina Frost, September 12th, 2013.

455 Quoted in Richard Pyle, *Schwarzkopf, In His Own Words* (Signet, 1991), 40–1.

456 JF to NH, January 27th, 2015.

457 JF to NH, January 27th, 2015.

458 JF to NH, January 27th, 2015.

459 JF to NH, January 27th, 2015.

460 JF to NH, April 1st, 2015.

461 TP to NH, December 15th, 2014.

462 Noted in *Eastern Daily Press*, May 1st, 1991.

463 Anne Frith to Jean, Margaret and David Frost, April 27th, 1991.

464 DK to NH, April 2nd, 2015.

465 TH to NH, April 29th, 2015.

466 BJ to NH, January 26th, 2015.

467 JM to WF, CNN, March 9th, 2014.

468 Quoted in *Observer*, December 1992.

469 JB to NH, February 3rd, 2015.

470 BJ to NH, January 26th, 2015.

471 JO'L to NH, January 27th, 2015.

472 Alastair Campbell, *Diaries*, 28, 296–8.

473 Campbell, *Diaries*, 326, 386, 408.

474 AC to NH, May 19th, 2015.

475 SDY to NH, 3 July, 2015.

476 TP to NH, December 11th, 2014.

477 TB to NH, March 11th, 2015.

478 BJ to NH, January 26th, 2015.

479 *TV's 50 Greatest Stars* (ITV, 2006)

480 TH to NH, April 29th, 2015.

481 BJ to NH, January 26th, 2015.

482 JL to NH, February 4th, 2015.

483 John Florescu, MS.

484 MR to NH, March 26th, 2015.

485 HS to NH, December 12th, 2014.

486 JF to NH, April 1st, 2015.

487 VB to NH, February 24th, 2015.

488 MGB to NH, February 3rd, 2015.

489 SWA to NH, June 16th, 2015.

490 CF to NH, February 26th, 2015.

491 SWA to NH, June 16th, 2015.

492 MN, May 12th, 2015.

493 AC to NH, May 19th, 2015.

494 TB to NH, March 11th, 2015.

495 AC to NH, May 19th, 2015.

496 AG to NH, February 4th, 2015.

497 Naim Attallah, "My soulmate Daily Frost and I were bound by our love of women", in *Daily Telegraph*, September 6th, 2013.

498 GF to NH, May 25th, 2015.

499 Goldsmith, *No Invitation Required*, 158.

500 BJ to NH, January 26th, 2015.

501 MF to NH, December 11th, 2014.

502 BJ to NH, January 26th, 2015.

503 CF to NH, February 26th, 2015.

504 MGB to NH, February 3rd, 2015.

505 GF to NH, December 11th, 2014.

506 JF to NH, January 27th, 2015.

507 GD to NH, January 29th, 2015.

508 WF to NH, May 25th, 2015.

509 AM to WF, May 21st, 2015.

510 MGB to NH, February 3rd, 2015.

511 MS to NH, March 30th, 2015.

512 MBS to NH, March 3rd, 2015.

513 MS to NH, March 30th, 2015.

514 PM to NH, March 20th, 2015.

515 MBS to NH, March 3rd, 2015.

516 David Frost with Bob Zelnick, *Frost/Nixon: Behind the Scene of the Nixon Interviews* (Harper Perennial, 2007), 4.

517 David Frost to Peter Morgan and Matthew Byam Shaw, October 6th, 2005.

518 PM to NH, March 20th, 2015.

519 MBS to NH, March 3rd, 2015; PM to NH, March 20th, 2015

520 MBS to NH, March 3rd, 2015

521 JB to NH, February 3rd, 2015

522 *Guardian*, August 22nd, 2006.

523 *New York Times*, April 23rd, 2007.

524 RH to NH, May 30th, 2015.

525 MS to NH, March 30th, 2015.

526 WF to NH, May 25th, 2015.

527 AA to NH, February 4th, 2015.

528 Quoted in *OnForm* magazine, Spring, 2012.

529 BJ to NH, January 29th, 2015.

530 Charlie Courtauld, blog: charliecourtauld.tumblr.com

531 MGB to NH, February 3rd, 2015.

532 TP to NH, December 15th, 2015.

533 GF to NH, December 1st, 2014.

534 AA to NH, February 4th, 2015; JL to; CCG to NH, February 4th, 2015; JL to NH, February 4th, 2015.

535 JF to NH, February 4th, 2015.

536 CC to NH, January 23rd, 2015.

537 TP to NH, December 15th, 2015.

538 TB to NH, March 11th, 2015.

539 WF to NH, May 25th, 2015.

540 ALA to NH, May 31st, 2015

541 David Frost, quoted in *OnForm* magazine, Spring 2012.

542 Charlie Courtauld, blog: charliecourtauld.tumblr.com

543 AM to NH, May 25th, 2015.

544 JM to WF, CNN, March 9th, 2014.

545 Lewis Hamilton, blog, September 6th, 2013: bbc.com/sport/formula1

546 EJ to NH, May 27th, 2015.

547 LN to NH, May 21st, 2015.

548 Charlie Courtauld, blog: charliecourtauld.tumblr.com

549 Charlie Courtauld, blog: charliecourtauld.tumblr.com

550 JL to NH, February 4th, 2015.

551 AA to NH, February 4th, 2015.

552 TB to NH, March 11th, 2015.

553 Tony Blair, *A Journey* (Hutchinson, 2010), 213.

554 WF to NH, February 27th, 2015

555 Prince of Wales to Wilfred Frost, April 2015.

556 WF to NH, February 27th, 2015.

557 WF to NH, February 27th, 2015.

558 Quoted in *Observer*, December 1992.

559 Quoted in *Independent*, 17 June, 1995.

560 *TV's 50 Greatest Stars* (ITV, 2006)

561 TP to NH, December 15th, 2014.

562 JB to NH, February 3rd, 2015.

563 MP to NH, April 16th, 2015; JL to NH, February 4th, 2015.

564 JS to NH, January 16th, 2015.

565 RB to NH, February 25th, 2015.

566 MF to NH, May 31st, 2015.

567 JF to NH, March 13th, 2015.

568 WF to NH, May 31st, 2015.

569 BG to NH, March 16th, 2015.

570 GF to NH, February 27th, 2015.

571 JB to NH, February 3rd, 2015.
572 GF to NH, May 25th, 2015.
573 Quoted in *Sunday Times* magazine, February 23rd, 2013.
574 Greg Dyke, Memorial Service for Sir David Frost, Westminster Abbey, March 13th, 2014.
575 DC to NH, April 16th, 2015.
576 Tony Hall, BBC Broadcasting House, October 8th, 2013.
577 JL to NH, February 4th, 2015.
578 Charlie Courtauld, blog: charliecourtauld.tumblr.com
579 MF to NH, November 11th, 2014.
580 MPB to NH, November 11th, 2014.
581 CF to NH, February 27th, 2015.
582 GD to NH, January 29th, 2015.
583 MN to NH, May 7th, 2015.
584 MP to NH, April 16th, 2015.
585 EJ to NH, May 27th, 2015.
586 *TV's 50 Greatest Stars* (ITV, 2006)
587 CF to NH, May 23rd, 2015.
588 DK to NH, April 2nd, 2015.
589 TB to NH, February 25th, 2015.
590 GHB to WF, May 21st, 2015.
591 John Florescu, MS.
592 MJ to NH, April 9th, 2015.
593 John Florescu, MS.
594 Cited in *Guardian*, March 6th, 2012.
595 NS to NH, April 21st, 2015.
596 Muhammad Ali, quoted in "From the Vault: the Poetry of the Rumble in the Jungle", in *Guardian*, October 12th, 2012.
597 CCG to NH, February 5th, 2015.
598 Frost, *An Autobiography*, 89.
599 JS to NH, January 14th, 2015.
600 Frost, *An Autobiography*, 121
601 Frost, *An Autobiography*, 473.
602 *A Prophet with Honour*, Channel 4, 1989.
603 Frost, *Autobiography*, 327.
604 LRP to NH, March 25th, 2015
605 LRP to NH, March 25th, 2015
606 Birt, *The Harder Path*, 205.
607 *Radio Times*, March, 2012.
608 *Radio Times*, March, 2012.
609 LRP to NH, 25 March, 2015.
610 Birt, *The Harder Path*, 205; Nigel Ryan to David Frost, October 30th, 1979
611 Birt, *The Harder Path*, 212.
612 LRP to NH, March 25th, 2015
613 HK to NH, May 21st, 2015.

Index

(the initials DF in subentries refer to David Frost)

434